Human Sacrifice
in Jewish and Christian Tradition

Numen Book Series

Studies in the History of Religions

Edited by

Steven Engler
Kim Knott
P. Pratap Kumar
Kocku von Stuckrad

VOLUME 112

Human Sacrifice

in Jewish and Christian Tradition

Edited by

Karin Finsterbusch
Armin Lange
K.F. Diethard Römheld

In association with

Lance Lazar

BRILL

LEIDEN · BOSTON
2007

This book is printed on acid-free paper.

Cover design and illustration by Celine Thorsten

Library of Congress Cataloging-in-Publication Data

A C.I.P. record for this book is available from the Library of Congress.

ISSN 0169-8834
ISBN 90 04 15085 4
ISBN 978 90 04 15085 0

PRINTED IN THE NETHERLANDS

Table of Contents

HUMAN SACRIFICE IN MEDIEVAL AND MODERN JUDEO-CHRISTIAN TRADITIONS

INDICES

Preface

> If sacrifice resembles criminal violence, we may say that there is, inversely, hardly any form of violence that cannot be described in terms of sacrifice—as Greek tragedy clearly reveals.[1]

The core of this volume goes back to a small conference on "Human Sacrifice in Ancient Mediterranean Religion and Its Reflections in Modernity" held at the University of North Carolina at Chapel Hill in October 2002 which was organized by Professors Yaakov Ariel and Armin Lange. The contributions of Yaakov Ariel, Armin Lange, Bennie H. Reynolds, and Christopher Roberts go back to talks held at this conference.

The conference and the present volume ask in how far ancient practices and traditions of human sacrifice are reflected in medieval and modern traditions. In antiquity, the volume focusses especially on rituals of human sacrifice and ancient polemics against it or transformations of it in the Israelite-Jewish (see the contributions of Michaela Bauks, Karin Finsterbusch, Armin Lange, Bennie H. Reynolds, Kathell Berthelot, and Tal Ilan) and Christian cultures (see the contribution of Peter Lampe) while the Ancient Near East and ancient Greece is not excluded (see the contributions of Beate Pongratz-Leisten and Gabriele Weiler).[2] For medieval and modern times the volume discusses human sacrifice in Jewish (see the contributions of Rainer Walz and Yaakov Ariel) and Christian traditions (see the contributions of Jasper Hopkins and Christopher Roberts) as well as the debates about euthanasia and death penalty in the western world (see the contributions of Udo Benzenhöfer, Wilhelm Rimpau, and Randall Styers).

---

[1] René Girard, *Violence and the Sacred* (trans. P. Gregory; Baltimore, Md.: Johns Hopkins University Press, 1977), 1.

[2] For human sacrifice in the Phoenicio-Punic cultures see also the article of Bennie H. Reynolds.

Beate Pongratz-Leisten surveys the Ancient Near Eastern ideas and practices out of which the concepts of the expiatory death of the Servant of the Lord (Isa 53:10) and of the sacrificial death of Christ developed. "Mesopotamian religious tradition displays a whole range of concepts of ritual killing, eliminatory rites and substitute rites, the idea of the offering with communicative function as well as the idea of guilt and sin, and the legal tradition knows of the idea of the ransom paid to redeem one's life. The crucial difference between the Old Testament theology and Mesopotamian tradition is that in Mesopotamia there is no direct connection between sacrifice and purification rites which consequently also implies that there is no sacrifice to atone for the sin or sacrifice to atone for the guilt."[3] Ancient Near Eastern and Christian thought also differ from one another: "If there is death involved, which is mostly symbolically performed by killing a substitute, then this substitute person dies for his own sins. The idea of atoning death for others is nonexistent. Christian soteriological theology then by introducing the elements of trust and obedience in God transforms the material substance as ransom into the idea of Christ giving himself as ransom for the many (Mark 10:45) whose life otherwise would be lost in the final judgment."[4]

Gabriele Weiler discusses nine texts from ancient Greece, which deal with human sacrifice. These examples reveal conceptions which find their expression in permanently modified myths, but which do not reflect historical realities or events. Especially archeological evidence and inscriptions show that human sacrifices were at best only very rare in ancient Greek culture. While Weiler's sample texts are best regarded as fiction they reveal nevertheless that human sacrifice was an essential part of the ancient Greek perception of being.

Michaela Bauks deals with the two most important biblical narratives on human sacrifice, i. e. The Sacrifice of Isaac (Gen 22:1–19) and The Sacrifice of Jephtah's Daughter (Judg 11:29–39). Bauks argues that both Gen 22:1–19 and Judg 11:29–39 contain a theological reflection of the infinite within god. According to Bauks, both texts belong to the genre of theological commentary and both texts assume the idea of absolute dependency of every creature on god. In Israel, this absolute dependency would also be present in the dedication of all first-born to god. In Gen 22:1–19, Abraham is tested and Isaac is redeemed. In Judg 11:29–39,

---

[3] 32.

[4] 32.

Jephtah tests God and his daughter is lost. Especially the story about Jephtah's daughter reminds of the numerous variations of the sacrifice of Iphigenia in Aulis.

Karin Finsterbusch analyses the relevant texts in the Hebrew Bible concerning sacrifice or redemption of the first born of humans and animals. In preexilic times, Exod 22:28–29 (7th cent. B. C. E.) prescribes the sacrifice of the first-born child to YHWH and Ezek 20:25–26 attests to such a prexilic pratice of Yahwistic childsacrifice. Postexilic Jewish literature, however, speaks about the redemption of the first-born son. In all Torah-laws, both the sacrifice of the first-born and the substitute for it are understood as offerings to YHWH. However, neither the child sacrifice nor its substitutes are voluntary offerings in order to express thankfulness to God as the giver of life, but instead are a tribute owed to YHWH. A good example is the late post-exilic text, Exod 13, which justifies YHWH's continued claim to the first-borns of humans and animals by way of the Passover events. Israel owes YHWH its first-born because he released them out of Egypt.

After an extensive discussion of the history of child sacrifice in Israel and other Canaanite successor cultures, as well as in the Canaanite cultures themselves, Armin Lange analyses the references to child sacrifices (Jer 7:31; 19:5; 32:35) in the Deuteronomistic Jeremiah redaction (= DtrJer). Lange shows that in its polemics DtrJer condemns a Yahwistic cult of child sacrifice as Baalistic. The polemics of the DtrJer against child sacrifice are part of its rejection of the resurfacing Jerusalem cult and its Zion theology. Jer 7 in particular shows that the DtrJer uses child sacrifice as the quintessential negative paradigm in the extreme. This paradigm showed what lengths the sacrificial cult was willing to go in order to achieve its goals of salvation and protection. A similar line of argument can be found in the deuteronomistic Micah redaction (Mic 6:6-8).

For Bennie H. Reynolds the Biblical term למלך is best understood as a causative participle of the root הלך. An analysis of Phoenician inscriptions as well as biblical references demonstrates that in the Phoenician and Israelite cultures the *mōlek* designates a type of sacrifice and not a deity: "the god *Molek* should once again be put to rest. He never existed in the minds of Iron Age Israelites."[5]

[5] 150.

According to Katell Berthelot, human sacrifice is neither a major theme of pre-Rabbinic ancient Jewish literature nor is it completely absent. Three points are emphasized: the relative dearth of references to pagan human sacrifices, the tendency to present human sacrifices as inspired by demons, and the reinterpretation of specific biblical human sacrifices (Jephtah's daughter, in Judg 11:29–39) or near-sacrifices (Isaac, in Gen 22:1–19) as self-sacrifices to which a positive value is attached. Even if condemnation of human sacrifices prevails in Jewish literature from this period, the moral judgement passed on human sacrifices remains ambivalent, as illustrated by the very notion of self-sacrifice.

Tal Ilan analyses the Jewish reception of The Sacrifice of Jephtah's Daughter. The rabbis regarded Jephtah's acts as horrific and impious. For the rabbis, Jephtah's behaviour reflects the injustice of the time of the Judges. In better times, they believed, several legal objections would have prevented the sacrifice of Jephtah. *Midrash Tanḥumah* is an especially comprehensive example of these objections. The editor of this midrash takes the strongest arguments he can muster against Jephtah's sacrifice and puts them directly into her mouth. She quotes scripture to prove that the God of Israel did not institute human sacrifice. *Midrash Tanḥumah* employs a principle also found in feminist reading strategies, i. e. it places the woman at the center, thus giving a voice to the marginalized. That Jephtah's daughter is not heard is a strong indictment of a system which ignores a wise woman.

For Christianity, the crucifiction of Christ is a key issue. New Testament scholars debate extensively whether the death of Christ should be understood as an atonement or atonement sacrifice. In his study, Peter Lampe shows that in Paul's writings Christ's death on a Roman cross can be seen as an analogy to the offering of a Passover lamb, as well as an analogy to the covenant "burnt offerings" and "peace offerings" of Exod 24. Contrary to popular belief, however, Paul did not interpret Christ's death as a "sacrifice of atonement" for sins, nor did he not see an analogy to the attempted offering of Isaac in Gen 22.

For medieval Judaism, Rainer Walz discusses the topic of human sacrifice in the context of Jewish martyrdoms during the 1096 crusade. When threatened with enforced conversion or death by the crusaders male Jews often opted for killing their own family and themselves. While recent interpretations have focused on infanticide in particular as a sacrifical act which was supposed to accelerate the coming of the messianic revenge,[6] Walz points to the multiple influences which where combined in the Jewish martyrdoms of 1096. While the interpretation of martyrdom as sacrifice stresses the continuity of Jewish religion after the interruption of the Temple sacrifices, Jewish martyrdom differs from Christian martyrdom by the inclusion of suicide and even active killing of the persecuted co-believers. Furthermore, Jewish aggression against the persecutors, even killing them, if the circumstances allowed for it, shows that martyrdom was not an aim in itself as with Christianity.

In medieval Christianity the crucifixion of Christ was understood in terms of human sacrifice. A good example of this belief is expressed in the treatise *Cur deus homo* by Anselm of Canterbury. Jasper Hopkins, in his contribution, shows that Anselm "teaches that incarnation and death were the only means whereby God could accomplish the reconciliation of human beings with Himself, once the human race had fallen. In and through Jesus—who is the God-man, two natures in one person—God lovingly effects the supreme sacrifice of Himself qua human to Himself qua divine. This salvific sacrifice of a human being by the Divine Being, to the Divine Being, on behalf of all human beings who will avail themselves of it—this sacrifice is unique and unrepeatable."[7] According to Hopkins, such a divine self-sacrifice would be unparalleled in the history of religion.

Christopher Roberts describes Kirkegaard's reading of the the biblical story of the Sacrifice of Isaac (Gen 22) in his 1843 treatise *Fear and Trembeling* as "the most portentous religious polemic of the nineteenth century."[8] For "Kierkegaard's text the public motions of the ritual were merely the conditions of possibility for demonstrating the criterial characteristic of the knight of faith. In this way, for Kierkegaard the whole of Gen 22, wherein the protagonist 'resigned everything infinitely, and then he grasped everything again by virtue of the absurd,'[9] takes place all at once and without cessation ... With the focus no longer on sacrifice as a specific kind of act but rather on faith as a unique mode of being, Derrida's observation that 'this land of Moriah ... is our habitat every second of every day'[10] derives directly from Kierkegaard's insistent claim

[6] Israel Jacob Yuval, "Vengeance and Damnation, Blood and Defamation: From Jewish Martyrdom to Blood Libel Accusations," *Zion* 58 (1993): 31–90 [Hebrew].

[7] 257.

[8] 259.

[9] Kierkegaard, *Fear and Trembling*, and *Repetition*, 40.

[10] Derrida, *The Gift of Death*, 69.

that Abraham's trial is not safely relegated to a past historical stage, but stands as a challenge to would-be Christians down to the present day."[11]

In the 20th century the rhetoric of human sacrifice resurfaced in different contexts. Examples are its transformation in the Jewish ritual of the *Pidyon Haben*, and the use of sacrificial rhetoric in the contexts of capital punishment (see the contribution of Randall Styers) and Euthanasia. This is the topic of the study of Viktor von Weizsäcker, which is published in this volume for the first time in English translation. Von Weizsäcker's study is introduced and set into the broader context of human sacrifice by Udo Benzenhöfer and Wilhelm Rimpau. Entitled "Euthanasie und Menschenversuche" ("Euthanasia and Experiments on Human Beings"), von Weizsäcker published his study in 1947 in conjunction with the Nürnberg medical trial. By asking for potential "medical" reasons of the Nazi-Euthanasia, von Weizsäcker discusses the subject of human sacrifice. While in medical science there are cases which might justify the sacrifice of individuals for the greater public good (e. g. during an epidemic), Nazi-Euthanasia does not fall into this category: "One can say that any appeal to the prevalent right of a majority, of the healthy, the efficient or the racially preferred, does not create a solidarity, for this can be only based on mutuality. This means that the 'sacrifice' of another is never a real sacrifice and that the latter can be demonstrated only in the sacrifice of one's self."[12]

By way of the *Pidyon Haben*, 20th century Judaism retained an ancient transformation of childsacrifice, the ransoming of the firstborn sons. According to Yaakov Ariel, what was originally a substitute for child sacrifice became a rite of passage: "First-borns were particularly vulnerable, as they were precious 'first fruits' that signified the fertility of their mothers and the beginning of a family, with more children to follow. Moreover, an awareness that God, like the gods of their neighbors, saw the first-borns as 'His,' prompted the Israelites to make every effort to 'ransom' their boys and liberate them from whatever demands the Deity might have over them, so as to ensure a favorable attitude on the part of God and his angels. Giving up on a rite of passage that comes to protect the new-borns, especially first-born sons, was something Jews would not easily do."[13] Influenced by the Enlightenment, liberal Jews abondened the ritual, but at the turn of the twenty-first century, hav-

[11] 276.
[12] 283.
[13] 319.

ing reexamined 'irrational' elements in their tradition, liberal Jews have reinstituted the ritual.

Randall Styers discusses parallels between capital punishment in the present-day United States and human sacrifice. In discussing the sacrificial nature of state violence, he concludes: "Error is inevitable in any human legal regime, and the sacrifice of the innocent is thus an inescapable risk within the system of death. In the face of this possibility, many proponents of capital punishment actively embrace this form of human sacrifice as the proper means to attain higher social and spiritual rewards. But the rewards of this sacrificial scheme are surely illusive."[14]

It is a welcome obligation to us to express our gratitude and thanks to all participants of the Chapel Hill conference on "Human Sacrifice in Ancient Mediterranean Religion and its Reflections in Modernity," as well as to the additional contributors to our volume. We wish to express our gratitude to Yaakov Ariel for co-organizing the Chapel Hill conference and to Bennie H. Reynolds for helping with its organization. We are further obliged to Lance Lazar for working with us on editing this volume at an early stage. Special thanks go also to the staff of Brill publishers, Mattie Kuiper and Ingeborg van der Laan, as well as to the editors of the Numen Book Series, Steven Engler, Kim Knott, Pratap Kumar, and Kocku von Stuckrad.

Karin Finsterbusch, Armin Lange, Diethard Römheld
Landau, Vienna, and Bonn May 25th 2006

[14] 351.

Human Sacrifice in Judeo-Christian and Other Ancient Mediterranean Religions

Ritual Killing and Sacrifice in the Ancient Near East

BEATE PONGRATZ-LEISTEN, Princeton University, Princeton, N. J.

1. Introduction

In cultural, religious, and biblical studies there is a perennial interest in the cultural conditions that give rise to collective killing.[1] This type of killing may take the form of *homo militaris*[2] who goes to war,[3] of *homo interfector* who commits murder and of *homo necans*[4] who kills and offers a victim within a "cultic" context. Certain types of communal killing, especially human sacrifice so often associated with cannibalism[5] have been used to characterize the "primitive," the "savage," *in short* "the Other." In many instances such characterizations formed the basis for a rhetoric which ideologically justified colonial dominion. These notions also infected the study of the Near East contributing to a type of "Orientalism" which created descriptions of "foreign" cultures which both fascinated and repelled the observer. Walter Burkert and René Girard have argued

---

[1] I am grateful to Jerrold S. Cooper, Daniel Fleming, Burkhard Gladigow, Mark S. Smith, Annette Krüger and Michael Davis for their comments and stimulating insights they provided during various discussions.

[2] For collective killing see Adolf Ellegard Jensen, "Über das Töten als kulturgeschichtliche Erscheinung," *Paideuma* 4 (1950): 23–38. Burkhard Gladigow, "Homo publice necans: Kulturelle Bedingungen kollektiven Tötens," *Saeculum* 37 (1986): 150–65.

[3] Yvon Garlan, *War in the Ancient World: A Social History* (Ancient Culture and Society; London: Chatto & Windus, 1975); Heinrich von Stietencron and Jörg Rüpke, eds., *Töten im Krieg* (Veröffentlichungen des Instituts für historische Anthropologie e. V. 6; Freiburg i. Br.: Alber, 1995).

[4] Walter Burkert, *Homo Necans; Interpretationen altgriechischer Opferriten und Mythen* (Berlin: Walter de Gruyter, 1972); English translation: *Homo Necans: The Anthropology of Ancient Greek Sacrifical Ritual and Myth* (Berkeley: University of California Press, 1983).

[5] Maurice Bloch and Jonathan Parry, eds., *Death and the Regeneration of Life* (Cambridge: Cambridge University Press, 1987).

that violence, far from being abhorrent, is a central element in religious practice.[6]

New Testament scholars as well as scholars of the history of the Christian church, and scholars of religious studies have recognized and studied in great detail the symbolization[7] of sacrifice in the Christian scriptures, in Christian theology, and its ritual practice. This symbolization, of course centers upon the death and resurrection of Christ and plays an important role in the soteriological thinking of Christianity. The willingness of Jesus to become a "sacrificial victim" has been taken, at various times in the history of the Christian Church, as call to identify with the sufferings of Christ and to engage in similar "self-sacrifice." In extreme cases this religious impulse has lead to the glorification of violence, redefining self-injury or even suicide as martyrdom undertaken for the common good. Such notions have obviously become a challenge for modern societies in their contemporary war against religiously sanctioned terrorism.[8] By glorifying violence and redefining suicide as a sacrifice or martyrdom for the common good, religion has become a challenge for modern societies in their war against terror.[9]

The portrayal of Jesus' death as sacrificial in the New Testament literature is complex and is present in varying ways and to different degrees in the Gospel narratives, in the Pauline and Deutero-Pauline epistles, in the epistle to the Hebrews, in the Epistles of Peter, James, and John, and in Acts and Revelation. In this essay, I intend to take this complex of sacrificial concepts and imagery and break it down into its various basic components which I take to be the following: restoration of order, expiation, atonement, and redemption, as well as the vicarious nature of the sacrificial act involved in Jesus' death found in various passages in the New Testament corpus. Such concepts appear to belong to a wider cultural *koine* which might be found throughout the history of the Mediterranean and ancient Near East.

---

[6] See below.

[7] I prefer to speak of symbolization instead of symbolism to denote the cultural process in conceptualizing this idea of human self-sacrifice, see also my remarks in 5. 1.

[8] Rainer Albertz, ed., *Kult, Konflikt und Versöhnung: Beiträge zur kultischen Sühne in religiösen, sozialen und politischen Auseinandersetzungen des antiken Mittelmeerraumes* (AOAT 285; Münster: Ugarit-Verlag, 2001).

[9] Marc Juergensmeyer, *Terror in the Mind of God: The Global Rise of Religious Violence* (Comparative Studies in Religion and Society 13; Berkeley: University of California Press, 2000); Walter Reich, ed., *Origins of Terrorism: Psychologies, Ideologies, Theologies, States of Mind* (Woodrow Wilson Center Ser.; Cambridge: Cambridge University Press, 1990).

It has been shown by Alberto R. W. Green,[10] that the Mesopotamian archaeological and textual material presents a considerable range of examples for ritual killing.[11] But following Dietz Otto Edzard one should be careful not to categorize any of them as human sacrifice.[12] Further, there is no evidence that there existed any terminology relating specifically to human sacrifice in Sumerian or in Assyro-Babylonian language. However, it is not the literal practice of human sacrifice that is relevant here. Rather, these concepts are related to various forms of ritual killing as told in ritual and myth in the ancient Near Eastern communities coupled with notions found in the expression of personal piety and "redemption" attested in the context of legal concepts and procedures as well as purification rites. These provide the template for the various concepts embedded in the expiatory suffering and death of the Suffering Servant, who appears to atone for the sins of others[13] in Isaiah (Isa 53:10), the refusal of sacrifice (Hos 6:6) in favor of love for and knowledge of god as formulated in Isaac's Aqedah (Gen 22), and the sacrificial self-offering of Christ (Heb 2:2).[14]

2. Terminology

English and French scholars distinguish between the two terms offering / *offrande*, deriving from Latin *offere* "to offer" and *sacrifice* / *sacrifice*, deriving from Latin *sacrificium*. This latter term is to be constructed of *sacer* "sacred" and *facere* "to make," that is, "to transfer an object into the sphere of the sacred" or "to make an offering to the gods."[15] The German term "Opfer" embraces both meanings and not only denotes the ritual act of offering but also the material offered (English: also *offering*). The New Testament and Christian interiorization and spiritualization of the notion of sacrifice is organized around an inner disposition rather

---

[10] Alberto R. Whitney Green, *The Role of Human Sacrifice in the Ancient Near East* (ASOR Diss. Ser. 1; Missoula, Mont.: Scholars Press, 1975).

[11] Green combines ritual killing and humans sacrifice in his investigation.

[12] Dietz Otto Edzard, "Menschenopfer," *RlA* 8, 60–61.

[13] Tryggve N. D. Mettinger, *A Farewell to the Servant Songs: A Critical Examination of an Exegetical Axiom* (Scripta Minora Regiae Societatis Humaniorum Litterarum Lundensis 1982/83, 3; Lund: Gleerup, 1983). The Servant has to be understood as a metaphor for the exiled community of Israel, not a single individual (Mettinger, 43).

[14] On the connection between Isaac's Aqedah and Jesus see James Swetnam, *Jesus and Isaac: A Study of the Epistle to the Hebrews in the Light of the Aqedah* (AnBib 94; Rome: Biblical Institute Press, 1981).

[15] Hubert Seiwert, "Opfer," in *Handbuch religionswissenschaftlicher Grundbegriffe* IV (ed. H. Cancik, B. Gladigow, and K.-H. Kohl; Stuttgart: Kohlhammer, 1998), 268–84, 270.

than an outer form.[16] Its metaphorical use of the terminology of offering has had its impact on the modern German vernacular which uses "Opfer" in the context of renunciation and self-sacrifice, in the context of crime, traffic accidents, etc., while the English would speak of victims.[17] However, while the term "offering" is generally used as the umbrella term, the word "sacrifice" is treated as having a far more narrow, specialized sense.[18]

3. Approaches in Religious Studies

Comparative religious studies of the nineteenth century shaped important approaches to the interpretation of sacrifice or human sacrifice. I would like to draw the reader's attention to some of these approaches that still remain important in the discussion on sacrifice and even ritual in general. The nineteenth century tended to de-contextualize offering and sacrifice taking it out of its ritual context and blurring its rationale with the notion of the sacred and its mystique.[19] This approach was revived in the theories of Burkert and Girard. In contrast, Edward B. Tylor[20] proposed that the offering was a medium of communication involving the divine realm. The sacrifice, therefore stood in analogy to human social behavior. The sacrifice was a gift and was intended to have a *do ut des* effect (I give that you may give). Tylor's theory of sacrifice involved an evolutionary scheme consisting of "gift," "homage," and "abnegation." Abnegation represented the latest and therefore higher form of religion (monotheism) encompassing systems of morality. In 1889 William R. Smith[21] advanced his idea of sacrifice as a communion between man and god during a sacramental meal. The function of the

[16] Jill Robbins, "Sacrifice," in *Critical Terms for Religious Studies* (ed. M. C. Taylor; Chicago: University of Chicago Press, 1998) 285–97.

[17] Seiwert, "Opfer," 271; Richard Schenk, "Einführung in die Thematik 'Zur Theorie des Opfers'," in idem, ed., *Zur Theorie des Opfers: Ein interdisziplinäres Gespräch* (Collegium Philosophicum 1, Stuttgart: Frommann-Holzboog, 1995), 1–7.

[18] Seiwert, "Opfer," 270. Victor Turner, "Sacrifice as quintessential process: Prophylaxis or abandonment?" *HR* 16 (1977): 189–215.

[19] Burton Mack, "Introduction: Religion and Ritual," in *Violent Origins: Walter Burkert, René Girard, and Jonathan Z. Smith on Ritual Killing and Cultural Formation* (ed. R. G. Hamerton-Kelly; Stanford: Stanford University Press, 1987), 1–70, 2.

[20] Edward B. Tylor, *Primitive Culture:Researches into the Development of Mythology, Philosophy, Religion, Language, Art, and Custom* (1871; reprint: *Primitive Culture 2: Religion in Primitive Culture*; New York: Harper & Row, 1958), 461–96

[21] William R. Smith, *Lectures on the Religion of the Semites: The Foundational Institutions* (London: Black, 1914).

sacrifice was to re-affirm the union between the social community and their deity. Famine, plague and other disasters were signs of the deterioration of the community's link with the deity, and the sacrificial meal was the only means by which to re-establish this union. Smith's idea was that the blood of the sacrificial animal connected humans and gods, and therefore the idea of expiation and atonement became part of the communion. His idea of atonement was linked to the idea of the deity's presence in the sacrificial meal. While concentrating on Sanskrit and Hebrew texts, Henri Hubert and Marcel Mauss[22] in their important contribution on the nature and function of sacrifice tried to show the likeness between the structure of Christian sacrifice and earlier rites. Hubert and Mauss concentrated upon the idea of absolute sanctity pervading all persons and things involved in the sacrifice. Much emphasis was placed upon the rites involving the consecration of the sacrificial place and the instruments used in the sacrificial act. These rites also implied their disposal after the sacrificial meal. This sacrifical communion sanctified the sacrifier and thereby changed his / her status. The essential legacy of Hubert's and Mauss' work lies in their attention to the complex character of sacrificial rites that prohibits isolating single aspects or intentions.

Based on the ethological research that ritual communication preceeds language,[23] Walter Burkert developed his theory of ritual behavior as a successful strategy for human survival.[24] He makes two observations: the first is that sacrifice accompanies all major religious institutions in Greek culture such as festivals, seats of oracles, games, cults mysteries, funerary rites, state ceremonies, or mythologies and drama. The second observation is that the special care taken in the handling of the bones of sacrificial animals in later Greek cult reflects the earlier practices performed among Paleolithic hunters. From these two observations he develops a theory of ritual and religion with which he investigates classical Greek texts.[25] According to Burkert, sacrifice evolved from the basic human need for survival especially from hunting. The whole range of

[22] Henri Hubert and Marcel Mauss, *Essai sur la nature et la fonction du sacrifice* (Paris: Alcan, 1899; English trans.: *Sacrifice: Its Nature and Function*; trans. W. D. Halls; Chicago: Chicago University Press, 1964).

[23] Rick Franklin Talbott, *Sacred Sacrifice: Ritual Paradigms in Vedic Religion and Early Christianity* (American University Studies 9, 150; New York: Lang, 1995).

[24] Burkert, *Homo necans*.

[25] Mack, ""Introduction," 24.

human behavioral patterns related to territory, feeding, pairing and reproduction can be traced back to the preparation and coordination of the hunt. Killing becomes part of the *conditio humana*. Similar to Burkert, the French literary critic and cultural philosopher René Girard understands religion as a social construction and tries to clarify its role in the formation of society. In his psychosocial approach as presented in *La Violence et le sacré*[26] he claims that *scapegoating*[27] is integrated into religious systems through the ritual of sacrifice as a ritually controlled answer to the uncontrolled violence and killing Girard sees as endemic to human society. Through the selection of a surrogate victim or scapegoat, which becomes the object of a common violence, aggression is channeled away from the community onto the scapegoat whose sacrifice aims at restoring harmony to the community and reinforcing the social fabric.[28] Ritual sacrifice and the origin of the sacred imply each other and can be traced back to a *violence fondatrice*. It is surprising that a philologist and a cultural philosopher with his uncritical reading of scapegoat rituals and a sacrificial theory that implicitly takes the Christian Sacrifice of the Mass as a model could have such an impact on theoretical approaches in religious studies.[29] Since the 1980s Girard's approach of this "dramatic theology" has been very influential in Anglo-American academics. It seems that the idea of an inherent relationship between religion and violence has recently again become a question of such high topical interest that it can serve for either ritual theory or as a pattern of explanation for actual politics.

Unlike the approaches of Burkert and Girard the German religious historian Burkhard Gladigow[30] moves away from defining a universal theory of sacrifice. He instead re-anchors sacrifice into the larger set

---

[26] René Girard, *La Violence et le sacré* (Paris: Grasset, 1972; English trans.: *Violence and the Sacred*; trans. P. Gregory; Baltimore: Johns Hopkins University Press, 1977).

[27] See also his article "Generative Scapegoating" in *Violent Origins* (ed. Hamerton-Kelly), 73–105; Girard, *Le bouc émissaire* (Paris: Grasset, 1982; English trans.: *The Scapegoat*, trans. Y. Freccero; Baltimore: Johns Hopkins University Press, 1986).

[28] Girard, *Violence*, 8.

[29] Burkhard Gladigow, "Religion und Gewalt: Religionsgeschichtliche, kulturanthropologische und systematische Aspekte," in preparation. I am grateful to Burkhard Gladigow for having shared his thoughts with me.

[30] Burkard Gladigow, "Die Teilung des Opfers: Zur Interpretation von Opfern in vor- und frühgeschichtlichen Epochen," *Frühmittelalterliche Studien* 18 (1984), 19–43; idem, "Opfer und komplexe Kulturen," in *Opfer: Theologische und kulturelle Kontexte* (ed. B. Janowski and M. Welker; Frankfurt: Suhrkamp, 2000), 86–105.

of a complex ritual while considering the historical context, place, and time of the ritual, the material of the sacrifice, the transfer of the sacrifice, the ritual acts preceding and following the act of sacrifice, cathartic rites,[31] processions, verbal acts such as prayers and recitations, divination, as well as the division of the sacrifice among the participant. This understanding of sacrifice precludes an interpretation of the pre-Christian Mediterranean sacrifice in terms of imaginary patricide, killing mechanisms or violence. Instead of being understood as a dramatic event, sacrifice is therefore seen as a routine maintenance of the cult which has daily course of ritual practices involving economic, political, and social considerations.[32]

Gladigow's characterization of "offering" and "sacrifice" is certainly to be preferred from a theoretical perspective in accounting for offering and sacrifice in the ancient Near Eastern context because of the attention to the actual complexity of the ritual. Assyro-Babylonian culture displays a whole range of terms denoting vegetal offerings and animal offerings such as *ginû* for small livestock and cattle, wine and dates; *ginû* occurs very often together with *sattukku* (dates cereals, sheep); terms such as *niqû* (sheep offering or offering in general), *guqqû* (small cattle, dates, wine), and *nindabû* (cereal offering) are also used as complementary to *sattukku*. Other terms such as *sirqu* and *surqinnu* derived from *sarāqu* "to sprinkle" denote the sprinkling of flour.[33] All these terms are used to describe the regular offerings given to the gods in the context either of the daily cult or on specific days in the cultic calendar such as the *eššešu* festival. The Mesopotamian practice of offering and a general theory of sacrifice do, however, not suffice to explain complex theological concepts such as human self-sacrifice, and, consequently, we have to search for other explanations. Before I do so, however, I would like

---

[31] I use the term "cathartic" as an umbrella term to describe all kinds of purificatory and exorcistic rites.

[32] Gladigow, "Opfer und komplexe Kulturen," 104.

[33] The Assyro-Babylonian Culture displays a whole range of terms denoting various vegetal offerings and animal offerings such as *ginû* for small livestock and cattle, wine, dates, it occurs very often together with *sattukku*; *niqû*, *guqqû*, *nindabû* (also complementary to *sattukku*), *sirqu* (derived from *sarāqu* "to sprinkle, scatter") and *surqinnu*, *maqlūtu* (burnt offerings), *karummatu*. See also Wilfred G. Lambert, "Donations of Food and Drink to the Gods in Ancient Mesopotamia," in *Ritual and Sacrifice in the Ancient Near East: Proceedings of the International Conference Leuven 1991* (ed. J. Quaegebeur; OLA 55; Leuven: Peeters, 1993) 191–201; for the Sumerian siskur see Henri Limet, "Le sacrifice siskur," in loc. cit., 243–55.

to address various forms of killing that were not considered to be illegal in ancient societies.[34]

4. Sacrifice, Ritual Killing, Cannibalism

Human sacrifice not only involves the killing of a person or the use of the human blood, flesh, or bones for ritual purposes; the victim must also be offered to a deity.[35] The distinction of this type of sacrifice obviously lies in the material involved. Other offerings would be animal sacrifice, vegetal offering, drink-offering, blood offering, etc. Considering the intention and the form of the ritual actions underlying the offering it may differ according to the context.[36] If one considers the form or way of treating the offering material sacrifice might be categorized as burnt offering, offering of slain animals, libation, building offering, etc. On the other hand, a typology emphasizing the intention of the offering person / sacrifier, might distinguish between the supplicatory offering, thank-offering, purificatory and propitiatory sacrifice.[37]

Seiwert's distinction between the two basic intentions of the sacrifice, the communicative and the distancing intention,[38] is helpful for distinguishing between sacrifice in the cultic context of ritual interaction between humans and gods, which in analogy to human interaction primarily conveys the idea of gift giving or sharing of a meal (communicatory intention), and ritual killing in order to eliminate illness, sin or other harmful effects (distancing intention). A distancing intention also applies to sacrifices to ward off divine wrath. Consequently, ritual killing of a human being with a distancing function should not be categorized as human sacrifice because there is no offering of the victim to a deity involved.

It is important to note that in the ancient Near East "sacrifice" with communicatory intention remains a province of highly specialized experts.[39] In the daily cult, the consumption of the sacrifice, consequently,

---

34 Hildegard Cancik-Lindemaier, "Menschenopfer," in *Der Neue Pauly: Enzyklopädie der Antike* 7 (ed. Hubert Cancik et al.; Stuttgart: Metzler, 1999), 1254–55.

35 Jan van Baal, "Offering, Sacrifice, and Gift," *Numen* 23 (1967), 161–78.

36 Sabine Hensel, "Menschenopfer," in *Metzler Lexikon Religion* 2 (ed. Chr. Auffarth, J. Bernard, and H. Mohr; Stuttgart: Metzler, 1999) 427–29.

37 Hensel, "Menschenopfer," 427; Seiwert, "Opfer," 280.

38 Seiwert 1998, 280.

39 A point made by John Gregory McMahon, "Cultural Boundaries in Hittite Ritual," in *Hittite Studies in Honor of Harry A. Hoffner Jr.* (ed. G. M. Beckman, R. H. Beal, and J. G. McMahon; Winona Lake: Eisenbrauns, 2003), 265–80, 275.

remains restricted to a specific group within the elite, with ritual experts performing the cult and other groups running the economics of the temple.[40] All these individuals got their share of the offering. An essential function of the offering was establishing and maintaining the social position of the temple household. In contrast to other cultures of the Mediterranean Mesopotamian tradition shows no traces of a *communio* between the deity and the worshippers. Nor are there any signs of channeling aggression and violence in the sacrificial act as assumed by Burkert and Girard.

Cannibalism, or anthropophagy, is sometimes considered to be a form of human sacrifice. There are three sorts of cannibalism: a) the real cannibalism that occurs in extreme situations such as famine; b) the symbolic cannibalism based on the idea that vitality and strength of a human being are concentrated in his organs and blood, and that by consuming them one can inherit that vitality—thus symbolic cannibalism may be part of warfare as well as of ritual context; and c) the phantasies of cannibalism which may occur in myths, theogonies, folktales and as a literary device.[41]

Only the last type (c) is attested in the ancient Near East. In Mesopotamian literature, anthropophagy[42] is said to happen in most distressing times of famine and extreme suffering. Thus the later version of the Babylonian *Atraḫasīs* describes how the gods try different methods of decimating the overpopulation of humankind such as plagues and famine, and after six years people start to consume their family members:

> [When the sixth year arrived], [they served up] the daughter
> for meal,
> They served up the [son for food] ...
> One [house] consumed another.[43]

---

[40] Assyrian royal decrees are especially illuminating regarding the lists of beneficiaries of the offering, see the texts published by Laura Kataja and Robert M. Whiting, *Grants, Decrees, and Gifts of the Neo-Assyrian Period* (SAA 12; Helsinki: Helsinki University Press, 1995).

[41] Sabine Hensel, "Kannibalismus," in *Metzler Religion* 2, 157–59; William Arens, *The Man-Eating Myth: Anthropology and Antropophagy* (New York: Oxford University Press, 1979); Bloch and Parry, eds., *Death and Regeneration*; Lutz Röhrich, "Die Volksballade von 'Herrn Peters Seefahrt' und die Menschenopfer-Sagen," in *Märchen, Mythos, Dichtung: Festschrift F. von der Leyen* (ed. H. Kuhn; Munich: Beck, 1963) 177–212

[42] Dietz Otto Edzard, "Kannibalismus," *RlA* 5, 389–90

[43] *Atraḫasīs* II v 22 ff.

Old Babylonian omina[44] refer to anthropophagy as do the curse formula in the treaty between Aššurnīrārī and Mati'-ilu,[45] royal inscriptions of Ashurbanipal,[46] and a Neo-Babylonian letter.[47]

In the following, I will show that anthropophagy is not of importance for our discussion, and that instead of dealing with sacrifice I will deal with patterns of ritual killing.

5. Patterns of Ritual Killing in the Ancient Near East: Preparing the Way for the Concepts of Atonement and Redemption

5. 1. Introduction

Before I set out to survey on various forms of killing as transformative act or ritual killing in Mesopotamia I would like to mention one example that might be categorized as ritual killing but does not have to be so. Charles Leonard Woolley, the excavator of Ur, interpreted the death of the retainers and their burial with the kings and queens of Early Dynastic Ur as human sacrifice,[48] postulating that the Ur I kings were divine. Susan Pollock emphasized that the inclusion of retainers in the burials of kings and queens must be seen as an "extreme form of display of

---

44 YOS 10, 45:51: *sunqu iššakkamma aḫu šīr aḫi ikkal* "There will be famine and the brother will eat the flesh of his brother."

45 SAA II, 2 rev. iv 10–11 *šīr mārēšunu mārātišunu lēkulūma kīma šīr ḫurāpi ḫurāpti liṭib* "May they eat the flesh of their sons and daughters, and may it taste as good to them as the flesh of the spring lambs."

46 Rykle Borger, *Beiträge zum Inschriftenwerk Assurbanipals: Die Prismenklassen A, B, C=K, D, E, F, G, H, J und T sowie andere Inschriften* (Wiesbaden: Harrassowitz, 1996), 67 prism A ix 59: *ana būrišunu ēkulū šīr mārēšunu* "in their hunger they ate the flesh of their children"; VAB 134, viii 18.

47 *ABL* 1274:10: *ana bubūtiya šīra ša mārēni u mārātini [nīt]akal* "should we eat the flesh of our sons and daughters in our! hunger?" See Manfried Dietrich, *Die Aramäer Südbabyloniens in der Sargonidenzeit (700–648)* (AOAT 7; Kevelaer: Butzon & Berker, 1970). The evidence has been collected by Brigitte Groneberg, "Atramhasis, Tafel II iv–v," in *Marchands, diplomates et empereurs: Ètudes sur la civilisation méopotamienne offertes à P. Garelli* (ed. D. Charpin and F. Joannès; Paris: Éd. Recherche sur les Civilisations, 1991), 397–410.

48 Charles Leonard Woolley, *The Royal Cemetery: A Report on the Predynastic and Sargonid Graves Excavated between 1926–31* (Ur Excavations 2; London: Trustees of the British Museum, 1934), 42. This interpretation was carried on by people outside the field, see for instance Brenda Ralph Lewis, *Ritual Sacrifice: An Illustrated History* (Stroud: Sutton, 2001), 28; Michael M. Rind, *Menschenopfer: Vom Kult der Grausamkeit* (Regensburg: Universitätsverlag Regensburg, 1996), 51 f.; Gunnar Heinsohn, *Die Erschaffung der Götter: Das Opfer als Ursprung der Religion* (Reinbeck bei Hamburg: Rowohlt, 1997), 16 f.

the power of certain individuals ... over the lives of others."[49] Green argued for an example of ritual killing in this instance in order to furnish the king with his wives, attendants, servants and all the gear of his earthly state[50] as described in the Sumerian tale *The Death of Gilgamesh*.[51]

> His beloved wife, his beloved son,
> His beloved favorite wife and junior wife,
> His beloved singer, cup-bearer and ...,
> His beloved barber, his beloved ...,
> His beloved attendants who all served (in) the palace,
> His beloved consignments—
> When they had lain down in their place with (him),
> As in the pure palace in Uruk,
> Gilgamesh, son of Ninsun,
> Weighed out the meeting-gifts for Ereshkigal,
> Weighed out the presents of Namtar.[52]

Archaeological and textual evidence refer to the concept of an afterlife where the privileged lifestyle for the deceased king had to be maintained in order to guarantee the continuity of his status when in the after-life. One could think of categorizing it as an example for maintaining the concept of order and in some way killing or self-killing must have been part of the burial ritual.

5. 2. Transformation and Violence: Striving to Maintain the Cosmic Order

The ancient Near Eastern idea of the cosmos is that of a *creatio continua*, an order that constantly has to be re-established. Unlike the Christian

---

[49] Susan Pollock, "Of Priestesses, Princes and Poor Relations: The Dead in the Royal Cemetery of Ur," *Cambridge Archaeological Journal* 1 (1991): 171–89.

[50] Green, *Role of Human Sacrifice*, 53.

[51] Antoine Cavigneaux and Farouk N. H. al-Rawi, *Gilgameš et la mort: Avec un appendice sur les textes funéraires sumériennes* (Textes de Tell Haddad VI; Cuneiform Monographs 19; Groningen: Styx, 2000), 59, ll. 262–67; Andrew George, *The Epic of Gilgamesh: The Babylonian Epic Poem and Other Textes in Akkadian and Sumerian* (London: Lane, 1999), 195 ff., 206.; Douglas Frayne in idem, Benjamin R. Foster, and Gary M. Beckman, *The Epic of Gilgamesh: A New Translation, Analogues, Criticism* (New York: Norton, 2001), 143 ff., 152.

[52] Translation Steve Tinney, "Death and Burial in Early Mesopotamia: The View from the Texts," in *Treasures from the Royal Tombs of Ur* (ed. Richard L. Zettler and Lee Horne; Philadelphia: University of Pennsylvania, Museum of Archeology and Anthropology, 1998), 26–28.

cosmology which adopted the Stoic concept of chaos by transforming it into the negative concept of *confusio*, antagonistic to the cosmic order,[53] disruptive elements in the ancient Near East were seen to be part of the cosmos, and it remains the continuous task of the king to integrate these elements into the existing order. Warfare, and, consequently, killing are necessary to establish and maintain the political order and with it, peace and prosperity. Creation remains part of the present and is not restricted to the cosmological narratives about the beginnings.[54] This concept is evident in the royal inscriptions as well as in the myths of the "battles of gods" such as *Enūma eliš* when Marduk does kill the monster Tiamat but does not annihilate her. Rather, her body is submitted to a transformation[55] as she becomes the material substance for building the cosmos. Killing here acquires a foundational aspect. This reintegrative aspect without killing is found in the *Anzû Myth* when Enlil, after his son Ninurta has defeated the Anzû bird, turns Anzû into the guardian of his temple. The same idea governs the Tiglath-Pileser's statement that he installed 25 gods of conquered lands to be doorkeepers of various temples in the city of Assur.[56] Order as the ultimate goal then allows for forms of violence embracing transformation, suppression or even killing. Under the auspices of maintaining or re-establishing order violence legitimates itself as counter-violence to ward off a threatening danger.

The aspect of transformation through killing also applies to the slaying of a god in order to create humankind in the mythical narratives. Interestingly, this motif is not known in the Sumerian creation accounts and is only introduced with the Old Babylonian version of *Atraḫasīs* in the first half of the second millennium B. C. E. When the younger generation of the gods rebels because of their workload in taking care of the canal building, Ea suggests to the chief god Enlil to let the goddess

---

[53] Christoph Auffarth, "Chaos," in *Handbuch religionswissenschaftlicher Grundbegriffe* 2 (ed. H. Cancik; Stuttgart: Kohlhammer, 1990), 193–95 with reference to Augustinus.

[54] Christoph Auffarth, *Der drohende Untergang: "Schöpfung" in Mythos und Ritual im Alten Orient und in Griechenland am Beispiel der Odyssee und des Ezechielbuches* (Religionsgeschichtliche Versuche und Vorarbeiten 39; Berlin: Walter de Gruyter, 1991), 44.

[55] Bruce B. Lawrence, "Transformation," in *Critical Terms for Religious Studies* (ed. Marc C. Taylor; Chicago: University of Chicago Press, 1998), 334–48.

[56] Beate Pongratz-Leisten, "The Other and the Enemy in the Mesopotamian Conception of the World," in *Mythology and Mythologies: Methodological Approaches to the Intercultural Influences. Proceedings of the Second Annual Symposium of the Assyrian and Babylonian Intellectual Heritage Project, Paris 1999* (ed. Robert M. Whiting; Melammu Symposia II; Helsinki: The Neo-Assyrian Text Corpus Project, 2001), 195–231.

Bēlet-ilī create man so that he can bear the load of the gods. Atraḫasīs I col. IV 192ff.:[57]

> They summoned and asked the goddess,
> The midwife of the gods, wise Mami,[58]
> 'Will you be the birth goddess, creatress of mankind?
> Create a human being that he bear the yoke!
> Let him bear the yoke, the task of Enlil,
> Let man assume the drudgery of god!'
> Nintu made ready to speak,
> And said to the great gods,
> 'It is not for me to do it.
> The task is Enki's;
> He it is that cleanses all,
> Let him provide me clay so I can do the making.'
> Enki made ready to speak,
> And said to the great gods,
> 'On the first, seventh, and fifteenth days of the month
> let me establish a purification, a bath.
> Let the one god[59] be slaughtered,
> The let the gods be cleansed by immersion.
> Let Nintu mix clay with his flesh and blood.
> Let that same god and man be thoroughly mixed in the clay.
> Let us hear the drumbeat for the rest of time,
> From the flesh of the god let a spirit remain,
> Let it make the living know its sign,
> Lest he be allowed to be forgotten, let the spirit remain.'
> The great Anunna-gods who administer destinies
> Answered 'Yes!' in the assembly.

[57] Translation Benjamin R. Foster, *Before the Muses* I: *An Anthology of Akkadian Literature* (Bethesda: CDL Press, 1993), 165f.

[58] After the creation process, Mami then in the assembly of the gods is renamed Bēlet-ilī.

[59] On *ilam išten* as the "leader-god," see William L. Moran, "The Creation of Man in Atrahasis I 192–248," in idem, *The Most Magic Word: Essays on Babylonian and Biblical Literture* (ed. R. S. Hendel; CBQMS 35; Washington: Catholic Biblical Association of America, 2002), 75–86, 81.

The god Enki / Ea who, due to his cunning and his practical and incantatory knowledge, assumes the role of the trickster[60] in Mesopotamian mythology, now enters in the role of the second creator who provides the idea and the material for creating mankind. It is due to his possession of secret knowledge that he is able not only to provide the clay but also to transform the substance of the slaughtered god into the first human being. Later when the mythical narrative proceeds to the actual description of the creation of humankind the myth plays on the words *eṭemmu* and *ṭēmu* "intelligence" or "scheme" as William L. Moran[61] prefers to translate (I col. iv 223–24):

> We-ila[62] who had the scheme [*ṭēma*] (to overthrow Enlil),
> they slaughtered in their assembly.

The gods' partaking in the slaughtering is the reason why Ea establishes the purification rites performed in a bath (*rimku*) on specific days of the months to allow the gods to cleanse themselves from the defilement generated through the contact with the dead god. Although man is created out of the flesh and blood of a god who partook in the rebellion against Enlil, the aspect of guilt of the rebellious god is not elaborated on in the myth and should also not be read into it on the basis of later texts.[63] Rather the divine material provides the substance for the ghost or disembodied spirit of man. Killing the rebel god establishes the new order with humankind now assuming the role of the younger gods in building the canals. An interesting aspect of when to apply punishment is disclosed in Ea's speech[64] addressed to Enlil after the flood. Enlil had imposed the flood as punishment on humankind and Ea now cautions against arbitrary wrongdoing by suggesting to punish only the

---

[60] William J. Hynes and William G. Doty, eds., *Mythical Trickster Figures: Contours, Contexts, and Criticisms* (Tuscaloosa: University of Alabama Press, 1993); Michael Weis, "Trickster," in *Metzler Lexikon Religion* 3 (ed. Chr. Auffarth, J. Bernard, and H. Mohr; Stuttgart: Metzler, 2000), 533–35.

[61] Moran, "Creation," 81.

[62] It is noteworthy to mention that the sign WE may be read Sumerian GEŠTUG = Akkadian *ṭēmu*.

[63] Pace Robert A. Oden Jr., "Divine Aspirations in Atrahasis and in Genesis I–II," *ZAW* 93 (1981): 197–216, 199–200; William L. Moran, "Some Considerations of Form and Interpretation in Atrahasis," in William L. Moran, *The Most Magic Word: Essays on Babylonian and Biblical Literture* (ed. R. S. Hendel; CBQMS 35; Washington: Catholic Biblical Association of America, 2002), 46–58, 55.

[64] Tablet III VI 16 ff.; see also Gilgamesh XI 183 ff., Foster, *Gilgamesh*, 90 f.

transgressors and otherwise to control the number of people by forbidding marriage and procreation to certain groups of people and ordaining mortality for all.

The rationale in *Atraḫasīs* is that man, although having fulfilled his duty, due to forces beyond his control was drawn into a situation that approached the chaotic represented in overpopulation. "He acquired a kind of guilt simply by being, and its very inevitability gives it a tragic dimension."[65]

Unlike *Atraḫasīs* the creation epic *Enūma eliš* transmitted in texts dating to the first millennium B. C. E.[66] elaborates on the slaying of a god as being performed as a consequence of his wickedness or rebellious character. For the first time mythical discourse explicitly introduces the notion of guilt and sin into the context of the slaughtering of the rebellious god Qingu. *Enūma eliš* VI 1 ff.:[67]

When [Mard]uk heard the speech of the gods,
He was resolving to make artful things (*niklāte*).[68]
He would tell his idea to Ea,
What he thought of in his heart he proposes,
'I shall compact blood, I shall cause bones to be.
I shall make stand a human being, let ‹Man›be its name.
I shall create humankind,
They shall bear the gods' burden that those may rest (*pašḫu*).[69]
I shall artfully double the ways of the gods,
Let them be honored as one but divided in twain.'[70]

---

[65] William L. Moran, "A Mesopotamian Myth and its Biblical Transformation," in Moran, *Most Magic Word*, 59–74, 71.

[66] Wilfred G. Lambert linked the promotion of Marduk to Nebuchadrezzar's I retrieval of Maruk's statue from Elam in the twelfth century, Wilfred G. Lambert, "The Reign of Nebuchadrezzar I: A Turning Point in the History of Ancient Near Eastern Religion," in *The Seed of Wisdom: Essays in honor of T. J. Meek* (ed. William Steward Mc Cullough; Toronto: University of Toronto Press, 1964), 3–13; Stephanie Dalley, on the contrary traces the origin back into the Old Babylonian period, "Statues of Marduk and the Date of Enūma eliš," *AoF* 24 (1997): 163–71; the text as it exists linguistically must date later but the origin of the idea may well go back into the Old Babylonian period.

[67] Foster, *Before the Muses*, 384 f.

[68] Dalley chooses the translation "miracle" instead. I would stay with the original meaning of "ingenuity, skillful work" for *nikiltu*, see CAD N/2, 220 f., because it is the technological aspect which is referred to primarily.

[69] "Appeased" would be the literal meaning.

Ea answered him saying these words,
He told him a plan to let the gods rest (*tapšuḫti*).
'Let one of their brothers be given to me,
Let him be destroyed so that people can be fashioned.
Let the great gods convene in assembly,
Let the guilty one (*ša anni*)[71] be given up that they may abide.'[72]
Marduk convened the great gods in assembly,
He spoke to them magnanimously as he gave the command,
The gods heeded his utterance.
As the king spoke to the Anunna-gods (these) words,
'Let your first reply be the truth![73]
Do you speak with me truthful words![74]
Who was it that made war,
Suborned Tiamat and drew up for battle?
Let him be given over to me, the one who made war,
I shall make him bear his punishment (*arnu*), you shall sit quietly (*pašāḫiš tišbā*).'[75]
The Igigi, the great gods, answered him,
To Lugal-dimmer-ankia, sovereign of all the gods, their lord,
'It was Qingu who made war,
Suborned Tiamat and drew up for battle!'
They bound and held him before Ea,
They imposed the punishment on him and shed his blood.
From his blood he made mankind,
He imposed the burden of the gods (on man) and exempted the gods.

The killing of a rebel god in the Mesopotamian world view, consequently, results in a positive consequence[76] because killing the disruptive

[70] This is a reference to the division of the Mesopotamian pantheon into the Anuna-gods and the Igigi-gods, see Foster, *Before the Muses*, 384 cf. n. 3.

[71] Literally "the one of guilt" (*annu* < *arnu*).

[72] *ša anni linnadinma šunu liktūnu* "the guilty / criminal should be extradited so that they become reinstated / loyal / well-disciplined" (CAD K, 162 s. v. *kânu* 2).

[73] *Enūma eliš* VI 21 *lu kīnamma maḫrû nimbakun*.

[74] *Enūma eliš* VI 22 *kīnāti atammâ* (var. *tatammâ*) *inimma ittija* "Speak truthful words with me!"

[75] Foster's translation "you shall be released" imports a connotation which to my understanding reminds too much the idea of vicariousness.

[76] Hyam Maccoby, *The Sacred Executioner: Human Sacrifice and the Legacy of Guilt* (London: Thames & Hudson, 1982), 8.

force re-establishes the concept of order as schemed by the gods. Unlike our modern world view killing in Mesopotamia primarily is part of a concept of order and not of ethical considerations.[77] Qingu belongs into the category of the *dema*-deities[78] who through their violent death contribute to the foundation of the actual world order. Qingu dies to provide the material for creating humankind which then relieves the gods of their tasks. The message is that humankind has to take care of the cult of the gods. Given Qingu's guilt, his death definitely takes on the character of an execution. Killing now acquires a legal significance. Qingu dies as a substitute for the rest of the rebellious gods and with his execution the chaotic force threatening the cosmic order has been eliminated. However, there is no hint either to atonement or to sacrifice.

Mythology thus reflects the same concept as is promoted in the royal inscriptions that conceive of warfare as an act of creation because it defeats chaos. War and chaos are antithetical, not war and peace. War is viewed as *creatio continua*.[79] Peace is a state resulting from the political action of the king who by means of warfare establishes *kittu* (right) and *mīšaru* (justice), *mitgurtu* (consent) and *nēḫtu* (peace).[80] This practical wisdom is already stated in the Middle Assyrian *Tukultī-Ninurta Epic* III A 15'–16':

> There will be established no peace (*salīmu*) without combat (*mitḫuṣu*),
> A good relationship (*ṭūbtu*) does not come without fighting (*šitnunu*).

---

[77] For these different concepts of thought see also Mary Douglas, *Leviticus as Literature* (Oxford: Oxford University Press, 1999), esp. chapter 2.

[78] This category was introduced by Adolf E. Jensen, *Die getötete Gottheit: Das religiöse Weltbild einer frühen Kultur* (Stuttgart: Kohlhammer, 1966) who borrowed the term from the language of the Marind-Anim in the South of New Guinea where it denotes exceptional forces that can be inherent in objects and persons but also exist independently, see also Karl-Heinz Kohl, "Dema-Gottheiten," in *Handbuch religionswissenschaftlicher Grundbegriffe* 2 (ed. H. Cancik; Stuttgart: Kohlhammer, 1990), 215 f.

[79] Eckhart Otto, "Human Rights: The Influence of the Hebrew Bible," *JNSL* 25 (1999): 1–20.

[80] Eva Cancik-Kirschbaum, "Rechtfertigung von politischen Handeln in Assyrien im 13. / 12. Jh. v. Chr.," in *Ana šadî Labnāni lū allik: Beiträge zu altorientalischen und mittelmeerischen Kulturen, FS Wolfgang Röllig* (ed. B. Pongratz-Leisten, H. Kühne, and P. Xella; AOAT 247; Kevelaer: Butzon & Bercker, 1997), 69–77, 75.

The mythical narratives provide a template for Ashurbanipal's description of the killing of the Elamite king Teumman after the battle of Til-Tuba at the Ulaj river.[81] Similar to Qingu in the *Enūma eliš* Teumman is characterized as one who is guilty of rebellion. Because of this Teumman is described as having disrupted the political and cosmic order. Therefore, the Elamite king has to die. It is only through his death that the cosmic and political order is restored. According to his inscription, Ashurbanipal having defeated Teumman takes his head and presents it opposite the city gate of Niniveh like an offering in order to reveal the power of the gods Aššur and Ištar.[82] In a corresponding scene of the relief in the North Palace at Niniveh as in the depiction of the whole battle in the Southwest Palace the Assyrian king is absent. Teumman is beheaded by an Assyrian soldier. The severed head of Teumman is then shown at a gate with two standards, which must be a temple gate. Left of the head one can discern the figure of the Assyrian king and part of his bow which reminds one of a libation scene typical of libations scenes over the dead lion after the hunting. The information from the inscription and the relief scene agree perfectly with the information provided by tablets with epigraphs intended to accompany the relief scenes.[83] The epigraphs, however, provide additional information.[84] According to the epigraphs Ashurbanipal sets off for a triumphal procession starting at Niniveh and proceeding to Arbela to celebrate the *akītu* of Ishtar-Shatri[85] who had predicted his victory and delivered Teum-

---

[81] See the recent monograph by Oskar Kaelin, *Ein assyrisches Bildexperiment nach ägyptischem Vorbild. Zur Planung und Ausführung der "Schlacht am Ulai"* (AOAT 266; Münster: Ugaritverlag, 1999).

[82] Borger, *Beiträge*, 107 Prism B vi 66–67: *nikis qaqqad* ^{I}*Teumman ina irat abulli qabal āli ša Nina*^{ki} *umaḫḫira maḫḫuriš* "I displayed the severed head of Teumman opposite the inner city gate of Niniveh like an offering."

[83] Borger, *Beiträge*, 301 f. A 2 I 14' ff.: *anāku* ^{I}*Aššurbanipal šar māt Aššur*^{ki} *qaqqad* ^{I}*Teumman* [*šar*] *māt Elamma*^{ki} / *ina irat abulli qabal āli muḫḫuriš umaḫḫir* / *ša ultu ulla ina bārûti qabû umma* [*qaq*]*qadāti* / *nakrūti tana*[*kkis*] /. Borger then continues with the first tablet A 1 II 1–3 linking the libation scene to the offering: *karāna elīšunu tanaqqi ša* x. . . / *enen*[*na* ^{d}*Šam*]*aš u* ^{d}*Adad ina* l a l-*ya* x. . . / *qaqqadāti nakrūtiya akkis karāna aqq*[*a elīšunu*] "I, Assurbanipal, king of Assyria, presented the head of Eumman, king of Elam opposite the inner city gate like an offering. What has been said since long in extispicy: 'You will cut the heads of the enemies'; I libated wine upon them ... Now Šamaš and Adad ... I severed the heads of my enemies and libated wine upon them." See also Kaelin, *Bildexperiment*, 55 and his plate 3.

[84] Kaelin, *Bildexperiment*, 120 TD A 1 24 (34) and p. 124 TD E 5 (34) as well as TD E 7 (p. 307).

[85] Beate Pongratz-Leisten, "The Interplay of Military Strategy and Cultic Practice in Assyrian Politics," in *Assyria 1995: Proceedings of the 10th Anniversary Symposium of the Neo-*

man into his hands. During his *triumphus* the Assyrian king carries along Dunanu, king of Gambulu and his brothers Samgunu and Aplāja as captives as well as the severed head of Teumman. Elnathan Weissert suggests that the procession then proceeded to Assur, the religious center of the Assyrian empire as the final station of the procession.[86] If we accept Borger's reconstruction of the sequencing of the tablets containing the epigraphs, we may reconstruct the following steps: killing of the enemy, entering of the royal residence Niniveh with the trophies of war, offering a libation over the head of the enemy. Thereby, the act of killing is transformed into a ritualized action after the model of the hunting rituals.[87] The close connection of hunting and war also shows in the prism fragment published by Weissert[88] which juxtaposes the hunt and the procession to Arbela. In this case nothing is said regarding the battle against Teumman. The entire narrative is framed by the topos of the hunt. The triumphal procession with the captives and the head of Teumman to the temples of Arbela and Aššur represents the additional element typical of war rituals.

5. 3. Ritual of the Substitute King

The ritual of the substitute king (*šar pūḫi*) likewise fits into this concept of order because it aims at re-establishing the harmonic relationship between the king and the gods. It is evidenced extensively in the correspondence of the Sargonid kings Esarhaddon and Ashurbanipal in the seventh century B. C. E.[89] as well as in a ritual text[90] and must be categorized as ritual killing to dispose of an infected *materia magica*. The ritual of the substitute king belongs to the category of eliminatory rites in which a living or dead animal, and in this specific case a human be-

---

Assyrian Text Corpus Project, Helsinki, 1995 (ed. S. Parpola and R. M. Whiting; Helsinki: Neo-Assyrian Text Corpus Project, 1997), 245–53, 250; and Elnathan Weissert, "Royal Hunt and Royal Triumph in a Prism Fragment of Ashurbanipal," in ibid., 339–58.

86 Weissert, "Royal Hunt," 348 f.

87 For the ritualizing of killing see Burkard Gladigow, "Religion und Gewalt."

88 Prism fragment 82-5-22,2 edited by Weissert, "Royal Hunt."

89 For a catalogue of texts referring to the ritual see Simo Parpola, *Letters from Assyrian Scholars to the Kings Esarhaddon and Assurbanipal Part II: Commentary and Appendices* (AOAT 5,2; Kevelaer: Butzon & Bercker, 1983), XXVI ff.; see also Jean Bottéro, *Mesopotamia: Writing, Reasoning, and the Gods* (Chicago: University of Chicago Press, 1995), 138 ff.

90 Wilfred G. Lambert, "A Part of the Ritual for the Substitute King," *AfO* 18 (1957 / 58): 109–12 and "The Ritual for the Substitute King: A New Fragment," *AfO* 19 (1959 / 60): 119.

ing, had to assimilate the elements or events threatening the real king and take them down to the Netherworld. The ritual of the substitute king was triggered by certain kinds of solar and lunar eclipses portending the death of the reigning king. In order to prevent his death the king temporarily abdicates his throne for a surrogate "who having ruled his predetermined period, is put to death, after which the king reascends his throne and continues ruling as if nothing had happened."[91] As soon as the need was established the chief exorcist not the king himself would choose a suitable substitute, a prisoner of war, a criminal condemned to death, a political enemy of the king or a gardener, a person whose life would have deserved death anyway or did not matter. As soon as the substitute king was installed on the throne the real king no longer was to be addressed as "king" but as "peasant" or "farmer" (*ikkaru*) to cover his real identity. While the substitute king was supposed to sit on the throne the real king would retire into a structure called *qirsu* where he would exercise his royal duties but also perform numerous purification rites to re-establish the communication with the gods on whose behalf he is supposed to partake in maintaining the cosmic order. After the substitute king had fulfilled his duty he had to die. To secure the safety of the legitimate king all the regal requisites used by the substitute king such as the royal table, throne, weapon and scepter had to be burnt. The substitute king then was buried with royal honors in a mausoleum, and subsequently, the whole palace of the king underwent purification rites. The substitute king serves as a carrier of impurity as do animals or puppets in other elimination rituals. The ritual of the substitute king, which is also attested in Hittite context[92] clearly belongs into the category of eliminatory rites.[93]

5. 4. The Scapegoat Ritual

The integration of the so-called "scapegoat" ritual into the survey needs justification since killing of the substitute is not a part of these rituals. The scapegoat ritual, consequently, represents a special form of substitution rituals. Two components, however, seem of special interest, one is the transferal of the impurity by laying hands on the ram and the other

---

91 Parpola, *Letters*, xxv.

92 Hans Martin Kümmel, *Ersatzrituale für den hethitischen König* (Studien zu den Bogazköy Texten 3; Wiesbaden: Harrassowitz, 1967).

93 Daniel P. Wright, *The Disposal of Impurity: Elimination Rites in the Bible and in Hittite and Mesopotamian Literature* (SBLDS 101; (Atlanta: Scholars Press, 1987).

is the collective component: the substitute acts on behalf of a group or community. Both components are present in the Hittite ritual and reappear in Leviticus 16. A third feature is that the substitute might also be human. The "scapegoat ritual" also known as *apopompe*[94] likewise belongs to the eliminatory rites but is distinct insofar as it involves the rite of laying the hands on the ram (LXX: ἀποπομπαῖος / Vulgata: *emissarius*) to transfer the pollution onto the substitute, and then the scapegoat is sent into the enemy land or across the border of the city. The English and French translation have maintained this original connotation in their translation of the "scapegoat" and the "bouc émissaire." It is only with the seventeenth century A. D. that language use emphasizes the aspect of the role of the victim which again laid the basis for Girard's theory of the role of violence in religions.[95]

Some scholars trace the origin of the scapegoat ritual as far back as Ebla between 2400 and 2300 B. C. E.[96] Among the ritual texts which came to light in the archive of palace G there are two texts which in a narrative way refer to the scapegoat ritual:

> (And) we purge the mausoleum.
> Before the entry (of the gods) Kura and Barama a goat,
> a silver bracelet (hanging from the) goat's neck,
> towards the steppe of Alini we let her go.[97]
>
> And we purge the mausoleum.
> A goat, a silver bracelet (hanging from the) goat's neck,
> before the entry of Kura and Barama,
> towards the steppe of Alini we *enclose (her)*.[98]

As has been emphasized by Ida Zatelli[99] both texts refer to the queen's wedding and to the queen's and king's enthronement. Apparently the king's desire is to legitimate his wife by the means of a journey to the temple of Kura and to the mausoleum of NE-*naš*. Before the arrival of

94 Renate Schlesier, "Apopompe," in *Handbuch religionswissenschaftlicher Grundbegriffe* 2 (ed. H. Cancik; Stuttgart: Kohlhammer, 1990), 38–40.

95 Andreas Bendlin, "Sündenbockrituale," in *DNP* II: 1082.

96 Paolo Xella, "Il ‹capro espiatorio› a Ebla," *SMSR* 62 (1996): 677–84.

97 Pelio Fronzaroli, *Testi rituali della regalità: Archivo L 2769* (Archivi di Ebla: Testi XI; Rom: Missione Archeologica Italiana in Siria, 1993), 1 v. I 19 – II 7.

98 Fronzaroli, *Testi XI*, 2 v. I 7–21.

99 Ida Zatelli, "The Origin of the Biblical Scapegoat Ritual: The Evidence of Two Eblaite Texts," *VT* 48 / 2 (1998): 254–63.

the royal couple, the gods Kura and Barama, the mausoleum has to be purified by means of an adorned goat which takes on the defilement and is subsequently sent onto the steppe.

Around a thousand years later evidence for the scapegoat ritual is attested in ritual texts from Ugarit, on the Mediterranean coast, as well as from Bogazköy, the capital of the Hittite empire, both within a military context. A clay model of a lung from Ugarit is inscribed with a ritual to be performed in a situation of crisis, i. e. the siege of the city.[100]

> (29) If the city is about to be conquered, if death wickedly treats man,
> (30) a person will take a goat in the steppe
> (31) and send her out.[101]

A Hittite scapegoat ritual dating from ca. 1350 B. C. E. involves elaborate ritual prescriptions concerning the reason of the ritual (pestilence), the time when it is to be performed (*ad hoc*), a designation of the substitute (rams and a woman), the adornment of the scapegoat, and the sending away of the scapegoat into the enemy's land. Here it is the king and the army which need to be purified, while the rams function as the substitute for the officers, the woman assumes the role of the substitute for the king. As has been shown by D. Schwemer,[102] the use of a woman as a substitute can be traced back to Babylonian eliminatory rites in which the relationship between the demon having caused the illness and the patient was considered as if a marriage. The substitute performed the role of the bride of the patient to whom the patient transferred his illness while he speaks the courting words.

This Hittite scapegoat ritual and two other texts that belong to the same context[103] show that the scapegoat ritual was always performed to rid the community of pestilence and therefore was not instituted in the

[100] *KTU* 1.127, *Ugaritica* 6 (1969): 166–72; ed. by Manfried Dietrich and Oswald Loretz, *Mantik in Ugarit: Keilalphabetische Texte der Opferschau—Omensammlungen—Nekromantie* (Münster: Ugarit-Verlag, 1990), 17 ff. and recently treated by Volkert Haas, "Betrachtungen zur Traditionsgeschichte hethitischer Rituale am Beispiel des 'Sündenbock'-Motivs," in *Hittite Studies in Honor of Harry A. Hoffner* (ed. G. Beckman, R. Beal, and G. Mc Mahon, (Winona Lake: Eisenbrauns, 2003), 131–47.

[101] *Ugaritic Scapegoat Ritual KTU* 1.127: 29 ff.

[102] Daniel Schwemer, *Akkadische Rituale aus Ḫattuša: Die Sammeltafel KBo* XXXVI *29 und verwandte Fragmente* (Texte der Hethiter 23; Heidelberg: Winter, 1998), 60, cf. n. 170.

[103] Oliver R. Gurney, *Some Aspects of Hittite Religion* (The Schweich Lectures of the British Accademy; London: Oxford University Press, 1977), 47–52; *CTH* 410, *CTH* 407, *CTH* 394, *CTH* 425b. See also Kümmel, *Ersatzrituale*.

calendar but performed as needed. Either rams or a woman may serve as a substitute. The substitute is always adorned before it is sent off which, as has been emphasized by Jan Bremmer[104], distinguishes it from other eliminatory rites in which the carrier of defilement is removed without adornment.[105]

> When evening comes, whoever the army commanders are, each of them prepares a ram—whether it is a white ram or a black ram does not matter at all. Then I twine a cord of white wool, red wool, and green wool, and the officer twists it together, and I bring a necklace, a ring, and a chalcedony stone and I hang them on the ram's neck and horns, and at night they tie them in front of the tents and say: 'Whatever deity is prowling about (?), whatever deity has caused this pestilence, now I have tied up these rams for you, be appeased!' And in the morning I drive them out to the plain, and with each ram they take 1 jug of beer, 1 loaf, and 1 cup of milk (?). Then in front of the king's tent he makes a finely woman sit and puts with her a jar a beer and 3 loaves. The officers lay their hands on the rams and say: 'Whatever deity has caused this pestilence, now see! These rams are standing here and they are very fat in liver, heart and lions. Let human flesh be hateful to him, let him be appeased by these rams.' And the officers point at the rams and the king points at the decorated woman, and the rams and the woman carry the loaves and the beer through the army and they chase them out to the plain. And they go running on to the enemy's frontier without coming to any place of ours, and the people say: 'Look! Whatever illness there was among men, oxen, sheep, horses, mules, and donkeys in this camp. And the country that finds them shall take over this evil pestilence.'[106]

---

[104] Jan N. Bremmer, "The Scapegoat between Hittites, Greeks, Israelites, and Christians," in *Kult, Konflikt und Versöhnung: Beiträge zur kultischen Sühne in religiösen, sozialen und politischen Auseinandersetzungen des antiken Mittelmeerraumes* (ed. R. Albertz; AOAT 285; Münster: Ugarit-Verlag, 2001), 175–86.

[105] Bremmer, "Scapegoat between Hittites," 177.

[106] Gurney, *Aspects*, 49; *CTH* 394.

Together with Oliver R. Gurney[107] and Bernd Janowski[108] Bremmer stresses the fact that these rituals are ascribed to "practioners from outlying parts of the Hittite empire, Kizzuwatna, Ḫapalla, and Arzawa, that is city-states in South-East Anatolia and present Northern Syria."[109] It is in these regions that this specific eliminatory ritual originated and then traveled into Palestine-Israel as well as into Greece.

The use of a woman as scapegoat in eliminatory rites has been adopted by Neo-Assyrian religious experts. A royal ritual against the threatening attack of the enemy describes that on a specific day a virgin is brought before the king who inseminates her. She will "eventually expel the evil in the form of a new-born in enemy territory."[110] The evil, as explained by Jerrold S. Cooper, is transferred by intercourse from the king to the virgin, and is then externalized in a birthing process.

Patrick D. Miller recently classified the Israelite expiation ritual performed on the *Day of Atonement* (Lev 16; 23:26–32; Num 29:7–11) as originally being an emergency purification ritual that only somewhere along the line became a fixed ritual in the cultic calendar. In Israel, this ritual was performed on the tenth day of the seventh month, Tishri, in the fall.[111] There were two aspects to the ritual involving two animals: a goat for Yahweh and a goat for Azazel (Lev 16:8–10; cf. v. 26). The goat for Yahweh was slaughtered as a *ḥaṭṭāʾt* offering and its blood sprinkled in the sanctuary to purge it of impurities. As for the other goat, "the priest would lay hands on it and confess the 'iniquities,' that is, the deliberate sins and transgressions of the people. Having been confessed, they were now transferred to the goat who was sent away into the wilderness 'for

---

107 ibid., 51.

108 Bernd Janowski and Gernot Wilhelm, "'Der Bock, der die Sünden hinausträgt,'" in *Religionsgeschichtliche Beziehungen zwischen Kleinasien, Nordsyrien und dem Alten Testament: Internationales Symposium Hamburg 1990* (ed. B. Janowski et al.; OBO 129; Fribourg: Universitätsverlag, 1993), 109–69, 129–30; Bernd Janowski, "Azazel und der Sündenbock: Zur Religionsgeschichte von Leviticus 16,10. 21 f.," in *Gottes Gegenwart in Israel* (ed. idem; Beiträge zur Theologie des Alten Testamentes 1; Neukirchen-Vluyn: Neukirchner Verlag, 1993), 284–302.

109 Bremmer, *Scapegoat between Hittites*, 177.

110 Jerrold S. Cooper, "Magic and M(is)use: Poetic Promiscuity in Mesopotamian Ritual," in *Mesopotamian Poetic Language: Sumerian and Akkadian* (ed. M. E. Vogelzang and H. L. J. Vanstiphout; Proceedings of the Groningen Group for the Study of Mesopotamian Literature 1,2; Cuneiform Monographs 6; Groningen: Styx, 1996), 47–57, 53 with n. 24; for the ritual text see also Werner Mayer, "Ein neues Königsritual gegen feindliche Bedrohung," *Or* 5 (1989): 145–64.

111 Patrick D. Miller, *The Religion of Ancient Israel* (Library of Ancient Israel; London: SPCK, 2000), 115 f.

Azazel' (Lev 16:10, 20–22). Verse 16 (cf. vv. 21–22) identifies the dual purpose of the ritual, the removal of impurities and the removal of sins."[112] Leviticus 17–26 then specifies the transgressions and links cultic purity and moral conscience.[113]

By comparing Anatolian and Greek scapegoat rituals (*pharmakos*) that primarily seem to be eliminatory in character, Bremmer claims that it is especially the Greek concept of sacrificial ideology that might have inspired the Christian concept of Christ's death as an atoning sacrifice[114] and not the Jewish tradition.[115] He bases his theory on the differences he sees between Greek and Anatolian rituals. While there are similarities between the Greek and the Anatolian rituals such as the occasion for the ritual (plague), the timing of its execution as needed, the adornment of the substitute and chasing out the scapegoat of the city, the Greeks did not send their scapegoats into the enemy country. More important, there is the aspect of willingness of the victim as portrayed in Greek myth and which played an important part in Greek sacrificial ideology.[116] The Greek tales stress that in times of crisis the member of the community who was designated to avert catastrophe must be a very significant individual, i. e. a member of the aristrocracy and members of the royal family as was the Athenian king Kodros, for instance, who saved the Athenian community by his death.[117]

The willingness of the scapegoat also emerges in the Rabbinic interpretation of Isaac's Aqedah (Gen 22) in which Isaac not Abraham becomes the hero because of his conscious willingness to sacrifice him-

[112] Ibid., 116.

[113] For the second part of Leviticus see recently Eckhart Otto, "Innerbiblische Exegese im Heiligkeitsgesetz Levitikus 17–26," in *Levitikus als Buch: Tagung der deutschsprachigen Alttestamentlerinnen und Alttestamentler, Trier 1997* (ed. H.-J. Fabry and H. W. Jüngling; Bonner Biblische Beiträge 119; Berlin: Philo, 1999), 125–217.

[114] Jan N. Bremmer, "Scapegoat Rituals in Ancient Greece," *HSCP* 87 (1983): 299–320 with a postscript reprinted in *Oxford Readings in Greek Religion* (ed. R. G. A. Buxton; Oxford: Oxford University Press, 2000), 271–93; Bremmer, "Scapegoat between Hittites", 184 ff.

[115] Otto Kaiser likewise advocates a close intercultural relationship between Greek and Judaic tradition, see Otto Kaiser, "Athen und Jerusalem: Die Begegnung des spätbiblischen Judentums mit dem griechischen Geist, ihre Voraussetzungen und ihre Folgen," in *Die Griechen und der Vordere Orient: Beiträge zum Kultur- und Religionskontakt zwischen Griechenland und dem Vorderen Orient im 1. Jahrtausend v. Chr.* (ed. M. Witte and S. Alkier; OBO 191; Fribourg: Universitätsverlag, 2003), 87–134.

[116] Bremmer, "Scapegoat Rituals in Ancient Greece," 279 f., and "Scapegoat between Hittites," 179.

[117] Bremmer, "Scapegoat Ritual in Ancient Greece," 276.

self.[118] As Bremmer,[119] however, also emphasizes in an earlier article, the New Testament drew on different traditions with different theological aims to express the self-sacrifice of Christ: one is the Israelite concept of atonement which accounts for the use of the Hebrew verb *kipper* translated in the Septuagint with *hilaskomai* as in Rom 3:25 ("whom God put forward as sacrifice [*hilasterion*] of atonement by his blood"), Hebr 2:17 and above all 1 John 2:2 (noun: *hilasmos*); the other is the formula "Christ died for our sins" in Pauline soteriology expressed implicitly or explicitly.[120] 1 Corinthians 15:3 is the most explicit reference in this context: "... Christ died for our sins in accordance with the scriptures." It is obviously only the latter that could be linked to Greek tradition. It is also interesting to note that blood is still important as a medium of salvation warding off God's wrath (Rom 5:9). Bremmer does not follow Versnel's approach, who in addition brought the Roman *devotio* to the fore in which soldiers or private persons were willing to sacrifice their life for the health of the Roman emperor.[121]

6. Guilt and Sin in Personal Piety, and the Idea of Redemption and Replacement in Purification Rituals and in Legal Contracts

Another domain which should be explored in order to explain the relationship between ethics and sacrifice is the aspect of personal piety,[122] as well as redemption and restoration in purification rituals and in legal

[118] Robbins, "Sacrifice," 294 ff. (see fn. 16); Edwart Noort and Eibert J. C. Tigchelaar, eds., *The Sacrifice of Isaac: The Aqedah (Genesis 22) and Its Interprestations* (Themes in Biblical Narrative 4; Leiden: Brill, 2002); Maren R. Niehoff, "The Return of Myth in Genesis Rabbah on the Akeda" *JJS* 46 (1995): 69–87.

[119] Jan N. Bremmer, "The Atonement in the Interactions of Greeks, Jews, and Christians," in *Sacred History and Sacred Texts in Early Judaism: Symposium in Honour of A. S. van der Woude* (ed. J. N. Bremmer and F. García Martínez; Contributions to Biblical Exegesis and Theology 5; Kampen: Pharos, 1992), 75–93.

[120] See the references collected by Bremmer, "Atonement," 76 f. n. 5: Rom 5:6,8; 14:9,15; 1 Cor 1:13; 8:11; 15:3; 2 Cor 5:14, 15, 21; Gal 3:13; 1 Thess 5:10.

[121] Hendrik S. Versnel, "Self-Sacrifice, Compensation and the Anonymous Gods," in *Le sacrifice dans l'Antiquité: Huit exposés suivis de discussions* (ed. Jean Rudhardt and Oliver Reverdin; Entretiens sur l'antiquité classique 27; Genève: Fondation Hardt, 1981), 135–85.

[122] Wolfgang von Soden, "Das Fragen nach der Gerechtigkeit Gottes im Alten Orient," *MDOG* 96 (1965): 41–59; Hermann Vorländer, *Mein Gott: Die Vorstellungen vom persönlichen Gott im Alten Orient und Alten Testament* (AOAT 23; Kevelaer: Butzon & Bercker, 1975); Dietz Otto Edzard, "Private Frömmigkeit in Sumer," in *Official Cult and Popular Religion in the Ancient Near East: Papers of the First Colloquium on the Ancient Near East 'The City and Its Life' Tokyo 1992* (ed. E. Matsushima; Heidelberg: Winter, 1993) 195–208.

contexts (*kasap ipṭirī*) in Mesopotamia.[123] To my knowledge, Assyriologists have only been dealt with these subjects separately.[124] A full treatment of these two subjects would go beyond the scope of the subject of this volume, but I cannot refrain from drawing the reader's attention to their importance in the development of the idea of self-sacrifice.

There is in Mesopotamia a group of texts in the form of hymn, lament or dialogue that deal with the misfortune and suffering of a person who at some point is saved by his god.[125] In these texts pain, agony, social marginalization and disruption of divinatory communication with the gods are thought to be the expression of an angered personal deity who due to an inadvertent offense turned away from man and exposed him to all kinds of afflictions brought about by demons. The terminology found in these texts use the same terms for sin and punishment (*arnu/annu*, *ḫīṭu*, *šē/īrtu*), and reflect the interrelationship between a person's action and its consequences. Thereby, suffering and recovery are seen as signs of divine power that withdraws the personal god to expose the person to demons, as is shown by the poem of *The Righteous Sufferer* (*Ludlul bēl nēmeqi*)[126] or the *Babylonian Theodicy*.[127]

Other texts are ritual in nature and describe purification rites involving offerings to the gods, to free the person of a demon inflicting illness

[123] See CAD I, 171 ff. s. v. *ipṭirū*. See also Klaas R. Veenhof, "Old Assyrian Period," in *A History of Ancient Near Eastern Law* (ed. R. Westbrook; HO I,72; Leiden: Brill, 2003), 464 f. with previous literature.

[124] See, however, the contribution by the German Hebrew Bible scholar Bernd Janowski, "Auslösung des verwirkten Lebens: Zur Geschichte und Struktur der biblischen Lösegeldvorstellung," *ZTK* 79 (1982): 25–59; idem, *Sühne als Heilsgeschehen: Traditions- und religionsgeschichtliche Studien zur Sühnetheologie der Priesterschrift* (2nd ed.; WMANT 55; Neukirchen-Vluyn: Neukirchner Verlag, 2000).

[125] For a collection of these texts see Foster, *Before the Muses*, 308 ff.; idem, in *The Context of Scripture: Canonical Compositions, Monumental Inscriptions, and Archival Documents from the Biblical World* (vol. I; ed. W. W. Hallo and K. L. Younger, Jr.; Leiden: Brill, 1997), 483 ff.; Manfried Dietrich, " 'Nur einer, der von Sünde weiß, eilt zu seinen Göttern,' " in Albertz, *Kult*, 73–97; for a survey see Joachim Krecher, "Klagelieder § 9: Persönliche Klage," *RlA* 6: 6; Dietz Otto Edzard, "Literatur § 3. 4. 4. Persönliche Klage," *RlA* 7: 43; Wolfgang Röllig, "Literatur § 4. 3. 4: Klage und Bußpsalmen," *RlA* 7: 55.

[126] See tablet III and IV that described how Marduk ordered recovery for the sufferer. For an edition of the text see Wilfred G. Lambert, *BWL*, 21–62; Andrew R. George and Farouq N. H. al-Rawi, "Tablets from the Sippar Library VII: Three Wisdom Texts," *Iraq* 60 (1998): 187–201; Wayne Horowitz/Wilfried G. Lambert, "A New Exemplar of Ludlul Bēl Nēmeqi Tablet I from Birmingham," *Iraq* 64 (2002): 237–45, for a recent translation see also Benjamin R. Foster in Hallo and Younger, *Context*, 486 ff.

[127] Lambert, *BWL*, 63–89; Foster in Hallo and Younger, *Context*, 492 ff.

or any kind of misfortune.[128] Among these purification rites are texts that express the idea that the ransom paid to the gods could compensate for the life of the person who was threatened by death as is the case in the following ritual text dating to the first millennium B. C. E.: "He will hold the balance and weigh out the silver for his ransom (and say): 'O Šamaš, the silver for the ransom of myself, my first wife, my (other) wives (and) [my sons and daughters] has been given to you.'"[129] The compensating function of ransom is also found in the price Ishtar has to pay to be released from the Netherworld in the myth *Ishtar's Descent*: "If she cannot give you a substitute for herself bring her (Ishtar) back (to the netherworld.)"[130]

As has been emphasized by Bernd Janowski, the idea of ransom is closely bound to the idea of the substitute (*andunānu/dinānu*, *nakkuššu*, *pūḫu*) as it becomes obvious in an Old Assyrian letter, *CCT* 4 2a 26 ff.: "Because of your journey / the god / is filled with anger against you. Get up / and come here! / The ten minas of silver which you are giving me in addition will serve as substitute for your life."[131]

As has been shown, we find already in the ancient Near Eastern purification rites the complex concept of guilt and sin in relationship with notions of substitution and ransom. Therefore, the element of sin remains, yet, anchored in the idea of an impure substance that can be washed off or carried off by a substitute.[132] Nonetheless these purification rites are understood as reconciliation with the deity. The conceptualization of sin and guilt thus reflect a personal relationship with the deity assuming an anthropomorphic deity.

[128] For an overview see Erica Reiner, "La Magie Babylonienne," in *Le monde du sorcier: Egypte, Babylone, Hittites, Israel* . . . (Sources orientales 7; Paris: Ed. du Seuil, 1966), 69–98.

[129] Erich Ebeling, "Ein neuassyrisches Beschwörungsritual gegen Bann und Tod," *ZA* 51 (1955): 167–79, AMT 72,1 rev. 28 f.: *gišrinna ina*[*ššīma kasap*] *ipṭirīšu iddan* ᵈ*Šamaš* . . . *kasap ipṭirīya ḫīrtiya aššātiya* [*mārēya mārātiya*] *nadnuka*.

[130] Rykle Borger, *Babylonisch-Assyrische Lesestücke* (AnOr 54; Rom: Pontificium Inst. Biblicaum, 1979), 103 Niniveh version 126: *šumma napṭirīša la iddanakkama ana šâšama tirraši*.

[131] Hans Hirsch, *Untersuchungen zur altassyrischen Religion* (AfOB 13 / 14; Graz: Weidner, 1972), 19; see Janowski, "Auslösung," 39 n. 67.

[132] Gernot Wilhelm's evaluation of the Hittite idea of impurity and the material aspect of cleanliness and ritual purity also applies to the Mesopotamian ritual, see Gernot Wilhelm, "Reinheit und Heiligkeit. Zur Vorstellungswelt altanatolischer Ritualistik," in *Levitikus als Buch*, 197–217.

7. Conclusion

This short survey aimed at illuminating the variety of ideas that at some point in history lead to the idea of the expiatory death of the servant of God (Isa 53:10) and finally to the sacrifice of Christ for the sins of humankind. In the course of the discussion the following patterns in the religious thinking and practice of ancient Near Eastern community have been found that might have contributed to the idea of this type of human sacrifice:

Killing as Transformation Intended to Re-establish the Cosmic Order:

1. In mythical narratives and royal inscriptions: killing to re-establish the cosmic order (Tiamat to build the cosmos; killing of the enemy king).
2. In mythical narratives: killing of a god to provide the substance for the creation of humankind.

The Substitute with a Distancing Function:

3. The substitute in eliminatory rites (puppet, wax figurines or animal).
4. The substitute king in times of eclipse.
5. The scapegoat ritual in times of plagues to transfer the impurity onto an animal.

The Offering with Communicative Function

6. Any kind of dedicatory offering in the cult to feed, to communicate with or appease the deity.

Personal Piety

7. Idea of conflict between deity and human being generated through an inadvertent offense → idea of guilt and sin; suffering and redemption are seen as signs of divine power.

Legal Context

8. Idea of redemption and substitute.

Mythical context

9. Idea of ransom given for the life of a deity.

Mesopotamian religious tradition displays a whole range of concepts of ritual killing, eliminatory rites and substitute rites, the idea of the offering with communicative function as well as the idea of guilt and sin, and the legal tradition knows of the idea of the ransom paid to redeem one's life. The crucial difference between the Old Testament theology and Mesopotamian tradition is that in Mesopotamia there is no direct connection between sacrifice and purification rites which consequently also implies that there is no sacrifice to atone for the sin or sacrifice to atone for the guilt. What is more, the Akkadian verb *kuppuru* "to wash off, clean, purify" is never used together with the words for sin.[133] Janowski's analysis of the root *kpr* in the Semitic languages has shown that the difference in the use between Hebrew *kpr* and Akkadian *kuppuru* cannot be solved by etymological explanations.[134] In the Hebrew Bible the idea of redemption (*kpr*) occurs in legal context by imposing a ransom to redeem one's life (Exod 21:30; 30:12).[135] Besides in the legal context *kpr* also occurs in theological context denoting the redemption of Israel through Yahweh (Isa 43:3 f.); Yahweh addresses Israel with the following words: "Do not fear, for I have redeemed you ... I give Egypt as your ransom (*nāṯattī kåpr*^{e}*ḵā*), Ethiopia and Seba in exchange for you." Additionally, "another difference that separates the sacrificial rituals in the two cultures is the 'blood consciousness' of the West, its awareness of the magic power of blood, which is not paralleled in Mesopotamia."[136]

The most important difference between the ancient Near Eastern and Christian concepts remains that if there is death involved, which is mostly symbolically performed by killing a substitute, then this substitute person dies for his own sins. The idea of atoning death for others is non-existent. Christian soteriological theology then by introducing the elements of trust and obedience in God transforms the material substance as ransom into the idea of Christ giving himself as ransom for the many (Mark 10:45) whose life otherwise would be lost in the final judg-

[133] Janowski, *Sühne*, 59 f.

[134] ibid., 27–102.

[135] This did not apply for a murderer. Murderers were put to death (Num 35:31 f.).

[136] A. Leo Oppenheim, *Ancient Mesopotamia: Portrait of a Dead Civilization* (Chicago: University of Chicago Press, 1977), 192.

ment.[137] In Paul's theology, "the division in humankind is constituted not by those faithful to the Torah and those who are wicked and 'Gentile sinners' (Gal 2:15), but rather by the death of Jesus Christ as the focal point of God's universal wrath and judgment."[138] In Paul's conceptualization there is no atonement that is periodically reiterated, rather the death of Christ is thought to overcome the sin and baptism as purification ritual turns into a conversion ritual. Sin then is not an accidental offense against norms but the sum of non-Christian life-style.[139] Salvation is linked both to death and to the resurrection of Christ (Rom 4:24–25).[140] Later on, Christian theologians by intersecting ethics and sacrifice created the concept of Christ's self-sacrifice while they could rely on all these cultural concepts developed throughout the millennia by the larger ancient Near Eastern intellectual communities either in the legal or religious domain.

---

137 Janowski, "Auslösung," 56.

138 Johan C. Beker, *Paul's Apocalyptic Gospel: The Coming Triumph of God* (Philadelphia: Fortress, 1982) 35.

139 Andreas Bendlin, "Sünde," in *Handbuch religionswissenschaftlicher Grundbegriffe* V (ed. H. Cancik, B. Gladigow, and K.-H. Kohl; Stuttgart: Kohlhammer, 2001), 125–34, 129.

140 Graham N. Stanton, "Paul's Gospel," in *The Cambridge Companion to St. Paul* (ed. James D. G. Dunn; Cambridge Companions to Religion; Cambridge: Cambridge University Press, 2003), 173–84, 178.

Human Sacrifice in Greek Culture*

GABRIELE WEILER, University of Cologne

Before dealing with human sacrifices in Greek culture, it is necessary to define the term and the meaning of "human sacrifice." In a narrow sense, "human sacrifice" means the sacrifice of a human being to a divinity, carried out like an animal sacrifice (the terminology is also the same, i. e. Greek: θύειν or σφάζειν). In a broader sense, the term implies also the forms of "ritual killing," either at the grave of a deceased person, before or after a battle, during a drought, famine, epidemic or a similiar catastrophe dangerous to an individual life or that of a community. Finally it is possible to offer living human beings to a divinity in order to comply with their cult. Therefore, human sacrifices belong to the rituals of offering, which are generally accepted by the religion and culture in question and which are therefore not considered as an illegal killing and consequently are not punished.

Quite a number of human sacrifices, in the narrow and in the broader sense, are revealed by the Greek myths and their flexible adaption in the fields of literature—especially of tragedies—as well as in the domains of art, particularly of vase-painting, plastic art or history painting.[1] In addition, there are inscriptions, findings and facts of archaeological nature, which however are and will be difficult to interpret.[2] Another category are the statements made until Roman times by historiographical and biographical sources as well as those made by periegetic writers. The first lists of human sacrifices were set up by philosophers, subsequent lists

* I am grateful to Annette Haensch for writing the English of this article. Thanks also to Johannes Heinrichs with whom I discussed all that is essential in this article.

[1] As for the representation in the Etruscan art generally acknowlegded as highly influenced by the Greek one, see for example Dirk Steuernagel, *Menschenopfer und Mord am Altar: Griechische Mythen in etruskischen Gräbern* (Palilia 3; Wiesbaden: Reichert, 1998).

[2] For example Anemospilia, see below n. 52 and 55; Lefkandi: see below n. 64 and 66.

by Christians.[3] Especially the late written sources however hardly reflect the historical reality, but they are rather literal fictions, rhetorical exercises, aitiological models or last, but not least, propaganda.

The research has tended to deny human sacrifices in ancient developed cultures. This is especially true for the Greek culture. Either the respective customs are attributed to a very distant, prehistorical past.[4] Or the influence of the civilizations of the Near East or the "barbarian" neighbouring tribes are held responsible for the human sacrifices which cannot be negated in the fields of written sources or art.[5] We have evidence that many tribes living around the Mediterranian Sea in ancient times and other Indo-European peoples practiced the sacrifice or ritual killing of human beings (Etruscans, Romans, Germans, Celts). We find the earliest archaeological testimonies in the region of Crete. They can be dated with great certainty to the first period of the palaces. But the interpretation of these findings are not undisputed. The first traditions we dispose of can be found in the context of the legend of Theseus and the myths about the argonauts and the war of Troy. Thus they evoke contexts referring back to a Minoan-Mycenaean background. For these reasons, one should not reject right from the start an indigenous tradition of this "extreme" practice of sacrifice independent of external influences.

Especially Walter Burkert has demonstrated by a further development of the theses made by Sigmund Freud, Karl Meuli and Konrad Lorentz that bloody sacrificial rituals—and these include not only animal sacrifices—have their origin in the migrating (middle-) palaeolithic groups of hunters ("hunting hypotheses" of hominization).[6] Today we are apparently able to trace back a tradition lasting for many generations up

---

[3] Thus for example the new Platonist Porphyry (source: Theophrastus; Porphyry, *Abst.* 2, 52 ff.), Tertullian (*Apol.* 9), Clement of Alexandria (*Protr.* 3, 42 p. 31 Stählin), Eusebius (*Praep. ev.* 4, 16), Cyrillus of Alexandria (*C. Iulianum* 4, 127 f.).

[4] Karl Meuli, "Griechische Opferbräuche," in: *Phyllobolia: FS Peter von der Mühll* (Basel: Schwabe, 1946), 185–288, 207 (repr. in *Gesammelte Schriften* [ed. Th. Gelzer; Basel: Schwabe, 1975], vol. 2, 907–1021); Konrad Lorenz, *Das sogenannte Böse: Zur Naturgeschichte der Aggression* (25th ed.; Vienna: Borotha-Schoeler 1970), 72 ff. concerning the rite.

[5] See more in detail Pierre Bonnechère, *Le sacrifice humain en Grèce ancienne* (Kernos Suppl. 3; Athènes: Centre International d'Etude de la Religion Grecque Antique, 1994.

[6] Sigmund Freud, *Das Unbehagen in der Kultur* (Gesammelte Schriften XII; Leipzig: Internat. Psychoanalytischer Verlag, 1934, 27–114). Robert Ardrey, *The Hunting Hypothesis: A Personal Conclusion Concerning the Evolutionary Nature of Man* (New York: Atheneum, 1976).

to historical times. The interchangeability of human and animal sacrifices is quite common in Greek myths. Memories of human sacrifices as an extreme form—and at the same time also the most valuable form—of sacrifice, especially in cases of particular emergencies or of wrongdoings, are reflected in later sources. These memories of human sacrifices could have been the basis for the development of an explaining myth, but they could have been also used for aitiological and etymological explanations of cults and epiteths of divinities. The Greeks' familiarity with this motive which can increasingly be observed from the 5th cent. on is completed by testimonies of human sacrifices celebrated by neighbouring peoples. In this context, one should mention the evidence transmitted by Herodotus or later Diodorus.[7] The practice of human sacrifices is often imputed to the respective enemies, but also to political agitators. However, it can be noticed that the contemporaries shrinked back from these acts more and more considered as cruel and uncivilized. Especially the written sources from the 5th cent. on[8] express the fact that people in a civilized culture could not any more imagine divinities which require human sacrifices. But does this really mean a humanization of society or rather a purer idea of God?

The first philosophical approaches in this direction date back to the times of Socrates and Plato. Both refer to the "divine" (τὸ θεῖον), which is not considered as a person, but as a principle and which is therefore far superior to the Homeric gods described as individuals with all the human weaknesses. These Olympian gods act like humans: They love and cheat, win and loose battles, they take revenge and intrigue, all this with respect to their equals as well as to human beings. The newly conceived "divine principle" contrasts with these Homeric gods. The divine principle is not thought of as a person, but it is ultimately above all people, even above ideas. Thus it is recognized and defined as the supreme principle, which creates itself the ideas and consequently also the more or less perfect images. Being the supreme principle, it is of particular quality: it must inevitably be good in order to create the ideas of the good. This philosophical model was also familiar to Plutarch and there is no doubt that it influenced his philosophical attitude. So it does not surprise us that he makes gods and humans shrink back from the

---

[7] Herodotus, *Hist.* 1, 216,2–3; 4, 62; 4, 71,4–72; 4, 94,2–3; 4, 103,1–2; 5, 5 (Thracians, Scythians, Getae, Persians); Diodorus 13, 86,3 (Carthaginians in Sicily).

[8] Euripides, *Iph. taur.* 380–91, source II.; cf. Plutarch, *Pel.* 21, source V.

realization of a human sacrifice. His world of ideas does not accept gods whishing such acts.[9]

But one should not forget that the ideas of the philosophers do not reflect the Greeks' general attitude towards gods or religious phenomena, but that they represent at that time a negligible number of elitist and educated persons. However, it was already Herodotus who made a deliberate separation, even if this is not explicitly formulated. On the one hand, he describes with a certain fascination the seemingly exotic rituals for the dead carried out by the Scythians and by some Thracian tribes with their ritual killings of women, servants and horses.[10] On the other hand, he regards the Persian practice of human sacrifice as a negative characteristic of civilisation and culture.[11] These types of sacrifice must have been known by his Greek contemporaries, but it is more likely that they celebrated human sacrifices only in isolated cases.

The paintings, especially the vase-paintings, reveal a changed representation of such acts. During the 6th cent., the moment of the killing, for example of Iphigenia, is the preferred thematic, whereas the emotional aspect, for example the girl forced to the altar, is more and more favoured from the 5th cent. on. Nevertheless, the motive of human sacrifice continues to be a popular subject. Thus, we cannot observe a deliberate break with this practice. The Etruscan paintings however place until their breakdown the act of killing, sometimes in a drastical way, into the foreground.[12]

Most of the human sacrifices are mentioned in connection with the virgin huntress Artemis and with Dionysus.[13] Artemis includes all facits of nature and thus also life and death. She seems to be connected with the realm of the prehistoric hunter via innumerable generations

---

9 Plutarch, *Pel.* 21, source V.; cf. Euripides, *Iph. Taur.* 380–91, source II.

10 Herodot, *Hist.* 4, 71,4–72; 5, 5.

11 *Hist.* 7, 114; 7, 180.

12 Cf. the famous Oinochoe vessel of the so-called Schuwalow painter, created approx. between 430–420 B.C., today part of the collection of antiquities in Kiel, Inv. B 538; it represents Iphigenia desperately offering resistance when forced to the altar; Steuernagel, *Menschenopfer*, 19–28 (slaughtering of Trojans), 28–36 (Iphigenia); Thomas Fontaine, "Blutrituale und apollinische Schönheit: Grausame vorgeschichtliche Opferpraktiken in der Mythenwelt der Griechen und Etrusker," in: *Morituri: Menschenopfer, Todgeweihte, Strafgerichte* (ed. H.-P. Kuhnen; Schriftenreihe des Rheinischen Landesmuseums Trier 17; Trier: Rheinisches Landesmuseum, 2000), 49–70, 51–53 with illustration 1.

13 Dennis D. Hughes, *Human Sacrifice in Ancient Greece* (London: Routledge, 1991), 88–92.

and predecessors[14] whose names are unknown to us. She combines the pre-Greek divinities of the "great mother goddess," Cybele of Asia Minor or the Near East, *Potnia Theron* (mistress of the animals) and other local divinities of nature which can hardly be identified in detail. This explains her many-sided activities. She owes for instance her importance for quite a number of female rites of initiation to her prominent role as the protectress of the virgins and the mothers as well as companion in case of births.[15] But she has the same function for example in Sparta when boys pass into adulthood (Artemis Orthia). Especially these initial rites are mythologically often connected with human sacrifices or traced back to them. Artemis, as mistress of the animals, protects the creatures under her command and often persecutes their killing relentlessly. Sometimes she can only be reconciled by a human sacrifice. The most famous example in this context is the one of Iphigenia.[16]

Dionysus in his quality of the embodied drunkenness, frenzy and madness also expects human sacrifices.[17] Zeus, Core, Persephone, Ares, Athena, Poseidon, Amphitrite or the Nereids expect them far more seldom. Even heroes like Achilles can require the death of a mortal person (Polyxena).[18] The Delphic Apollo can recommend such a sacrifice on

---

[14] As for Artemis: Walter Burkert, *Griechische Religion der archaischen und klassischen Epoche* (Die Religionen der Menschheit 15; Stuttgart: Kohlhammer, 1977), 233–38 with further literature.

[15] Cf. for example the initiation of girls in Brauron and Munichia, both apparently based on human sacrifices, Susanne Aretz, *Die Opferung der Iphigeneia in Aulis: Die Rezeption des Mythos in antiken und modernen Dramen* (Beiträge zur Altertumskunde 131; Stuttgart: Teubner, 1999), 41–46 with numerous pieces of evidence; see also Ken Dowden, *Death and the Maiden: Girls' Initiation Rites in Greek Mythology* (London: Routledge, 1989).

[16] *Cypria* (early history of the *Iliad*, created before 650: Iphigenia is replaced by an animal, oldest version): Proclus, *Chrestomathia*, Suppl. ex Apollodorus, *Epit.* 3,1–33 = Proclus, *Chrest.* 80 (Severyns); *Poetarum epicorum Graecorum testimonia et fragmenta* (*PEG*) (ed. A. Bernabé; 2nd ed.; Leipzig: Saur, 1996), vol. 1, *Cypria argumentum* 42–49, p. 41; for English translation see now Martin L. West, ed., *Greek Epic Fragments from the 7th to the 5th Centuries C. C.* (LCL 497; Cambridge, Mass.: Harvard University Press, 2003), *Cypria, Argument* 1, 8, p. 75; Hesiod, *Fr.* 23 Merkelbach-West (Ehoiai); Euripides, *Iph. aul.* 1540–1612; Aeschylus, *Ag.* 104–247; 176 ff. (chorus); 232 ff.; 1525–29; 1555–59 (Iphigenia dies, Clytemnestra has a reason for the killing of Agamemnon); Pindar, *Pyth.* 11 ia resp. 11, 22–23 (Iphigenia dies); Euripides, *Iph. taur.* 359; local variations: Attica > Brauron, Munichia: Aretz, *Opferung*, 41–46; Ovid, *Metam.* 12, 27–38; 13, 181–95 (indirect).

[17] As for Dionysus see: Burkert, *Griechische Religion*, 251–60; and Bonnechère, *Sacrifice*, 181–228.

[18] Euripides, *Hec.* 1–628; esp. 37–41; 107–15; further evidence: Friedrich Schwenn, *Die Menschenopfer bei den Griechen und Römern* (Religionsgeschichtliche Versuche und Vorarbeiten 15,3; Gießen: Töpelmann, 1915), 62–64; Hughes, *Human Sacrifice*, 62–64.

the grounds of an oracle as a last resort from a crisis.[19] This is mostly a young girl, i. e. a virgin, or a boy from the upper classes, who sometimes sacrifice themselves even voluntarily which corresponds with the positive value attached to this action. More rarely, the choice of the person to be sacrificed is left to chance.[20]

Especially the myths about (voluntary) sacrifices of virgins are often linked to certain sanctuaries and their mostly purely local cults and rites in the context of aitiological or etymological explanations.[21] In connection with the stories giving subsequent elucidations or explanations, one should not forget for example the stories about the cult of Zeus Lycaon in Arcadia with its human sacrifices.[22] Other human sacrifices, for example offered to Apollo, are known from Etruria.[23]

The types of human sacrifices as well in the narrow as in the broad sense of ritual killing or consecrating can be divided into nine models. On the following pages they are listed and described by some examples.

1. The Sacrifice as Expiation

A man or a woman violates consciously or unconsciously divine rules or insults the divinity who demands as a punishment a special form of reparation, i. e. the sacrifice of a person close to the perpetrator, mostly a relative. Ultimately it is up to the divinity to claim the sacrifice or

---

[19] As for Apollo: Burkert, *Griechische Religion*, 225–33. Boys sacrificed to Dionysus Aigobolus in Potneae according to the instructions of Apollo: Pausanias, *Descr.* 9, 8,2.

[20] Sources see Stella Georgoudi, "À propos du sacrifice humain en Grèce ancienne," *ARG* 1.1 (1999): 61–82.

[21] For example the Leochores and the Erechthides in Athens, or Heracles' daughter Macarea, also in Athens: Hughes, *Human Sacrifice*, 73–79; Virgins from Leuctra: Plutarch, *Pel.* 21 (see source V).

[22] Hughes, *Human Sacrifice*, 96–107.

[23] The Etruscans also made human sacrifices to Apollo. During the siege of Lipara they swore for example to sacrifice in case of a victory the bravest opponent to this god on an altar. After the seizure, they fulfilled their pledge and chose Theodotus to this end. Other human sacrifices of the Etruscans in an enlarged sense are mentioned by Herodotus and Livius; Ovid, *Ib.* 465–66, ed. R. Ellis; medieval *Scholia commenting Ovid, Ib.* 465, acccording to the edition of R. Ellis; Ovid's poem depends on Callimachus. Herodotus, *Hist.* 1, 166: lapidation of prisoners from Phocaea in Caere after the sea battle of Alalia (about 540–535 B. C.); Livius, *Ab urbe condita* 7, 15,10 referring to 358 B. C.: 307 roman prisoners of war are sacrificed on the forum of Tarquinia (*immolare*), probably in front of one of the most important sanctuaries of the town (Ara della Regina); Livius, *Ab urbe condita* 7, 19,2–3: The Romans take revenge on prisoners from Tarquinia in 354.

to replace it in the last moment by an animal sacrifice. The numerous variations of the sacrifice of Iphigenia by her father Agamemnon before the army of the Greek coalition leaves for Troy[24] is the most prominent example. The replacement of the girl by an animal can already be found in the oldest tradition. However it becomes the most decisive element of the action in the most famous tragedies written by Euripides, that is *Iphigenia aulidensis* and *Iphigenia taurica*.[25] The figure of Iphigenia is linked with many local traditions, for example in Brauron where she is venerated with Artemis among the divinities of birth.[26] The replacement of an animal sacrifice by a human sacrifice in the same ritual manner is a motive much preferred by the Greek writers of tragedies during the

---

[24] See n. 16. According to the oldest tradition, the girl is replaced on the altar of Artemis by an animal, so that her life is saved. However Aeschylus, the writer of tragedies, during the first half of the 5th cent., clearly changes the accents by the death of the virgin. This offers her mother Clytaimnestra the mobile for the murder of her husband on his return from Troy, which she planned and carried out together with Aegisthus. This murder is in a way the revenge of her daughter's death; the author's trilogy known as *Orestea* is based on this idea; in detail Albert Henrichs, "Human Sacrifice in Greek Religion: Three Case Studies," in: *Le sacrifice dans l'antiquité: Huit exposés suivis de discussions, Vandoeuvres—Genève 1980* (ed. J. Rudhardt, O. Reverdin, and J. P. Vernand; Entretiennes sur l'antiquitè classique 27; Geneva: Fondation Hardt, 1981), 195–242, 198–208 with all variations and discussion. As for the tragedy concerning the sacrifice of Iphigenia in Aulis and the manifold literary receptions until modern times see Aretz, *Opferung*.

[25] According to Bernhard Zimmermann, "Euripides," DNP 4 (1998): 284, they have been performed posthumously between 405 and about 400 B. C. For the replacement of the human by an animal cf. Abraham / Isaak, Gen 22,13; Iphigenia in Aulis: Euripides, *Iph. aul.*; *Iph. taur.*; Apollodorus, *Epit.* 3, 22; virgin / goat in Munichia: Zenobios, *Epithome*, Cod. Athous 1, 8, p. 350 (Miller), see Emmanuel Miller, *Mélanges de littérature grecque contenant un grand nombre de textes inédits* (Paris: Impr. Impériale, 1868; repr. Amsterdam: Hakkert, 1965), 341–84 (*Recueil de Proverbes*); new edition: Winfried Bühler, ed., *Zenobii Athoi proverbia* (Göttingen: Vandenhoeck & Rupprecht, 1987–99), vol. 1, 41 ff. (*Codex Athous*, now Paris Suppl. Gr. 1164); Pausanias, *Descr.* 1, 33,1; Hughes *Human Sacrifice*, 82–86; Walter Burkert, *Homo necans: Interpretation altgriechischer Opferriten und Mythen* (2nd. ed.; de Gruyter Studienbuch; Berlin: de Gruyter, 1997), 29; (English trans.: *Homo necans: The Anthropology of Ancient Greek Sacrificial Ritual and Myth* [trans. P. Bing; Berkeley: University of California Press, 1983].)

[26] Research on the etymology of her name have favoured this theory; Clement: "She who causes the birth of strong offspring"; Platner: "the strong in birth"; Wilamowitz: "die Gewaltgeborene"; cf. Aretz, *Opferung*, 33–36. It is possible that Iphigenia as an old divinity of birth was gradually subordinated as hypostasis to Artemis. According to Ken Dowden, *Death and the Maiden: Girl's Initiation Rites in Greek Mythology* (London: Routledge, 1989), 43–46, Iphigenia was the first priestess in the sanctuary of Artemis in Brauron. In her function as heroine she was closely connected with the initiation of the girls practiced there.

5th cent.[27] But we know also the contrary, that is the replacement of a human sacrifice by an animal one.[28]

In this context, one should also mention a Boeotian tradition: According to Pausanias, a priest of Dionysus was killed in the temple of Dionysus Aegobolus in Potneae during the sacrifice due to drunkenness and intoxication. This was immediately followed by an epidemic, the pestilence. The Delphic oracle recommended as a replacement the annual sacrifice of a boy; some years later, the god even replaced the human sacrifice by that of a goat.[29]

2. Self-Sacrifice for Victory

Before winning a battle or a war, it was necessary to offer a "human sacrifice."[30] According to Porphyry from Tyre, a Neoplatonist of the 3rd cent. A. D. who refers to Phylarchus (3rd cent. B. C.), it was common practice in Greece to make a human sacrifice before the army went to war.[31] However this is not confirmed by the earlier sources which are to be taken more seriously into account and which only mention animal sacrifices (σφάγια, σφαγιάζεται). The examples quoted by Plutarch in this context (Themistocles and Pelopidas, see below) are not historical. Therefore the human sacrifice has rather to be considered as a relic from prehistorical-mythological times.

Porphyry enumerates in a long list of 16 examples the cases of human sacrifice known to him.[32] Apart from the famous practices of sacrifice of the Phoenicians and the Cathaginians, he gives eight examples from the Greek world. All cases of historical times however can be explained as projections of mythological events. A typical example is the story of a human sacrifice before the battle at Salamis or the one at Leuctra:[33]

---

27 Burkert, *Homo necans*, 29 (German edition).

28 For example the killing of a calf instead of a child in Tenedos mentioned by the Sophist Claudius Aelianus (second half of the 2nd cent. A. D.), *Nat. an.* 12, 34. Replacement of a sacrificed boy by a goat in case of the cult of Dionysus Aegobolus in Potneae in Boeotia.

29 Pausanias, *Descr.* 9, 8,2; cf. Locrian maiden tribute, below n. 87–89.

30 For example Protestilaus: Homer, *Il.* 2, 695–702; *Schol. Il.* 2, 700 f.; Herodotus, *Hist.* 9, 116; Pausanias, *Descr.* 4, 2,3; Plutarch, *Them.* 13, 2–5 = Phainias, frg. 25 Wehrli (Salamis); Plutarch, *Pel.* 21 (Leuctra), source V.

31 Porphyry *Abst.* 2, 56,7 = Phylarchus, *FGrHist* 81 F 80.

32 Porphyry, *Abst.* 2, 53,3 – 56,10.

33 Plutarch, *Them.* 13, 2–5 = Phainias, frg. 25 Wehrli (Salamis); Plutarch, *Pel.* 21 (Leuctra), source V.; Hughes, *Human Sacrifice*, 111–15.

(a) "Human Sacrifice" at Salamis[34]

According to Plutarch, this alleged sacrifice refers to three Persian brothers of the upper classes. They were presumably sacrificed by Themistocles on the urgent request of the masses. It is supposed that the sacrifice was made to Dionysus (the raw-eater).[35] This episode is neither mentioned by the contemporary Aeschylus nor by the historiographer of the Persian wars, Herodotus. Plutarch is in this matter contradictory. If this case was an historical event, it would be an absolute exception. But it should be considered as unhistorical, as other historical emergencies well covered by the available sources do not refer to such a practice.[36]

(b) Human Sacrifice before the Battle of Leuctra:[37]

The Boeotian general Pelopidas had a dream in his camp before the battle, according to which lamenting girls, the Leuctrids, curse in their graves the Spartans. Their father, Scedasus, told the general that he should sacrifice a fair-haired virgin if he wanted to win the battle. The general is horrified and reports this to his officers and his seer. In the following discussion, quite a number of previous "human sacrifices" are mentioned[38] as well as the Persian prisoners sacrificed by Themistocles at Salamis.[39] In all cases this led to a successful outcome of the respective war. But there are also examples demonstrating the opposite, that means a refused sacrifice resulted in a lack of success.[40] Pelopidas and his advisers however shrink back from a human sacrifice with the argument that no supreme being could demand such a barbarian and criminal sacrifice. Finally, a foal which had run away is recognized as a sacrificial

---

34 Henrichs, "Human Sacrifice," 208–24 with detailed discussion and the whole evidence.

35 Plutarch, *Them.* 13, 2–5 = Phainias, frg. 25 Wehrli; against: Plutarch, *Arist.* 9, 2 with contradictory statements.

36 pap. Oxyrhynchus (XVIII) 2165 = Alcaeus, frg. 129, 9 Lobel-Page; the earliest evidence concerning Dionysus (the raw eater) can be found in a poem by Alcaeus from the 7th cent B. C.; it mentions the trias venerated in Lesbos consisting of Zeus, the Aeolian Hera and the above-mentioned Dionysus (the raw eater). But most importantly, his cult is limited to Lesbos, Dionysus Omadius (raw one) to Chios and the one of Dionysus Anthroporrhaistes (render of men) to Tenedos. According to tradition, human sacrifices were made to all three of them. However, there can be found no evidence of these divinities in the Greek mother land. This renders the statement of Phaeneas from Lesbos regarding the sacrifice of three Persians incredible and therefore that of Plutarch, too.

37 Plutatch, *Pel.* 21, source V.

38 Cf. Herodotus, *Hist.* 7, 219,1; 220; 224,1 concerning the Thermopylae; source I.

39 Plutarch, *Them.* 13, 2–5.

40 Plutarch, *Ages.* 6, 4–6, source IV.; *Pel.* 21,3, source V.

replacement and therefore is killed at the virgins' graves accompanied by prayers.[41]

A variant of this model concerns a self-sacrifice: On the recommendation of an oracle or a seer, the king, the agitator, or a relative must sacrifice himself (or herself).[42] Mythological examples in this context are Codrus[43], the Erechthidae[44], or the figures of Menoeceus and Macaria invented by Euripides[45]: Codrus, the legendary king of Athens, had to defend the town against the Peloponnesians. He was informed of an oracle promising his enemies the victory on condition that the king of Athens would not be killed. In order to rescue the town, Codrus, dressed as a beggar, went into the hostile camp and thus sacrificed himself voluntarily. When the Peloponnesians heard of his deed, they allegedly left without a fight.[46]

The death of the Spartan king Leonidas in 480 B. C. can be interpreted as the most prominent example of historical times. According to a certain tradition, he knew about a Delphic oracle saying that either a Spartan king from the dynasty of the Heraclidae would perish or the whole town of Sparta—and therefore also Greece. Therefore he sacrificed himself and his men in the battle for the liberty of the Hellenes.[47] This corresponds to the *devotio* we find in the Roman tradition.[48]

3. The Model of Catastrophes

In order to prevent a catastrophe, an epidemic, a famine or something similar, a human sacrifice has to be made on recommendation of an or-

---

[41] Plutarch, *Pel.* 21–22 (whole context), source V.; esp. 21,3; concerning a respective oracle about the Thebans' victory at the virgins' graves who, according to a local legend, had killed themselves after having been raped by Lacedaemoneans, cf. Xenophon, *Hell.* 6, 4,7; Diodorus, *Bibl.* 15, 54; Pausanias, *Descr.* 9, 13,5–6; 9, 14,3.

[42] Cf. Xenophon, *Hell.* 2, 4,18–19 (seer of the democrats around Thrasybulos).

[43] FGrHist 4 F 125; Hellanicus, FGrHist 3 F 154; principal source: Lycurgus, *Leocr.* 84 ff.; Pompeius Trogus / (M. J.) Justinus, *Epit.* 2, 6,16 ff.

[44] Lycurgus, *Leocr.* 98–101.

[45] Menoeceus: Euripides, *Phoen.* 834 ff.; Pausanias, *Descr.* 9, 25,1; Plutarch, *Pel.* 21, source V.; Macarea: Euripides, *Heracl.* 408–601; *Schol. Plat. Hipp. Maior* 293 a.

[46] According to an older version Codrus was killed in the battle; Strabo, *Geogr.* 9, 393; 14, 653; Cicero, *Nat. d.* 3, 49; *Fin.* 5, 62; represented on the bowl representing Codrus from Bologna, 5th cent. B. C.; cf. also the so-called painter of Codrus: painter of bowls, Attic, about 430–410 B. C.

[47] Herodotus, *Hist.* 7, 220, source I.

[48] Cf. Livivius, *Ab urbe condita* 8, 9,4–12: In the context of the battle against the Latins in 340 B. C. the consul P. Decius Mus sacrificed himself in compliance with the ritual of the *devotio*.

acle or a seer.[49] In this context we often find in the literary sources local traditions. The example of the daughters of the mythological king Leon of Athens (*Leokorai*) have to be mentioned who sacrificed themselves in order to prevent a famine (according to another tradition they tried to prevent the pest).[50] Parallels with this story can be found among many other myths in the one about Orion's daughters who sacrifice themselves in order to rescue their hometown in Boeotia.[51]

Perhaps we can place one of the earliest archaeological evidence in Crete in this context. This evidence regards the striking findings in Anemospilia.[52] During excavations in 1979, a building with several rooms of unusual shape has been discovered which the excavators called "shrine" (νάος), surrounded by a precinct well. In one room they found large quantities of ceramics, in an adjacent room—in the centre of the installation—perhaps the relics of a ξόανον,[53] in a third room three skeletons in different positions, a fourth outside in an anteroom (προθάλαμος, corridor). Three persons, two men and one woman (about 28 years old, 1,54 m high) probably died when the building crashed down or during the following fire, the fourth person however, a man of about 18 years and around 1,65 m high, was found in a striking (lateral) position on a low, altar-like structure. On his body was a solid blade with a length of about 40 cm which the excavators considered to be a sacrificial knife.[54] Strangely enough, the bones of the skeleton were of different colours. The bones of the upper left side of the body were white, the bones of the lower right side of the body were black-stained. The excavators have interpreted the scene as a human sacrifice made in an extreme emergency. Either it was offered during the first preliminary earthquakes to prevent a more important catastrophe or following the principal earth-

---

49 Archaeological evidence: probably Anemospilia, cf. below n. 52 and 55; literary evidence: for example Leokorai in Athens (see below).

50 Demosthenes, *Epitaph.* 29; Aelian, *Var. Hist.* 12,28; Pausanias, *Descr.* 1, 5,2; the sanctuary called Leokoreum erected in their honor was near the Panathenaean way in Athens.

51 Corinna, frg. 3 Page; Dowden, *Death and the Maiden*, 168; Hughes, *Human sacrifice*, 73–79 with further examples.

52 Anemospilia, near Archanes, was towards 1700 B. C. destroyed by an earthquake which was responsible for the destruction of the older palaces. Yannis Sakellarakis and Efi Sapouna-Sakellaraki, "Anaskaphe Archanon," *Praktika (tes en Athenais Christianikes Archaiologikes Hetaireias)* (1979), 331–92; idem and idem, *Archanes: Archanes Excavations* (Athens: Ekdotike Athenon, 1991), 137–56.

53 *JHS Archeological Reports* (1979–80), 50.

54 Blade; bronze weapon, spear (?) or sword; fig. 85, *JHS Archaeological Reports* (1980–81), 44; sacrificial weapon, Sakellarakis, *Archanes*, 154.

quake in order to reconcile the divinities. In this case the destruction of the building caused by an aftershock would have put an end to this action. Almost every element of the interpretation made by the excavators has been contradicted, for example with regard to the building as a "shrine," to the so-called *xoanon* and above all with regard to the human sacrifice itself.[55] Despite possible objections one should nevertheless take these findings into consideration. Perhaps further research will clarify the circumstances.

4. The Model of Killing and Revenge

We know of ritual killings of persons, often prisoners of war or criminals, during the funeral or at the grave of a deceased person. The most famous example in the literature is the *Iliad*. During the funeral of Patroclus killed by Hector, Achilles slaughters 12 noble Trojan boys whose corpses subsequently are completely burnt together with skinned sheep, cattle, four horses, two dogs and other sacrificed animals.[56] It is therefore a typical sacrifice of annihilation as it is due to chthonic deities.[57] One has to make the difference between this *holokaustion* (ὁλοκαύτωμα) and the sacrificed and slaughtered animals for the meal in remembrance of the dead.[58] The killing of the Trojans during the funeral of Patroclus has become in the following period a mythological paradigm. While pictural representations of this scene remain rather rare in Greek art, they are a favourite motive of sepulchral art in Etruria, central and south Italy in the middle of the 4th cent. B. C. The most famous example in this context is a fresco in the Tomba François in Vulci (about 340–310 B. C.), which clearly designs the persons by means of annotations and which obviously refers to a death-offering.[59]

---

[55] Cf. already *JHS Archaeological Reports* (1980-81), 42; in detail Hughes, *Human Sacrifice*, 13–17; Yannis Sakellarakis and Efi Sakellaraki, Praktika (1979) 331–92; Yannis Sakellarakis and Efi Sakellaraki, "Drama of Death in a Minoan Temple," *National Geographic* 159.2 (1981): 204–22; Yannis Sakellarakis and Efi Sakellaraki, *Archanes*, (Athen: Ekdotite Athenon, 1991); brief information in: *JHS Archaelogical Reports* (1979–80), 50–51; *JHS Archaelogical Reports* (1980–81), 42; *Bulletin de Correspondance Hellénique* 104 (1980): 673–75.

[56] Homer, *Il.* 23, 114–176; Hughes, *Human Sacrifice*, 49–56; as for the iconography of the representation in Etruscan contexts see Steuernagel *Menschenopfer*, 19–28.

[57] But see also the huge burnt-offering for Artemis Laphria in Hyampolis in the region of Phocis and in Patrae.

[58] Homer, *Il.* 23, 30–34.

[59] Cf. Steuernagel, *Menschenopfer*, 19–28.

The sacrifice of Polyxena at Achilles' grave at the request of his spirit also belongs to this cycle of Trojan legends. We know many variants of this episode. The *Iliou persis* (an epic poem dealing with the fall of Troy) mentions for the first time that Achilles' spirit demands the sacrifice of Polyxena at his grave. Euripides is probably also influenced by the myth of Iphigenia. The sacrifice of Iphigenia is necessary in order to have good winds for the army departing for Troy. The equivalent is the sacrifice of Polyxena for the return, so that good conditions for the ships sailing back from Troy to their home town are guaranteed.[60] Her blood is considered as a drink-offering for Achilles' shadow.[61]

Alexander the Great had recourse to these mythological models: The persons who conspired against his father Philipp II. are killed on Alexander's request at his father's grave in a ritual manner. As the excavations in Aegae / Vergina carried out by M. Andronikos have shown, even the funeral of Macedonian kings at that time apparently were much influenced by epic writings. Therefore, Alexander orchestrates the killing as a sacrifice according to the Homeric example.[62] This action is the start-

60 According to the tradition of the Cypria, Polyxena, the daughter of Priamus and Hecabe, is killed by Odysseus and Diomedes and is then buried by Neoptolemus, see *PEG* I (*Cypria*), frg. 34., p. 62 (*Schol. Euripides Hec.* 41). According to another tradition however, she is sacrificed by the Greeks at Achilles' grave, as his spirit demands the sacrifice and threatens to prevent otherwise good winds for the return of the Greek fleet: *PEG* I (*Iliou persis argumentum*), p. 89 (Proclus, *Chrestomatia* 239 [Severyns], suppl. ex Apollodorus, *Epit.* 5,16–25); for an English translation see M. L. West, *Greek Epic Fragments*, 143–47, 147; Hyginus, *Fab.* 110; Apollodorus, *Epit.* 5, 23; Euripides, *Hec.* 37–41; 107–15 (according to Zimmermann, "Euripides," 283 performed in the twenties of the 5th cent.); Ovid, *Metam.* 13, 441–48; Quintus Smyrnaeus, *Posthom.* 14, 234–45. Occasionally Neoptolemus is mentioned as the one who carries out the sacrifice, cf. Ibycus frg. 307 Page. Especially Euripides gives a detailed description, *Hec.* 1–628; cf. however also later Virgil, *Aen.* 3, 321–24; Ovid, *Met.* 13, 439–80; Seneca, *Tro.* 1132–64; a respective tragedy by Sophocles is only available in fragments: TrGF 4 p. 403–7; Sophocles Frgm. 522–28 Pearson. According to another version Achilles falls in love with Polyxena, allegedly when Hector is ransomed or when Troilus is watched secretly, cf. Diktys, *Ephem.* 3, 2 f.; 4, 10 f.; when Achilles finally wants to negotiate a marriage, he is killed at the sanctuary of the Apollo of Thymbra by Paris' arrow: Hyginus, *Fab.* 110; *Schol. Eur. Tro.* 16; Servius, *Aen.* 3,321. According to Philostratus, Polyxena commits suicide at Achilles' grave because of her unhappy love: *Vit. Apoll.* 4, 16,4.

61 Euripides, *Hec.* 536–38; cf. 392–93.

62 Pompeius Trogus / (M. J.) Justinus, *Epit.* 11, 2,1; cf. as for the Homeric rites of death Manolis Andronikos, *Totenkult* (Archaeologia Homerica W 4; Göttingen: Vandenhoeck & Ruprecht, 1968); as for the funerals idem, *Vergina: The Royal Tombs and the Ancient City* (Athens: Ekdotike Athenon, 1984).

ing point of a series of further immitations of his idol Achilles which we find in the literary sources referring to his reign.[63]

Plutarch's report on Messenian prisoners of war who were lapidated in 183 B. C. at the grave of Philopoemen in Megalopolis can be compared with these immitations (Plutarch, *Phil.* 21,5; source VI). Certainly, there is no stylization as a death-sacrifice, but the context leaves no doubt about this. The Achaeans took revenge for the killing of their great leader.

A variant of the model of death-sacrifice is the model of death-sacrifice combined with a gift: Women and servants are given as companions into the graves of high-ranking deceased persons. From this we must differentiate the practice to kill servants at their master's funeral or even wives at the funeral of their respective husband; both practices assume the belief that there is a life after death. These practices have been documented on a literary level and probably also on an archaeological level.[64] This practice is limited to funerals of high-ranking persons ("kings" or very wealthy persons).[65] A prominent example is perhaps the protogeometrical grave at Lefkandi on the island of Euboea. In a shaft grave were found next to an incinerated man in a precious imported bronze amphora a woman's skeleton with valuable offerings. Her hands and feet were crossed, beside her head lay an iron knife with an ivory handle. It is especially the striking position of the corpse and the knife which made the excavators think of a ritual killing. The second shaft grave contained the remains of four horses. Above the grave was a house with an apsis,

---

[63] Justinus probably follows the example of Cleitarchus; the modern research on Alexander is based on the presumption that not all examples of this *immitatio* are historically proven, but that they are the result of a deliberate stylization. However it cannot be denied that Alexander orientated himself in a particular way to Homer and Achilles.

[64] Cf. Mycenaean graves in the form of a Tholos with a funeral in the Dromos; possibly in Dendra, "King and Queen," with servant and dog for being accompanied in the underworld: Axel W. Persson, *The Royal Tombs at Dendra Near Midea* (Skrifter 15, ed. Kungliga Humanistiska Vetenskapssamfundet i Lund, 1931), 68–70; contra Georgios E. Mylonas, *Mycenae and the Mycenaean Age* (Princeton: Princeton University Press, 1966), 128–29; cf. Lefkandi: Gabriele Weiler, *Domos Theiou Basileos: Herrschaftsformen und Herrschaftsarchitektur in den Siedlungen der Dark Ages* (Beiträge zur Altertumskunde 136; München: Saur, 2001), 111–14.

[65] Possible archaeological evidence of Mycenaean graves: Hughes, *Human Sacrifice*, 26–35; 43–47; for the written tradition see Herodotus, for example referring to Scythians and Thracians, *Hist.* 4, 71,4 – 72: the Scythians strangle during the funeral of a king one of his concubines and bury her with him; further persons are the cupbearer, favourite cook as well as horses and drinking cups; *Hist.* 5, 5: some Thracians tribes practice at their king's death the custom to have his favourite wife killed at the grave by one of her relatives.

with 45 × 50 m the biggest known building of this period. During or rather after the funeral, the house was burnt down and the whole construction was covered with a tumulus.[66] Thanks to the discovered ceramics, we can date the funeral to the period between 1000 and 950 B. C.

5. Model of Initiation

In order to become a member of the community with full rights, symbolic barriers have to be overcome. In this scenario, human sacrifices can be of importance in different ways.[67] A good example is the cult of Zeus Lykaios. According to Hughes it is the only cult connected with human sacrifice for which we have several historical sources. Furthermore, we dispose of some written pieces of evidence referring to this cult.

In the west of the plain of Megalopolis in Arcadia is situated mount Lykaion. On its peak was found a circular sacrificial place where allegedly human sacrifices had been celebrated in compliance with the cult of Zeus Lykaios.[68] The festivals of the Lykaia hold there by the Arcadians had their origin in combative games. Even if the sanctuary and the festivities are known by the literature since Alcman and Pindar, the earliest evidence which can be connected with human sacrifices dates from the 4th cent. B. C.[69]

Socrates mentions in Platon's Politeia (565 D–E) that the consumption of human flesh on the altar transforms a man into a wolf.[70] Appararently several authors mention "human sacrifices" in this context. But it is

---

[66] Hughes, *Human sacrifice*, 46–47; Weiler, *Domos*, 111–14; in detail see Mervyn R. Popham, Peter G. Calligas, and L. Hugh Sackett, *Lefkandi II: The Protogeometric Building at Toumba 2: The Excavation, Architecture and Finds* (Annual of the British School of Athens, Suppl. 23; London: Thames & Hudson, 1993), especially 81–96.

[67] Zeus Lykaios, Arcadia; apparently human flesh of a person sacrificed on the altar is consumed which results in a temporary transformation into a "wolf," see below.

[68] Meuli, *Opferbräuche*, 278–280; Burkert, *Homo necans*, 98–108 (German edition); Hughes, *Human Sacrifice*, 96–107.

[69] Alcman, frg. 24 (Page); Pindar, *Ol.* 9, 96–97; 13, 107–8; *Nem.* 10, 48; Plato, *Pol.* 565 D–E.

[70] Also Theophrastus frg. 13, 22–26 Pötscher; about 370–288 / 285 B. C.; cf. Porphyry, *Abst.* 2, 27; Polybios, *Hist.* 8, 13,7 and Pausanias, *Descr.* 8, 2,6 know the cult and the story of the Arcadian wolf-men; a further testimony—even if it cannot be taken literally—offers Pausanias, *Descr.* 8, 38,7; variants concerning an Olympic champion called Damarchos or Demaenetus are mentioned by Pausanias, *Descr.* 6, 8,2; cf. Pliny the Elder, *Nat.* 8, 34 and Augustine, *Civ.* 18, 17.

not excluded that the sources depend on each other. Doubts are quite justified, at least for the historical times.

According to the myth, Lykaon, the oldest king of Arcadia and the initiator of the Lycaean games, sacrificed and offered one of his sons to Zeus on the mountain. In consequence, Lykaon was transformed into a wolf. But was this *aition* the reason for real human sacrifices in the 4th cent. B. C.? According to Otto Kern,[71] this story of a "werewolf" refers to a pre-Greek wolfslike god who was later replaced by Zeus. Most recently, Burkert has tried to draw from the written tradition the conclusion that they refer to rites of initiation which however cannot clearly be reconstructed.[72] The described transformation into a "wolf" could symbolize a rite of transition into a certain age, according to Burkert probably the admission into a society of adult men and warriors.[73] After a certain but indefinit lapse of time (one year?, ten years?) these persons would get into another age class, they would not remain for ever a "wolf," but become again a 're-transformed' human being or another animal. According to Pausanias (*Descr.* 4, 11,3), the Arcadian soldiers wore wolf skins or bear furs. Thus, it is quite possible that this was the term for a certain age group. But we could also think of a kind of secret society (a wolf brotherhood?) or some kind of priesthood for Zeus Lykaios.[74]

The sanctuary of Zeus Lykaios has always been surrounded by secrets even for contemporaries. Entrance was forbidden. According to Polybius, the illegal entry led to the loss of one's shadow.[75] Later sources are even more clear. Persons who deliberately dared to enter were lapidated by the Arcadians, those who entered by accident, were sent "to Eleutherae."[76] Pausanias reports that every person who entered the district without permission had to die within a year; access to the sanctuary in Megalopolis was not permitted, either.[77]

---

[71] Otto Kern, *Die Religion der Griechen 1: Von den Anfängen bis Hesiod* (Berlin: Weidmann, 1926), 187 f.; cf. also Apollon Lyceius, who kills wolves in Sparta.

[72] Burkert, *Homo necans*, 98–108 (German edition).

[73] Burkert, *Homo necans*, 105–107 (German edition).

[74] Cf. Pliny the Elder, *Nat.* 8, 34 referring to Euanthes; transformation into a wolf for nine years; restricted to the members of Anthos' family, the Anthides; the person who carried out the sacrifice was determined by lot.

[75] Polybios, *Hist.* 16, 12,7 = Theopomp, FGrHist 115 F 343.

[76] Plutarch, *Quaest. Graec.* 39, 300 A–D = Architimos, FGrHist 315 F 1.

[77] Pausanias, *Descr.* 8, 36,6; 8, 30,2.

In 1902, excavations by Konstantinos Kourouniotis discovered the circular sacrificial place on the mountain of Lykaion. On the natural soil was found a layer of about 1,50 m consisting of earth, stones, ashes and the remains of bones. On the basis of ceramics and coins, the place was used from about 600 up to the 4th cent. B. C.

Tests on bones have revealed that they mostly belonged to smaller animals like birds, but cattle and pigs could also be identified. Contrary to the literary tradition, no human rests were found. Therefore, human sacrifices on the occasion of the festival of the Lykaia cannot be proven, at least not for historical times. Burkert's thesis of rites of initiation[78] is probably the best explanation.[79]

Another prominent example is the lashing of Spartian boys in the sanctuary of Artemis Orthia in Sparta, a cult practiced up to Roman imperial times.[80] Within the framework of the education (ἀγωγή), all future male full citizens had to undergo this rite of initiation. In conformity with the tradition, quite a number of these people lost their lives in doing so. According to one tradition, the cult statue of Artemis Orthia came from the Taurans and was brought by Iphigenia and Orestes to Sparta. The ritual flogging of boys whose blood had to sprinkle the altar, is reported only by authors of Roman times. As some scholars think it replaced apparently an older, bloody human sacrifice. But there are also still serious objections to this oppinion.[81]

6. Model of Envy and Ill Will

A famous story has its origin in the legend of the "Golden Fleece" and thus in the legend of the Argonauts: Ino, the second wife of Athamas, profits from a drought in Boeotia to have her stepson Phrixus sacrificed to Zeus with the help of a falsified Delphic oracle. When Athamas leads

---

78 Cf. Lycaeae in honour of Apollon Lyceius (who killed wolfs in Sparta).

79 The cult for Zeus Laphystius in Halus in Achaea Phthiotis also belongs to this context, Herodotus, *Hist.* 7, 197.

80 Hughes, *Human Sacrifice*, 79–81 with further reference.

81 Plutarch, *Lyc.* 18,1; Pausanias, *Descr.* 3, 16,7–11; cf. *Suda* s. v. *Lykourgos*; discussion by Herbert J. Rose, "The Cult of Arthemis Orthia," in: *The Sanctuary of Arthemis Orthia at Sparta: Excavated and Described by the Members of the British School at Athens* (ed. R. M. Dawkins; The Society for the Promotion of Hellenic Studies, Suppl. 5; London: Macmillan, 1929), 399–407, 404 ff. The flogging is not mentioned in earlier sources. But Xenophon describes another rite in which boys try to steal cheese from the altar of the goddess while opposed by others, who scourge them; cf. Xenophon, *Lac.* 2, 9 and Platon, *Leg.* 1, 633 B; Hughes, *Human Sacrifice*, 80.

his son to the altar, his first wife Nephele, mother of Phrixus, sends a golden ram, who carries the boy and his sister Helle off to Colchis. There Phrixus sacrifices the animal to Zeus; as in the case of Iphigenia, a human sacrifice is ultimately replaced by an animal sacrifice.[82]

7. Model of Xenophobia and Aversion to Foreigners

When foreigners are found, they are sacrificed to a local divinity.[83] The most famous literary example is the story of Orestes and Pylades. During her sacrifice, Iphigenia was carried off by Artemis and brought to Colchis where Thoas, king of Colchis, appointed her priestess of Artemis. Thus, Iphigenia has to carry out herself human sacrifices firmly rooted in the Tauran cult. When Orestes and Pylades appear by order of Apollo to take away the cult image of Artemis, they are discovered and are supposed to be sacrificed by the divinity's priestess as it is the custom. Iphigenia however recognizes her brother and all three of them can escape with the cult image.[84] According to Euripides Athena instructs Orestes and Iphigenia to bring the image of the goddess to Attica and to build a temple at Halai. As atonement for their sacrifice a new created custom demands a man's blood to flow during the future celebrationes, for holiness's sake.[85] A cult practiced in honour of the divinity Artemis Orthia in Sparta refers also to this myth of Artemis Tauropolos.[86]

---

[82] Legend of the "Golden fleece"; Apollodorus, *Bibl.* 1, 9,1; cf. Bonnechère, *Sacrifice*, 96–107, who considers the cult dedicated to Zeus Laphystius in Halus in Achaea Phthiotis as one of the rites of initiation; cf. Herodotus, *Hist.* 7, 197.

[83] For example Herodotus, *Hist.* 4, 103,1–2 (Taurans); *Hist.* 9, 119,1 (Thracians).

[84] It is possible that this myth goes already back to the *Cypria* (created before 650 B. C.), but it is above all embellished by Euripides in the tragedy of *Iphigenia Taurica*; according to Zimmermann, "Euripides," 284 it was performed in 414 B. C.; as for the representations of this myth in the Hellenistic Etruscan sepulchral art see Steuernagel, *Menschenopfer*, 36–42; cf. Herodotus, *Hist.* 4, 103,1–2: The Taurans sacrifice shipwrecked persons and captive Hellenes to the "virgin" by decapitation; according to the Taurans Iphigenia was this divinity.

[85] Euripides, *Iph. taur.* 1458–61; cf. source III.; Hughes, *Human Sacrifice*, 81: "... the lines would appear to be senseless if Euripides did not refer to an actual, contemporary ritual which involved the (non-fatal) cutting of a male's neck with a sword."

[86] According to the tradition, a priestess holds the cult image of Artemis Orthia in her arms when Spartian boys are flogged in the sanctuary. If the flogging is too weak, the image will become too heavy for the priestess. The goddess requires blood. But do we really see here the replacement of a bloody human sacrifice by lashing boys? Only authors of the Roman times report these rite; cf. Pausanias, *Descr.* 3, 16,7–11; Hughes, *Human Sacrifice*, 79–80.

8. The Model of Tribute

The following tradition from Locris belongs to this model: From Locris, every year girls are sent as a tribute to Troy in order to atone Aias' violent behaviour towards Cassandra (another later variant speaks of rape) in the temple of Athena, in the face of the altar and image of the virgin goddess.[87] This subject was also appreciated by vase-painters. On their arrival, the girls are lapidated by the Trojans. In case that one of them gets away and makes her way up to the temple of Athena, her life is saved and she becomes the priestess of the goddess.[88] An inscription found in Western Locris dating from the 3th cent. B. C. permits to reconstruct the real circumstances. It mentions the "tribute of Locrian maiden"[89]

Some passages deal with money which is spent for the girls' clothes and food, with the indemnification for the parents and the exemption of the citizens from other tributes in times of war. The analysis of these sources probably reveal that since archaic times, two girls were sent each year by the Locrians to Troy in order to serve there one year as a priestess of Athena. It seems historically not proven that the girls were lapidated and it would make no sense in the context as an expiatory offering for Aias' act of violence.

We find similar correlations in the far more famous legend about Theseus which probably is based on older traditions: In regular intervals, the Athenians had to send as a kind of tribute a fixed number of boys and girls to Cretan Cnossus where they were led to the Minotaur who was held captive in a labyrinth. By killing the monster the Attic hero Theseus puts an end to this habit which is justified as an expiation for the murder of the Cretan Androgeon, the king's son. But more likely it goes back to sacrifices to a Cretan divinity. In the version of the myth known to us, this divinity is replaced by the monster Minotaur, the sacrifice itself is thus replaced by a surrender as we can find them also in other fabulous traditions (for example Andromeda).

---

[87] This story must have its origin in the epic cycle poems where the competing variants can probably also be found; Homer, *Homeri opera V: Hymnos, Cyclum, fragmenta, Margiten, Batrachomyomachiam, Vitas continens* (ed. Th. W. Allen; Oxford: Clarendon, 1912), *Iliou persis* frg. 2–6, p. 108 = *PEG* 1, *Iliou persis frg.* 4, p. 91–92; *Iliou persis argumentum*, p. 89; Burkert, *Homo necans*, 72 (German edition), considers the rape as an apocryphal invention; cf. n. 10 with evidence; evidence and discussion see Hughes, *Human Sacrifice*, 166–84.

[88] First mentioned by Aeneas Tacticus in about 350 B. C., *Poliorc.* 31, 24; see also Lycophron, *Alex.* 1141–73; *Scholion Lycoph. Alex.* 1141 = Callimachos, fr. 35 Pfeiffer.

[89] *IG* IX^2 1,3 no. 706; Klaffenbach.

9. Sacrificing Living People as Personnel of Cult

In this context, the PY Tn 316 tablet in linear B script found in the layers of destruction of the Mycenaean palace in Pylos in Messenia ruined in about 1200 B. C. caused a sensation.[90] Names of divinities in the dative case, for example Zeus, Hera, Potnia and others are listed; to each item is added an ideogram for a vessel and an ideogram for gold. In most cases a further ideogram designates a man or a woman. The reading seems to be clear: for example "for Hera, a golden bowl and a woman." The tablet lists a total of 12 proven divinities, 13 golden vessels as well as 8 women and 2 men.

As for the interpretation of these findings, the first editors have not taken human sacrifices into account. But in a later edition John Chadwick ventured a new interpretation on the grounds of the observation that not on all sacrificed vessels is added the notion "man" or "woman": "Hence the alternative, that these people were committed to divine service by being sacrificed, begins to appear more likely."[91] Compared to further similar tablets from Pylos and Thebes, this seems plausible if one takes into account that these texts deal with a more limited number of actions than has been thought until now. One should not forget that the documentation of the tablets only records a part of one single calendar year. If we take the evidence from Pylos for example, the sacrifice of several dozen people and gold vessels respectively would have been necessary. But this would have exceeded the resources of the palace as well as the needs of the cult centres. For this reason one should look for other explanations, such as the recourse of the palace to persons and vessels which were already in the possession of the temple in order to let pass by them ceremonially offerings like odorous oils from the palace to the temple. This does not exclude however that from time to time also humans were sacrificed and that they were thus made for ever available to the divinities.

At this point, a connection to the sacrifice of Iphigenia in Aulis can be established. In most variants of the tradition, the girl is not killed, but is

[90] Leonard. R. Palmer, *The Interpretation of Mycenaean Greek Texts* (Oxford: Clarendon, 1963), 261–68; John Chadwick and Michael Ventris, *Documents in Mycenaean Greek* (2nd. ed.; Cambridge: Cambridge University Press, 1973), 284–89; Hughes, *Human Sacrifice*, 199–202.

[91] Chadwick and Ventris, *Documents*, 460; John Chadwick, *The Mycenaean World* (Cambridge: Cambridge University Press, 1976), 91–92; more cautious Palmer, *Interpretation*, 266.

brought by a divinity to another place where she serves as a priestess. A comparable practice can apparently be proven up to the 4th cent. A. D., which is supported by numerous inscriptions found in several Greek temples, for example in supra-regional centres like Delphi, but also in smaller sanctuaries. Recently, 194 texts have been discovered in a sanctuary in the mountains near the Macedonian Beroea,[92] which all deal with so-called sacral liberations. This means that male and female slaves were assigned to the local "autochthon" mother goddess, in most cases they were sold (the purchase price, a kind of price of liberation, was most probably fixed by the slaves themselves). Thus the rights of ownership expired—but in no case the claims regarding the παραμονή of the original owner. As for the privileges acquired in the legal act, the divinity can only in a limited way have made use of them, for example at the yearly celebrated *Panegyris*. In reality, the assigned or purchased persons became free from any master, which was in opposition to the Greek sense of justice however. This made the fictious assignment to a divinity necessary. So we cannot really speak of human sacrifices in this context.

These nine models reveal conceptions and concepts which find their expression in permanently modified myths, but which do not reflect historical situations or events. As especially some archaeological findings and inscriptions have shown, the reality was always different. Nevertheless, one should not underestimate the importance of the myth or even consider it as a falsification of reality. In fact, the myth translates ideas which were well rooted in the Greek society and religion.[93]

According to Claude Lévi-Strauss and Jean-Pierre Vernant,[94] the myth, besides language, rituals and religion, serves as a system of com-

---

[92] Photios M. Petsas et al., *Inscriptions du sanctuaire de la Mère des Dieux Autochtone de Leukopétra (Macédoine)* (Melethemata 28; Athens: Boccard, 2000). As for some necessary restrictions of their interpretation see the review by Johannes Heinrichs, in: *Gnomon* 75 (2003): 74–76.

[93] Glenn Most, "Strenge Erforschung wilder Ursprünge: Walter Burkert über Mythos und Ritus," preface to: Walter Burkert, *Wilder Ursprung: Opferritual und Mythos bei den Griechen* (Kleine kulturwissenschaftliche Bibliothek 22; Berlin: Wagenbach, 1990), 8: "Mythos ist nicht gleich Fiktion: auch wenn seine Loskoppelung einer Ästhetisierung gleichkommt, bleibt an ihm ein unauslöschlicher Hinweis auf jenen fernen Kontext haften, in dem er entstand und aus dem heraus er wuchs."

[94] Jean-Pierre Vernant, *Mythe et société en Grèce ancienne* (Fondations; Paris: Maspero, 1981); German trans.: *Mythos und Gesellschaft im alten Griechenland* (Edition Suhrkamp 1381; Frankfurt: Suhrkamp, 1987).

munication within a society. It can be a concrete explanation for collective rituals and trace back, justify and sanction religious norms and ideas, as particularly the scholars from the Cambridge-School, especially Jane Ellen Harrison point out.[95] The respective context of the sacrifical scenes gives us the necessary background information. As a whole, an existential submission of man to the divinity is expressed, who can not only require animals and things under the power of men, but even human beings themselves. This demand defines the distance between divinity and man. In this context, it does not matter whether such demands really were made or fulfilled in historical times. The possibility expressed by the myth is sufficient to concretisize and thus to define the relation between divinity and man in a permanently new way. Thus, the mythological human sacrifices influenced the Greeks' lives and became a reality which later could be criticized by philosophers and Christians.

This development required that the myth was not considered as a literary fiction, but as a historical tradition. The parting line the Greeks drew between myth and historical reality was not so narrow as it is the case in the enlightened society of modern times. In the Greeks' eyes, the myth reflected in principle a real past even if this was presented in an artificially elaborated way. They considered the myth and its descriptions as historical and therefore real. For these reasons the modern separation between myth and reality implies a simplification, even if it can objectively be justified. As the Greeks did not consider the myths as constructions, but as reflections of a distant reality in the past, the human sacrifices described in the myths have to be interpreted as projections of events the Greeks regarded as real and in no way as fictional.

Human sacrifices cannot directly be proven for the Greek world, but they were considered as real by the Greeks and influenced their life. The killing orchestrated by Alexander as a sacrifice of those who conspired against his father Philipp II. as well as the lapidation of Messenians at the grave of Philopoemen also carried out as a sacrifice illustrate the value attached to the myth. Human sacrifices however were at the most only very rare exceptions. The listed examples, which we consider as fictions, reveal however that they were an essential part of the Greek understanding of the world.

---

[95] Jane Ellen Harrison, *Themis: A Study in the Social Origins of Greek Religion* (Cambridge: Cambridge University Press, 1912).

Literary Sources

I. Herodotus, *Historiae* 7, 220
(Thermopylai 480 B. C.; Oracle from Delphi)[96]

Fated is for you, ye dwellers in wide-wayed Sparta,
Either your city must fall, that now is mighty and famous,
Wasted by Persian men, or the watcher of fair Lakedaemon
Mourn for a king that is dead, from Heracles' line descended.
Yea, for the foe thou hast nor bulls nor lions can conquer;
Mighty he cometh as Zeus, and shall not be stayed in his coming;
One of the two will he take, and rend his quarry asunder.

II. Euripides, *Iphigenia taurica* 380–91
(414–412 B. C.)[97]

Iphigeneia: "Out on this Godess's false subtleties,
Who, if one stain his hands with blood of men,
Or touch a wife new-travailed, or a corpse,
Bars him her altars, holding him defiled,
Yet joys herself in human sacrifice!
It cannot be that Zeus' bride Leto bare
Such folly. Nay, I hold unworthy credence
The banquet given of Tantalus to the Gods,—
As though the Gods could savour a child's flesh!
Even so, this folk, themselves man-murderers,
Charge on their Goddess their own sin, I ween;
For I believe that none of Gods is vile.

III. Euripides, *Iphigenia taurica* 1458–11
(414–412 B. C.)

"And institute this custom: when the people celebrate,
as atonement for your sacrifice let them hold a sword
to a man's neck and cause blood to flow,
for holiness's sake and that the goddess have due honour."

---

[96] Herodotus, *The Persian Wars: With an English Translation* (ed. and trans. A. D. Godley; LCL 119; Cambridge, Mass.: Harvard University Press, 1922, repr. 1971).

[97] Edwin B. England, ed., *The Iphigeneia among the Tauri of Euripides* (London: MacMillan, 1883, repr. 1986); cf. Euripides, *Trojan Woman, Iphigenia Among the Taurians, Ion* (ed. and trans. D. Kovacs; LCL 10n; Euripides, vol. 4; Cambridge/Mass.: Harvard University Press, 1999), 145–311.

IV. Plutarch, *Agesilaus* 6, 4–5
(Aulis 396 B. C.)[98]

While his forces were assembling at Geraestus (spring 396) Agesilaus himself went to Aulis with his friends and spent the nigth. As he slept, he thought a voice came to him, saying: "King of the Lacedaemonians, thou art surely aware that no one has ever been appointed general of all Hellas together except Agamemnon, in former times, and now thyself, after him. And since thou commandest the same hosts that he did, and wagest war on the same foes, and settest out for the war from the same place, it is meet that thou shouldst sacrifice also the godess the sacrifice which he made there before he set sail." Almost at once Agesilaus remembered the sacrifice of his own daughter which Agamemnon had there made in obedience to the soothsayers. *He was not disturbed, however, but after rising up and imparting his vision to his friends, declared that he would honor the goddess with a sacrifice in which she could fitly take pleasure, being a goddess, and would not imitate the cruel insensibility of his predecessor.* So he caused a hind to be wreathed with chaplets, and ordered his own seer to perform the sacrifice, instead of the one customarily appointed to this office by the Boeotians.

V. Plutarch, *Pelopidas* 21
(Leucta 371 B. C.)[99]

After Pelopidas had lain down to sleep in the camp, he thought he saw these maidens [the Leuctridae] weeping at their tombs, as they invoked curses upon the Spartans, and Scedasus bidding him sacrifice to his daughters a virgin with auburn hair, if he wished to win the victory over his enemies. The injunction (*prostagma*) seemed a lawless and dreadful one to him, but he rose up and made it known to the seers and the commanders. Some of these would not hear of the injunction being neglected or disobeyed, adducing as examples of such sacrifice among the ancients, Menoeceus, son of Creon, Macaria, daughter of Heracles; and, in later times, Pherecydes the wise man, who was put to death by the Lacedaemonions, and whose skin was preserved by their kings, in accordance with some oracle; and Leonidas, who in obedience to the oracle, sacrificed himself, as it were, to save Greece [cf. Herodotus, *Hist.* 7,

[98] Plutarch, *Parallel Lives* V: *Agesilaus and Pompey, Pelopidas and Marcellus* (ed. and trans. B. Perrin; LCL 87; Cambridge/Mass.: Harvard University Press, 1914–18, repr. 1967–75), 1–113.

[99] Ibid., 339–433.

220]; and, still further, the youth who were sacrificed by Themistocles to Dionysos [Carnivorous] before the sea fight at Salamis [cf. Plutarch, *Themistocles* 13, 2–3]; for the successes which followed these sacrifices proved them acceptable to the gods. Moreover, when Agesilaus, who was setting out on an expedition from the same place as Agamemnon did, and against the same enemies, was asked by the goddess for his daughter in sacrifice, and had this vision as he lay asleep at Aulis [cf. Plutarch, *Agesilaus* 6, 4–5], he was too tender-hearted to give her, and thereby brought his expedition to an unsuccessful and inglorious ending. *Others, on the contrary, argued against it, declaring that such a lawless and barbarous sacrifice was not acceptable to any one of the superior beings above us, for it was not the fabled typhons and giants who governed the world, but the father of all gods and men; even to believe in the existence of divine beings who take delight in the slaughter and blood of men was perhaps a folly, but if such beings existed, they must be disregarded, as having no power; for only weakness and depravity of soul could produce or harbour such unnatural and cruel desires.*

VI. Plutarch, *Philopoemen* 21,5
(Megalopolis 182 B.Ċ.)[100]

He (Philopoemen) was burried, then, as was fitting, with conspicuous honours, and at his tomb the captive Messenians were stoned to death.

"Human Sacrifice" described by Herodotus

Herodotus, *Hist.* 1, 216,2–5:[101]

And they (the Massagetae) have no appointed limet of live but this, that whensoever a man waxeth exceeding old, all his kinsmen come together and slay (θύειν) him, and much cattle also; and then they seethe the flesh and devour it. This is held by them to be the most blessed lot; but the man that perisheth of sickness they consume not but bury in the earth, and they deem it a calamity that he lived not to be slain. (...) The only god (θεός) they worship is the sun (Helios), to whom they sacrifice horses; and the meaning of this

[100] Plutarch, *Parallel Lives* X: *Agis and Cleomenes, Tiberius and Gaius Gracchus, Philopoemen and Flaminius* (ed. and trans. B. Perrin; LCL 102; Cambridge/Mass.: Harvard University Press, 1914–18, repr. 1967–75), 255–319.

[101] J. Enoch Powell, trans., *Herodotus* (2 vols.; Oxford: Clarendon Press, 1949).

sacrifice is this, that they apportion to the swiftest of the gods the swiftest of all mortal things.

Herodotus, *Hist.* 2, 119[102]

And Menelaus came to Egypt and sailed up to Memphis; and when he had spoken the truth about these matters, he received great hospitality and got back Helen and all his riches besides. Howbeit, when he had gotten them, Menelaus did the Egyptians wrong. As he purposed to sail away, contrary winds stayes him; and when this had lasted a great while, he imagined an unholy deed. He took two children of the people and made sacrifices of them (ἔντομά σφεα ἐποίησε). Then, when it came to be bruited about that he had done this deed, he was hated and pursued after; and he departed and fled with his ships unto Libya.

Herodotus, *Hist.* 4, 62[103]

Such is their (the Scythians) way of sacrificing (θύειν) to all other gods and such are the beast offered; but their sacrifices to Ares are on this wise. Every district in each of the governments has in it a structure sacred to Ares, to wit, a pile of fagots of sticks three furlongs broad and long, but of a less height, on the top of which there is a flattened four-sided surface; (...) On this sacred pile there is set for each people an ancient scimitar of iron, which is their image of Ares; to this scimitar they bring yearly sacrifice of sheep and goats and horses, offering to these symbols even more than they do to the other gods. Of all their enemies that they take alive, they sacrifice (j'uein) one man in every hundred, not according to their fashion of sacrificing sheep and goats, but differently. They pour wine on the men's head and cut their throats over a vessel; then they carry the blood up on to the pile of sticks and pour it on the scimitar. So they carry the blood aloft, but below by the sacred pile they cut off all the slain men's right arms and hands and throw these into the air, and presently depart when they have sacrificed the rest of the victims; the arm lies where it has fallen, and the body apart from it.

---

102 Ibid.
103 Trans. Godley, LCL 119.

Herodotus, *Hist.* 4, 71,4–72[104]

> Then, having laid the dead (king) in the tomb on a couch, they (the Scythians) plant spears on each side of the body and lay across them wooden planks, which they then roof over with plaited oziers; in the open space which is left in the tomb they bury, after strangling, one of the king's concubines, his cup-bearer, his cook, his groom, his squire, and his messenger, besides horses, and first-fruits of all else, and golden cups; for the Scythians make no use of silver or bronze. Having done this they all build a great barrow of earth, vying zealously with one another to make this as great as may be.
>
> With the completion of a year they begin a fresh practice. Taking the trustiest of the rest of the king's servants (and these are native-borne Scythians, for only those serve the king whom he bids to do so, and none of the Scythians have servants bought by money) they strangle fifty of these squires and fifty of their best horses and empty and cleanse the bellies of all, fill them with chaff, and sew them up again. (...) Then they take each of the fifty strangled young men and mount him on the horse. (...) So having set horsemen of this fashion round about the tomb they ride away.

Herodotus, *Hist.* 4, 94[105]

> As to their claim to be immortal, this is how they (the Getae, Thracians) show it: they believe that they do not die, but that he who perishes goes to the god (δαίμων) Salmoxis or Gebeleizis, as some of them call him. Once in every five years they choose by lot one of their people and sent him as a messenger to Salmoxis, charged to tell of their needs; and this is their manner of sending: Three lances are held by men thereto appointed; others seize the messenger to Salmoxis by his hands and feet, and swing and hurl him aloft on the spear-points. If he be killed by the cast, they believe that the god regards them with favour; but if he be not killed, they blame the messenger himself, deeming him a bad man, and send another messenger in place of him whom they blame. It is while the man yet lives that they charge him with the message. Moreover when there is thunder and lightning these same Thracians shoot arrows skyward as a threat to the god (θεός), believing in no other god (θεός) but their own.

---

104 Ibid.
105 Ibid.

Herodotus, *Hist.* 4, 103,1–2[106]

> Among these, the Tauri have the following customs: all shipwrecked men, and any Greeks whom they take in their sea-raiding, they sacrifice (θύειν) to the Virgin goddess (παρθένος) as I will show: after the first rites of sacrifice, they smite the victim on the head with a club; according to some, they then throw down the body from the cliff. This deity (δαίμων) to whom they sacrifice is said by the Tauri themselves to be Agamemnon's daughter Iphigenia.

Herodotus, *Hist.* 5, 5[107]

> Those (Thracians) who dwell above the Crestonaeans have a custom of their own: each man having many wives, at his death there is a great rivalry among his wives, and eager contention on their friends' part, to prove which wife was best loved by her husband; and she to whom the honour is adjudged is praised by men and women, and then slain (σφάζειν) over the tomb by her nearest of kin, and after the slaying she is buried with her husband. The rest of the wives take this sorely to heart, deeming themselves deeply dishonoured.

Herodotus, *Hist.* 7, 114[108]

> Having used these enchantments and many other besides on the river (Strymon in Thrace), they (the Persian army of Xerxes in 480 B. C.) passed over it at the Edonian town of Nine Ways (Ἐννέα Ὁδοί), by the bridges which they found thrown across it. There, learning that Nine Ways was the name of the place, they buried alive that number of boys and maidens, children of the people of the country. To bury alive is a Persian custom; I have heard that when Xerxes' wife Amestris attained to old age she buried fourteen sons of notable Persians, as a thank-offering on her own behalf to the fabled god of the nether world.

Herodotus, *Hist.* 7, 180[109]

> The ship of Troizen, whereof Prexinus was captain, was pursued (near Sciathus) and straightway taken by the foreigners (the fleet of the Persian king Xerxes in 480 B. C.), who thereupon brought the

[106] Ibid.
[107] Ibid.
[108] Ibid.
[109] Ibid.

goodliest of its fighting men and cut his throat on the ship's prow, so making a common sacrifice (διαδέξιος; διαδέχεσθαι?) of the first and goodliest of their Greek captives. The name of him that was thus offered up was Leon; and mayhap it was his name that he had to thank for it.

Herodotus, *Hist.* 7, 197[110]

When Xerxes (Persian king invading Greece in 480 B.C.) was come to Alus (Halos) in Achaea, his guides, desiring to inform him of all they knew, told him the story that is related in that country concerning the worship of Laphystian Zeus: how Athamas son of Aeolus plotted Phrixus' death with Ino, and further, how the Achaeans by an oracle's bidding compel Phrixus' posterity to certain tasks; namely, they bid the eldest of that family forbear to enter their town hall (λήιτον; which the Achaeans call the People's House, the πρυτανήιον) and themselves keep watch there, if he enter, he may not come out, save only to be sacrificed (θύειν); and further also, how many of those that were to be sacrificed had fled away in fear to another country, but if they returned back at a later day and were taken, they had been brought into the town hall; and the guides showed Xerxes how the man is sacrificed (θύειν), with fillets covering himall over and a procession to lead him forth. It is the descendants of Phrixus's son Cytissorus who are thus dealt with, because when the Achaeans by an oracle's bidding made Athamas son of Aeolus a scapegoat for their country and were about to sacrifice him, this Cytissorus came from Aea in Colchis and delivered him, but thereby brought the god's wrath on his own posterity. Hearing all this, Xerxes when he came to the temple grove forbore to enter it himself and bade all his army do likewise, holding the house and the precinct of Athamas' descendants alike in reverence.

[Commentary A.D. Godley: "The legend, in its main features, originates in the cult of 'Zeus Laphystius,' a tribal god who, like the Jehova of the Old Testament and the Moloch and Melqart of the Phoenicians, has a right to all first-born, especially of the priestly house. In time human sacrifice is avoided by the substitution of a ram; but even then the first-born child must leave the country."[111]]

---

110 Ibid.
111 Godley, LCL 119; vol. 3, p. 514 f. n. 1

Herodotus, *Hist.* 9, 119,1[112]

> Oeobazus made to escape into Thrace; but the Apsinthians of that country caught and sacrificed him (θύειν) after their fashion to Plistorus the god (θεός) of their land; as for his companions, they slew them in another manner.

Further Readings

Burkert, Walter, *Anthropologie des religiösen Opfers: Die Sakralisierung der Gewalt* (Carl-Friedrich-von-Siemens-Stiftung, Themen 40; München: Carl-Friedrich-von-Siemens-Stiftung, 1984).

Burkert, Walter, *Creation of the Sacred: Tracks of Biology in Early Religions* (Cambridge, Mass.: Harvard University Press, 1996); German trans.: *Kulte des Altertums: Biologische Grundlagen der Religion* (Munic: Beck, 1998).

Girard, René, *La Violence et le Sacré* (Paris: Grasset, 1972).

Hamerton-Kelly, Robert (ed.), *Violent Origins: Walter Burkert, René Girard, and Jonathan Z. Smith on Ritual Killing and Cultural Formation* (Stanford, Calif.: Stanford University Press, 1987).

Harder, Ruth Elisabeth, *Die Frauenrollen bei Euripides: Untersuchungen zu 'Alkestis,' 'Medeia,' 'Hekabe,' 'Erechtheus,' 'Elektra,' 'Troades' und 'Iphigeneia in Aulis'* (Drama, Beiheft 1; Stuttgart: M. & P., 1993).

Mikalson, Jon D., *Honor Thy Gods: Popular Religion in Greek Tragedy* (Chapel Hill: University of North Carolina Press, 1991).

112 Ibid.

The Theological Implications of Child Sacrifice

in and beyond the Biblical Context in Relation to Genesis 22 and Judges 11[1]

Michaela Bauks, Université de Montpellier

A serious problem is posed by the theme that is at the heart of Gen 22 and Judg 11: that of human sacrifice, and more explicitly, that of child sacrifice together with redemption by means of the substituted sacrifice of an animal. In general, commentators tend to present one of three positions in response to this problem:

1. Some exegetes assume that human sacrifice is unacceptable and therefore inadmissible on anthropological and religious grounds. They affirm that child sacrifice does not occur in the Bible. As a result, passages that deal with the practice are perceived simply as a polemic against foreign cults.[2] However, since Gen 22 contains no polemic, it has to be considered as a case apart, which requires an alternative explanation. Texts like Judg 11 contain a polemic against the *character* of an individual.[3]

---

[1] I am grateful to Andrew Buckler, Pasteur de l'Eglise Réformée de France at Mantes la Jolie, who translated a first draft of this paper, which was presented in June 2002 at the University of Groningen (Netherlands) on the Symposium "Religion and the Irrational" organised by Prof. R. Kessler (Marburg) and Prof. P. Vandermeersch (Groningen), and sponsored by the European Community Program (Erasmus).

[2] See Otto Kaiser, "Den Erstgeborenen Deiner Söhne sollst du mir geben: Erwägungen zum Kinderopfer im Alten Testament", in *Von der Gegenwartsbedeutung des Alten Testaments: Gesammelte Studien zur Hermeneutik und Religionsgeschichte* (ed. Volkmar Fritz, Karl-Friedrich Pohlmann, and Hans-Christoph Schmitt; Göttingen: Vandenhoeck & Ruprecht, 1984), 142–66; 148–52.

[3] Most exegetes interpret Judg 11 in this way because of the social status of Jephthah, a son of a prostitute (Judg 11:1); see e. g. Phyllis Trible, *Texts of Terror: Literary-Feminist Readings of Biblical Narratives* (OBT 13; Philadelphia: Fortress Press, 1984), 93–116; Mieke Bal, *Death and Dissymmetry: The Politics of Coherence in the Book of Judges* (CSHJ; Chicago: Chicago University Press 1988), 41–68; Jan Alberto Soggin, *Judges: A Commentary* (OTL; Philadelphia: Westminster, 1981), 207 f.; critically David Marcus, *Jephthah and His Vow*

Thus, already *Jub* 17:15–16 and 4QpsJub[a] 2 II 7–8 (2nd–1st cent. B. C. E.) as well as later on the Jewish commentator Rashi (12th cent. C. E.) consider the person that "tests" [Abram] to be Satan (cf. Job 2:1). Rashi himself prefers an alternative solution, commenting on the "offer him" (literally "take him up") of v. 2 in the following manner: "God did not say to him: Offer him as a sacrifice. The Holy One, Blessed be his name, certainly did not seek that, commanding instead that he climb up the mountain in order to give Isaac the appearance of an offering to God. Once he had made him climb [the mountain], he instructed him: Now take him down."[4]

2. Others consider human sacrifice to have been a real characteristic of Syro-Palestinian culture, of which traces remain in the Bible. For example, Roland de Vaux considers such references to be of relatively late date.[5] He alludes to 2 Kgs 16:3 and 21:6 as examples of the sacrifice to the god Molech[6] that is condemned in Leviticus, Deuteronomy and the prophetic literature. Once again, however, this approach sheds little light on the role played by Gen 22. It is suggested simply that Gen 22 offers an etiological form of substitution or redemption of the first-born (cf. Exod 13:13b; 34:20b).[7]

(Lubbock: Texas Tech Press, 1986), 7 ff., who thinks that the sacrifice is not realised (34, 47 ff.) and that Judg 11 rejoins Gen 22. I think that the case is more complicated. See the new study of Andreas Michel, *Gott und Gewalt gegen Kinder im Alten Testament* (FAT 37; Tübingen: Mohr-Siebeck 2004), 48–53 (who lists the scriptural references attesting the phenomenon).

4 Rashi, *Commentaire de la Genèse* (vol. 1 of *Le Pentateuque*; 3d ed.; Paris, Fondation S. et O. Levy, 1976), 133; cf. *Ber. Rab.* 56,8 in *The Midrash Rabbah: Genesis* (trans. Harry Freedman and Maurice Simon; London: Soncino, 1977), 498.

5 Roland de Vaux, *Les institutions de l'Ancien Testament* (2 vols.; Paris: Cerf, 1991), 2:328 f., 332; Kaiser, "Den Erstgeborenen", 145, n. 11. But Philippe Derchain, "Les plus anciens témoignages de sacrifices d'enfants chez les sémites occidentaux," *VT* 20 (1970): 351–55 and Anthony John Spalinger, "A Canaanite Ritual Found in Egyptian Reliefs," *JSSEA* 8 (1978): 47–60 point out that the Canaanite practice of human sacrifice is attested in the middle of the 2nd millenium B. C. on Egyptian temple-wall-inscriptions.—Armin Lange ("They burn their sons and daughters" Excursus) points out in this volume that human sacrifaces in Israel know a long history of tradition.

6 See also John Day, *Molech: A God of Human Sacrifice in the Old Testament* (University of Cambridge Oriental Publications 41; Cambridge: University Press, 1989), 62–63.

7 For example Hans-Peter Müller, "Genesis 22 und das *mlk*-Opfer," *BZ* 41 (1997): 237–46, 239–42 describe *mlk(t)* in the Punic context as a type of offering (and not as the name of a god / king), which substitutes a human sacrifice after an oath (*ndr*). See also Müller, "Umgang mit dem Negativwertig-Numinosen in der Phönizisch-Punischen Religion,"

3. Certain exegetes attempt to follow the second reading metaphorically. They accord to the account in Gen 22 the nature of an exception, by which the testing of Abraham employs the motif of child sacrifice to demonstrate the patriarch's profound and exceptional faith.[8] In this way, Gen 22 does not deal with human sacrifice as such, but rather centres on the divine promise by which Abraham will become a great nation. This approach reduces the theme of Gen 22 to a simple test, by suppressing the crucial aspect of the human sacrifice required and then prevented by God.

I. Translation and Context of Genesis 22

> 1 After these things God tested Abraham, and said to him, "Abraham!" And he said, "Here am I." 2 He said, "Take your son, your only son Isaac, whom you love, and go to the land of Mori'ah, and offer him there as a burnt offering upon one of the mountains of which I shall tell you." 3 So Abraham rose early in the morning, saddled his ass, and took two of his young men with him, and his son Isaac; and he cut the wood for the burnt offering, and arose and went to the place of which God had told him. 4 On the third day Abraham lifted up his eyes and saw the place afar off. 5 Then Abraham said to his young men, "Stay here with the ass; I and the

---

in *Die Dämonen—Demons: Die Dämonologie der israelitisch-jüdischen und frühchristlichen Literatur im Kontext ihrer Umwelt—The Demonology of Israelite-Jewish and Early Christian Literature in Context of Their Environment* (ed. Armin Lange, Hermann Lichtenberger, and Diethard Römheld; Tübingen: Mohr-Siebeck, 2003), 108–21, 114–17) and Edward Noort, "Human Sacrifice and Theology in the Hebrew Bible," in *The Sacrifice of Isaac: The Aqedah (Genesis 22) and Its Interpretation* (ed. E. Noort, E. J. C. Tigchelaar; Themes in Biblical Narrative 4, Leiden: E.J. Brill, 2002), 1–20, 10 ff. with a detailed discussion of the problem; Michel, *Gott und Gewalt*, 276 ff., 313–16, reintroduces the god Molech and underlines that Gen 22 intends to contrast the different texts of sacrifices to Molech in the OT; Michel assumes the practice of child sacrifice in exilic time. Jon D. Levenson, *The Death and Resurrection of the Beloved Son: The Transformation of Child Sacrifice in Judaism and Christianity* (New Haven: Yale University Press, 1993), 111 ff. qualifies the case of Gen 22 not "as an etiology of the substitution of animal for human sacrifice" (111), because "nothing in Gen 22:1–19 suggests that God's command to immolate Isaac was improper ... It may, nonetheless, reflect a situation in which the father's substitution of a sheep for the special son can meet with God's favour" (113 f).

[8] See Gen. Rab. 55,2 in *The Midrash Rabbah*, 482 f. (test of the righteous, cf. Ps 11:5), and Timo Veijola, "Das Opfer des Abraham—Paradigma des Glaubens aus dem nachexilischen Zeitalter," *ZThK* 85 (1988): 129–64, 159 f.

> lad will go yonder worship, and come again to you." 6 And Abraham took the wood of the burnt offering and laid it on Isaac his son; and he took in his hand the fire and the knife. So they went both of them together. 7 And Isaac said to his father Abraham, "My father!" And he said, "Here, am I, my son." He said, "Behold, the fire and the wood; but where is the lamb for an burnt offering?" 8 Abraham said, "God will provide himself the lamb for a burnt offering, my son." So they went both of them together. 9 When they came to the place of which God had told him, Abraham built an altar there, and laid the wood in order, and bound Isaac his son, and laid him on the altar, upon the wood. 10 Then Abraham put forth his hand, and took the knife to slay his son. 11 But the angel of the Lord called to him from heaven, and said, "Abraham, Abraham!" And he said, "Here am I!" 12 He said, "Do not lay your hand on the lad or do anything to him; for now I know that you fear God, seeing you have not withheld your son, your only son, from me." 13 And Abraham lifted up his eyes and looked, and behold, behind him was a ram, caught in a thicket by his horns; And Abraham went and took the ram, and offered it up as a burnt offering instead of his son. So Abraham called the name of that place The Lord will provide. ...
> 19 So Abraham returned to his young men, and they arose and went together to Beer-Sheba; And Abraham dwelt at Beer-Sheba. (Gen 12,1–14a. 19 NRSV)

I consider Gen 22:1–14a, 19 as the basic text and I prefer to see verses 14b–18 as a parenthesis.[9] In line with this perspective, I shall consider the central drama, leaving in suspense the testing motif (1aβ *nsh*), together

[9] See John van Seters, *Abraham in History and Tradition* (New Haven: Yale University Press, 1975), 229 ff.; George W. Coats, "Abraham's Sacrifice of Faith: A Formcritical Study of Gen 22," *Int* 27 (1973): 389–400; R. W. L. Moberley, "The Earliest Commentary on the Aqedah", *VT* 38 (1988): 302–23 (v. 15–18). Recently Omri Boehm, "The Binding of Isaak: An Inner-Biblical Polemic on the Question on 'Disobeying' a Manifestly Illegal Order", *VT* 52 (2002): 1–12 criticised the interpolation of vv. 14–18 for compositional reasons. Exegetes have given very different chronological datings to Gen 22: pre-exilic ("elohistic") by Horst Seebass, *Genesis II: Vätergeschichte I (Gen 11,27–22,24)* (Neukirchen-Vluyn: Neukirchener Verlag, 1997), 199 f., 213 ff.; or post-exilic see Veijola, "Opfer", 155 (in the 5th cent.). See for the discussion Claus Westermann, *Genesis 12–36* (trans. John J. Scullion; Minneapolis: Fortress, 1995), 363 ff.; Victor P. Hamilton, *The Book of Genesis: Chapters*

with the interpretation of the events given by divine oracle and the reaffirmation of the promise. The narrative elements within our chosen verses may be resumed as follows: the theme of Abraham's trust in God, that of child sacrifice, and the concept of the holy place.[10]

1. Abraham's Trust in God: The Sacrifice of the Past

The mention of promise functions as an allusion to Gen 12:1–8, a passage with which Gen 22 has important parallels. Abraham leaves for a land, which God will show him, accompanied by Lot his adopted son. This departure is not simply the beginning of an itinerary; it represents at the same time a complete reversal of his nomadic life. In leaving his family and tribe, Abraham gives himself and his family over in trust to the providence of God. In so doing, he finds himself in opposition to the rules of nomadic life, which encourage the formation of networks with surrounding families.[11] Abraham leaves Syria for a far-off land. In other words, he sacrifices the past.[12]

2. Abraham's Obedience: The Sacrifice of the Future

We observe a similar pattern in Gen 22. Abraham receives a second command to depart. This time accompanied by his own son Isaac and two servants he leaves for a specific destination—Mori'ah—in order to offer a sacrifice to God. Once more, he finds himself in an existentially overwhelming situation. Everything is accounted for, except the sacrifice itself. Isaac asks about it, surprised that there is no animal to sacrifice.

Abraham's reply has a double reference, since, grammatically, *beny*, "my son," can represent either a vocative or a complement whose pur-

---

18–50 (NICOT; Grand Rapids: Eerdmans, 1995), 99 ff.; Noort, "Human Sacrifice," 14–20 and Michel, *Gott und Gewalt*, 267–72, 306–13 (for the discussion of the latest research).

[10] This important aspect is excluded in my study. See Levenson, *Death and Resurrection*, 114 ff.; Siegfried Mittmann, "ha-Morijja-Präfigurationen der Gottesstadt Jerusalem (Gen 22,1–14. 19)", in: *La Cité de Dieu—Die Stadt Gottes: 3. Symposium Tübingen 1998* (WUNT 129; ed. M. Hengel, S. Mittmann, and A. M. Schwemer; Tübingen: Mohr-Siebeck, 2000), 67–97; Alfred Marx, "Sens et fonction de Gen XXII,14," *VT* 51 (2001): 197–205.

[11] Seebass, *Vätergeschichte I*, 13.

[12] Thomas Römer, *Le Dieu obscur: Le sexe, la cruauté et la violence dans l'AT* (Essais bibliques 27; Genève: Labor & Fides, 1996), 62.

pose is to clarify the object of the sacrifice, hence: "it is you, my son."[13] Verses 9–10 make it clear that Abraham understands the sacrifice to be that of Isaac. Isaac himself does not react, in all probability because he suspects nothing, a reading confirmed by the remainder of the account.[14] Thus, the text presents a situation that appears unpalatable to the reader of today: Abraham chooses (once again) to obey God, and is even ready to sacrifice his own son as the ultimate test of his faith.

Genesis 22 is in fact the culmination of a series of tests or obstacles for Abraham[15], which led successively to the fulfilment of the promise first given in Gen 12:1 ff.:

- Gen 12:10 ff. and Gen 20 both recount the forcible rescue of Abraham's wife from the harems of a neighbouring king.
- Gen 14 describes how the patriarch leaves for war.
- Gen 16 explains how the patriarchal couple, believing themselves unable to have children, attempt to bring about the realisation of the promise by using Hagar the servant as a surrogate mother (Gen 17–18). In Gen 21 the promise does, in fact, appear to be fulfilled through the birth of Isaac.
- The following chapter, Gen 22, thus presents a second great moment of testing. Whereas Gen 12, 14, and 20 focus on the threat hanging over the life of the patriarchal couple, a threat which could prevent the fulfilment of the promise, Gen 22 portrays the threat overshadowing a promise now partially fulfilled. In this case, the sacrifice is no longer that of the past or the present, but of the future. The promise, and everything it represents, seems to be on the brink of collapse.

This requirement to sacrifice the future giving up the only child, is not unknown elsewhere in ancient literature. However, such a demand can only be understood within the framework of a culture, which attempts to make sense of the experience of an infinite God by allowing him to

[13] Rashi, *Genèse*, 135; André Wénin, *Isaac ou l'épreuve d'Abraham: Approche narrative de Genèse 22* (Le livre et le rouleau 8; Bruxelles: Lessius 1999), 68, and Römer, *Dieu obscur*, 62.

[14] Wénin, *Isaac*, 65, 68; for the transformation of the expression in v. 19 see Römer, *Dieu obscur*, 63.

[15] Römer, *Dieu obscur*, 60.

make infinite demands of man. How could it be possible to limit the action of a God who himself knows no limits? Viewed from this perspective, the sacrifice of one's own child represents the most significant sacrifice imaginable.[16] Such a sacrifice is superior even to the sacrifice of self, since the child symbolises the continuity of a life limited by death. By means of his descendants, an individual is able to gain a kind of immortality.

This is precisely the dimension that we see in Gen 22. However, the account goes beyond the infinite demands made by God, for it appears at the same time that through his command God is destroying the very foundations of his work up to this point. The entire history of salvation would be lost with the sacrifice of Isaac, who is after all the progenitor of Israel.

Wénin notes that the end of v. 5, in which Abraham tells the two servants to wait for the two of them "so that we may worship and then return to you," does not simply imply an indecision concerning what will happen, a "white lie." He rather points to elements of an indistinct trust in God, that God does not really desire the sacrifice of Isaac. Wénin concludes: It is thus possible to state that his obedience puts God himself to the test.[17]

However, if we focus too quickly on the substitution of a ram as a burnt offering in place of the son, we will be too easily satisfied. We will overlook the tension inherent in the account, a tension created precisely by the insertion of the theme of child sacrifice in the text. It is far too simple to sideline the theme of child sacrifice, since it is in this very practice, which seems so cruel to us, that the infinite requirements of the divine command and the infinite obedience of the human response are played out in the reality of lived experience. This is true of Gen 22, as indeed it is of the whole account of Abraham's dealings with God.

It is my thesis that the divine command to Abraham to sacrifice his own son is neither simply a rhetorical device, nor—as is claimed by the French psychoanalist Marie Balmary—a profound misunderstanding on the part of Abraham.[18] In my opinion, the theme of child sacrifice in

---

[16] See Hartmut Gese, "Die Komposition der Abrahamserzählung," in *Alttestamentliche Studien* (ed. H. Gese; Tübingen: Mohr-Siebeck, 1991), 29–51, 41.

[17] Wénin, *Isaac*, 63 f. with n. 7 (with citation of Rashi).

[18] Marie Balmary, *Le sacrifice interdit: Freud et la Bible* (Paris: Grasset, 1986), 197 f., 205; see also Römer, *Dieu obscur*, 61 f.: This misunderstanding reveals the psychic mindset of a father who has abdicated his responsibility.

this text implies a theological reflection concerning the *infinite* within God (*altérité* in French), without which no explanation of the narrative paradox is possible.

Before we explore further this theological reflection, it is appropriate to examine the contexts in which the theme appears elsewhere in the Bible.

II. A Further Account of Child Sacrifice (Judges 11.29–39)

There is in the Old Testament a second account that includes child sacrifice: that of the daughter of the judge Jephthah.[19]

> 29 Then the spirit of the Lord came upon Jephthah, and he passed through Gilead and Manasseh. He passed on to Mizpah of Gilead, and from Mizpah of Gilead he passed on to the Ammonites. 30 And Jephthah made a vow to the Lord, and said, "If you will give the Ammonites into my hand, 31 then whoever comes out of the doors of my house to meet me, when I return victorious from the Ammonites, shall be the Lord's, to be offered up by me as a burnt offering." 32 So Jephthah crossed over to the Ammonites to fight against them; and the Lord gave them into his hand. 33 He inflicted a massive defeat on them from Aroer to the neighbourhood of Minnith, twenty towns, and as far as Abel-keramim. So the Ammonites were subdued before the people of Israel. 34 Then Jephthah came to his home at Mizpah; and there was his daughter coming out to meet him with timbrels and with dancing. She was his only child; he had no son or daughter except her. 35 When he saw her, he tore his clothes, and said, "Alas, my daughter! You have brought me very low; you have become the cause of great trouble to me. For I have opened my mouth to the Lord, and I cannot take back my vow." 36 And she said to him, "My father, if you have opened your mouth to the Lord, do to me according to what has gone forth from your mouth, now that the Lord has avenged you on your enemies, on the Ammonites."

[19] See Wolfgang Richter, "Die Überlieferungen um Jephtah," *Bib* 47 (1966): 485–556, 503–17; Thomas Römer, "Why would the Deuteronomists tell about the sacrifice of Jephthah's Daughter," *JSOT* 77 (1998): 27–38; Heinz-Dieter Neef, "Jephta und seine Tochter (Jdc 11,29–40)," *VT* 49 (1999): 206–17.

> 37 And she said to her father, "Let this thing be done for me; let me alone two months, that I may go and wander on the mountains, and bewail my virginity, I and my companions." 38 And he said "Go." And he sent her away for two months; and she departed, she and her companions, and bewailed her virginity upon the mountains. 39 At the end of two months, she returned to her father, who did with her according to the vow he had made. She had never known a man. And it became a custom in Israel 40 that the daughters of Israel went year by year to lament the daughter of Jephthah the Gileadite four days in the year. (Judges 11:29–35, 39 NRSV)

When we place Judg 11 and Gen 22 in parallel, certain differences emerge between the two stories:

- The sacrifice of Jephthah's daughter, performed by her father himself, is the consequence of a vow taken in the context of a war (Judg 11:30 ff.). This vow does not specify the victim; the choice of victim is due to chance (v. 34); the text ends with a simple statement concerning the realisation of the vow (v. 39).[20]
- The daughter of Jephthah accepts the role to which her father's vow has condemned her (v. 36). She asks simply for a delay of two months in order to "bewail her virginity" (v. 37 ff.), that is, in fact, that she will not have any descendants before she is sacrificed. Her posterity will be assured thanks to the insertion into the worship calendar of a festival in her memory (v. 39b–40).[21]

[20] The case of the daughter of Jephthah recalls Iphigineia in the two versions of Euripides. See Jan N. Brenner, "Sacrificing a child in Ancient Greece: The case of Iphigineia" in *The Sacrifice of Isaac: The Aqedah (Genesis 22) and its Interpretation* (ed. E. Noort and E. J. C. Tigchelaar, Leiden: Brill, 2002), 21–43. With the reference to Iphigineia is associated a tragic connotation which corresponds to a critical evaluation of the institution of vow; cf. Römer, "Why," 37 f. with an allusion to Qoh 5:3–4 ("When you make a vow to God, do not delay in fulfilling it, for there is no favour for fools; fulfil your vow. It is better not to vow than to make a vow and not to fulfil it"): "Judg 11:30–40 is a narrative application of Qohelet's sceptical maxim" (38).

[21] Judg. 11 seems to include an etiology, but without any historical background because the rite of v. 40 knows no testimony in biblical or Jewish literature—see J. Cheryl Exum, "On Judges 11", in *A Feminist Companion to Judges* (ed A. Brenner, Sheffield: Academic Press, 1993), 131–45, 140 f. with n. 3, who confirms that those verses should be understood as a rite of passage. See also Marcus, *Jephthah*, 35.

- At no point in this account does God intervene, a fact that leads Römer to the following interpretation: God is silent in the face of human aberrations, preferring to place human beings before the consequences of their own cruelty.[22] This is an important point of divergence from Gen 22. Alternatively, the fact that it is the daughter of Jephthah who comes out of the house could imply a divine act of providence: in this way, God is seen to have accepted the vow of Jephthah and has now chosen to put it to the test. Certainly the privileged relationship that Jephthah enjoyed with God is underlined by the expression employed in v. 29a: "the Spirit of the LORD came upon Jephthah."

Gen 22 contrasts with Judg 11 in the following ways:[23]

- The sacrifice is not the result of a vow made by a protagonist who finds himself in a situation of distress; rather it is a simple command (a 'test') of God. Thus, it is God himself who provokes the dilemma. In Judg 11 it is Jephthah who is testing God, by attempting to ensure his victory by his vow.
- Right up to moment of the sacrifice itself, Isaac does not appear to be aware of the real situation. His reaction is not mentioned in any passage (except perhaps in v. 19). Hence, the action takes place between Abraham and God. Jephthah's daughter is conscious of her father's intent.
- Divine intervention causes the sacrifice to take on another form, God himself choosing a substitute in order to redeem Isaac. Consequently, God acts finally in accordance with his promise of Gen 12, which is repeated in oracular form in Gen 22:14 ff. The nature of the sacrifice in Judg 11 is doubtful: is it literal or figurative, an act of mourning or human sacrifice?[24]

---

[22] Römer, *Dieu obscur*, 68 f. But this interpretation does not agree with v. 29 (see for the literary-critical implications of his opinion Römer, "Why", 28 ff., with whom I do not agree).

[23] Marcus (*Jephthah*, 39) observes other differences: Abraham's son has a name, but the daughter of Jephthah is not named; Isaac comes from a 'good' family, the father of the daughter is born illegitimately, and her mother is never mentioned; Abraham passes God's test of faith and will have descendants, Jephthah's lack of faith embarrass descendants. I do not agree with his observation that Jephthah does not show compassion (see v. 35).

[24] See Marcus, *Jephthah*, 35 ff. (who suggests "the intentional ambiguity of the present state of the Jephthah story," 43).—In this context the history of reception of the biblical

- The theological commentary characterises the story as a test of the patriarch's faith (cf. v. 1 aβ).

The common theme to both texts is that of child sacrifice in the form of a burnt offering (*ʿolāh;* cf. Judg 11:31; Gen 22:2; 2 Kgs 3:27). The narrative framework of Gen 22 implies that Abraham understands that Isaac will be the object of the sacrifice, an indication at the very least that the existence of such a practice was well known. As for Jephthah, his vow (v. 30) demonstrates that he believes human sacrifice to be an acceptable practice in certain extreme situations (crisis). Both Abraham and Jephthah have in common the fact that each is the father of an only child[25]: their child is the single most precious thing they possess, a fact that explains both the mourning of Jephthah (Judg 11:35) and the indecision of Abraham (see above). Moreover, both accounts are of an etiological nature.

The existence in the Bible of two such different narratives indicates the relative importance attributed to the theme of child sacrifice. Because the accounts do not specify which god is the object of the child sacrifice, we have to suggest that they were offered to the God of Israel, YHWH, rather than referring to a pagan ritual.

III Observations Concerning Child Sacrifice in Biblical Text and in the Ancient Near East

In which other biblical contexts does this theme appear?

1. The Legal Texts and Their Prophetic Commentaries

The legal texts identify a particular form of child sacrifice: that of the first-born. Moreover, the Israelite is not required merely to offer as a sacrifice the first-born from among his livestock and the first fruits of his harvest. He is also required to sacrifice his first-born son. The command

text is important, see Phyllis Silverman Kramer, "Jephthah's Daughter: A Thematic Approach to the Narrative as Seen in Selected Rabbinic Exegesis and in Artwork," in *A Feminist Companion to Judges* (ed A. Brenner, Sheffield: Academic Press, 1993), 67–92; Alexandra und Dirk U. Rottzoll, "Die Erzählung von Jiftach und seiner Tochter (Jdc 11,30–40) in der mittelalterlich-jüdischen und historisch-kritischen Bibelexegese," *ZAW* 115 (2003): 210–30.

[25] See Levenson, *Death and Resurrection*, 21 f.; Marcus, *Jephthah*, 38 ff.

occurs for the first time in the Book of the Covenant in Exod 22:29–30 [28–29][26]:

> You shall not delay to make offerings from the fullness of your harvest and from the outflow of your presses. The first-born of your sons you shall give to me. You shall do the same with your oxen and with your sheep: seven days it shall remain with its mother, on the eighth day you shall give it to me.

It is significant that in this context there appears to be no form of substitution that would allow the human first-born to be spared. Such a clarification does occur, however, in Exod 34:19 ff.:

> All that first opens the womb is mine, all your male livestock, the first-born cow and sheep. The first-born of a donkey you shall redeem with a lamb, or if you will not redeem it you shall break its neck. All the first-born of your sons you shall redeem. No one shall appear before me empty-handed."[27]

A similar passage occurs Exod 13:2 following the account of the Passover:

> Consecrate to me all the first-born; whatever is the first to open the womb among the Israelites, of human beings and animals, is mine.

According to Exod 12, the substitution for the first-born Israelites is the result of a supernatural act. By marking their doorposts with the blood

---

[26] Exod 22:28 is the beginning of the second collection of laws of the Book of the Covenant. So corresponds the law of the sacrifice of the first-born to the majesty of God (cf. Eckart Otto, *Theologische Ethik des Alten Testaments* [Theologische Wissenschaft 2; Stuttgart: Kohlhammer, 1994], 100). For Levenson, *Death and Resurrection*, 9 "Exod 22:28 b articulates a theological ideal about the special place of the first-born son, an ideal whose realisation could range from literal to non-literal implementation, that is, from sacrifice to redemption, or even to mere intellectual assent without any cultic act whatsover." For a broader examination of these texts see John van Seters, "The Law on Child Sacrifice in Exod 22,28b–29," *ETL* 74 (1998): 364–72 and in this volume Karin Finsterbusch.

[27] See Jörn Halbe, *Das Privilegrecht Jahwes Ex 34,10–26: Gestalt und Wesen, Herkunft und Wirkung in vordeuteronomistischer Zeit* (FRLANT 114; Göttingen: Vandenhoeck & Ruprecht, 1975), 444 f., 448 f. He argues that Exod 34:19 is older than Exod 22:28–29 (cf. Kaiser, "Den Erstgeborenen," 164 f.). Therefore the idea of redemption would be absent from the more recent version of the law; see Otto, *Theologische Ethik*, 100 ff.

from the Passover sacrifice, the Israelites were spared by the exterminator who visited only the houses of the Egyptians. In Exod 13:11–13, the events of ch. 12 are reframed as a pattern to be repeated once the people have arrived in the Promised Land: the human first-borns are to be redeemed through animal sacrifice (cf. Exod 34:19 ff.).[28]

Notice here certain elements concerning these first-born sacrifices:

- The form of redemption is not specified.
- The redemption is realised by a supernatural act; the sacrifice indeed takes place with the first-born Egyptians as victims who have not been able to benefit from the supernatural deliverance.
- The redemption is realized through the substitution of first-born livestock.
- Two texts (Num 3:40–51 and 8:17–18) present a further form of redemption. In this case, it is not animal sacrifice that redeems the human first-born, but the consecration of the Levites. It is thus a symbolic redemption: the fact that the Levites constitute a chosen tribe consecrated to God suffices to suspend the sacrifice of the first-born.[29]
- In the Holiness Code (Lev 27:26), the commandment to sacrifice the first-born is limited to livestock and makes no reference to human first-born.[30]

It would be misleading to conclude from this diverse collection of laws that an ancient law originally requiring the sacrifice of all first-born had subsequently been modified with the course of history. It seems highly unlikely that there ever existed a primitive form, which envisaged real

[28] Cf. Exod 34:19–20 and Num 18:15–16; see Levenson, *Death and Resurrection*, 4 f. and Brevard S. Childs, *The Book of Exodus* (OTL; Philadelphia: Westminster Press, 1974), 195.

[29] The donation or dedication of the Nazirites (Exod 13:2–7; 1 Sam 1:11; Gen 49:26) belongs probably also to this concept. See Levenson, *Death and resurrection*, 46 ff.

[30] See the innerbiblical polemics against human sacrifice in Lev 18:21; 20:2–5; cf. Deut 12:31; 18:10, cf. to the deuteronomistic context of the polemic Udo Rüterswörden, "Die Stellung der Deuteronomisten zum alttestamentlichen Dämonenwesen," in *Die Dämonen—Demons: Die Dämonologie der israelitisch-jüdischen und frühchristlichen Literatur im Kontext ihrer Umwelt—The Demonology of Israelite-Jewish and Early Christian Literature in Context of Their Environment* (ed. A. Lange, H. Lichtenberger, K. F. D. Römheld; Tübingen: Mohr Siebeck, 2003), 197–210, 201 f.

child sacrifice, followed later by a more "modern" one, which allowed for redemption.[31]

Roland de Vaux underlines that it would be indeed absurd to suppose that there could have existed in Israel or any other people at any moment in their history a permanent and all embracing religious law that required the elimination of all the first-born, precisely those who constituted the future hope of the race.[32] Instead, the requirement should be understood as a proof of the absolute dependence of every creature on its creator. Ancient anthropology allows for this recognition through the dedication of all the first-born. Thus, in fact, the sacrifice takes place either as an act of redemption or in symbolic form.

The prophetic literature represents a critical, even polemical, response to the law given in Exod 22:29–30. Thus, we find in Mic 6:6–8:

> 6 With what shall I come before the Lord, and bow myself before God on high? Shall I come before him with burnt offerings, with calves a year old? 7 Will the Lord be pleased with thousands of rams, with ten thousands of rivers of oil? Shall I give my first-born for my transgression, the fruit of my body for the sin of my soul? 8 He has told you, O mortal, what is good; and what does the Lord require of you but to do justice, and to love kindness, and to walk humbly with your God?

In this context, child sacrifice is an exaggerated form of expiatory cultic practice. It intends to highlight the basis for a true worship of YHWH, translated concretely thus: a respect for the law, the love of faithfulness, and a right behaviour before God are more important than even the most sophisticated sacrifices. Such cultic polemic seeks to introduce alternative theological values in order to replace indigenous practices.[33]

---

[31] Kaiser, "Den Erstgeborenen," 159 ff. underlines the late exilic origin of the polemic passages.

[32] Roland de Vaux, *Les sacrifices de l'Ancien Testament* (CahRB 1; Paris: Gabalda, 1964), 65, cf. Kaiser, "Den Erstgeborenen," 65.

[33] De Vaux, *Institutions*, 329. Levenson, *Death and Resurrection*, 10 ff. discusses the different positions and concludes: It "is an ideal of sacrifice, the Israelite father's offering to God of what is most beloved to him, his first-born son, the first fruit of his body presented lovingly to his lord" (12).

Of particular interest in this respect is the passage in Ezek 20:25–26:[34]

> 25 Moreover I gave them statutes that were not good and ordinances by which they could not live. 26 I defiled them through their very gifts, in their offering up all their first-born, in order that I might horrify them, so that they might know that I am the Lord.

According to this passage, it is God himself who commanded the sacrifice of the first-born "to defile the Israelites by their very gifts." Ezekiel describes fatal practices of the religious and cultic history of Israel. Cultic forms inherited from their forefathers (v. 18, 30) do not constitute good theology. Ezekiel thus demands a change of theological paradigm, while acknowledging that these abhorrent practices did indeed exist within the Yahwist cult, and that they had been carried out as acts of common piety. Nevertheless, they belong to an inappropriate cultic tradition, which God himself introduced as a test for the people, a test that the people had failed to understand. The text is thus of particular interest because it reveals the theological problem posed by this type of precept. By describing it as a test, Ezekiel distances himself from a theological concept widely accepted as a description of divine otherness.

2. The Narrative Texts

Those narrative texts that treat the subject of child sacrifice generally do so in a polemical and negative manner.

In 2 Kgs 3:26–27, the king of Moab takes his first-born son (!), who would have reigned after him, and he offers him as a sacrifice on the city walls. This action is undertaken in a situation of military defeat. On this occasion, child sacrifice is neither the consequence of a vow nor in response to a divine command, but a spontaneous impulse to offer an exceptional sacrifice in a political crisis. It is the king of the Moabites

---

[34] Cf. Levenson, *Death and Resurrection*, 8 f. and Hartmut Gese, "Ez 20,25 und die Erstgeburtsopfer," in *Alttestamentliche Studien* (ed. H. Gese; Tübingen: Mohr-Siebeck, 1991), 72–83. Cf. recently Scott W. Hahn and John S. Bergsma, "What Laws were 'Not Good'? A Canonical Approach to the Theological Problem of Ezekiel 20:25–26," *JBL* 123 (2004), 201–218, 208 f., who suggest the correspondance of the "not good laws" with the giving of the Deuteronomic code (Deut 11:32 and 12:1 חקים). V. 26 is a reference to Exod 13:12 which distinguishes human frist-born from "every opener of the womb in order to exclude them from being offered" (212). The laws are not good because they degraded the "pristine Priestly standards" (217).

himself who makes this exceptional offering: he offers his son as a sacrifice within his besieged city. The text does not stipulate whether the indignation experienced by the Israelites is a sign of the effectiveness of the sacrifice (the god Kemosh accepting the sacrifice and acting immediately),[35] or the expression of the Israelites' horror at such an abominable act.[36]

The sacrifice of the Moabite prince on the city walls may be explained on the basis of Phoenician texts, which testify to acts of a similar nature. In the case of a national danger, the Phoenicians would offer their children dearest to them "according to a secret ritual" (Eusebius, *Praep. Ev.* 1. 10. 44 or 4. 16. 11 or by the Egyptian Temple Wall Inscriptions cited in n. 5).

Among the writings of Eusebius of Caesarea, we find a quote "which comes from Book 1 of Philo's Phoenician History [= from the Byblos]":

> Among ancient peoples in critically dangerous situations it was customary for the rulers of a city or nation, rather than lose everyone, to provide the dearest of their children as a propitiatory sacrifice to the avenging deities. The children thus given up were slaughtered according to a secret ritual. Now Kronos had an only son by a local bride named Anobret, and therefore they called him Ieoud [= *yāḥîd* "the only"][37].—Even now among the Phoenicians the only son is given this name.—When war's gravest dangers gripped the land, Kronos dressed his son in royal attire, prepared an altar and sacrificed him."[38]

A second text, this time from Diodorus of Sicily, enables us to specify further the nature of this type of sacrifice. Faced with a disastrous threat to their city, the Carthaginians

> also alleged that Kronos had turned against them inasmuch as in former times they had been accustomed to sacrifice to this god the noblest of their sons, but more recently, secretly

[35] Cf. Levenson, *Death and Resurrection*, 14 f.

[36] Cf. de Vaux, *Institutions*, 328.

[37] Cf. *yāḥîd* "the sole / only": Müller, "Genesis 22," 245 with n. 49 and Levenson, *Death and Resurrection*, 37 f.

[38] Philo of Byblos, *The Phoenician History, Fragment 3: Praeparatio evangelica* 1. 10. 44 (trans. H. W. Attridge and R. A. Oden; CBQMS 9; Washington: Catholic Biblical Association of America, 1981), 61, 63; cf. de Vaux, *Institutions*, 332 f.

> buying and nurturing children, they had sent these to the sacrifice; and when an investigation was made, some of those who had been sacrificed were discovered to have been supposititious. When they had given thought to these things and saw their enemy encamped before their walls, they were filled with superstitious dread, for they believed that they had neglected the honour of the gods that had been established by their fathers. In their zeal to make amends for their omission, they selected two hundred of the noblest children and sacrificed them publicly; and others who were under suspicion sacrificed themselves voluntarily, in number not less than three hundred. There was in their city a bronze image of Kronos, extending its hands, palms up and sloping towards the ground, so that each of the children when placed thereon rolled down and fell into a sort of gaping pit filled with fire. It is probable that it was from this that Euripides has drawn the mythical story found in his works about the sacrifice in Tauris, in which he presents Iphigeneia being asked by Orestes: "But what tomb shall receive me when I die? / A sacred fire within, and earth's broad rift." Also the story passed down among the Greeks from ancient myth that Kronos did away with his own children appears to have been kept in mind among the Carthaginians through this observance."[39]

This text confirms that child sacrifice was neither banal nor commonplace. It was rather a harrowing custom for parents who would have sought every possible means to avoid giving up their son as an offering. Nevertheless, in a time of crisis, the god whose aid was sought for the people could not be deceived. "False" sacrifices were considered a waste and were invalid.

These examples all derive from a pagan context. However, the Old Testament also contains allusions to such customs. In 2 Kgs 3:27, the sacrifice is probably offered to the Moabite god Kemosh. But two further Old Testament passages also speak of such practices, and this time

[39] Diodorus Siculus, *Bib. Hist.* XX. 14.4–7 (ed. and trans. Russel M. Geer, *Diodorus of Sicily: Library of History 10, Books 19–20* (LCL 390, London: 1954), 179. 181. Cf. de Vaux, Sacrifices, 72f; Kaiser, "Den Erstgeborenen," 151 f., 156 (including passages mentioning the Tophet like 2 Kgs 23:10; cf. Jer 7:31 and Is 30:33). See the critical study about the Tophet from Rüterswörden, "Stellung des Deuteronomisten," 205 ff.

they are performed by the Judean kings Ahaz (2 Kgs 16:3) and Manasseh (2 Kgs 21:6, cf. the critique in 2 Kgs 23:10). These kings burn their sons as an offering, the first in order to remove the threat of a syro-ephraimite war, and the second when faced with the threat from Assyria (cf. 2 Chr 33:11 ff.). This rite of child sacrifice seems to have little in common with the sacrifices mentioned in Judg 11 and 2 Kgs 3:25 ff. Instead, here it is a matter of a different religious practice altogether. Some exegetes suppose that the two Judean kings fulfil a rite that corresponds to a sacrifice offered to the god Molech.[40] The polemic against this sacrificial act is strong. Passages such as Ezek 16:21, Jer 7:31, and 19:5 offer powerful critiques of the practice of delivering children up as an offering by fire, without, however, revealing with any degree of certainty whether the acts formed part of a pagan cult (Ezek 16:20, Jer 19:4–6) or a cult to YHHWH (Jer 7:31).[41]

It is important to distinguish these forms of sacrifice from those of the first-born, since the practice described here does not necessarily concern the first-born and may also extend to the offering of female children (cf. Jer 7:31). Moreover, the sacrifice and its ritual context as an offering made by fire fulfil a different theological function: they do not represent an act of dedication to God the creator, but rather an act of appeasement in a time of crisis.

In addition, the passage quoted above provides a further element of interest to our present study. It is evident that the custom of child sacrifice in the event of a national catastrophe also provoked a substitutionary practice with regard to the victims. Thus, Diodorus speaks of the children of noble families being replaced by children from poorer origins. It is probable that this modification paved the way for the eventual substitution of animals for human victims in line with the biblical prescriptions concerning the sacrifice of the human first-born. However, according to Diodorus, it also appears that in a time of extreme crisis, there was little possibility of any acceptable substitute for the sacrifice of children.

---

40 Cf. de Vaux, Sacrifices, 333; George C. Heider, "Molech," in *Dictionary of Deities and Demons in the Bible* (ed. K. van der Toorn, B. Becking, and P. W. van der Horst; 2nd ed.; Leiden: Brill, 1999), 583 f. and Day, *Molech*, 82–85. For the critical reception of this interpretation see Müller, "Genesis 22," 240–44 and above note 6.

41 Day, *Molech*, 84 f.—For the apologetic use of the references to pagan human sacrifice see also Katell Berthelot in this volume ("Jewish Views of Human Sacrifice", § I.2); for Human sacrifice as a cult of YHWH (Jer 7:31) see Armin Lange, "They burn their sons and daughters."

IV Conclusion

Having thus presented the range of forms of child sacrifice that appear in the Old Testament, we shall now attempt to define how Gen 22 and Judg 11 might relate to those passages. Three principle themes emerge from our study:

1. In various legislative texts and in two commentaries on these texts within the prophetic literature, the issue revolves around an act of dedication of the first-born to the Creator. A substitute is provided which may be either real (in the case of an animal) or symbolic (in the case of the consecration of an individual or tribe). It seems unlikely in these cases that the law was applied systematically. Rather, it acted as a figurative representation of the ultimate right exercised by God over all creation. The first-born owes his life to God in a twofold sense since, firstly, all human beings are created by God and, secondly, the first-born has been redeemed that he might live in spite of the fact that he ultimately belongs to God.

The patriarchal cycle repeats on several occasions that Isaac is a gift, born of a barren woman and of a couple far too advanced in years to be able to procreate. Given the exceptional character of this birth, therefore, it is not surprising that Isaac should be consecrated to the Lord (cf. 1 Sam 1–2). In 1 Sam 1–2, the redemption of the first-born given by God is realized symbolically: the boy Samuel ministers in the Temple (in line with the dedication of the Levites according to Num 3:40–51 and 8:17 ff.). In Gen 22 the redemption takes place in a more classic manner since a ram substitutes for the son. The theological issues in Gen 22, together with the prescriptions concerning the sacrifice of the first-born, focus around the response given to the infinite demands made by God of his created beings. Isaac, the first-born of the patriarchal couple is at the same time the seed of Israel. Through him God redeems all Israel.

2. When compared with the accounts of 2 Kgs 3 and Judg 11, Gen 22 offers certain parallels concerning the sacrificial motif. All three accounts are concerned with human sacrifices given in the form of a burnt offering. The first texts are silent on the details of the sacrifices, underlining instead their function as a means of deliverance for a whole people in crisis. By contrast, Gen 22 provides a detailed description of the sacrifice itself, but its context is completely different. Unlike Judg 11, which follows a vow or 2 Kgs 3:25 ff. where the event is simply stated, the initiative in Gen 22 lies not with Abraham but with God.

The long description concerns the preparations for the sacrifice and underlines the paradoxical nature of the situation. On the one hand, the divine command that sets the events in motion places Gen 22 within the general context of the sacrifice of the first-born. On the other hand, the form of the sacrifice corresponds to the pattern found in Judg 11 and 2 Kgs 3, which deals rather with an elitist form of sacrifice that derives from a common notion of the only child or crown prince.

3. Gen 22, Judg 11 and 2 Kgs 3 need to be clearly distinguished from the sacrifice to *mlk*, which the Bible presents unequivocally as a sacrifice inherited from pagan cults. Furthermore, the polemical context in which such traditions are transmitted serves to exclude any positive identification with such rites. It is therefore unlikely that Gen 22 contains any such references. It is possible to conclude that Gen 22, together with Mic 6 and Ezek 20, and also Judg 11 belongs to the genre of theological commentary. In the first case, the commentary has chosen a narrative form. The first-born son of the patriarchal couple is the only beloved son, a fact that reinforces the value of the narrative within a sacrificial context. God commands the sacrifice as a response to the legal requirement by which all the first-born belong to him. Abraham takes this command seriously and accepts it, even if it is in contradiction with the promise that is the leitmotif for the whole story. This narrative interpretation reveals a further aspect of the story: whereas, according to certain accounts, child sacrifice seems to have formed the response to a situation of national crisis, Gen 22 presents a paradoxical reworking of this theme. On the one hand, Abraham is not responding to a situation of distress by performing a free act or uttering a vow, but is reacting to the command of God. On the other hand, it is this very command that puts the promise of God in danger and risks bringing the divine plan to nothing. Gen 22 makes use of the two themes—dedication of the first-born and the sacrifice of the beloved son for the salvation of the people. The narrative transforms them in such a way that the dedication through an act of obedience will alone be sufficient since Abraham has proved himself faithful to the point of sacrificing his own interests. As a result, God does not in fact demand the life of the victim. Thus, the beloved son is not sacrificed, but becomes the medium by which the promise is fulfilled and Israel brought into existence.[42] Gen 22 has of-

[42] Cf. the quotation of Noort, "Human Sacrifice," 19, who underlines: "The story about Abraham and his child of promise, who at the last moment is not sacrificed, is a tale about a deadly threat and the rescue from it. It is the deeply reflective story of a God who

ten been cited as an example of an etiology of the substitution for child sacrifice, which would demonstrate a sort of "religious progress" with regard to neighbouring cultures. Such an explanation is hardly satisfactory.[43] The rhetoric by which such substitution is claimed goes beyond the simple pattern of obedience-redemption. In reality, the "religious progress" is not to be found in the concept of substitution—this idea existed also in contemporary neighbouring cultures—but in the reciprocal trust exercised between God and man. The command is not given in a time of crisis, but in a situation of comfort and fulfilment. The believer is free either to trust in God and thus continue his walk with him, or to trust in himself and his own intelligence. According to Gen 22, Abraham chooses to continue his way with God despite his own personal concerns. Because Abraham is willing to leave these behind, God renews to him the promise, which God wishes to realize through him.

Judg 11 aims at another, tragic perspective in the narrative.[44] Jephthah, who has the spirit of the Lord (v. 29), had success in his military aims. He becomes a successful judge, who will merit a good evaluation by the Deuteronomistic redaction (cf. 1 Sam 12:11), which is generally very critical of the ritual form of human sacrifice. Judg 11:29–40 stresses another polemic feature: The price of the military victory of Jephthah contains the loss of his personal future. It is less important if he sacrifices his girl or if he dedicates her to eternal virginity. He loses his daughter and with her, his descendant.[45] If Abraham is at the end of the story of

threatens to draw back everything he has promised, who threatens to destroy the future. Isaac is not only the son, he is also the embodied promise."

[43] See also Noort, ibid., 20: "It is not a story telling that YHWH is a God who does not want children to be sacrified. The story reflects a stage [for him a date in the late 8th/7th century would fit, 19] in which the possibility that child sacrifice belongs to the YHWH cult is present. It uses a well known theme and practice to tell about experiences in which YHWH, this God of life, of promise, of future, change sides, and shows the dark side of the death and destruction, apparently recanting the promises."

[44] Römer, "Why," 37 speaks about fatality which knows a theological interest: "By inserting his story in the Dtr context of the Jephthah cycle, he makes Jephthah less heroic and confronts him with a courageous daughter thus creating an open and ambiguous text. By making the Hebrew Iphigineia accept her sacrifice the narrator sacrifices the Dtr ideology of divine pedagogics and confronts her reader ... with theological problems which have still not been solved." See also above n. 20.

[45] At this point I disagree with Bal, *Death and Dissymmetry*, 113: "Both sacrifices figure the rite of passage that initiates the separation between father and child. In the case of father and son, the common interest of the establishment of patriliny helps them solve the problem, dissolve the anxiety caused by the threat. ... In the case of father and daughter, there is no such common interest, only separation. The giving up of the daughter is the

the Aqedah the elected patriarch, Jephthah is a very limited institution in the history of Israel. Both narrations testify to human sacrifice as a possible cultic institution in Israel, but only Gen 22 knows a happy end. While Abraham delivers himself to God, Jephthah has delivered himself to his vow. Abraham is tested and Isaac is redeemed. Jephthah tests God and his daughter is lost. It is probably that both conceptions belong to latest theological redactions of the Hebrew Bible.[46]

As I have stated above, Gen 22 and Judg 11 both contain a theological reflection concerning the infinite within God. Both passages assume the idea of the absolute dependence of every creature on God[47], also present in the dedication of all first-born. There is one difference; Gen 22 points out that God reclaims the offering, while in Judg 11 Jephthah delivers himself to the oath. Having a serious request, Abraham obeys God, Jephthah acts to save his people. But only the first knows a happy end. Jephthah is damned because there is no *Deus ex machina* who resolves his ambiguous situation. He remains the tragic hero.

---

giving up of self, as long as virilocal patriliny is the motivation that generates the stories. Jephthah's fire is futile. No patriliny can be established through it."

[46] See Katell Bertheolot ("Jewish Views about Human Sacrifice", § III), who points out that the history of Jewish reception of Gen 22 and Judg 11 knows the pattern of human sacrifice as self-sacrifice with a positive value.

[47] Gese has connected this concept with Gen 22: "Das größte Opfer, mehr als die eigene Hingabe des Menschen, ist das Opfer dessen, der die eigene Zukunft repräsentiert, die Dahingabe des Sohnes. Hat Gott ihn gegeben, kann Gott ihn auch zurückfordern. . . . Die Forderung an Abraham in Gen 22 entspricht also durchaus einem allgemein empfundenen wenigstens theoretischen letzten göttlichen Anspruch an den Menschen."

The First-Born between Sacrifice and Redemption in the Hebrew Bible[1]

Karin Finsterbusch, University of Koblenz-Landau

Almost all the law codes in the Pentateuch include a law concerning sacrifice or redemption of the first-born of humans and animals. Several studies have considered these laws—with altogether contradictory conclusions.[2] One major source of dispute is whether the law in the Book of the Covenant can be understood as prescribing the sacrifice of

[1] This article is a shorter version of "Vom Opfer zur Auslösung: Analyse ausgewählter Texte zum Thema Erstgeburt im Alten Testament," *VT* 56 (2006): 21–45. I am very grateful to Maria Urban, member of the American Protestant Church in Bonn, who translated this paper. The following translations from the Hebrew are my own.

[2] Compare particularly Evaristus Mader, *Die Menschenopfer der alten Hebräer und der benachbarten Völker: Ein Beitrag zur alttestamentlichen Religionsgeschichte* (BibS[F] 14,5/6; Freiburg: Herdersche Verlagshandlung, 1909); Otto Eissfeldt, *Molk als Opferbegriff im Punischen und Hebräischen und das Ende des Gottes Moloch* (Halle a. d. Saale: M. Niemeyer, 1935), 48 ff.; Johannes Hempel, "Eine Vorfrage zum Erstgeburtsopfer," *ZAW* 13 (1936): 311–13; Roland de Vaux, *Studies in Old Testament Sacrifice* (Cardiff: University Press of Wales, 1964), 63 ff.; Joseph Henninger, "Zum Erstgeborenenrecht bei den Semiten," in *Festschrift W. Caskel zum siebzigsten Geburtstag* (ed. E. Gräf, Leiden: Brill, 1968), 162–83; George Buchanan Gray, *Sacrifice in the Old Testament: Its Theory and Practice* (LBS; New York: Ktav Publishing House, 1971), 33–36; Walter Zimmerli, "Erstgeborene und Leviten: Ein Beitrag zur exilisch-nachexilischen Theologie," in *Studien zur alttestamentlichen Theologie und Prophetie: Gesammelte Aufsätze, Band II* (München: Ch. Kaiser, 1974), 235–46; Alberto R. Whitney Green, *The Role of Human Sacrifice in the Ancient Near East* (ASOR Diss. Ser. 1; Missoula, Mont.: Scholars Press, 1975), 343–51; Otto Kaiser, "Den Erstgeborenen deiner Söhne sollst du mir geben. Erwägungen zum Kindopfer im Alten Testament," in *Denkender Glaube: Festschrift C. H. Ratschow* (ed. O. Kaiser, Berlin: W. de Gruyter, 1976), 24–48; Jon D. Levenson, *The Death and Resurrection of the Beloved Son: The Transformation of Child Sacrifice in Judaism and Christianity* (New Haven: Yale University Press, 1993); Gershon Brin, *Studies in Biblical Law: From the Hebrew Bible to the Dead Sea Scrolls* (JSOTSup 176, Sheffield: JSOT Press, 1994); John van Seters, "The Law on Child Sacrifice in Exod 22:28b–29," *ETL* 74 (1998): 364–72; Jacob Milgrom, "Were the Firstborn Sacrificed to YHWH? To Molek? Popular Practice or Divine Demand?" in *Sacrifice in Religious Experience* (ed. A. I. Baumgarten; Leiden: Brill, 2002), 49–55. See also the contributions of Armin Lange and Michaela Bauks in this volume.

the human first-born. In addition, one question central to the understanding of the laws of the first-born has not been satisfactorily settled, namely, what exactly is meant by first-born.[3] There has not been sufficient discussion of whether instructions for sacrifice or redemption of the first-born, in so far as explicit instructions are not present in the texts, refer only to male or also to female first-born. Finally, almost no consideration has been given to how the first-born sacrifices should be interpreted in the sense of a theory of sacrifice.[4] Therefore, a further detailed interpretation of the most important relevant texts may well be advisable.[5] First of all the occurrence of relevant texts outside the Books of the Torah and in particular Ezek 20:25 f. will be considered. Then the individual laws in the law codes will be interpreted in diachronic order. Both the pre-exilic and pre-deuteronomic laws in the Book of the Covenant (Exod 22:28 f.) and in the Dodecalogue (Exod 34:19 f.) will be discussed. The example in the deuteronomic law (Deut 15:19–22) will be briefly interpreted. Finally, the early post-exilic priestly law (Num 18:15–18) and the law in Exod 13, probably attributable to the so-called Pentateuch editor, will be interpreted. It should be pointed out from the beginning that the diachronic arrangement of these texts cannot be exhaustively substantiated within the scope of this discussion.

1. Ezek 20:25 f.

The first fact to establish is that, excluding the Books of the Torah in the Hebrew Bible, the dedication or sacrifice of first-born only appears in four passages. Three of these do not add much information to our subject: Neh 10:37 is merely a personal commitment to offer the first-born of human and animal in accordance with a not-specified law of the Torah. 2 Kgs 3 relates that the Moabite King, Mescha, sacrificed his first-born son at a time of crisis. As Hartmut Gese states, this is "in the strictest sense not the sacrifice of a first-born, ... because it is not the

---

[3] See already Hempel, "Vorfrage."

[4] A review of general sacrifice theories is offered in Josef Drexler, *Die Illusion des Opfers. Ein wissenschaftlicher Überblick über die wichtigsten Opfertheorien ausgehend vom deleuzianischen Polyperspektivismusmodell* (Münchner ethnologische Abhandlungen 12; München: Akademischer Verlag, 1993).

[5] Lev 27:26 f. is neglected as it is not a law of the first-born in the strict sense, but rather a direction concerning animal first-born in the context of votive offerings, see Brin, *Studies*, 188; Eckard S. Gerstenberger, *Das dritte Buch Mose: Leviticus* (6th ed.; ATD 6, Göttingen: Vandenhoeck & Ruprecht, 1993), 407 f.

birth of a first-born as such that gives rise to the sacrifice, but rather the exceptional situation, in which the first-born functions as a particularly valuable and highly-prized sacrifice."[6] In the context of Mic 6:6–8 the question from an individual Israelite whether he could give YHWH his first-born child[7] as a sin offering for a not-specified transgression, is rejected on the part of the prophet.[8] The crucial factor here too is not that the first-born as such causes the sacrifice, but that the first-born child would be an especially valuable sin offering in a specific situation.

The fourth instance, Ezek 20:25 f.,[9] does illuminate a first-born law of sacrifice. To briefly sketch the context, according to Ezek 20:1–4, the elders come to Ezekiel to consult YHWH.[10] YHWH refuses a consultation and gives as his reason a review of the history of Israel from the Exodus up to their existence in the Promised Land (vv. 5–29), in the course of which God's chosen people without exception are accused of disobedience to the laws of YHWH. Hossfeld divides the review into 4 phases: Israel in Egypt (vv. 5–10); Israel in the wilderness (vv. 11–17); the second generation in the wilderness (vv. 18–26); Israel in the Promised

[6] Hartmut Gese, "Ezechiel 20,25 f. und die Erstgeburtsopfer," in *Beiträge zur alttestamentlichen Theologie: FS W. Zimmerli* (ed. H. Donner, R. Hanhart, and R. Smend; Göttingen: Vandenhoeck & Ruprecht, 1977), 140–51, 144.

[7] Usually *bekhory* is translated as "my first-born son"or "my eldest son," see e.g. Francis I. Andersen and David Noel Freedman, *Micah: A New Translation with Introduction and Commentary* (AncB 24 E; New York: Doubleday, 2000), 503. However, it cannot be excluded that *bekhory* here means "my first-born child."

[8] The sacrifice of the first-born has only in this instance in the Hebrew Bible the function of a sin offering. See van Seters, "Law," 367: "The sacrifice of the first-born, whether of humans or animals, certainly had quite a different significance from that of sin offerings. It is a rather late, post-exilic development that tends to make all offerings into sin offerings."

[9] For Ezek 20:25 f., other than the commentaries and literature cited in n. 2, see in particular Gese, "Erstgeburtsopfer"; Corrine Patton, "'I Myself gave them Laws that were not good': Ezekiel 20 and the Exodus Traditions," *JSOT* 69 (1996): 73–90; George C. Heider, "A Further Turn on Ezekiel's Baroque Twist in Ezek 20:25–26," *JBL* 107 (1988): 721–28; Thomas Krüger, *Geschichtskonzepte im Ezechielbuch* (BZAW 180; Berlin: W. de Gruyter, 1989), 238–47; Franz Sedlmeier, *Studien zu Komposition und Theologie von Ezechiel 20* (SBB 21; Stuttgart: katholisches Bibelwerk, 1990), 277–86; Frank-Lothar Hossfeld, "Die Verteilung der Gesetze im Geschichtsaufriss von Ez 20," in *Gottes Wege suchend: Beiträge zum Verständnis der Bibel und ihrer Botschaft, FS. R. Moses* (ed. F. Sedlmeier, Würzburg: Echter Verlag, 2003), 171–84, 180 f.

[10] There is nothing against dating at least the basic text of Ezek 20 to the time given in v. 1, i.e. adapted to our calendar 14. 8. 591 B. C., see Walter Zimmerli, *Ezechiel: 1. Teilband Ezechiel 1–24* (2nd ed.; BKAT XIII/1; Neukirchen-Vluyn: Neukirchener Verlag, 1979), 441; Moshe Greenberg, *Ezechiel 1–20* (HThK, Freiburg i. Br.: Herder, 2001), 425; Hossfeld, "Verteilung," 172.

Land (vv. 27–29).[11] Consequently, vv. 25 f. conclude the description of the third phase. Before quoting these two verses, it should first be noted that the recognition formula at the end of v. 26 is mostly considered as a later addition and will therefore not be dealt with in the following discussion.

(25aα) I for my part gave them
(25aβ) decrees that were not good
(25bα) and laws
(25bβ) by which they could not live.
(26aα) And I defiled them by their gifts
(26aβ) when they handed over every first-birth of the womb
(26bα) in order that I might devastate them
[(26bβ) that they may know
(26bγ) that I am YHWH.][12]

The correlation of the two verses is thus, that the laws in v. 25 are exemplified in v. 26. Those decrees and laws in v. 25, which YHWH revokes for the second wilderness generation as not good and not life-giving, thus include directions concerning the cult offerings mentioned in v. 26 (*mattanot*).[13] Here it must deal with offerings for YHWH, unless one argues for the, in my opinion unlikely, assumption, that YHWH himself would have required gifts for other gods. The offering up of every "first-birth of the womb" (*peter rekhem*, v. 26aβ) is then to be understood as an example of such an offering for YHWH.

The phrase *peter rekhem* (פטר רחם) signifies the child or young animal that first comes from the womb and is therefore gender-neutral.[14] The verb *ʿbr* hiphil in v. 26aβ denotes an act of sacrifice with a fatal outcome.[15] This develops from the intention given in v. 26bα, that YHWH wants

[11] Hossfeld, "Verteilung," 172.

[12] Regarding the final sentence see Zimmerli, *Ezechiel*, 436; Daniel I. Block, *The Book of Ezekiel: Chapters 1–24* (NICIOT; Grand Rapids, Mich.: Erdmans, 1997), 634 f., n. 109.

[13] See Hossfeld, "Verteilung," 181.

[14] Compare Hempel, "Vorfrage," 311; Frank Crüsemann, *Die Tora: Theologie und Sozialgeschichte des alttestamentlichen Gesetzes* (München: Ch. Kaiser, 1992), 165; contrast Gese, "Erstgeburtsopfer," 144 f.

[15] According to Heider, "Turn," 723, *ʿbr* hiphil "had become a standard description for the sacrificial act of the cult of Molek," see also Block, *Ezekiel*, 637. In contrast Gese, "Erstgeburtsopfer," 146, rightly maintains that the verb "in Exod 13,12 zur Bezeichnung der Erstgeburtsweihe im legitimen Jahwekult [verwendet wird]; es ist also als kultischer Terminus gar nicht auf den Molochkult beschränkt," see also Krüger, *Geschichtskonzepte*, 246; Sedlmeier, *Studien*, 284. In my view there is a clear distinction between the sacrifice

to make the Israelites desolate (*šmm* hiphil).[16] Thus disobedient Israel should be decimated by laws of sacrifice. The intention after all indicates quite clearly, that by *peter rekhem* only the first-born of the *Israelites* and not those of the animals are meant.[17]

The unusual YHWH word in Ezek 20:25 f., always understood as a crux interpretum, supports in my view the idea that in Ezekiel's time first-born children were indeed sacrificed and apparently in the belief that a law of YHWH was being observed.[18] However, it cannot be determined how widespread such child sacrifice was in ancient Israel.[19] Nevertheless, it is clear from Ezek 20:25 f. that the treatment of first-born was a recurring theme in Israel's law codes.

2. Exod 22:28 f.

The probably oldest preserved law referring to first-born is found in the Book of the Covenant, in Exod 22:28f.[20] These two verses are extremely difficult and will therefore first be quoted in Hebrew:

---

of the first-born and the molk-sacrifice, see also the contribution of Armin Lange in the present volume.

[16] The translation of *šmm* hiphil by "fill with horror" or "horrify" is in this instance too harmless; for the other opinion see Mader, *Menschenopfer*, 109; Zimmerli, *Ezechiel*, 433. Important to note is that according to v. 25 Israel "could not live by" the laws given by YHWH, compare also Edward Noort, "Human Sacrifice and Theology in the Hebrew Bible," in *The Sacrifice of Isaac: The Aqedah (Genesis 22) and Its Interpretation* (ed. E. Noort and E.J.C. Tigchelaar; Themes in Biblical Narrative 4; Leiden: Brill, 2002), 1–20, 8; Patton, "Ezechiel 20," 79, n. 18; Block, *Ezekiel*, 637, 639; Greenberg, *Ezechiel*, 433.

[17] Contrary opinion in Gese, "Erstgeburtsopfer," 146.

[18] For the frequently posed question, to which law Ezekiel could be referring, see Patton, "Ezekiel 20," 84: "Ezekiel knew pre-exilic law, but whether this law was identical to any in the extant law codes is impossible to determine. This liberal attitude to pre-existant traditions hinders any attempt to reconstruct the exact law codes and historical traditions that the prophet may have known, and raises the real possibility that even when Ezekiel and a Pentateuchal tradition may agree, the 'original text' may be in the prophetic text, rather than the legal one."

[19] According to Kaiser, "Erwägungen," 31 ff. and Levenson, *Death*, 8, the archaeological findings do not suggest a wide-spread practice. However, see the contribution of Armin Lange to this volume.

[20] Referring to Exod 22:28 f. compare, in addition to the commentaries and the literature given in n. 2, in particular Michael Fishbane, *Biblical Interpretation in Ancient Israel* (Oxford: Clarendon, 1985), 181–87; Ludger Schwienhorst-Schönberger, *Das Bundesbuch (Ex 20,22–23,33): Studien zu seiner Entstehung und Theologie* (BZAW 188; Berlin: W. de Gruyter, 1990), 360–77; Cornelis Houtman, *Das Bundesbuch: Ein Kommentar* (Documenta et Monumenta Orientalis Antiqui 24; Leiden: Brill, 1997), 241–55

(28a) מלאתך ודמעך לא תאחר
(28b) בכור בניך תתן לי
(29a) כן תעשה לשרך לצאנך
(29bα) שבעת ימים יהיה עם אמו
(29bβ) ביום השמיני תתנו לי

V. 28 a is usually interpreted as an instruction relating to harvest offerings,[21] although no consensus could be reached on the precise meaning of *meleah* (מלאה) and of *dema*ʿ (דמע).[22] This discussion will introduce a different reading of v. 28 a. Accordingly, it is best understood as a general formula[23] and translated as follows:

> You shall not withhold your fullness and your treasure.[24]

In any case it is the male Israelite who is addressed. This is clear from the context, in which the wives of those addressed are mentioned.[25] The three subsequent instructions are understood as the elaboration of v. 28 a, in the course of which they explain the meaning of *dema*ʿ ("treasure") and *meleah* ("fullness") and also what is intended by "not to delay" (אחר piel) the offering of *dema*ʿ and *meleah*.

The first instruction in v. 28b is understood as the specification of what offering the *dema*ʿ means. The verse reads: בכור בניך תתן לי and without exception in the literature is translated as follows:[26]

---

[21] Only exception to my knowledge is Armin Lange, "The Meaning of Demaʿ in the Copper Scroll and Ancient Jewish Literature," in *Copper Scroll Studies* (ed. G. J. Brooke and Ph. R. Davies; JPSSup 40; Sheffield: Sheffield Academic Press, 2002), 122–38, 137 f.

[22] According to Brevard S. Childs, *The Book of Exodus: A Critical, Theological Commentary* (OTL, Louisville, Ky.: Westminster, 1974), 450 both terms relate to grapes; according to Schwienhorst-Schönberger, *Bundesbuch*, 363 *meleah* refers to wine harvests and *dema*ʿ to oil harvests; according to Houtman, *Bundesbuch*, 244 *meleah wedema*ʿ is to be read as hendiadys ("the best of your harvest"). These interpretations are not convincing. Of importance is that the verb *ʾkhr* piel in the Hebrew Bible is not used in the context of agricultural offerings (grain, oil and wine) for YHWH. Furthermore, in the Book of the Covenant there is a corresponding directive concerning the "first-fruits of the land," see Exod 23:19.

[23] The majority of the laws of the first-born begin with a general formula, compare Brin, *Studies*, 174. However, Brin does not mention the possibility of reading Exod 22:28 a as a general formula.

[24] Following Lange, "Meaning," 137 *dema*ʿ is translated as "treasure."

[25] See Exod 22:23.

[26] See de Vaux, *Studies*, 70; Zimmerli, "Erstgeborene," 239; Childs, *Exodus*, 445; Paul G. Mosca, *Child Sacrifice in Canaanite and Israelite Religion: A Study of Mulk and Klm* (Ph.D. diss.; Cambridge, Mass.: Harvard University, 1975), 237; Fishbane, *Interpretation*, 181 f.; John I. Durham, *Exodus* (Word Biblical Commentary 3; Nashville: Thomas

The first-born of your sons you shall give to me.

In this case the Israelite would be instructed to give his first-born child, should it be a son, to YHWH. Should it be a girl, the rule would not apply. In fact, the noun *bekhor* (בכור) in many instances in the Hebrew Bible indicates the male first-born, that is the first child of a woman or man, if it is a son[27]. However, *bekhor* can also mean the first-born *child*.[28] One indication to support this comes in the context of two passages concerning first-born in the Torah, Num 3:40–43 and Deut 15:19, where *bekhor* is clearly specified as "male" (*zakhar*).[29] Consequently v. 28 b would be better translated as follows:

The first-born of your children you shall give to me.

Therefore, the Israelite should give YHWH his first-born child, be it daughter or son. Every Israelite is thus concerned, unless he is childless. From the outset it should be stated that this instruction represents a peculiarity in comparison with the other laws of the first-born: Exod 22:28 b refers to the first-born of the male Israelite (father). All other instructions refer to the first-born of the respective wife of the Israelite (i. e. of the mothers).[30]

The second instruction in v. 29 a is not difficult to interpret: the Israelite should act in the same way with his cattle or small livestock. Hence the meaning of offering the "fullness" mentioned in the general formula becomes clear: the Israelite should give YHWH the first-born (be it male or female) of each female animal.

Nelson Publishers, 1987), 309; Houtman, *Bundesbuch*, 242; Schwienhorst-Schönberger, *Bundesbuch*, 360; Levenson, *Death*, 3; Shimon Bar-On, "The Festival Calendars in Exod XXIII:14–19 and XXXIV:18–26," *VT* 48 (1998): 161–95, 167; van Seters, "Law," 365; Milgrom, "Firstborn," 49 f.

27 The eldest son is not necessarily the first-born child: Saul's son Jonathan, who appears in the genealogical lists on the first place (1 Sam 14:49 f.; 1 Chr 8:33; 9:39), is not called *bekhor*. Saul's daughter Merab is called *bekhirah* in 1 Sam 14:49. Jonathan was presumably Saul's first son, but not his first-born child.

28 See also Brin, *Studies*, 213, n. 14 and *The Dictionary of Classical Hebrew II* (ed. D. J. A. Clines; Sheffield: Sheffield Academic Press, 1995), 170–72. The verb *bkhr* hiphil (in the Hebrew Bible only in Jer 4:31) means "to give birth first," see also the later use of *bkhr* piel in *m. Bek.* VIII.

29 In Exod 22:28 f. there is no such specification, but see the translation of *Tg. Neof.*: בכור זכר בניך תתן לי ("the male first-born of your children give to me").

30 However, see the text of LXX of Exod 22:28 b: τὰ πρωτότοκα [!] τῶν υἱῶν σου δώσεις ἐμοί.

The third instruction found in v. 29bα and 29bβ gives a clear deadline, illustrating the statement in the general formula that there should be no delay in giving the *meleah* ("fullness") and *dema*ᶜ ("treasure"). Nevertheless in v. 29bα and 29bβ the instruction is mostly restricted to the first-born of *animals*.[31] To refute this theory v. 28b–29 are quoted first in translation:

> (28b) The *first-born* of your children you shall give to me.
> (29a) You shall do the same with your oxen (and) with your livestock.
> (29bα) Seven days *it* (i. e. the firstborn) shall remain with its mother,
> (29bβ) on the eighth day you shall give *it* to me.

The subject of v. 29 bαbβ ("it") is without doubt the noun *bekhor* ("first-born") mentioned explicitly only in v. 28 b. This noun is to be assumed in reading v. 29 bαbβ. In my opinion, it is most unlikely that in v. 29 bαbβ one should add *bekhor* but that the instruction in this section should not apply to the *bekhor* of the Israelite referred to in v. 28 b. Contrary to the majority view therefore, v. 29 bαbβ should be interpreted that the first-born of human and animal are to be given to YHWH on the 8th day. Under no condition should the offering—wherever the Israelite is to make it[32]—be delayed, that is take place after the 8th day.

Finally, the meaning of "give" (*natan* qal) in v. 29 bβ should be considered. Often "give" is understood here in the sense of "dedicate." Reference is then made to Hannah's giving her son, Samuel, to Eli, the Priest (1 Sam 1:11), as well as to the redeeming of the first-born of Israel by the Levites (Num 3:11–13; 8:16 f.).[33] Only a few interpreters understand "give" in Exod 22:28 f. in the sense of "sacrifice."[34] One argument

[31] See, e. g. Eckart Otto, *Wandel der Rechtsbegründungen in der Gesellschaftsgeschichte des antiken Israel: Eine Rechtsgeschichte des 'Bundesbuches' Ex XX 22–XXIII 13* (Studia Biblica 3; Leiden: Brill, 1988), 45; Durham, *Exodus*, 309, 330; Schwienhorst-Schönberger, *Bundesbuch*, 360; Milgrom, "Firstborn," 50; Houtman, *Bundesbuch*, 242.

[32] The directive of v. 29 bαbβ is a clear indication that the centralization of cult was not yet anchored in law. For it is inconceivable that the Israelite should be urged to travel to Jerusalem for the offering of each first-born on each relevant eighth day. See also Schwienhorst-Schönberger, *Bundesbuch*, 367; Houtman, *Bundesbuch*, 249.

[33] See Moshe Weinfeld, "The Worship of Melech and of the Queen of Heaven," *UF* 4 (1972): 133–54, 154; Durham, *Exodus*, 330; Brin, *Studies*, 209; Houtman, *Bundesbuch*, 253; Milgrom, "Firstborn," 50 f.

[34] For the earlier literature see the summary of Houtman, *Bundesbuch*, 250 f. For more recent contributions see Levenson, *Death*, 17: " 'You shall give Me the first-born amoung

for such an interpretation would be that giving the first-born animals to YHWH definitely implies their complete sacrifice, and consequently the giving of the human first-born also implies their sacrifice.[35] In any case, the openness of the wording of Exod 22:28 f. is remarkable. This openness clearly includes the possibility that the verse can be understood such that YHWH requires the sacrifice of the first-born child. In any case, the law of YHWH does not retain this openness. As a result the last word on this theme does not rest with Exod 22:28.

3. Exod 34:19 f.

The Dodecalogue Exod 34:11–26 can be divided into two parts:[36] the first part dealing with contract and marriage prohibitions (v. 11–17); the second part with cultic regulations (v. 18–26). This section, v. 19 f., includes various directions concerning the first-born:

> (19a) Every first-birth of the womb belongs to me.
> (19bα) And all your herds 'you should remember'[37]
> (19bβ) the first-birth of cow and sheep.
> (20aα) And the first-birth of an ass you shall redeem with a lamb
> (20aβ) And if you will not redeem (it), you must break its neck.

your sons' (Exod 22:28 b). Most fathers did not have to carry out this hideous demand. But some did. Abraham knew it was his turn when he heard God in his own voice, ordering the immolation of Isaac. Jephta knew when it was his only child who met him at his home on that day of triumph turned to tragedy. Mesha knew when all earthly strategy failed to break Israel's siege and only the supreme sacrifice could reverse the dire situation."

35 See Childs, *Exodus*, 480: "[...] the same verb is used for both men and animals, which lies at the heart of the problem." Refer also to Mic 6:7: here the offering (*ntn* qal) of the first-born means its sacrifice.

36 For Exod 34:19 f. see, apart from the commentaries and the literature given in n. 2, in particular Jörn Halbe, *Das Privilegrecht Jahwes Ex 34,10–26: Gestalt und Wesen, Herkunft und Wirkung in vordeuteronomischer Zeit* (FRLANT 114, Gsttingen: Vandenhoeck & Ruprecht, 1975), 176–85; Crüsemann, *Tora*, 163 f.; Bar-On, "Calendars"; Frank-Lothar Hossfeld, "Das Privilegrecht Ex 34,11–26 in der Diskussion," in *Recht und Ethos im Alten Testament: Gestalt und Wirkung, FS H. Seebass* (ed. S. Beyerle; Neukirchen-Vluyn: Neukirchener Verlag, 1999), 39–59, 49 f.

37 The verb in the MT *tizzakhar* (niphal) is often read as *hazakhar* ("the male") see e. g. Childs, *Exodus*, 604; Durham, *Exodus*, 457 n. 19 a. Crüsemann, *Tora*, 163 argues against this interpretation and reads with good reasons the verb as *tizkor* (qal: "you should remember"): "Die vorliegende passivische Nifalform gibt freilich auf das angeredete Du bezogen wenig Sinn und kann nicht auf den 'Besitz' (*miqneh* fem. [this is a mistake, read: mask., K. F.]) bezogen werden."

(20bα) Every first-born of your children you shall redeem.
(20bβ) None shall appear before me empty-handed.

The passage begins in v. 19 a with a declaration: every first-birth of the womb (*kol peter rekhem*), that is, every first-birth of human and animal, belongs to YHWH. It is thus unequivocally stated that YHWH is the *true* owner of every *peter rekhem*. The subsequent instructions can be understood as an elaboration of v. 19 a. Hence, there is a similar structure to the law of first-born in the Book of the Covenant: a general formula functions as an introduction, the other clauses constituting the elaboration of this introductory formula.

The meaning of the first directive in v. 19bαbβ can be deduced without difficulty: the first-born of the entire livestock of sheep and cow belong to YHWH. The exhortation that the *entire* livestock (*kol mikneh*) should be remembered makes sense considering that a farmer's herds could be scattered in various areas; no herd should be forgotten by the farmer for the offering of the first-born.[38]

The following two instructions in v. 20aα and v. 20aβ concern an unclean animal: the *peter* of the ass, considered unclean, should be either redeemed or slaughtered by the owner.

The fourth instruction in v. 20bα concerns the human first-born. It is quite clear from the wording *every bekhor* that the person addressed has several *bekhorim*. From this fact can be deduced that the male Israelite is the one addressed. Only for him—not for a female Israelite—is the mention of several *bekhorim* meaningful, in so far as the male Israelite with several wives can have several first-born from the respective women.

The wording כל בכור בניך is usually translated as "every first-born of your sons."[39] However, not to be overlooked is the assertion of the general formula v. 19 a, that *every* first-birth, be it male or female, belongs to YHWH. In this respect it can also be assumed that the specification of the general formula in v. 20bα should be understood in the sense that every first-born of the Israelite's children, be it male or female, is to be redeemed. If the v. 20bα had intended only the male first-born, then an explicitly restrictive wording would be expected, for example every

[38] See Crüsemann, *Tora*, 163.

[39] Halbe, *Privilegrecht*, 176; Durham, *Exodus*, 456; Crüsemann, *Tora*, 163; Bar-On, "Calendars," 167.

male *bekhor* of your children (כל בכור זכר בניך)[40] such as is found in other laws concerning the first-born. In any case the first-born are clearly to be redeemed, and thus the for this point unclear wording of the Book of the Covenant is quasi corrected. Nevertheless, still not clarified is with what the human first-born are to be redeemed.

V. 20bβ specifies that one should not appear before YHWH without offerings. In the context of the first-born "without offerings" (*reqam*) can only mean: without the offering of the first-born of human and animal or their substitute. The time of the appearance before YHWH can be pinpointed with the assistance of the further statements in the Dodecalogue. According to v. 23 f. the male members of Israel should appear before YHWH three times a year during the pilgrimage festivals. The place of appearance is indicated in v. 26 a as "the House of YHWH, your God," meaning therefore the Temple in Jerusalem. The first-born of human and animal or their substitute are therefore to be presented in the course of these three pilgrimages in the Sacred Place of YHWH.

To summarize, the wording of the law of the first-born is clearer and more detailed in the Dodecalogue than in the Book of the Covenant; in my opinion this indicates the earlier date of Exod 22:28 f. Two points should be particularly noted. In the Dodecalogue a motive for the offering of the first-born is indicated: since YHWH in v. 19 a claims the first-born belong to him, the offering of them or their redemption appears to be the payment of a debt (and not, for example, as an act of gratitude).[41] Secondly, in comparison with Exod 22:28, a tendency can be detected to impose more tributes on the Israelite, in so far as *every* first-born child of the Israelite's women (and not only *his* first-born child) must be redeemed and in so far as one direction also refers to the first-born of the ass.

4. Deut 15:19–23

The deuteronomic law has no law concerning the sacrifice or redemption of human first-born. However, Deut 15:19–23 does contain a law

---

40 It is noticeable that the noun *peter* is not used also for the human first-born. The reason could derive from the male perspective of the verse: it concerns the children of the male Israelites addressed; the form כל פטר רחם [!] בניך could thus possibly have appeared curious.

41 See also William H. C. Propp, *Exodus 1–18: A New Translation with Introduction and Commerntary* (AncB 2, New York: Doubleday, 1999), 455.

concerning the giving of the first-born of animals.[42] Several aspects of this law assist the interpretation of the other laws of first-born and therefore will be discussed briefly. Finally, the significance of the silence in the deuteronomic law code concerning respectively sacrifice and redemption of human first-born will be considered.

> (19aα) Every first-born who is born among your cattle and your livestock, the male
> (19aβ) you shall consecrate to YHWH, your God.
> (19bα) You shall not do work with the first-born of your ox
> (19bβ) nor shear the first-born of your livestock.
> (20aα) Before YHWH, your God, you shall eat it (i. e. every first-born), annually,
> (20aβ) at the place that YHWH will choose,
> (20b) you together with your household.
> (21aα) But if it has any defect, such as lameness or blindness
> (21aβ) any serious defect,
> (21bα) you shall not sacrifice it
> (21bβ) to YHWH your God.
> (22a) Within your towns you may eat it,
> (22bα) the unclean and the clean alike,
> (22bβ) as you would a gazelle or deer.
> (23a) Its blood, however, you must not eat
> (23b) you shall pour it out on the ground like water.

It is noteworthy that this law is not constructed in the form of general formula and elaboration, but consists rather of several complementary instructions. The first point (v. 19aααβ) is that the farmer addressed should consecrate every *bekhor* of cattle and small livestock to YHWH, but, as is clearly emphasized, only the male (*zakhar*). This shows that the noun *bekhor* does not mean "male first-born" per se, but is rather gender-neutral.[43] Should the *bekhor* of cattle and small livestock be female, then it need not be consecrated to YHWH.

---

[42] For Deut 15:19–23 see, apart from the commentaries and the literature given in n. 2, Crüsemann, *Tora*, 262 f.; Eckart Otto, *Theologische Ethik des Alten Testaments* (Theologische Wissenschaft 3,2; Stuttgart: W. Kohlhammer, 1994), 181 f.

[43] In Deut 12:17 and 14:23 the first-births are not restricted to "male" and "unblemished." In my opinion the knowledge of the law Deut 15:19–23 is assumed in these passages.

Consecration to YHWH signifies, as v. 19bα and 19bβ show, that the animals may not be used for work and are therefore to be withheld from profane agricultural use. However, consecration to YHWH does not imply that the animals are to be sacrificed, nor that he is the sole beneficiary of the animals. On the contrary, v. 20 shows that the Israelite together with his family should every year slaughter the first-born and eat them in the presence of YHWH. Intended is probably the annual Feast of the Booths in the Holy Place in Jerusalem, during which the entire offering of the tithe of the annual harvest and the first-born should be eaten in the presence of YHWH—so that the people learn to revere YHWH (Deut 14:23).[44] The emphasis is therefore instructive; the Feast in the presence of YHWH, the abundance of which includes the meat of first-born animals, should inspire reverence of YHWH as the true source of the gifts.

V. 21 f. comprise instructions in case the first-born male animal has a blemish: it should not be brought to the Temple for the Feast of Booths, but may be slaughtered and eaten on the scene.

The law can be seen as decidedly "farmer-friendly."[45] First, the Israelite must indeed consecrate the male first-born of cattle and small livestock to YHWH, but he and his family nevertheless remain the beneficiary of the animals. Secondly, the female animals, so valuable for milk and young, are excluded from the law. The omission in the deuteronomic law concerning human first-born and the first-born of an unclean animal like the ass can also be explained as an expression of this "farmer-friendly" tendency. The omission of relevant instructions can only indicate that according to the deuteronomic law-maker these first-born need *not* be consecrated *nor* redeemed. This would mean a considerable material relief for the Israelite families. In this way the earlier drafts in the Book of the Covenant and in the Dodecalogue are clearly corrected.

---

44 The wording of Deut 15:19 f. refers to Deut 14:22 f. The annual time of the feasts is in both probably the Feast of Booths, see Georg Braulik, *Deuteronomium 1–16,17* (EB; Würzburg: Echter, 1986), 116; Duane L. Christensen, *Deuteronomy 1:1–21:9* (revised ed.; WBC 6A; Nashville: Thomas Nelson, 2001), 325; in contrast see Brin, *Studies*, 189 ("Festival of Spring").

45 See also Crüsemann, *Tora*, 262.

5. Num 18:15–18

The so-called Holiness Code Lev 17–26 contains no law corresponding to the other law codes concerning the first-born of human and animal. However, there is a priestly text in Num 18:15–18, which states:[46]

> (15a) Every first-birth of the womb of all creatures, human and animal, which they (i. e. the Israelites) offer to YHWH, shall be yours (i. e. Aaron).
> (15bα) But you must provide for the redemption of the first-born of humans
> (15bβ) and redeem as well the first-born of unclean animals.
> [(16aα) You shall collect their redemption payment on behalf of all over one month of age
> (16aβ) according to the estimated value
> (16aγ) with five shekels of silver, according to the shekel of the sanctuary
> (16b) that is twenty gerahs.]
> (17a) But the first-born of an oxen, or the first-born of a sheep or the first-born of a goat you shall not redeem; they are holy.
> (17bα) You shall dash their blood on the altar, and shall turn their fat into smoke
> (17bβ) as an offering by fire for a pleasing odour to YHWH.
> (18a) And their flesh shall be yours,
> (18b) like the breast of the presentation offering; like the right thigh—they shall belong to you.

V. 15a fundamentally lays down that every first-birth of the womb (*peter rekhem*) of human and animal, which the Israelites offer to YHWH, shall belong to Aaron or the Aaronic priests. This sentence represents a general formula, which is illustrated in detail. Hence Num 18:15–18 conforms to the structure of the corresponding laws in the Book of Covenant and Dodecalogue.

From the point of source criticism Num 18:15–18 cannot be considered as homogenous. According to Horst Seebass, v. 16 should be designated as a note added later.[47] Therefore, it should not be considered when

[46] For Num 18:15–18, apart from the commentaries, see the literature given in n. 2.

[47] Horst Seebass, *Numeri 2. Teilband: Numeri 10,11–22,1* (BKAT IV/2; Neukirchen-Vluyn: Neukirchener Verlag, 2003), 232.

interpreting the specific clauses following the general formula, v. 15bαbβ and 17 f.

The first specific clause, v. 15bα, directs the priest in question to ensure that the human first-born (*bekhor*) be redeemed. Most interpreters understand *bekhor* here in the sense of male first-born.[48] However, one important fact contradicts this interpretation, i. e. the general formula, v. 15 a, refers to "every first-birth of the womb"(*kol peter rekhem*). This excludes any restriction for example to male first-born. The subsequent explanations of the general formula consistently use the noun *bekhor* for first-birth. This use of vocabulary suggests that *bekhor* can be considered a synonym of *peter rekhem*. It therefore follows that v. 15bα can be understood to mean the first-born of a female Israelite, be it male or female, should be redeemed.

According to the second instruction in v. 15bβ the first-born of the unclean animal must also be redeemed. It should be noted, that in the law of the Dodecalogue only the ass is mentioned. Futhermore the intended alternative to redemption in the Dodecalogue, the slaughter of the first-born ass by the Israelite, is not mentioned here. In any case the animal is to be given to the priest.

The final instruction v. 17 f. concerns clean animals; their first-born are "holy"and therefore not redeemable (v. 17 a). According to v. 17 b, YHWH's claim to the animal is discharged by sprinkling the altar with the animal's blood and by sacrificing the fat. V. 18 states that the priest is the beneficiary of the entire flesh of the first-born.

Now v. 16 will be considered. This verse supplements v. 15bα in so far as it contains an instruction with a concrete description of how the human first-born should be redeemed—the only such specification in the laws of the first-born. The at least one month old first-born is to be redeemed with 5 shekels. This sum appears in another context: according to Lev 27:11 f. 5 shekels is the monetary value of a male child between the age of one month and five years. The given amount supports the interpretation that, according to v. 16, only the *male* human first-born are to be presented to YHWH or redeemed. Thus v. 16 restricts the instruction of v. 15bα. We can only speculate about the reasons for this restriction. Possibly it arose at a time when the instruction to redeem

[48] See for example Brin, *Studies*, 214; Baruch A. Levine, *Numbers 1–20: A New Translation with Introduction and Commentary* (AncB 4; New York: Doubleday, 1993), 436. 447; Milgrom, "Firstborn," 50.

the human *bekhor* was applied only to the male child in all the laws (see the summary below).

If Deut 15:19–23 can be termed "farmer-friendly," then Num 18:15–18 can be considered "priest-friendly." The general formula of this law indicates the intention to impose as many offerings of first-born as possible on the Israelite, since these offerings were intended as a part of the living support for the priests. All the first-born, male and female, acceptable as an offering to YHWH were to belong entirely or in part to the Aaronic priests. Contrary to this maximum demand is clearly the—probably subsequently added—restriction concerning the human first-born in v. 16.

The law formulated in the scope of P presupposes that there was again a functioning temple cult. Num 18:15–18 leaves open on what occasions the first-born of human and animal or their substitute are to be presented to YHWH or the priests.

6. Exod 13:1 f., 11–16

Exod 13:1–16 includes the theme of first-born in two passages.[49] First of all a rough plan of the apparently irregular section will be made:

(1 f.) YHWH's command to Moses to consecrate the first-born to YHWH
(3 f.) Moses' command to Israel to commemorate the Exodus from Egypt
(5–10) Moses' declaration of the law for the Promised Land regarding the Mazzot
(11–16) Moses' declaration of the law for the Promised Land regarding the first-born.

Childs comments on this arrangement: "The formal structure is particularly interesting because it disrupts the natural content units by separating the first-born stipulation in 13.2 from its detailed explication in vv. 11 ff." His explanation for the noticeable separation is: "Section 13.1–2 is presented as a divine speech which is then interpreted by Moses in

[49] For Exod 13:1 f., 11–16, apart from the commentaries to these passages and the literature given in n. 2, see in particular Masseo Caloz, "Exode, XIII, 3–16 et son rapport au Deutéronome," *RB* 75 (1968): 5–62; Heinz-Josef Fabry, "Gott im Gespräch zwischen den Generationen: Überlegungen zur 'Kinderfrage' im Alten Testament," *Katechetische Blätter* 107 (1982): 754–60; Mose Weinfeld, *Deuteronomy 1–11: A New Translation with Introduction and Commentary* (AncB 5; New York: Doubleday, 1991), 328–30.

13.3 ff."[50] However, one objection is that the section can only be understood as an interpretation of the sanctity of the first-born with great difficulty.[51] In addition v. 1 f. hardly forms a "natural unity" with v. 11 f. In order to cast light on the problem, v. 1 f. should first of all be considered closely:

> (1) And YHWH said to Moses:
> (2aα) Consecrate to me every first-born.
> The first-birth of every womb among the Israelites,
> (2aβ) both human an animal,
> (2b) belongs to me.

According to the first sentence of v. 2aα Moses—and not Israel!—is to consecrate all first-born (*bekhor*) to YHWH. The instruction seems to state that Moses should comply without delay. The second connected sentence (up to v. 2b) is clearly to be understood as an explanation of this directive; YHWH claims the first-birth of every womb (*peter kol rekhem*) of human and animal in Israel.

Moses in v. 11–16 declares a law concerning how the Israelites are to deal with the first-born in the Promised Land. It is most unlikely that this future law for the Israelites concerning the first-born can be explained as Moses' interpretation of YHWH's currently required consecration of the first-born.[52] Nevertheless, the question arises, when and how Moses complied with the divine command to consecrate the first-born.

The answer can, in my opinion, be found in Num 3, whilst Israel is still at Sinai. According to Num 3:12 YHWH tells Moses that as a substitute for all the first-born he will take all the Levites and that they should from then on belong to him. He furthermore refers to his action in Egypt, when he struck down the first-born of Egypt and consecrated all the first-born in Israel, human and animal to himself (*qdsh* hiphil). YHWH explains thus his claim to the first-born. Since Egypt, Israel in

[50] Childs, *Exodus*, 203. See also van Seters, "Law," 368: "The law in 13:2 is stated as a general rule by P who has added it as an introduction to the laws that follow."

[51] See also Durham, *Exodus*, 177.

[52] See also Brin, *Studies*, 171: "Had there been no 'general law' in 13:11–13, one might have seen 13:2 as serving this function, appearing separately from the other sections of the law of the first-born because of some literary consideration. However, since v. 12a constitutes the 'general part' of this law, serving as an introduction to 13:11–13 [...], we must conclude that Exodus 13 contains two separate sections addressing themselves to the laws of the first-born."

this respect is indebted to its God.[53] Moses then receives the following commission, which to some degree limits the declaration of intent in v. 12 f. He is to count the *male* Levites a month old or more and all the *male* first-born Israelites a month old or more (v. 14–39). Then he should take the Levites in place of the male first-born Israelites and the first-born livestock of the Levites in place of that belonging to the Israelites (v. 40–51). It should be noted briefly that Num 8 gives information on the function of the Levites singled out by Moses. They are to be given to Aaron and his sons to do the duties at the Tent of Meeting and to make atonement for the Israelites (Num 8:19).

Therefore, from a literary aspect Exod 13:1 f. has the function of an advance reference. This was doubtlessly inserted in the appropriate place, namely after Exod 12, the narration of the events of the Passover. From Exod 13:1 f. it becomes clear to the reader that YHWH's claim to the first-born of Israel is related to the events of the Passover and that this claim should take effect already for the Exodus-generation and not beginning with the first generation in the Promised Land.

One final comment should be made in connection with the gender of the first-born. The wordings *kol bekhor* and *peter kol rekhem* in Exod 13:2, which are to be read as synonymous, suggest that YHWH lays claim to male as well as female first-born. However Num 3:14 f. states explicitly that of the human first-born only the males are affected.[54] Quite clearly then the final editors of the Pentateuch did not consider it necessary to include this restriction in the advance reference Exod 13:2 (similarly in the references Num 3:12 and Num 8:16 f.).

Now the law of the first-born in Exod 13:11–16 will be examined in detail. To begin with only the first part of the law, v. 11–13 is quoted:

> (11aα) When YHWH has brought you into the land of the Canaanites,
> (11aβ) as he swore to you and your ancestors
> (11b) and has given it to you
> (12a) you shall set apart to YHWH every first-birth of the womb.

---

[53] See also Propp, *Exodus*, 457.

[54] Is this limitation for the human first-born explained by the fact that only male Levites may perform the sacred duties? With reference to the animals there is in any case no such limitation. It is also noticeable that neither in Exod 13:2 nor in Num 3 is any distinction made between unblemished and blemished animals.

> (12b) And all the first-birth of your cattle that are males, belong to YHWH.
> (13aα) And every first-birth of an ass you shall redeem with a sheep
> (13aβ) and if you will not redeem (it), you must break its neck.
> (13b) And every first-born among your children you shall redeem.

V. 11–12a form a temporal-condition sentence structure; v. 11 is taken as the anterior clause and v. 12a as the posterior clause. The anterior clause includes the condition that Israel will have brought in the Promised Land. V. 12a outlines what is then to apply; Israel must transfer to YHWH's possession every first birth of the womb (*ʿbr* hiphil). Also, v. 12a acts as the general formula in this law, which is then illustrated in detail.[55]

The first explanation v. 12b determines that with regards to the animals only the male first-born belongs to YHWH. The second explanation v. 13aαaβ contains a special rule concerning the male first-born of the animals; the first-born of the ass, considered unclean, is to be redeemed or slaughtered. The third explanation in v. 13b concerns human first-born; every first-born (*kol bekhor*) of the children is to be redeemed. From this wording, comparable with Exod 34:20, it is clear that the Israelite concerned can have several *bekhorim*, that is, if he has several wives, he can have several first-born.[56] As in Exod 34:20, the means of redemption is left open. In view of the limitation of the first-born animals to the males in this context, the question arises, in regards to the human first-born should the same apply as in the case of the first-born of animals, namely that only a male first-born is to be given to YHWH or redeemed?[57] This question can be answered by an analysis of the second part of the law, v. 14–16:

> (14a) And when in future your child asks you, 'What does this mean?'
> (14bα) you shall answer,
> (14bβ) 'By strength of hand YHWH brought us out of Egypt,

[55] See also Brin, *Studies*, 172; van Seters, "Law," 368.

[56] See also v. 15bβ: KOL *bekhor banay* ("EVERY first-born of my children") und Propp, *Exodus*, 421.

[57] See v. 12a according to the LXX: καὶ ἀφελεῖς πᾶν διανοῖγον μήτραν, τὰ ἀρσενικά, τῷ κυρίῳ. According to this all *male* first-born of human and animal belong to YHWH.

from the house of slavery.
(15aα) When Pharaoh stubbornly refused to let us go, YHWH killed all the first-born in the land of Egypt,
(15aβ) from human first-born to the first-born of animals.
(15bα) Therefore I sacrifice to YHWH every male first-birth,
(15bβ) but every first-born among my children I redeem.
(16aα) And it shall serve as a sign on your hand (16aβ) and as a frontlet on your forehead
(16bα) that by strength of hand
(16bβ) YHWH brought us out of Egypt.'

The child's question forming the beginning of the passage refers to the meaning of the just-proclaimed law of the first-born (v. 14a). The father's reply refers first of all to the events in Egypt (v. 14b–15a); YHWH led Israel from the house of slavery, Egypt, and, when Pharaoh refused to let the Israelites go, killed the first-born of human and animal in the land of Egypt. The father presents this action of YHWH as the reason for his sacrifice of first-born ("therefore" *ʿl ken*).[58] In the light of this statement the first-born appear as a tribute to the God who acted in Israel's interest or spared Israel. The father then considers the sacrifice of the first-born more closely. First of all he states that he sacrifices to YHWH *every* first-birth of the womb (*kol peter rekhem*), in as far as it is male (v. 15bα). This clarifies what remained open in v. 13b, namely that with regards to the first-born of animal *and human* solely the *male* is affected.[59] V. 15bβ comprises another limitation concerning the sacrifice; with regards to his first-born male children, the father does not sacrifice, but redeems them.

According to the father's closing instruction the child should from then on be reminded of the sacrificial practice by the symbols borne on his body (v. 16).[60] In this way the following generation will know the

58 In the so-called children's catechism the behaviour demanded according to the Torah is always explained by God's action on behalf of Israel in history, see Fabry, "Gespräch," 759.

59 Therefore the story of YHWH's action on the night of the Passover in Exod 12 is to be understood to the effect that YHWH killed every *male* first-born of human and animal. One indication of this is found in Exod 4:22 f. According to Werner H. Schmidt, *Exodus, 1. Teilband: Exodus 1–6* (BKAT II / 1, Neukirchen-Vluyn: Neukirchener Verlag, 1988), 211, Exod 4:21–23 is "eine spät hinzugefügte Antizipation" [...], die sowohl die Priesterschrift als auch den Jahwisten voraussetzt."

60 See Durham, *Exodus*, 178: "The antecedent of 'it' at the beginning of both vv. 9 and 16 remains unclear, but the instruction concerning the unleavened bread cakes and

meaning of the sacrifice of the first-born and is motivated to continue the practice.

7. Summary and Conclusion

The meaning of the sacrifice of the first-born is briefly discussed. According to Christian Eberhart, four theological sacrifice theories are above all relevant; sacrifice is interpreted as an offering, as contributions to communal feasts, as a means of substitution and as a means of controlling social aggression.[61] The sacrifice of the first-born or of the substitute are understood in all the laws of the Torah without doubt as an offering to YHWH. At the same time, the texts do not indicate that the offerings have the function of influencing YHWH, for example to make him gracious or forgiving.[62] Also the texts reveal no indication that the sacrifices are an expression of thankfulness or reverence to God as the giver of all life. According to the earliest law in the Book of Covenant it is rather YHWH who lays claim to the "treasure" of the Israelite, his first-born child, and to his "fullness," namely the first-born of his animals. According to the pre-exilic Dodecalogue, YHWH appears as the rightful owner of the first-born. With the sacrifice of first-born, therefore, the Israelite must present YHWH with what belongs to him. In the late post-exilic text, Exod 13, YHWH's continued claim to the first-born of human and animal in Israel is explained by the events of the Passover. Even in the light of this explanation the sacrifices are not voluntary offerings, but tributes owed to the God who freed Israel. Consequently YHWH can dispose of his property; according to Num 18 the flesh of the sacrifice or its substitute should be given for the priests' use. According to Deut 15 the israelite families should consume the flesh of the animals consecrated to YHWH once a year in his presence. The point of the Deuteronomic concept is educational in that, according to Deut 14:22, during this annual feast when the entire tithe and first-born offering should be consumed in the presence of YHWH, reverence of YHWH or the relationship of human and God should be represented.

---

the instruction concerning the firstborn are probably what is to serve as the 'sign,' the 'reminder,' and the 'bands.'" For the history of the consequences of these directives see Weinfeld, *Deuteronomy*, 341–43.

61 Christian Eberhart, *Studien zur Bedeutung der Opfer im Alten Testament: Die Signifikanz von Blut- und Verbrennungsriten im kultischen Rahmen* (WMANT 94, Neukirchen-Vluyn: Neukirchener Verlag, 2002), 188 ff.

62 But see Mic 6:7.

Next should be recorded in the case of Exod 22:28, that an Israelite could understand this instruction to mean that he should sacrifice his first-born child to YHWH. Ezek 20:25f. describes such first-born sacrifices for YHWH as practised. Therefore it cannot be ruled out that in early Israel at a particular time such a sacrificial practice could indeed have occurred.[63] It need not have been carried out by all families; no tofet such as in Carthage has up to now been found in the country. What can be documented is that all later laws are unmistakably clear on this point: that the first-born child or first-born son is to be redeemed.

Finally considering the terms for first-births *bekhor* and *peter rekhem* the following can be stated: In the laws of the first-born in the Book of Covenant, in the Dodecalogue and in the original layer of Num 18:15–18 (P) the corresponding terms *bekhor* and *peter rekhem* refer to the male and female first-born of human and animal. The regulation in Deut 15, to consecrate only the male first-born clean animals to YHWH and to consume them in YHWH's presence during the Feast, is connected with a clearly farmer-friendly tendency of the Deuteronomic law-maker. Apart from that a limitation to the male first-born prevails only in the later post-exilic period. According to the note in Num 18:16, the redemption of the human first-born applies only to male children; according to the law of the first-born in Exod 13 only the male first-born of human and animal (of female Israelites and animals) are affected.

To conclude with a "synchronic remark," Exod 13:11–16 is the first law of the first-born in the Torah. To this extent this law also carries a hermeneutic key function; it provides not only—representative of all laws of the first-born—its etiological explanation. Exod 13:11–16 gives clear indications in many aspects for the understanding of further laws; the instruction in the Book of Covenant to give YHWH the first-born is naturally to be understood in the light of Exod 13:11–16 in the sense of a redemption of the first-born. All general comments on the first-born (*bekhorim* and *pitre rekhem*) are interpreted as the *male* first-born. Indeed, this was also the interpretation of the rabbis,[64] which determines Jewish practice up to the present day.

---

[63] See also the contribution of Lange in the present volume.

[64] See *m. Bek.*; also Lk 2:23.

"They Burn Their Sons and Daughters— That Was No Command of Mine" (Jer 7:31)

Child Sacrifice in the Hebrew Bible and in the Deuteronomistic Jeremiah Redaction

Armin Lange, University of Vienna

In his famous novel Salammbo, Gustave Flaubert describes the theft of a sacred item called Zaïmph out of Carthage's Tanith temple. The people of Carthage are more than upset and look for ways to avoid the catastrophe necessarily following such an act of sacrilege.

> Thus all misfortunes came from the loss of the Zaïmph. Salammbo had taken part in this indirectly; she was included in the same resentment; she must be punished. The vague idea of some immolation soon circulated among the people. To appease the Baalim there must no doubt be offered something of inestimable value, some being who was young, beautiful, virgin, of ancient lineage, descended from the Gods, a human star.[1]

In 1862, Flaubert describes the intended sacrifice of Salammbo as an almost magic measure to appease the divine world. In this description of a Punic ritual in Carthage, Flaubert drew copiously on the Hebrew Bible, which mentions the sacrifice of children repeatedly.[2]

At least in deuteronomic / deuteronomistic thought, human sacrifice is compared with other despised acts of magic and divination. E.g., Deut 18:9–11 reads,

> (9) When you come into the land that the Lord your God is giving you, you must not learn to imitate the abhorrent

[1] Gustave Flaubert, *Salammbo* (translated with an introduction by A.J. Krailsheimer; London: Penguin Books, 1977), 165

[2] See op. cit., 9.

> practices of those nations. (10) No one shall be found among you who makes a son or daughter pass through fire, or who practices divination, or is a soothsayer, or an augur, or a sorcerer, (11) or one who casts spells, or who consults ghosts or spirits, or who seeks oracles from the dead.[3]

Deut 18:10 is not exceptional. In exilic times, several deuteronimistic texts are attacking or prohibiting child sacrifice (Deut 12:31; 2 Kgs 16:3; 17:17; 21:6).[4] The sacrifice itself is described with the phrases "who makes a son or daughter pass (*hʿbyr*)[5] through fire" (Deut 18:10; compare 2 Kgs 16:3; 17:17) and "to burn (*śrp*) in the fire" (Deut 12:31).[6] To the child sacrifice attacked, no age or gender restriction seem to be attached and the children to be sacrificed are not necessarily the firstborn. In the Dtn / Dtr literature, it is presumed, that sons and daughters at any age have been sacrificially burned. In every reference, the practice of child sacrifice is either evidence for Israel's straying away to pagan deities or at least connected with its idololatry. When in the Dtn and Dtr texts these deities are identified, they are described as the deities of Canaan (Deut 12:30; 18:9). Therefore, in Dtn and Dtr texts, child sacrifice is perceived as Canaanite. In deuteronomistic thought, the ritual of child sacrifice is understood as one of the pivotal crimes of Israel which necessitated the destruction of the northern kingdom (2 Kgs 17:17–18) and the punishment of the exile for the southern kingdom (see 2 Kgs 21:6, 10–15). This explanation of the exile as punishment for Judah's child sacrifices influenced Jewish thought for a very long time (see e. g. Isa 57:5, 9; Ezek 16:20–21; 20:31 (MT); 23:36–39: Ps 106:37–38) and is still attested in a 2nd century B. C. E. apocalypse (see 4QpsDan[a] 13 3 f. par. 4QpsDan[b] 12).

---

[3] If not noted otherwise, biblical quotations are taken from the NRSV.

[4] For Deut 18:10 and Deut 12:31; 2 Kgs 16:3; 17:17 see Brian B. Schmidt, *Israel's Beneficient Dead: Ancestor Cult and Necromancy in Ancient Israelite Religion and Tradition* (FAT 11; Tübingen: J. C. B. Mohr (Paul Siebeck), 1994), 179–90, 220–41.

[5] For עבר hifʿil as sacrificial language describing the burning of a child see Morton Smith, "A Note on Burning Babies," *JAOS* 95 (1975): 477–79, 478; Hans-Peter Müller, "מֹלֶךְ *mólek*," *TDOT* 8: 375–388, 385–86.

[6] For the sacrificial language used in Dtr literature in connection with child sacrifice, see Udo Rüterswörden, "Die Stellung der Deuteronomisten zum alttestamentlichen Dämonenwesen," in *Die Dämonen – Demons: Die Dämonologie der israelitisch-jüdischen und frühchristlichen Literatur im Kontext ihrer Umwelt – The Demonology of Israelite-Jewish and Early Christian Literature in Context of their Environment* (eds. A. Lange, H. Lichtenberger, and K. F. D. Römheld; Tübingen: Mohr Siebeck, 2003), 197–210, 197–204.

In the deuteronimistic redaction of the Book of Jeremiah (in the following DtrJer), which comes from late exilic times and argues against the rebuilding of the Jerusalem temple during the years 520–515 B. C. E.,[7] three polemics against Israel's child sacrifices can be found, i. e. Jer 7:31; 19:5; and 32:35.[8]

> 7:31 They have built a shrine of Topheth in the valley of Ben-hinnom, at which they burn their sons and daughters—that was no command of mine, says the Lord.
>
> 19:5 They have built shrines to Baal, where they burn their sons as whole-offerings to Baal. It was no command of mine; I never spoke it; it never entered my thought.
>
> 32:35 They have built shrines to Baal in the valley of Ben-hinnom, to surrender their sons and daughters as a Molk-sacrifice. It was no command of mine, nor did it ever enter my thought to do this abominable thing and lead Judah to sin.

As in the Dtr, Israel is accused of sacrificing their children to a Canannite deity (Jer 19:5; 32:35). As in the Dtr, *śrp* (7:31; 19:5) and *hʿbyr* (32:35) are used to describe the actual sacrifice. As in the Dtr children of both genders are sacrificed and again no age restrictions apply. But there is a significant difference between the DtrJer on the one hand and the Book of Deuteronomy and the Deuteronomistic History on other hand. With regard to the practice of child sacrifice, DtrJer emphasizes in all three references, "which I did not command." That there is a need for this clarification, could imply vice versa, practitioners of child sacrifice actually claimed that YHWH commanded this sacrifice. But such a claim would not agree with the accusation of Jer 19:5 and 32:35, that the child sacrifices were made in Baal shrines and that according to Jer 32:35 they were performed *lammolekh* ("for / as *molekh*").

---

[7] For the date of the DtrJer see Armin Lange, *Vom prophetischen Wort zur prophetischen Tradition: Studien zur Traditions- und Redaktionsgeschichte innerprophetischer Konflikte in der Hebräischen Bibel* (FAT 34; Tübingen: Mohr Siebeck, 2002), 198–199, 204–205, 266–267.

[8] For the Dtr character of Jer 7:31; 19:5 and 32:35 see e. g. James Philip Hyatt, "The Book of Jeremiah," *IB* 5, 775–1142, 867–68, 877, 967, 1047 and Winfried Thiel, *Die deuteronomistische Redaktion von Jeremia 1–25* (WMANT 41; Neukirchen-Vluyn: Neukirchner Verlag, 1973), 128–29, 221; idem., *Die deuteronomistische Redaktion von Jeremia 26–45* (WMANT 52; Neukirchen-Vluyn: Neukirchner Verlag, 1981), 30–31.

There are several possible interpretations of Jer 7:31; 19:5; and 32:35.

- Children have been sacrificed to a deity named Molekh, the mention of Baal is polemic.[9]
- Children have been sacrificed to Baal.[10]
- The practitioners of child sacrifice claimed that YHWH had commanded a child sacrifice to Baal and or Molekh.
- The mention of Baal is polemic and the children were sacrificed to YHWH.[11]

---

[9] Alberto R. Whitney Green, *The Role of Human Sacrifice in the Ancient Near East* (ASOR Diss. Ser. 1; Missoula, Mont.: Scolars Press, 1975), 177–78; Jürgen Ebach and Udo Rüterswörden, "ADRMLK, 'Moloch' und BAʿAL ADR," *UF* 11 (1979): 219–26, 222; George C. Heider, *The Cult of Molek: A Reassessment* (JSOTSup 43; Sheffield: JSOT Press, 1985), 336–46 (the three references refer to sacrifices made both to Molekh and Baal); Gunther Wanke, *Jeremia*, vol. 1: *Jeremia 1,1–25,14* (Zürich: Theologischer Verlag Zürich, 1995), 95 (in 19:5 the sacrifices are connected with the Baal cult, 185); Jack R. Lundbom, *Jeremiah 1–20: A New Translation with Introduction and Commentary* (AB 21A; New York, N.Y.: Doubleday, 1999), 495, 497, 839.

[10] Thus e.g. Roland de Vaux, *Ancient Israel: Its Life and Institutions* (translated by J. McHugh; London: Darton, Longman, and Todd, 1961), 221, 444; Robert P. Carroll, *Jeremiah: A Commentary* (Philadelphia, Pa.: Westminster, 1986), 388; (in 223–24, concerning Jer 7:31, Carroll claims that children were sacrificed to YHWH); Klaus Koch, "Molek astral," in *Mythos im Alten Testament und seiner Umwelt: Festschrift für Hans-Peter Müller zum 65. Geburtstag* (eds. A. Lange, H. Lichtenberger, and D. Römheld; BZAW 278; Berlin: 1999), 29–50, 43–45 (the molk-sacrifice is part of an astral cult which among other deities venerated the Baal of heaven); Christl Maier, *Jeremia als Lehrer der Tora: Soziale Gebote des Deuteronomiums in Fortschreibungen des Jeremiabuches* (FRLANT 196; Göttingen: Vandenhoeck & Ruprecht, 2002), 122–24.

[11] Bernhard Duhm, *Das Buch Jeremia: Erklärt* (KHC 11; Tübingen: J.C.B. Mohr (Paul Siebeck), 1901), 85 (Jer 19:5 and 32:35 are later insertions which misinterpret Jer 7:31 and attribute the child sacrifices wrongly to Baal or Molekh, which in turn were conceived as being mysteriously linked with YHWH, 161, 269); Paul Volz, *Der Prophet Jeremia* (2nd ed.; KAT 10; Leipzig: A. Deichersche Verlagsbuchhandlung D. Werner Scholl, 1928), 202–3; Otto Eissfeldt, *Molk als Opferbegriff im Punischen und Hebräischen und das Ende des Gottes Moloch* (Halle an der Saale: M. Niemeyer, 1935), 41–42; Wilhelm Rudolph, *Jeremia* (HAT 12; Tübingen: J.C.B. Mohr (Paul Siebeck), 1947), 50; John Bright, *Jeremiah: Introduction, Translation, and Notes* (AB 21; Garden City, N.Y.: Doubleday, 1965), 57; Paul G. Mosca, *Child Sacrifice in Canaanite and Israelite Religion: A Study of Mulk and Klm* (Ph.D. diss., Cambridge, Mass.: Harvard University, 1975), 228–31; Michael Fishbane, *Biblical Interpretation in Ancient Israel* (Oxford, U.K.: Clarendon, 1985), 186; William L. Holladay, *Jeremiah 1: A Commentary on the Book of the Prophet Jeremiah Chapters 1–25* (Hermeneia; Philadelphia, Pa.: 1986), 268; Wolfgang Werner, *Das Buch Jeremia: Kapitel 1–25* (Neuer Stuttgarter Kommentar Altes Testament 19/1; Stuttgart: Katholisches Bibelwerk, 1997), 102 (for Werner, in Jer 19:5 and 32:35, the child sacrifices are made

- All three references are polemic and attack the Jerusalem cult by comparing its practices with child sacrifice.[12]

Already at this stage of my investigation the reader can be referred to the contribution of Bennie H. Reynolds to this volume. Based on earlier work by Otto Eissfeldt and Hans-Peter Müller,[13] Reynolds shows that in Jer 32:35 and elsewhere the phrase *lammolekh* describes a specific type of sacrifice called molk and is not the proper name of a deity. This means, Jer 32:35 does not accuse Israel of sacrificing children to a deity called Molekh but of performing a molk-sacrifice. To ascertain which of the other four options applies to the DtrJer, in the following, I will briefly discuss the practice of child sacrifice during the iron age outside of Israel. Afterwards, Israel's attitude towards child sacrifice will be analyzed and excursus will discuss bronze age child sacrifices in Syro-Palestine. At the end of this essay, I will try to apply this survey to the interpretation of child sacrifices in the DtrJer.

1. Have Children Been Sacrificed to Baal? The Practice of Child Sacrifice Outside of Israel

Outside the Hebrew Bible,[14] except for the Punic and Phoenician peoples, the evidence for child sacrifice is sparse. According to 2 Kgs 3:26–

---

to Baal or Moloch respectively [see ibid., 181 and idem, *Das Buch Jeremia: Kapitel 25–52* (Neuer Stuttgarter Kommentar Altes Testament 19/2; Stuttgart: Katholisches Bibelwerk, 2003), 86]); John van Seters, "The Law on Child Sacrifice in Exod 22,28b–29," *ETL* 74 (1998): 364–372, 366. Similar of Roland de Vaux, *Studies in Old Testament Sacrifice* (Cardiff: University Press of Wales, 1964), 72–73.

[12] Compare Mose Weinfeld, "The Worship of Molech and of the Queen of Heaven," *UF* 4 (1972): 133–54, 140–41; Stig Norin, "Baal, Kinderopfer und 'über die Schwelle springen': Propheten und israelitische Religion im siebten Jahrhundert v. Chr.," in *"Wer darf hinaufsteigen zum Berg JHWHs?": Beiträge zu Prophetie und Poesie des Alten Testaments: Festschrift für Sigurður Örn Steingrímsson zum 70. Geburtstag* (eds. H. Irsigler and K. Ólason; Arbeiten zu Text und Sprache im Alten Testament 72; St. Ottilien: EOS, 2002), 75–100, 81–87, who thinks that all three representations are a polemic misrepresentation of an earlier rite, and Rüterswörden, 204–8, who thinks that all Dtr references to child sacrifice are a rhetorical construct.

[13] Eissfeldt, *Molk als Opferbegriff*; Müller, מֹלֶךְ. For a discussion of the extensive scholarly literature on the topic, see Bennie H. Reynolds' contribution to this volume.

[14] For the question of human sacrifices in Mesopotamia and Egypt, see Green, *The Role of Human Sacrifice* and the article of Beate Pongratz-Leisten to this volume. For human sacrifice in the Graeco-Roman world see the article of Gabriele Weiler to this volume and Jan N. Bremmer, "Sacrificing a Child in Ancient Greece: The Case of Iphigenia," in *The Sacrifice of Isaac: The Aqedah (Genesis 22) and Its Interpretations* (eds. E. Noort and E.J.C. Tigchelaar; Themes in Biblical Narrative 4; Leiden: Brill, 2002), 21–43.

27, when besieged, the Moabite king Mesha sacrificed his oldest son on the walls of his city.[15] Mesha's sacrifice thus responds to a situation of emergency. As no age restriction seems to apply with Mesha's son, in some respects, this sacrifice agrees with the child sacrifices attacked in the Dtn / Dtr literature. Comparably, 2 Kgs 17:31 relates that the Sepharvites burnt their children to Adrammelech and Anammelech. Again no age restriction seems to apply and as with the child sacrifices attacked in the Dtn / Dtr literature, both sexes have been sacrificed.

While we do not know who the Sepharvites have been, we know by way of their language and other indicators that the Moabites were of Canaanite heritage[16] and it seems that the child sacrifice described in 2 Kgs 3:26–27 conforms closely with an earlier Canaanite ritual (see below).

Another attestation to the practice of child sacrifice by a Canaanite successor culture may be found in the second combination of the Tell Deir ʿAlla plaster inscriptions (in the following DAT). The post-Canaanite character of the Tell Deir ʿAlla culture is evident in its language. Hans-Peter Müller describes the language of the DAT plaster inscriptions as a "relativ späten Rest eines nordwestsemitischen Zustands vor der endgültigen Trennung des Aramäischen vom Kanaanäischen, … wie er sich in einer ritardierenden Randgesellschaft des syrischen Kulturraumes erhalten konnte".[17] According Hackett's interpretation of DAT II, the word "scion" or "sprout" (*nqr*) mentioned in DAT II,5 is metaphorical language for a child. Combination II would begin with a description of the child to be sacrificed and continue with a description of the child's fate during the ritual. Regrettably, not enough text is preserved to gain more detailed knowledge about the ritual itself. But it seems possible, that DAT II describes the response of the DAT-people to the doom prophecy which Balaam uttered in DAT I. They would have

[15] For the child sacrifice described in 2 Kgs 3:26–27 see John Gray, *I & II Kings: A Commentary* (2nd ed.; OTL; Philadelphia, Pa.: Westminster, 1970), 490–91; Green, 169–71; Gerald L. Mattingly, "Moabite Religion," in *Studies in the Mesha Inscription and Moab* (ed. A. Dearman; Archeology and Biblical Studies 2; Atlanta, Ga.: Scholars Press, 1989), 211–38, 229–231 and the literature quoted there.

[16] See Mattingly, "Moabites," in *Peoples of the Old Testament World* (eds. A.J. Hoerth, G.L. Mattingly, and E.M. Yamauchi; Grand Rapids, Mich.: Baker Books and Lutterworth Press, 1994), 317–33, 321–25.

[17] Müller, "Die Sprache der Texte von Tell Deir ʿAllā im Kontext der nordwestsemitischen Sprachen: mit einigen Erwägungen zum Zusammenhang der schwachen Verbklassen," *ZAH* 4 (1991): 1–31, 31.

tried to appease the gods by way of a child sacrifice.[18] As the Moabite sacrifice mentioned in 2 Kgs 3:26–27, the child sacrifice described in DAT II would thus respond to a situation of emergency and crisis.

None of the references quoted so far mentions Baal. But at least the Moabites and the DAT-culture are Canaanite successor cultures. And Baal was a prominent deity in Canaanite religion.

The bulk of the evidence for iron age child sacrifices outside of Israel comes from the Phoenicio-Punic culture which is also a Canaanite successor culture. For a description of Phoenician and Punic child sacrifices, at this place, the reader can be referred to the contribution of Reynolds in this volume.[19] I agree with Reynolds, that both peoples sacrificed children regularly and that the Phoenician term *molk* as the Hebrew term *molekh* is not the designation of a deity but of a specific type of sacrifice. The ritual itself seems to have been quite different from the one described in 2 Kgs 3:26–27. The Moabite child sacrifice responded to a situation of desperate need and the same might be true for the sacrifice described in DAT II. But in the Phoenicio-Punic culture, children seem to have been sacrificed on a regular basis. As far as we can tell, both sexes have been sacrificed and the human victims were mostly toddlers. What is more important here though is the question if the Phoenicians and Punics sacrificed children to Baal.

To answer this question, at this place, a brief reminder to a Punic inscription from the 6th century B.C.E. which was found at a tophet on the island of Malta may suffice.

> (1) Stela of "the presentation instead (2) of an infant,"
> (3) which *NHM* erected (4) for Baal Hamon, the (5) Lord, because he (i.e. Baal Hamon) answered (6) the call of his words. (KAI 61 A)

As several other inscriptions, KAI 61 A attests to the fact, that Baal was at least one of the deities to whom children were sacrificed—another one being Tanith. In the case of the Malta inscription, it was Baal in his form as Baal Hamon. Furthermore, the inscription attests to the sacrifice and burning of an animal instead of a child. As this is the oldest reference to

[18] Jo Ann Hackett, *The Balaam Text from Deir ʿAllā* (HSM 31, Chico, Calif.: Scholars Press, 1980), 80–85; idem, "Religious Traditions in Israelite Transjordan," in *Ancient Israelite Religion: Essays in Honor of Frank Moore Cross* (eds. P.D. Miller, P.D. Hanson, and S.D. McBride; Philadelphia, Pa.: Fortress, 1987), 125–36, 126.

[19] For further reading see the literature quoted by Reynolds.

the use of animals instead of children, this means that at the latest from the 6th century B. C. E. onwards Punic and possibly also Phoenician religion allowed for a substitution of the child to be sacrificed. That the inscription needs to emphasize such substitution demonstrates also that in other cases children and not animals were sacrificed.

So far, it can be concluded that in different forms child sacrifices were practiced in three Canaanite successor cultures, the Phoenicio-Punic, the Moabite and the DAT-culture. But did iron age Israel as another Canaanite successor culture subscribe to this ritual, too?

2. Have Children Been Sacrificed to YHWH? The Practice of Child Sacrifice in Israel

In my opinion, for iron age Israel, at least three texts attest to the practice of child sacrifice. For the time shortly before the Babylonian exile, Ezek 20:25–26 seem to confirm the implication of Jer 7:31; 19:5 and 32:35 that there were religious laws commanding child sacrifices to YHWH.

> (25) Moreover I gave them statutes that were not good and ordinances by which they could not live. (26) I defiled them through their very gifts, in their offering up all their firstborn, in order that I might horrify them, so that they might know that I am the Lord.

In the perspective of this exilic text, in pre-exilic times, among other things, YHWH had commanded child sacrifices, to defile and devastate Israel, leading it thus unavoidably to the catastrophes of 597 and 587 B. C. E. as well as to Babylonian exile.[20] Here and now, is not the place to attempt an interpretation of Ezekiel's concept of a bad law consciously given to Israel by YHWH to drive it into exile. Whatever the assessment of the laws in question, for pre-exilic times, Ezek 20:25–26 documents the existence of a command of YHWH prescribing child sacrifice.[21] But there are differences between the child sacrifices mentioned

[20] For the idea that the Babylonian exile was caused at least in part by Israelite child sacrifices see also 2 Kgs 21:6, 10–15 and my discussion of this text above.

[21] For Ezek 20:26 as referring to a command to sacrifice the firstborn son to YHWH, see e. g. Eissfeldt, 42; Walter Zimmerli, *Ezekiel 1: A Commentary on the Book of the Prophet Ezekiel, Chapters 1–24* (translated by R. E. Clements; Hermeneia; Philadelphia, Pa.: Fortress, 1979), 410–11; Marc S. Smith, *The Early History of God: Yahweh and the Other Deities in Ancient Israel* (New York, N. Y.: Harper & Row, 1990), 132; Daniel I. Block, *The Book of Ezekiel: Chapters 1–24* (NICOT; Grand Rapids, Mich.: Eerdmans, 1997), 636–37;

in Jer 7:31; 19:5 and 32:35 and the child sacrifices prescribed in Ezek 20:25–26. In Jer 7:31; 19:5 and 32:35, all sons and daughters are sacrificed and the sacrifice is not restricted to the firstborn. According to Ezek 20:26, YHWH asks only for the *peter rekhem* (verbally "everything that breaks out first of the mother's womb").[22] The phrase designates both firstborn sons and daughters. Ezek 20:26 disagrees thus with the accusations of the DtrJer in sacrificing only the firstborn but agrees in sacrificing both sexes. Furthermore, as in Jer 7:31; 19:5 and 32:35, the child sacrifice mentioned in Ezek 20:26 is not exceptional but seems to apply to every firstborn. And as in Jer 32:35, Ezek 20:26 uses the verb *hʿbyr* ("to walk through fire") to describe the act of the actual sacrifice.

At least in one case, in Exod *20:22–23:19, the pre-exilic *Book of the Covenant*, a law is preserved which prescribes a child sacrifice.[23]

> (28) You shall not withhold your fullness and your treasure from me, the firstborn among your sons you shall give me. (29) You shall do the same with your oxen and sheep. They shall stay with the mother for seven days; on the eighth day you shall give them to me. (Exod 22:28–29)[24]

As the firstborn of cattle and sheep, the firstborn son is to be given to YHWH. While v. 28 as such could be interpreted in different ways, its continuation in v. 29 leaves no doubt as to how the phrase "the firstborn among your sons you shall give me" is to be understood. It is for

---

van Seters, 366; and the contribution of Karin Finsterbusch to this volume. Many interpreters deny that Ezek 20:25–26 refers to a child sacrifice and often consider the verses to refer to a misinterpretation of Exod 20:28–29 (see e. g. de Vaux, *Studies*, 71–72; idem, *Ancient Israel*, 444; Green, 175–79; Hartmut Gese, "Ezechiel 20,25 f. und die Erstgeburtsopfer," in *Beiträge zur alttestamentlichen Theologie: Festschrift für Walther Zimmerli zum 70. Geburtstag* (eds. H. Donner, R. Hanhart, and R. Smend; Göttingen: Vandenhoeck & Ruprecht, 1977), 140–51, 146; Otto Kaiser, "Den Erstgeborenen deiner Söhne sollst du mir geben," in O. Kaiser, *Von der Gegenwartsbedeutung des Alten Testaments: Gesammelte Studien zur Hermeneutik und zur Redaktionsgeschichte* (eds. V. Fritz, K.-F. Pohlmann, and H.-Chr. Schmitt; Göttingen: Vandenhoeck & Ruprecht, 1984), 142–66, 143, 159; Heider, 369–72.

22 See the contribution of Karin Finsterbusch to this volume.

23 For an interpretation of Exod 22:28–29 and the term *demaʿ* used in Exod 22:28 see Armin Lange, "The Meaning of Demaʿ in the Copper Scroll and Ancient Jewish Literature," in *Copper Scroll Studies* (eds. G. J. Brooke and Ph. R. Davies; JSPSup 40; Sheffield: Sheffield Academic Press, 2002), 122–138, 137. For a more detailed analysis and discussion of the scholarly literature see e. g. Kaiser, 144–48, and the contribution of K. Finsterbusch to this volume.

24 Translation A. L.

the same sacrificial purpose as the firstborn of oxen and sheep.[25] And contrary to what modern scholarly interpretations sometimes claim,[26] Exod 22:28–29 mentions no possibility to redeem the firstborn son in question. Different from both Jer 7:31; 19:5; 32:35; and Ezek 20:26, the law in Exod 22:28 prescribes a sacrifice only of the firstborn son. But as in Jer 7:31; 19:5; 32:35; and Ezek 20:26 this sacrifice is not exceptional but is concerned with every firstborn son. Verse 29 might hint to the fact, that like oxen and sheep the firstborn sons were sacrificed on there seventh day, while the Phoenicio-Punic child sacrifice seems to have been performed with toddlers.

For pre-exilic times, the story of Jephthah's daughter (Judg 11:29–40) might reflect another form of child sacrifice. In my opinion, Judg 11:29–40 goes back to an older source used by the author of the Dtr history. Judg 11:29–40 would thus date to pre-exilic times. Originally, it seems to have been an etiology explaining a yearly custom of a day of lamentation performed by Israelite women (see Judg 11:39–40). In this older version the story attests to a child sacrifice.[27]

Before a battle with the Ammonites, Jephthah makes an oath, that should he be victorious, he would sacrifice to God the first thing he would meet coming home:

> And Jephthah made a vow to the Lord, and said, "If you will give the Ammonites into my hand, then whoever comes out of the doors of my house to meet me, when I return victorious from the Ammonites, shall be the Lord's to be offered up by me as a burnt offering." (Judg 11:31)

When the victor comes home, the first thing he encounters is own daughter:

> Then Jephthah came to his home at Mizpah; and there was his daughter coming out to meet him with timbrels and with dancing. She was his only child; he had no son or daughter except her. (Judg 11:34)

---

[25] For the sacrifice of the firstborn oxen and sheep see e. g. Deut 15:19–20.

[26] See e. g. of de Vaux, *Studies*, 70–71; idem, *Ancient Israel*, 444; Weinfeld, 154; Fishbane, 181–87; van Seters, 370–72; Philip J. King and Lawrence E. Stager, *Life in Biblical Israel* (Library of Ancient Israel; Louisville, Ky.: Westminster John Knox, 2001), 359.

[27] See e. g. the interpretations of de Vaux, *Studies*, 65; idem, *Ancient Israel*, 442; Green, 161–63; and Jan A. Soggin, *Judges: A Commentary* (transl. J. Bowden; OTL; Philadelphia, Pa.: Westminster, 1981), 213–19.

After a time of two months, the obedient daughter is sacrificed:

> At the end of two months, she returned to her father, who did with her according to the vow he had made. (Judg 11:39)

The human sacrifice described in the older tradition of the Jephthah story does not document a regular custom but an exceptional event. And the age of Jephthah's daughter agrees well with the son Mesha sacrificed according to 2 Kgs 3:26–27. It thus relates to none of the Israelite child sacrifices discussed so far. And different from the DAT-culture and the Moabites Jephthah's sacrifice of his daughter does not respond to an emergency but is the fulfillment of a vow after a crisis-situation has been solved.

For the final version of the Jephthah-story, it has rightly been pointed out that God responds with silence to Jephthah's vow to sacrifice the first thing he sees when he comes home. It is not God's wish that Jephthah sacrifices his daughter but the consequence of human hubris. In this way, in its tragedy, the story of Jephthah's daughter reminds of the Greek idea of hubris. God does not respond to Jephthah's presumptuous vow. Jephthah is entangled in the consequences of his presumptuous vow and thus needs to sacrifice his own daughter.[28]

Another argument made for Israelite iron age child sacrifice, have been urns from burial caves in Gezer and other places.[29] But it has been shown that the bones in these jars display no traces of burning. The jars in question are thus part of a burial practice unrelated to any form of child sacrifice and today to say the least even their iron age dating is uncertain.[30] Actually, of what has been found so far, there seem to be no archeological remains of the child sacrifices practiced in iron age Israel.

It can be concluded that in iron age times, the DAT-culture, the Moabites, the Phoenicians, the Punics, and the Israelites practiced child sacrifices in different forms. The Moabites and maybe the DAT-culture responded to exceptional crises by way of a child sacrifice, while both the Phoenicio-Punic and the Israelite cultures performed child sacrifices on a regular basis. In iron age Israel, basically two forms of child

[28] Compare the interpretation of Daniel I. Block, *Judges, Ruth* (NAC 6; Nashville, Tenn.: Broadman & Holman, 1999), 364–79. For a more theological reading according to which the Jephthah-story would emphasize the infinite in God see the contribution of Bauks to this volume.

[29] See e.g. Robert Alexander Stewart Macalister, *The Excavation of Gezer: 1902–1905 and 1907–1909*, vol. 2 (London: John Murray, 1912), 401–2, 431–35.

[30] See Green, 152–56; Kaiser, 149–50 and the literature quoted there.

sacrifice can be distinguished. The sacrifice of the firstborn (Exod 22:28; Ezek 20:26) and the molk-sacrifice.[31] Both were performed on a regular basis. For the sacrifice of the firstborn, different customs seem to have existed. Sometimes both genders and sometimes only the firstborn son was sacrificed. Furthermore, the story of Jephthah's daughter attests to children of any age and gender sacrificed in fulfillment of a vow. The child sacrifices attacked in Jer 7:31; 19:5 and 32:35 do relate to neither the sacrifice of the firstborn nor the sacrificial fulfillment of a vow. Jer 32:35 shows that they belong to the category of molk-sacrifices also attacked in other Dtr texts.

To gain more information about the ritual attacked in Jer 7:31; 19:5 and 32:35, Israelite prohibitions and attacks of child sacrifice as well as Israelite substitution of the sacrificial victim need to be discusses. Before this can be done, the origin of Israelite child sacrifice needs to be analyzed in an excursus.

Excursus: Canaanite Child Sacrifices

As the languages of all cultures practicing child sacrifice belong to the Canaanite branch of north-west semitic languages or are otherwise related to the Canaanite language, it can be suspected that Phoenician, Punic, Moabite, and Israelite child sacrifices as well as the ritual described in DAT II go back to a Canaanite bronze age ritual. For the late bronze age such a ritual is attested by several Egyptian war reliefs from the times of Seti I, Ramesses II, Merneptah, and Ramesses III. The reliefs in question have been collected and interpreted by Anthony John Spalinger.[32] Depicted are Canaanite cities besieged by the armies of Seti I, Ramesses II, Merneptah, and Ramesses III. More or less well preserved, on the city walls or a rampart, the reliefs show a group of dignitaries raising their faces and hands towards heaven. One of the dignitaries holds a brazier burning

---

[31] For the distinction between molk-sacrifice and the sacrifice of the firstborn see Gese, 145; Day 65–67, 77; Koch, 35; and the contribution of K. Finsterbusch to this volume. To a certain extent, the distinction between the sacrifice of the firstborn and the molk-sacrifice seems to overlap with Weinfeld's distinction between sacrifices brought in an extraordinary situation and regular sacrifices (see Weinfeldt, 133–35; Ebach and Rüterswörden, 219–21), although there are no indications that the molk-sacrifice was performed only in extraordinary situations.

[32] Anthony John Spalinger, "A Canaanite Ritual Found in Egyptian Reliefs," *JSSEA* 7 (1978): 47–60; see also the earlier article by Philippe Derchain, "Les plus anciens témoignages de sacrifices d'enfants chez les sémites occidentaux," *VT* 20 (1970): 351–55, and the remarks by Marc S. Smith, 135–36.

incense while one or two others let dead children fall over the city walls, see figure 1[33]:

Fig. 1

The brazier in question is typical for the service of Baal Hamon. The scene reminds of the Moabite child sacrifice described in 2 Kgs 3:26–27.[34] Based on biblical references as well as other texts, Spalinger reconstructs the depicted ritual as follows:

> (1) Ba'al is invoked; (2) there is the sacrifice of infants; (3) the act occurs under duress—i. e., the city is besieged; (4) on one occas-

33 Stone relief from Karnak, cf. Derchain, "Les plus anciens témoignages" 352, fig. 1.

34 See Spalinger, 52; Baruch Margalit, "Why King Mesha of Moab Sacrificed His Oldest Son," *BAR* 12 (1986): 62–63, 76; James K. Hoffmeier, "Further Evidence for Infant Sacrifice in the Ancient Near East," *BAR* 13 (1987): 60–61.

sion a bag of flour is brought for the ritual; (5) incense braziers are present on all occasions; and (6) the heaven, and not the Pharaoh, is invoked."[35]

The depictions of the Egyptian military reliefs leave no doubt that different from Jer 7:31; 19:5; 32:35 and other Dtr references, the sacrificed children have not been burned. In fact, their dead bodies were thrown over the city walls.

That, in order to depreciate the conquered enemies depicted, the Egyptian reliefs are not inventing an abhorrent ritual practice for polemical purposes is evident from a cuneiform text found in Ugarit (RS 24.266 VI D = CTU 1.119 V 26–35). The tablet describes the ritual of a child sacrifice to be performed when a city is attacked by a strong foe.[36]

(26') When a strong foe attacks your gate,
a warrior (27') your walls,
You shall lift your eyes to *Baʿlu* and say:
(28') O *Baʿlu,* if you drive the strong one from our gate,
(29') the warrior from our walls,
a bull, (30') O *Baʿlu*, we shall sanctify,
a vow, O *Baʿlu*, (31') we shall fulfill;
a firstborn, O *Baʿlu*, we shall sanctify,
(32') a *htp*-offering, O *Baʿlu*, we shall fulfill,
a feast, O *Baʿlu*, we shall (33') offer;
To the sanctuary, O *Baʿlu*, we shall ascend,
that path, O *Baʿlu*, (34') we shall take.
And *Baʿ*[*lu* will h]ear [your] prayer:
(35') He will drive the strong foe from your gate,
[the warrior] (36') from yo[ur] walls.[37]

The evidence leaves no doubt that in the late bronze age, at least when a city was besieged by a strong enemy, Canaanites performed child sacrifices. According to the brief report of 2 Kgs 3:26–27, the Moabite practice is closest to the bronze age Canaanite ritual. The child sacrifice described in DAT II might also respond to an exceptional crisis. It seems therefore plausible, that the child sacrifices of these Canaanite successor cultures developed out of a Canaanite ancestor ritual.

But from late bronze age Canaan there might be even evidence for a more regularly performed child sacrifice which could thus have influenced the Israelite

---

35 Spalinger, 54.

36 For RS 24.266 VI D see Andrée Herdner, "Une priere a Baal des ugaritians en danger," *CRAI* 72 (1972): 693–97; Spalinger, 54–55; Margalit; 62–63, 76; Hoffmeier, 60–61.

37 Dennis Pardée, *Ritual and Cult at Ugarit* (Writings from the Ancient World 10; Atlanta, Ga.: SBL, 2002), 53, 149–150 (counting according to Pardée); for a different translation see Nick Wyatt, *Religious Texts from Ugarit: The Words of Ilimilku and his Colleagues* (The Biblical Seminar 53; Sheffield: Sheffield Academic Press, 1998), 421–22. See also the bibliography on p. 416.

and Phoenicio-Punic child sacrifices. In a small isolated temple in the area of today's Amman airport several thousand human bone fragments and a few animal bone fragments were found.[38] Major bone concentration were found in the in areas of the temple's cella and around an incinerator outside the building. The bones in the temple were fragmentary and burned. Their state of preservation makes an analysis difficult. Some fragments seem to come from a youth 14–18 years old and from a 40 year old woman.[39] The temple was in use only for over a century. And the small number of bodies identified indicates a somewhat occasional use. "There can be little doubt that a major concern of the ritual at the Amman airport temple was the burning of human bodies and the scattering of the remains within the building and possibly outside. There appear to be two possible explanations for the site. It was either a mortuary temple or a temple associated with human sacrifice."[40] In comparison with the bones of a human sacrifice victim found on Crete, the "condition and color of the bones could suggest the burning of freshly slaughtered bodies." Burned bones show a white coloration only if their flesh has been bled before they were burned. Therefore, the corpses from both Crete and Amman must have been slaughtered before they were burned. With some propability, the temple found at the Amman airport was thus dedicated to human sacrifice.[41] In this context, it is of great interest that a significant part the pottery found in and around the Amman temple are of Mycenean or Aegean character.[42] In light of the Cretan human sacrifice, it can be asked if the human sacrifices performed in this temple were

[38] For a description of the temple and a discussion of the bone fragments see John B. Hennessy, "Thirteenth Century B.C. Temple of Human Sacrifice at Amman," in *Phoenicia and its Neighbours: Proceedings of the Colloquium held on the 9th and 10th of December 1983 at the "Vrije Universiteit Brussel," in cooperation with the "Centrum voor Myceense en Archaïsch-Griekse Cultuur"* (ed. E. Gubel; Studia Phoenicia 3; Leuven: Peeters, 1985), 85–104. For earlier discussions of the evidence and an excavation report see George R. H. Wright, "The Bronze Age Temple in Amman," *ZAW* 78 (1966): 350–57; Larry G. Herr, "The Amman Airport Excavations," *ADAJ* 21 (1976): 109–11; and idem, ed., *The Amman Airport Excavations, 1976* (AASOR 48; American Schools of Oriental Research: Winona Lake, Ind., 1983).

[39] See Hennessy, 99.

[40] Hennessy, 99.

[41] Hennessy, 104; see also ibid., 99–100. For the Cretan human sacrifice see Yannis A. Sakellarakis and Efi Sapouna-Sakellarakis, "Drama of Death in a Minoan Temple," *National Geographic* 159, no. 2 (February 1981): 204–22, 213, 218–19, 222; idem, *Archanes: Archanes Excavations* (Athens: Ekdotike Athenon, 1991), 151–56. In case of the body found in Anemopsilia on Crete, there can be no doubt that it was the victim of a human sacrifice. The bones were found on an altar in the inner sanctum. The sacrificial ritual itself was interrupted by an earthquake and the ceiling of the temple fall on the victim (an 18 year old male) shortly after he was slaughtered. For the different bone colorations of burnt bled and unbled corpses see Sakellarakis and Sapouna-Sakellarakis, "Drama," 219.

[42] See Hennessy, 92, 94, 103; see also Vronwy Hankey, "A Late Bronze Age Temple at Amman, I. The Aegean Pottery," *Levant* 6 (1974): 131–159.

influenced by Aegean religion. Regrettably, there is not enough evidence left to answer this question. But should the answer be yes, the differences between Phoenicio-Punic and Israelite human sacrifices on the one hand and Canaanite human sacrifices on the other hand could be due to Aegean influence in Phoenicia and Israel. As in the 13th and 12th century, both areas of later Phoenicia and Israel have been exposed more significantly to the Sea People than e. g. Moab or Transjordania, such a development would be far from astonishing.

Different from Canaanite and Moabite child sacrifice as well as the child sacrifices of the DAT-culture, the Phoenicio-Punic and Israelite sacrifices seem to have been a regular ritual practice. At least with regard to the age of the children sacrificed and with regard to which deity the children have been sacrificed to the Phoenicio-Punic and the Israelite child sacrifices differ, too. As has been shown above, in iron age Israel itself, several different forms of regularly performed child sacrifices can be observed, while no case of an emergency-sacrifice is attested. A significant parallel between the Israelite and Phoenicio-Punic child sacrifices is that at the latest from the 6th century B. C. E. onwards both cultures allowed for a substitution of the children to be sacrificed. But Israel went further than the Phoenicio-Punic culture and at least in post-exilic times forbid child sacrifice all together. And the texts dealing with substitution and redemption of the sacrificial victims and the passages forbidding and / or attacking child sacrifices might give more insight into what form of sacrifice is attacked in Jer 7:31; 19:5 and 32:35.

(end of excursus)

3. Substitution for, Prohibition of, and Polemic against Child Sacrifice

As the Punic and Phoenician cultures, Israelite religion allowed for the substitution of a child to be sacrificed. In exilic and post-exilic times, several religious laws prescribe such substitutes: A good example is a Dtr addition to the Exodus story, Exod 13:2–16.[43] Exod 13:2, 11–13 prescribes:

> (2) Consecrate to me all the firstborn; whatever is the first to open the womb among the Israelites, of human beings and animals, is mine .... (11) When the Lord has brought you into the land of the Canaanites, as he swore to you and your ancestors, and has given it to you, (12) you shall set apart to

[43] For the Dtr character of Exod 13:2, 11–13, see e. g. Martin Noth, *Das 2. Buch Mose: Exodus, Übersetzt und erklärt* (6th ed.; ATD 5; Göttingen: Vandenhoeck & Ruprecht, 1978), 79–80; Brevard S. Childs, *The Book of Exodus: A Critical, Theological Commentary* (OTL; Louisville, Ky.: Westminster, 1974), 184; Erhard Blum, *Studien zur Komposition des Pentateuch* (BZAW 189; Berlin: W. de Gruyter, 1990), 167–68.

> the Lord all that first opens the womb. All the firstborn of your livestock that are males shall be the Lord's. (13) But every firstborn donkey you shall redeem with a sheep; if you do not redeem it, you must break its neck. Every firstborn male among your children you shall redeem.

The priestly source proceeds similarly: Without mentioning passover, Num 18:15–16 prescribes:

> (15) The first issue of the womb of all creatures, human and animal, which is offered to the Lord, shall be yours; but the firstborn of human beings you shall redeem, and the firstborn of unclean animals you shall redeem. (16) Their redemption price, reckoned from one month of age, you shall fix at five shekels of silver, according to the shekel of the sanctuary (that is, twenty gerahs).[44]

In other places, P understands even the Levites as a substitute God takes instead of the firstborn son:

> For they (i. e. the Levites) are unreservedly given to me from among the Israelites; I have taken them for myself, in place of all that open the womb, the firstborn of all the Israelites (Num 8:16).[45]

As in Ezek 20:26, the firstborn children redeemed in Exod 13:2, 11–13; Num 8:16; 18:15–16 are not restricted to the male gender. The use of *peter rekhem* (verb. "everything that breaks out first of the mother's womb") indicates that the law applies both to firstborn sons and to firstborn daughters.

A possible exception to the general practice of redemption might be Neh 10:37:

> Also bring to the house of our God, the firstborn of our sons and of our livestock, as it is written in the law.

On first glimpse, it seems as if the Nehemiah reference does not provide for any redemption. But Joseph Blenkinsopp has rightly pointed

---

[44] For Num 18 as part of P, see e. g. Philip J. Budd, *Numbers* (WBC 5; Waco, Tex.: Word Books, 1984), 201: "analysts are agreed in attributing it to P."

[45] For Num 8:5–26 as part of P, see Budd, 90. Compare also Num 3:11–13.

out: "It is noticeable, however, that the qualification 'as prescribed in the law' refers only to sons and livestock generally, distinguishing these from cattle and sheep which are destined for sacrifice. It may therefore be taken as an implicit allusion to redemption".[46] Another significant difference between Neh 10:37 and Exod 13:2, 11–13; Num 8:16; 18:15–16 remains though. Neh 10:37 concerns only male children.

Finally, in pre-exilic times, a pre-deuteronomistic version of the story of the sacrifice of Isaac (Gen *22:1–19)[47] may argue for a substitution of another form of child sacrifice. It is almost a consensus among the interpreters of Gen 22 that verses 15–18 are a later addition to the Aqedah-story.[48] In v. 15, the way the messenger calls Abraham a second time interrupts the flow of the narrative. It is only continued in v. 19. As opposed to the story told in vv. 1–14, vv. 15–18 provide a theological interpretation of the Aqedah in light of the promises to the patriarchs made elsewhere in the Pentateuch. Because Abraham obeyed god and was even willing to sacrifice his firstborn son, he is worthy of the promises and blessings made earlier and repeated later (compare Gen 22:16 with Gen 26:3 b; Gen 22:17 with Gen 15:3; 24:60; 32:13 and Gen 22:18 with Gen 13:3; 18:18; 26:4; 28:14). In this way, in Gen 22:15–18, the promises made to and the blessings of the patriarchs become conditional. In Gen 22:15–18, the Aqedah story thus mutates to a paradigm of exemplary obedience. The idea that the promises to the patriarchs are conditional and depend on obedience can also be found in the Book of Deuteronomy and in Dtr literature. Like in Gen 22:15–18, in the Book

---

[46] Joseph Blenkinsopp, *Ezra-Nehemiah: A Commentary* (OTL; Philadelphia, Pa.: Westminster Press, 1988), 318; compare e.g. also Hugh G.M. Williamson, *Ezra, Nehemiah* (WBC 16; Waco, Tex.: Word Books, 1985), 337.

[47] For Gen 22:1–19 and its interpretative history see Frédéric Manns, ed., *The Sacrifice of Isaac in the Three Monotheistic Religions: Proceedings of a Symposium on the Interpretation of the Scriptures Held in Jerusalem, March 16–17, 1995* (Studium Biblicum Franciscanum Analecta 41; Jerusalem: Franciscan Printing Press, 1995); and Edward Noort and Eibert J. C. Tigchelaar, eds., *The Sacrifice of Isaac: The Aqedah (Genesis 22) and its Interpretations* (Themes in Biblical Narrative 4; Leiden: Brill, 2002).

[48] See e.g. Gerhard von Rad, *Das erste Buch Mose: Genesis, übersetzt und erklärt* (11th ed.; ATD 2–4; Göttingen: Vandenhoeck & Ruprecht, 1981), 192–93; Claus Westermann, *Genesis*, vol. 2: *Genesis 12–36*, part 2: *Gen 21,8–36,43* (3rd ed.; BKAT 1.2.2; Neukirchen-Vluyn: Neukirchener, 2003), 434, 445; Erhard Blum, *Die Komposition der Vätergeschichte* (WMANT 57; Neukirchen-Vluyn: Neukirchener, 1984), 320; David M. Carr, *Reading the Fractures of Genesis: Historical and Literary Approaches* (Louisville, Ky.: Westminster John Knox, 1996), 153–59; Horst Seebass, *Genesis II: Vätergeschichte I (11,27–22,24)* (Neukirchen-Vluyn: Neukirchener, 1997), 200.

of Deuteronomy and in the Deuteronomistic History, it is the call to obedience on which the fulfillment of the promises rests. The Dtr character of the addition in Gen 22:15–18 is further confirmed by the fact, that like Gen 22:15–18 Deuteronomy understands the promise of the land as an oath of God (see Deut 1:8, 15; 6:10, 18, 23; 7:8, 13; 8:1; 9:5; 10:11; 11:9, 21; 19:8; 26:3, 15; 28:11; 30:20; 31:7, 20, 21; 34:4). Gen 22:15–18 are thus part of a Dtr redaction which links the Aqedah to the rest of the Pentateuch and interprets the patriarchal promises and blessings as conditional depending on the obedience of Israel.

Therefore, Gen 22:1–14, 19 represents a pre-deuteronomistic story belonging to the Pentateuch's Non-P material. How is the sacrifice of Isaac understood in this earlier narrative? This version of the story mentions neither obedience nor reward. The main point of the story is made in the words of the angel addressed to Abraham in vv. 12–13.

> He said: "Do not lay your hand on the boy or do anything to him; for now I know that you fear God, since you have not withheld your son, your only son, from me." And Abraham looked up and saw a ram, caught in the thicket by its horns. Abraham went and took the ram and offered it up as a burnt offering instead of his son. (Gen 22:12–13)

What is essential is the fear of God. It is not the sacrifice of Isaac but Abraham's fear of god that matters. But fear of God does not need to be expressed by an actual child sacrifice. God accepts a ram instead. In its older version, Gen 22:1–14, 19 thus argues for a substitution of the child to be sacrificed by an animal.[49]

The sacrifice of Isaac itself is described as a burnt offering (*ʿlh*). And although the phrases used by Dtn / Dtr literature as well as by P to describe the sacrifice of a child (*hʿbyr, śrp bʾš*) are not used in Gen *22:1–14, 19, and although Abraham wants to slaughter Isaac before he burns him, the fact that Isaac is supposed to be burnt brings the ritual described closest to the molk-sacrifice. The differences between Gen *22:1–14, 19 and the molk-sacrifice are most probably due to either original narrator's or a later redactor's lack of knowledge about the details of a molk-sacrifice.

[49] See e.g. the interpretation of Edward Noort, "Genesis 22: Human Sacrifice and Theology in the Hebrew Bible," in *The Sacrifice of Isaac: The Aqedah (Genesis 22) and its Interpretations* (eds. E. Noort and E. J. C. Tigchelaar; Themes in Biblical Narrative 4; Leiden: Brill, 2002), 1–20. For a different interpretation of Gen 22:1–14, 19 emphasizing the infinite character of God, see the contribution of Michela Bauks to this volume.

As the Pentateuch's non-P material is notoriously difficult to date, about the date of the original story no more can be said than that it might be pre-exilic. This means, that with the possible exception of Gen *22:1–14, 19, for ancient Israel, documentation for a substitution of child sacrifices starts at the same time as it starts in the Phoenician and Punic cultures, i. e. in the 6th century B. C. E.

But different from the Phoenician and Punic cultures, from exilic times onwards, child sacrifice was even forbidden in Israel. Should there be any historical truth to the brief note in 2 Kgs 23:10,[50] in Israel, child sacrifices were first abolished as part of Josiah's religious reforms. Although it seems quite possible that his successors revived the practice. Israel's rejection of child sacrifice is well documented by the Dtr polemics and laws mentioned at the beginning of this article. And the same prohibition of child sacrifice can also be found in the post-exilic Holiness Code Lev 17–26.[51] In this part of the Pentateuch's Priestly Source, Lev 18:21 (compare Lev 20:2–5)[52] reads,

> You shall not give any of your offspring to sacrifice them as a Molk, and so profane the name of your God: I am the Lord.

An examination of all prohibitions of child sacrifice reveals though, that the only form of child sacrifice attacked or forbidden is the molk-sacrifice. Although the law prescribing it is judged negatively in Ezek 20:25–26, no actual prohibition of the offering of the firstborn can be found. But this does not mean, that in exilic or post-exilic times firstborns were still sacrificed to Yhwh. Just the opposite, instead of a prohibition of the sacrifice of the firstborn, Jewish religious law provided for a redemption.[53] A prohibition of this type of sacrifice was thus unnecessary.

It can be concluded: In cases of crisis and emergency, already late bronze age Canaan practiced child sacrifices. The temple excavated at the Amman airport suggests that in addition to child sacrifices in emer-

---

50 See Gray, 735–36; Iain. W. Provan, *1 and 2 Kings* (NIBCOT; Peabody, Mass.: Hendrickson and Paternoster: 1995), 272–73; Koch, 37–41. Ernst Würthwein, *Die Bücher der Könige: 1. Kön. 17–2. Kön. 25, übersetzt und erklärt* (ATD 11.2; Göttingen: Vandenhoeck & Ruprecht, 1984), 459, regards the verse as part of a later idealization of king Josiah added by DtrN.

51 For the Holiness Code as a part of P, see e. g. Frank Crüsemann, *Die Tora: Theologie und Sozialgeschichte des alttestamentlichen Gesetzes* (München: Chr. Kaiser, 1992), 323–29.

52 For Lev 18:21 and 20:2–5, see Kaiser, 160–62.

53 For a discussion of the redemption of the firstborn in contemporary Judaism, see the contribution of Yaakov Ariel to this volume.

gencies, probably due to Aegean influence, a somewhat more regularly performed form of human sacrifice was practiced, too. Several of the iron age Canaanite successor cultures, i. e. the DAT-culture, Phoenicia, Israel, and Moab continued the practice of child sacrifice but developed their own specific forms. In Israel, child sacrifices to YHWH were practiced until late pre-exilic times. At least three different forms of child sacrifice can be distinguished in pre-exilic Israel, the sacrifice of a child in fulfillment of a vow, the molk-sacrifice, and the sacrifice of the firstborn child. The sacrifice of the firstborn was either concerned only with the firstborn son or with both the firstborn daughter and / or son. All other forms of Israelite child sacrifice were not gender specific. At the latest in exilic times, for the sacrifice of the firstborn, Dtr and non-Dtr texts allow for an animal substitute and prohibit the other forms of child sacrifice. Starting with Josiah's reforms and becoming dominant in exilic times, what was once an indigenous part of Israel's YHWH-cult was excluded by Deuteronomism from Israel's religion as pagan. In its laws concerned with child sacrifice, the priestly source leaves no doubt that the Dtr polemics were convincing. In Israelite-Jewish literature, from exilic times onwards, no evidence for child sacrifices can be found anymore.

4. Child Sacrifice in the Dtr Jeremiah-Redaction

How does the history of child sacrifice in Israelite religion relate to the three references to child sacrifice in the Dtr Jeremiah redaction? Jer 7:31; 19:5 and 32:35 do not restrict the sacrifice to firstborn and the polemics of these three references do not refer to an emergency or a vow connected with the child sacrifices. Therefore, as elsewhere in Dtr literature the child sacrifice attacked by the DtrJer redaction is the molk-sacrifice. This is confirmed by the phrase *lammolekh* ("as a molk-sacrifice") in Jer 32:35. In my opinion, the overall pre-exilic evidence for child sacrifices to YHWH as well as texts like Gen 22:*1–19 make it feasible that the molk-sacrifice attacked in Jer 7:31; 19:5 and 32:35 was dedicated to YHWH.[54] But why do Jer 19:5 and 32:35 claim the children have been sacrificed to Baal?

The way how the name Baal is used in the Book of Jeremiah provides an answer to this question. On the one hand, Baal is mentioned when the different layers of the Book of Jeremiah accuse Israel of the

[54] See e. g. Kaiser, 157–58.

veneration of other deities (Jer 7:9; 9:13; 11:13, 17; 23:13). At least some of these references go back to the prophet himself while others are part of the DtrJer or other later redactions. On the other hand, Baal can be used as a polemic term designating syncretism and pagan piety as such. In this way, it is often used to attack a religious practice that was part of Israel's YHWH cult. The word Baal is thus part of an anti-language and serves as a metaphor disqualifying anything which opposes monolatric or henotheistic YHWHism.[55] For example, in Jer 2:8, Jeremiah's prophetic opponents are accused of prophecying in the name of Baal although texts like Jer 28 show that they have been YHWH-prophets. Even more so, in Jer 2:23 the person accused of Baal worship claims not to have gone after Baal. And in the Dtr verse Jer 9:13,[56] what qualifies as walking after the Baalim is following one's own heart stubbornly but not YHWH's law. Here, Baal equals the stubbornness of the criticized.

In which way is Baal used in Jer 19:5 and 32:35? In these two verses, the meaning of Baal is determined by the disclaimer "which I did not command or decree." YHWH's clarification that he did not command child sacrifices implies that somebody actually claimed so. Why should YHWH otherwise clarify that he did not command a child sacrifice to Baal?[57] Furthermore, although in Jer 7:16–20, Israel is accused of worshipping other gods, Jer 7:31 speaks only about the high place of the tophet and not about Baal. In Jer 7:21–26, v. 7:31 is proceeded by the polemics against Israel's YHWH cult. Should the child sacrifices mentioned in Jer 7:31 have been made to Baal, it would have been much more appropriate for the Dtr redactor who wrote the temple speech to place Jer 7:31 after Jer 7:16–20, i. e. to continue the polemics against Israel's veneration of the queen of heaven with an attack of child sacrifices made to Baal. Furthermore, like Jer 19:5 and 32:35, Jer 7:31 emphasizes, that YHWH did not command child sacrifices. Therefore, Jer 7:31 must be understood as attacking Israelites who actually sacrificed children do YHWH. In turn, in Jer 19:5 and 32:35, the claim that Israel sacrificed children to Baal is

---

[55] Jörg Jeremias, "Der Begriff 'Baal' im Hoseabuch und seine Wirkungsgeschichte," in: idem, *Hosea und Amos: Studien zu den Anfängen des Dodekaprophetons* (FAT 13; Tübingen: J. C. B. Mohr [Paul Siebeck], 1996), 86–103, 96–100; Mosca, 230–31; William Robert Domeris, " When Metaphor Becomes Myth: A Socio-Linguistic Reading of Jeremiah," in *Troubling Jeremiah* (eds. A. R. P. Diamond, K. M. O'Conner, and L. Stulman; JSOTSup 260; Sheffield: Sheffield Academic Press, 1999), 244–262, 257–260; Norin, 77.

[56] For the Dtr character of Jer 9:13 see e. g. Wanke, 106.

[57] See e. g. Kaiser, 157; Marc S. Smith, 132.

a polemic disqualification of a YHWHistic sacrifice as non-YHWHistic. The Dtr Jeremiah redaction discredits these YHWHistic child sacrifices as sacrifices to Baal. This polemic agrees well with the approach to child sacrifice found elsewhere in Dtr literature (see e. g. Deut 12:31; 18:10).

But why does the Dtr Jeremiah redaction mention child sacrifices at all? And in Jer 7:21–34, why links the Dtr Jeremiah redaction Israel's temple cult with the practice of child sacrifice? To answer these questions, the dating of the Dtr Jeremiah redaction as well as its aims and opponents need to be discussed. Elsewhere, I have shown that in Jer 14:13, the Dtr Jeremiah redaction argues with Hag 2:9 and Zech 8:19.[58] The Dtr paragraph Jer 14:10–16 would thus attack the preaching and the Zion theology of the prophets Haggai and Zechariah. Which in turn means that the Dtr Jeremiah redaction was written shortly before or during the rebuilding of the Jerusalem temple 520–515 B. C. E. In my opinion, the DtrJer has dual aim. On the one hand, it explains the Babylonian exile as a consequence of Israel's behavior in pre-exilic times. On the other hand, it argues against a rebuilding of the Jerusalem temple by way of reasoning with the consequences which Zion theology evoked in the years 597 and 587 B. C. E. In the opinion of the Dtr Jeremiah redaction, the hope for a magical protection of Jerusalem due to its temple and sacrificial cult, has been one of the reasons for the destruction of Jerusalem in 587 B. C. E. In the temple theology of Haggai and Zechariah, the Dtr Jeremiah redaction sees the same opinions resurfacing. Again, a sacrificial cult promised to end natural disasters like a famine (Hag 1:2–11; 2:15–19). As soon as the temple would have been built, the nations would do pilgrimage to Mt. Zion (Zech 8:20–23) and their wealth would come to it (Hag 2:7–9).

Only a few verses before the attack on child sacrifice in Jer 7:31, Jer 7:22 argues against the sacrificial cult connected with these hopes:

> For in the day that I brought your ancestors out of the land of Egypt, I did not speak to them or command them concerning burnt offerings and sacrifices.

It is not the sacrificial cult which the God of Israel commanded, but it is obedience he asked for (Jer 7:23). It is not a temple and the sacrifices made in it which Israel should trust in. It is not from them, by way of magic rituals, that Israel will receive salvation. Instead, it should follow

58 See above.

the commands given to it.[59] The polemics of the Dtr Jeremiah redaction against child sacrifice are thus part of its rejection of the resurfacing Jerusalem cult and its Zion theology. Child sacrifice functions as a negative paradigm in the extreme. It demonstrates to what unbelievable length the sacrificial cult is willing to go to magically achieve its goals of salvation and protection.

This disqualification of the Jerusalem cult by way of child sacrifice is not exceptional. Likewise, a Dtr addition to the book of Micah (6:6–8) compares the sacrificial cult of the Jerusalem temple with child sacrifices:[60]

> (6) "With what shall I come before the Lord,
> and bow myself before God on high?
> Shall I come before him with burnt offerings,
> with calves a year old?
> (7) Will the Lord be pleased with thousands of rams,
> with ten thousands of rivers of oil?
> Shall I give my firstborn for my transgression,
> the fruit of my body for the sin of my soul?"
> (8) He has told you, O mortal, what is good; and what does the Lord require of you but to do justice, and to love kindness, and to walk humbly with your God?

That both the Dtr Jeremiah redaction and the Dtr Micah redaction argue in the same way against the temple cult suggests that the Dtr Jeremiah redaction's rejection of the revived Zion theology and the rebuilding of the temple was not an isolated effort. But to follow this line of argument leads beyond the scope of this article.

---

[59] For this interpretation of Jer 7:1–8:3, see Armin Lange, "Gebotsobservanz statt Opferkult: Zur Kultpolemik in Jer 7,1–8,3," in *Gemeinde ohne Tempel—Community without Temple: Zur Substituierung und Transformation des Jerusalemer Tempels und seines Kults im Alten Testament, antiken Judentum und frühen Christentum* (eds. B. Ego, A. Lange, and P. Pilhofer; WUNT 118; Tübingen: Mohr Siebeck, 1999), 19–35.

[60] For this passage see Hans Walter Wolff, *Micah: A Commentary* (trans. by G. Stansell; CC; Minneapolis, Minn.: Augsburg, 1990), 177–184; Alexander B. Ernst, *Weisheitliche Kultkritik: Zu Theologie und Ethik des Sprüchebuchs und der Prophetie des 8. Jahrhunderts* (Biblisch-Theologische Studien 23; Neukirchen-Vluyn: Neukirchener, 1994), 186–97; Rainer Kessler, *Micha: Übersetzt und ausgelegt* (HTKAT; Freiburg i.B.: 1999), 266–272.

Molek: Dead or Alive?

The Meaning and Derivation of *mlk* and מלך

BENNIE H. REYNOLDS, University of North Carolina

> You shall not give any of your offspring to sacrifice them to Molech, and so profane the name of your God: I am the LORD
>
> (Lev. 18:21, NRSV)

Leviticus 18:21 is the first of several mentions in the Hebrew Bible of a child sacrifice directed למלך.[1] Through the course of history, most interpreters have chosen to read למלך in precisely the same way that the NRSV chooses to: a compound of the preposition ל and a divine name מלך. Certain archaeological discoveries at the beginning of the 20th century, however, have modified our understanding of what the term למלך might have originally connoted. After nearly a century of debate, however, the question still remains: Was a god named Molek offered (human) sacrifices in Israel?

Serious discussion of the question began properly in 1935 with a monograph by Otto Eissfeldt.[2] His daring title, "Molk as Sacrificial-term in Punic and Hebrew and the End of the God Molok," declared that such a god was a later invention. Several contributions have been made to the subject over the last three quarters of the century, but there has been a renewed interest since the mid-1980's. Three major books have appeared in the last 25 years,[3] and three articles and/or book chapters

---

[1] Lev 18:21, 20:2–5; 1 Kgs 11:7; 2 Kgs 23:10; Jer 32:35.

[2] Otto Eissfeldt, *Molk als Opferbegriff im Punischen und Hebräischen und das Ende des Gottes Moloch* (Halle: Max Niemeyer, 1935).

[3] John Day, *Molech: A God of Human Sacrifice in the Old Testament* (New York: Cambridge University Press, 1989). George C. Heider, *The Cult of Molek: A Reassessment*, JSOTSup 43 (Sheffield: JSOT Press, 1985). Paul G. Mosca, "Child Sacrifice in Canaanite and Israelite Religion: A Study in Mulk and מלך" (Unpublished Harvard PhD diss, 1975). Only the first two of these books has been published, but I have received personal communication from the author of the third that it is soon to be published.

dealing with the subject have appeared in the 90's.[4] This paper will offer evidence why the Phoenician / Punic term *mlk* as well as the Hebrew term למלך are best explained as causative participles of the root *hlk*—not as divine names. This will be accomplished in four steps: (I) Gleaning pieces of research from published work and grafting together important elements, (II) Submitting some previously unconsidered evidence (or significant reinterpretations of some evidence) with respect to several Phoenician inscriptions, (III) Offering some fresh insights on several pieces of Biblical evidence, and (IV) Consideration of possible attestations of the sacrificial term *mlk* in Anatolia and the Levant.

I.

The first synthesis of research was presented by Eissfeldt. A small background to his position is needed. Since at least 1921, scholars have claimed to have found *tophetim*.[5] These are purported to be sites of child sacrifice (or at least the burial grounds of sacrificed children) throughout the Phoenician-Punic world, including mainland Phoenicia.[6] These sites were first identified based on the accounts of classical authors as

[4] Edward Lipinski, "Rites et sacrifices dans la tradition Phénico-Punique," in *Ritual and Sacrifice in the Ancient Near East: Proceedings of the International Conference organized by the Katholieke Universiteit Leuven from the 17th to the 20th of April 1991*, ed. J. Quaegebeur (Leuven: Peeters, 1993), 257–81. Klaas Smelik, "Moloch, Molekh or Molk-Sacrifice? A Reassessment of the Evidence Concerning the Hebrew Term Molekh," *SJOT* 9 (1995): 133–42. Klaus Koch, "Molek astral," in *Mythos im Alten Testament und Seiner Umwelt: Festschrift für Hans-Peter Müller zum 65. Geburtstag*, eds. Armin Lange, Hermann Lichtenberger, and Diethard Römheld (New York: Walter de Gruyter, 1999), 29–50.

[5] 1921 refers to the discovery of the *tophet* at Carthage. In reality, two others had already been discovered unwittingly at Nora (1889) and Motya (1919). It was the discovery at Carthage that marked a new moment in the discussion. Cf. Michel Gras, Pierre Rouillard, and Javier Teixidor, "The Phoenicians and Death," trans. Helga Seeden, *Ber* XXXIX (1991): 127–76, esp. 150–52.

[6] Ibid., 150 ff. Also, William F. Albright, *Yahweh and the Gods of Canaan: A Historical Analysis of Two Contrasting Faiths* (Winona Lake, Indiana: Eisenbrauns, 1968), 237–44. Shelby Brown, *Late Carthaginian Child Sacrifice and Sacrificial Monuments in their Mediterranean Context*, JSOR / ASOR Monograph Series 3 (Sheffield: Sheffield Academic Press, 1991), 37–75. John Andrew Dearman, "The Tophet in Jerusalem: Archaeology and Cultural Profile," *JNSL* 22 / 1 (1996): 59–71. Helga Seeden, "A Tophet in Tyre?" *Ber* XXXIX (1991): 39–82. Colette Picard, "Le Monument de Nebi-Yunis," *RB* 83 (1976): Charles Kennedy, "Tartessos, Tarshish and Tartarus: Tower of Pozo Moro and the Bible," (unpublished essay presented to the First International Meeting of the Society of Biblical Literature, Salamanca, Spain, 1983), quoted extensively in Heider, *The Cult of Molek*, 189–92. Lawrence Stager and Samuel R. Wolff, "Child Sacrifice at Carthage: Religious Rite

well as the descriptions of the site(s) in the Hebrew bible. The word *tophet* (תפת) is a Hebrew word used as a matter of convenience. There is no attestation of the word in Phoenician or Punic inscriptions.

Eissfeldt worked with inscriptions found on stelae at many *tophetim*. In these incscriptions, the term *mlk* appears often. Generally, *mlk* and its variations in the Semitic world are understood to be descriptive of royalty or even divinity.[7] Because of their frequency, however, three particular word combinations with *mlk* have puzzled scholars. The three expressions are *mlkʾmr*[8] *mlk ʾdm*,[9] and *mlk bʿl*[10]. Based on the inscriptions, Eissfeldt asserted that *mlk* was a sacrificial term.[11]

He began working with the terms *morcomor, morchomor, mochomor, and molchomor* which were found on Latin inscriptions from Ngaous (North Africa).[12] Previous scholarship had determined all of these to be variants of *molchomor* which would mean, "Gelübde, Opfer eines Schafes" ("A

---

or Population Control," *BAR* 10 (1984): 30–51. Lawrence Stager, "Carthage: A View from the Tophet," in *Phönizier im Westen* (Mainz: Philipp von Zabern, 1982), 159–61.

7 Indeed, some scholars who consider *tophetim* nothing more than infant cemetaries consider the term *mlk* to be nothing more than that. Cf. Helene Benichou-Safar, *Les tombes puniques De Carthage: Topographie, structures, inscriptions et rites funeraires* (Paris: Centre National de la Recherche Scientifique, 1982), 343. See also her article, "A propos des ossements humains du Tophet," in *Rivista di Studi Fenici* IX (Rome: Consiglio Nazionale dele Richerche, 1981), 5–9. Sergio Ribichine, "Beliefs and Religious Life," in *The Phoenicians*, ed. Sabatino Moscati, (New York: Rizzoli, 1998), 120–44, esp. 139–41. Ribichine does not deny that children were ever sacrificed, but holds that the practice was probably reserved for the most dire of circumstances. Generally, the idea of a child-necropolis seems appealing to him. Sabatino Moscati, *Il sacrificio Punico dei Fanciullu: Realtà o invenzione?*, (Rome: Accademia Nazionale dei Lincei, 1987). Moshe Weinfeld, "The Worship of Molech and of the Queen of Heaven and Its Background," *UF* 4 (1972): 133–54. Though see the comments by Berger which Heider rightly regards as prophetic, "non pas un titre divin, ni un titre royal, ni un ethnique, mais la designation de l'objet offert en sacrifice." Philippe Berger, "Les inscriptions de Constantine au Musée du Louvre," *Actes du onzième congrès international des orientalistes* (1897) 4th section (reprint; Nendeln / Liechtenstein: Kraus, 1968 [orig. 1898]). See also Heider, *The Cult of Molek*, 28–29.

8 This expression has been found on one stela at Carthage, three at Cirta, and one at Malta. Cf. Brown, LATE CARTHAGINIAN CHILD SACRIFICE, 29–32.

9 Multiple stelae at Cirta, one at Altiburus. Brown, Late Carthaginian Child Sacrifice, 32.

10 Numerous stelae at Carthage, Motya, and Sulcis, as well as two stelae from Sousse. Brown, *Late Carthaginian Child Sacrifice*, 32–33.

11 Eissfeldt did so based on work of Gsell, Chabot, and Carcopino which had not yet been tied together. For a marvelously thorough survey of the history of scholarship on this topic, see Heider, *The Cult of Molek*, 1–92.

12 Stéphane Gsell, *Atlas Archéologique de l'Algérie* (Alger / Paris: Jourdan 1911), leaf 26, no. 161. See idem, *Inscriptions latines de l'Algérie recueilles et publiées* (Paris: Champion, 1922–57).

vow, an offering of a lamb").[13] In making the same claim, however, Eissfeldt offered much more evidence for why *mlk* should not be read as a divine or royal title. His move is nicely described by Heider:

> Eissfeldt's crucial observation was that such references occurred at widely different places in the word order of the inscriptions, whether right after the name(s) of the god(s) to whom the gift was made (which regularly occur first in the texts), or after the name(s) of the human offerer(s), or near the end of the entire inscription (14–15, 23). This presented a syntactical conundrum, so long as one assumed that in all cases the *mlk* references were in apposition to the divine names with which the inscriptions began.[14]

Eissfeldt gained further support not only for the idea that *mlk* meant sacrifice, but that *mlk ʾmr* meant "sacrifice of a lamb" from the same Latin inscriptions, one of which read: "*Q(uod) b(onum) et f(austum) f(actum) s(it) d(omino) s(ancto) S(aturno) sacrum ma[gnum]* | *nocturnum anima p[ro]* | *anima sang(uine) pro san(guine)* | *vita pro vita pro Con[cess|a]⸢e⸣ salutem ex viso et vot[o]* | *[sa]crum reddiderunt* | *[molcho]mor Felix et ⸢D⸣iod⸢ora⸣* | *[lib]⸢ent⸣[es anim]o ⸢a⸣[gnum pro vikario]*."[15] The designation, "*anima pro anima, sanguine pro sanguine, vita pro vita . . . agnum pro vicario*" seems quite decisively to designate *ʾmr* as a lamb. "Breath for breath, blood for blood, life for life . . . a lamb as substitute."[16] Felix and Diodora sacrificed a lamb in place of their daughter, Concessa. What Eissfeldt apparently did

---

[13] Eissfeldt, *Molk als Opferbegriff*, 12. The "previous scholarship" refers largely to Chabot who makes these remarks in a supplementary note to Gsell's article. The *mlk ʾmr* inscriptions known to Chabot were *CIS* I. 307 and *JA* 10 / 11 (1917): 49–50, no. 58. Many more are now known.

[14] Heider, *The Cult of Molek*, 35. A nice example of the phenomenon isolated by Eissfeldt is *lʿdn lbʿl ḥmn ndr ʾš nʿdr ʾdnbʿl bn ʿbdʾšmn mlk ʾdm bšrm bnʿ tm šmʾ qlʾ brkʾ* = "To the Lord, to Baal-Hammon, a vow which Adonbaal son of Abdeshmun vowed, an offering of a man, his own child, his son in perfect condition. He heard his voice, he blessed him." See *KAI* 107 as well as Day's translation, *Molech*, 5. Day also reminds us that while Eissfeldt himself actually read *mlk ʾdm* as "offering of a layperson (not a priest)," the parallel nature of *mlk ʾmr* and *mlk ʾdm* seem to beg Day's translation. See Day, *Molech*, 5 n. 6.

[15] Eissfeldt, *Molk als Opferbegriff*, 3–4 @. The Latin inscriptions from Ngaous have been consistently dated between the 2nd and 3rd centuries C. E.

[16] It seems even clearer now that both Chabot and Eissfeldt were correct to understand *ʾmr* as lamb. We now have profuse cognate evidence: Ugar. *imr*; Akk. *immeru(m)*; Anc. Aram. אמר; Bib. Aram. אִמַּר; Emp. Aram. אמר; Jew. Aram. אִמְּרָא; Syr. *ʾemraʾ*; Mand. *ʾmbra*; Arab. *ʾimmarun*. See Richard S. Tomback, *A Comparative Semitic Lexicon of the Phoenician and Punic Languages*, SBL Diss. Series 32 (Missoula, Montana: Scholars Press, 1978), 24.

not know and has been pointed out by Mosca helps his case even more. Stelae I, II, III, and IV at Ngaous all bear representations of a ram.[17]

While Eissfeldt's contribution to the concept of *mlk* was large, he left work to be done. As scholars have noted, he perceived his own translation of *mlkbʿl* and *mlkʾdm* to be problematic. He basically considered both *bʿl* and *ʾdm* as offerers rather than offerings. Newer research, however, has gone farther in establishing both *ʾdm* and *bʿl* as genitive objects of *mlk*. Roland de Vaux seems to have settled *mlkʾdm* as a human offering with his translation of the inscription "*mlkʾdm bšrm btm*" "A human sacrifice, his own child, totally."[18] Thus, for de Vaux, *mlkʾmr* and *mlkʾdm* were parallel terms, one for animals and the other for humans.[19]

Mosca has taken *mlkʾmr, mlkʾdm*, and *mlkbʿl* and posited that they mean respectively, sacrifice of a lamb (as substitute), sacrifice of a commoner, and sacrifice of a noble. For Mosca, *mlk bʿl* and *mlk ʾdm* are both parallel to *mlkʾmr* and they represent respectively the upper and lower social classes. Mosca employs Diodorus and Plutarch to help make the connection. "Diodorus … explained how 'in former times' the Carthaginians sacrificed 'the noblest of their sons,' but more recently, secretly buying and nurturing children, they had sent these to the sacrifice."[20] He adds, "According to Plutarch, 'those who had no children would buy little ones from poor people and cut their throats as if they were so many lambs or young birds.' "[21]

The respective monographs of Heider and Day appeared almost simultaneously and around ten years after Mosca's dissertation. Heider takes a wide survey of the ancient Near East to find parallels for a god named *mlk*.[22] He concludes, based on inscriptions from the Ancient Near East (especially two from Ugarit) that there was indeed a god named *Molek* which the Hebrew Bible refers to.[23] Both he and Day ac-

[17] Mosca, "Child Sacrifice," 59.

[18] De Vaux does so by using bilingual, Latino-Punic inscriptions of Tripolitania to establish an equivalence between *btm* and *pro pecunia sua*. Roland de Vaux, *Studies in Old Testament Sacrifice* (Cardiff: University of Wales Press, 1964), 78.

[19] See Mosca's discussion, "Child Sacrifice", 67.

[20] Mosca, "Child Sacrifice", 76.

[21] Ibid.

[22] Heider, *The Cult of Molek*, chap. 11, esp. 115–28.

[23] There is no room for a full discussion of this point, however, I disagree that one can locate a god named *mlk* in the Ugaritic Literature. Cf. Theodore Lewis, *Cults of the Dead in Ancient Israel and Ugarit*, HSM 39 (Atlanta: Scholars Press, 1989) and Mark Smith, *The Early History of God: Yahweh and the Other Deities in Ancient Israel*, 2nd ed. (Grand Rapids: Eerdmans, 2002), 178–80.

cept Eissfeldts's argument that *mlk* is a sacrificial term in Punic inscriptions. He claims, however, that the practice was strictly intra-Punic.[24] Like Heider, Day argues that there was a god named *mlk* in the northern Levant who is the same one mentioned in the Hebrew Bible. For him, the particular form of מלך (i. e., למלך) militates against Eissfeldt and Mosca's reading of the word as a sacrificial term in the Hebrew Bible. He and Heider share the opinion that the Phoenician-Punic *mlk* sacrifices neither originated in the Phoenician homeland nor ever made it back. Yet, given what the epigraphic evidence says about the contents of the tens of thousands of urns at Phoenician / Punic *tophetim* the burden of explaining Biblical parallels remains theirs.

Every scholar I have mentioned so far considers all Levantine occurrences of *mlk* to derive from the radicals *mlk*. Day, however, considers the Punic references to *mlk* actually to derive from the root *hlk*.[25] Given the very similar contexts (i. e., sacrificial) of the usages of *mlk* in both Phoenician-Punic inscriptions and the Bible it seems fruitful to ask whether or not the Biblical references could derive from the root *hlk*. This proposal was actually made quite a long time ago. Unfortunately, it seems to have been largely ignored by those writing on the subject.

In an early review of Eissfeldt, Wolfram von Soden proposed that the term *mlk* in both Phoenician-Punic and Biblical contexts was taken from the root *hlk*. It is my contention that his position deserves a fresh look.[26] Von Soden's own proposal takes the thesis as almost self-evident and provides little discussion. He simply states: "Ich möchte daher in מֹלֶךְ vielmehr eine Defektivschreibung für מוֹלֶךְ sehen und das Wort dann von der Wurzel הלך ‚gehen' ableiten."[27] ("I prefer, rather, to see in מֹלֶךְ a defective spelling of מוֹלֶךְ and to derive the word from the root הלך 'to go.' ")

---

[24] Heider, *The Cult of Molek*, 185–88, 401.

[25] Day, *Molech*, 8.

[26] Wolfram von Soden, "A Review of Otto Eissfeldt: *Molk als Opferbegriff im Punischen und Hebräischen und das Ende des Gottes Moloch*," *TLZ* 3 (1936): 45–46. Albrecht Alt also briefly championed this idea in "Die Phönikischen Inschriften von Karatepe," *WO* 1 (1949): 581–87. However, Alt later withdrew this assertion. Also, in 1994 Smelik took up this view, however, he offers no new evidence and is simply willing to follow von Soden and Day. Since Day insists that the derivation of *mlk* from *hlk* is valid only for Phoenician-Punic inscriptions, it is interesting that Smelik would adopt this opinion without comment. Smelik, "Moloch, Mokekh, or Molk-Sacrifice?," 133–42.

[27] Von Soden, *TLZ* 3 (1936): 46.

The most recent defense of the proposal has come from Hans-Peter Müller.[28] Müller makes it clear that a number of 'motion' verbs in causative form are understood in terms of cultic offering in both Hebrew and Phoenician / Punic. (E.g., hiphil of עלה in Hebrew: Gen 8:20, 22:2 and of *ʿlʾ* [< *ʿly*] in Punic: Platus, *Poenulus*, 934).[29] This is true particularly for *hlk*.[30] Müller points out as exemplar a Phoenician inscription from Karatepe. I will begin part two of this project by offering a new translation of that inscription plus two other inscriptions that Müller does not discuss. All three of these inscriptions contain a causative use of the verb *hlk* meaning "to offer."

II.

The Karatepe inscriptions found in Anatolia are bilingual. They were written in Phoenician and hieroglyphic Luwian and date to the 8th century B. C. E.[31] The text of the inscriptions amounts to royal propaganda on the part of a certain king *ʾztwd*. The fortress containing the inscriptions was apparently destroyed by either Shalmanassar V around 720 B. C. E. or Essarhadon around 680 B. C. E.[32] In the section of the inscription that I am presenting, *ʾztwd* boasts about building the city (or citadel) where the inscription is located and dedicating it to *Baʿal krntryš* (whom he had given credit for establishing his reign earlier in the text). He furthermore outlines the cultic procedures that he plans to follow in gratefulness to *Baʿal krntryš*.

wbn ʾnk hqrt z št
ʾnk šm ʾztwdy yšb ʾnk bn
bʿl krntryš wylk zbḥ lkl
hmskt zbḥ ymm ʾlp 1 *wbʿ[t ḥ]rš*
š 1 *wbʿt qṣr š* 1

[28] Hans-Peter Müller, "mlk," in *TDOT* VIII, ed. G. Johannes Botterweck, Helmer Ringgren, and Heinz-Josef Fabry, trans. Douglas W. Stott (Grand Rapids, Michigan: William B. Eerdmans, 1984), 375–88.

[29] One may also note the hiphil of עבר in Hebrew and aphel of סלק / נסק in Aramaic. For more semitic references, see Müller, "mlk," 377. See also Mark Smith, "A Note on Burning Babies," *JAOS* 95 (1975): 477–79.

[30] See Tomback, *A Comparative Semitic Lexicon*, 80–81.

[31] See François Bron, *Recherches sur les inscriptions phéniciennes de Karatepe*, HEO **11** (Paris: Droz, 1979), esp. 163–69.

[32] Cf. the website of the Ministry of Culture and Tourism of Turkey: www.kultur.gov.tr/portal/default_EN.asp?BELGENO=723

wabanā ʾanaka haqarīta za šāta
ʾanaka šāma ʾazitiwadiya yyašibu ʾanaka biennu
baʿal karanturyš wayyalik zebaḥ likalu
hamsakot zabaḥa yomama ʾalpu 1 wabʿā[t ḥa]riša
šā 1 wabāʿt qaṣira šā 1

I (re?)built this city,
I named it *ʾAzitiwadiya* (and) I caused
Baʿal *Karanturyš* to dwell in it and I offered a sacrifice to him
at all the sacrifices (festivals?), an ox at the periodic sacrifice,
a sheep in the season of plowing, and a sheep in the season
of harvesting.[33]

The next two inscriptions are a Punic inscription from Carthage and a Neo-Punic inscription from Tripolitania, both of which use the causative form of *hlk* (i. e., *ylk*). For the first inscription, Tomback transcribes *wylk rbm ʾdnbʿl* and translates "and their chiefs *ʾdnbʿl* offered."[34] A section of this inscription is also translated by Charles Krahmalkov in his Phoenician-Punic Dictionary: "Generals Idnibal son of Gisco the Great and Himilco son of Hanno the Great proceeded at dawn; they seized Agrigentum, and they [the Agrigentines] made peace."[35] My translation is very different from both of these renderings for two reasons. First, I read *wylk* "to offer." Second, I read *ʿlš* not as "dawn" but as "sacrifice." The second reading is the critical one. Krahmalkov proposes the Arabic cognate *ghalas* (*ġalas*). This cognate seems rather uncertain to me. I have not found the lexeme in a single Arabic dictionary. It is absolutely *not* found in the Qurʾan or earlier Arabic.[36] It appears that the word may have come into Arabic much too late to be helpful in this discussion. Therefore, I prefer to see the closest parallel with the Hebrew עלה / עלת.

33 KAI 26 A II,17–A III,1. My vocalization and translation. I would like to thank Professor Orval Wintermute and my classmates from a course on Comparative Semitics in the fall of 2003 at Duke University for offering helpful suggestions concerning the vocalization for this and the following inscriptions. My translation is quite different from the transcription and translation of Tomback: *wylk zbḥ lkl hmskt* "And I established (?) a sacrificial order (?) for all the molten images." *A Comparative Semitic Lexicon*, 81.

34 Tomback, *A Comparative Semitic Lexicon*, 81.

35 Charles Krahmalkov, *Phoenician-Punic Dictionary*, OLA 90 (Leuven: Peeters, 2000), 373–74.

36 Cf. Abdul Mannan Omar, *The Dictionary of the Holy Qurʾan*, (Republic of Korea: Noor Foundation, 2003). There is indeed an Arabic word for dawn found in the Qurʾan: *fajr* (*faǧr*). See also Hans Wehr, *A Dictionary of Modern Written Arabic* (Ithaca, NY: Spoken Language Services, 1976).

Indeed the word appears in the form *ʿlt* meaning "sacrifice" in Hebrew, Syriac and the Proto-Siniatic Inscriptions.[37]

> *wylk hrbm ʾdnbʿl bn grskn hrb wḥmlkt bn ḥnʾ hrb ʿlš*
> *wtmk hmt ʾgrgnt wšt [h]mt šlm*
>
> *wayyaliku harabima ʾadonbaʿal bena garaskin haraba waḥamlakot bena ḥannaʾ haraba ʿolaša*
> *watamaku hēmata ʾagraginta wašūtu [hē]mata šalama*
>
> The generals offered Adonbaʿal, son of *Garaskin* the general and *Ḥamlakot* the son of *Ḥannaʾ* the general [as] a sacrifice, then they seized Agrigentum, and the Agrigentines surrendered (made peace).[38]

This Punic inscription from Carthage is quite reminiscent of two texts from the Bible: Judg 11:29–33 and 2 Kgs 3:4–27. The former tells the story of a certain *shopet* of Israel who made a bargain with YHWH. "If you will give the Ammonites into my hand, then whoever comes out of my house to meet me, when I return victorious from the Ammonites, shall be the LORD's, to be offered up by me as a burnt offering" (11:30–31, NRSV). The latter tells the story of King Mesha of Moab being besieged by Israel. When all his security measures failed, it is reported that, "he took his firstborn son who was to succeed him, and offered him as a burnt offering on the wall. And great wrath came upon Israel, so they withdrew from him and returned to their own land" (3:27, NRSV) The evidence for such a practice is even more widespread as we have a pictoral attestation in at least two different Egyptian reliefs of Egyptians conquering Canaanites. One dates to the time of Seti I, the other Ramses II.[39] Each of these reliefs depict children being sacrificed on the city wall as the Egyptian forces move in.

The final inscription I will discuss is part of an ostracon that was found in Tripolitania in 1957. Discussion of it remains confined to Tomback's

[37] See the discussion of the term and its appearances in the form in Ludwig Koehler and Walter Baumgartner, *The Hebrew and Aramaic Lexicon of the Old Testament*, vol. 1 (Leiden: Brill, 2001), 830–31 and 416. Most importantly, see William F. Albright, *The Proto-Sinaitic Inscriptions and Their Decipherment* (Cambridge: Harvard University Press, 1966), 42.

[38] CIS I 5510,9–10. My vocalization and translation.

[39] See Anthony John Spalinger, "A Canaanite Ritual Found in Egyptian Reliefs", *JSSEA* 7 (1978): 47–60. For further discussion cf. Armin Lange in this volume.

Lexicon (other than its original publication in an Italian article from 1964).[40] Based on that article, Tomback transcribes *ylk htm ʾt pry* and translates "the total (?) will produce (?) fruit."[41]

My translation is to be distinguished from both Tomback's and Della Vida's because of two different issues. Unlike Della Vida, I recognize *ʾt* as the direct object marker. Unlike Tomback, I read a bit further in the inscription (two more words).[42] The phrase *kn šlm* could be woodenly translated "to be established in peace." More idiomatically it means "to prosper." Here I understand the verb *kn* to be passive (though an active reading would not necessarily change the sense of the phrase).

> *ylk htm ʾt pry kn šlm*
> *yyalik hatamu ʾet pary kūna šalama*
> The upright one offers fruit and prospers[43]

This inscription does not offer evidence about human sacrifice, but rather the cultic use of the verb *hlk* in the causative stem. Indeed, it is valuable to have an instance of such a phenomenon outside the context of human sacrifice. To that end, one usage of *hlk* from the Hebrew Bible should be mentioned.

III.

There is a usage of הלך in the hiphil stem in Num 17:11 in the context of a cultic act. Here, Aaron is to take sacred items from the altar and "go out" quickly to the congregation and make atonement for them.

> And Moses said to Aaron: Take the censor and put fire on it from the altar and put incense on it and quickly go (וְהוֹלֵךְ) to the congregation and make atonement for them, for wrath has gone out from YHWH—the plague has begun.[44]

---

[40] Giorgio Levi Della Vida, "Ostracon Neopunico dalla Tripolitania," *Or* 33 (1964): 1–14.

[41] Tomback, *A Comparative Semitic Lexicon*, 81. He largely follows the Italian translation found in *Or* 33.

[42] To Tomback's credit, his translation is simply an attempt to give context to an entry in his Lexicon. The meaning of the lexeme *hlk*, however, is significantly clarified in the light of more text.

[43] *Or* 33 (1964): 4, line 6. My transcription, vocalization, and translation. I largely follow the Italian translation found in *Or*.

[44] All Biblical passages are my translation unless otherwise noted.

In light of these passages, it seems clear that the verb *hlk* in the causative stem can be an offering term. I will now see how this possibility accords with the actual form of the word in the Hebrew Bible. Concerning the form of מלך in the *LMLK* passages in the Bible, there is no doubt we are dealing with defective orthography. (I. e., we would rather have *hlk* > *ylk* > *mwlyk* [מוליך]). Müller rightly points out, however, that, "defective orthography of the preformative syllable occurs frequently in derivatives of nouns with *mem*-preformative from I *waw/yod* roots, cf., e. g., *mṣ*ʾ "place or act of going forth,"[45] or *mtnt* "gift."[46]

Concerning vocalization, we would prefer to have the clearly pointed *maqtil* (*Malik*).[47] The form is not completely unexplainable though. There is certainly precedence for a long *o*-vowel in the first syllable of hiphil participles of verbs beginning with *waw* / *yod* in the Hebrew Bible. For example, מוֹלִיךְ in Job 12:17 is derived from הלך, מוליד in Isa 66:9 is derived from ילד, and מוֹרִיד in 2 Sam 22:48 is derived from ירד.[48] When one considers that the word likely was derived from Phoenician where the so-called Canaanite shift from *ā* to *ō* was even more widespread, this should provide no surprise.[49] Dealing with the *segol* in the second syllable is slightly more difficult. What one can say is that it is, like the *hireq* we expect, an *i* class vowel. What we may see is a frozen form of a technical term which entered the language as such. While this is not clean-cut, it is probably a better option than recent revivals of Abraham Geiger's proposal.[50]

Following Geiger, John Day argues that the term *mlk* is a divine name which entered Hebrew vocalized differently (*segol—segol* and was revocalized to reflect the pronunciation of the Hebrew word for shame: בֹּשֶׁת (i. e., *holem—segol*). I would suggest that a powerful argument has already been made against such a proposal by Mosca: "The theory that a form *molek* would immediately suggest to the reader or hearer the word *boset* (rather than *qodes* or *ohel*) is the product of nineteenth century in-

---

[45] While Müller's comments are about Phoenician / Punic morphology, the statement also applies to Hebrew as one finds both *mṣ*ʾ and *mwṣy*ʾ from *yṣ*ʾ in the Hebrew Bible.

[46] Root is *ntn*. See, Müller, "mlk," 377.

[47] Heider offers some evidence for the possibility of a god named Malik at Ebla. Even he admits, however, that only one of his examples may prove correct. I am not convinced that his examples actually contain the divine determinative. Heider, *The Cult of Molek*, 96–101.

[48] See also the hiphil participle of ילד in Jer 16:3.

[49] Cf. Stanislav Segert, *A Grammar of Phoenician and Punic* (München: Beck, 1976), 66 f.

[50] Abraham Geiger, *Urschrift und Übersetzungen der Bibel* (Breslau: Heinauer, 1857), 301.

genuity, not of Massoretic or pre-Massoretic tendentiousness."[51] Mosca further reminds us that Greek versions of Lev 18:21 and 20:2–5 translate ἄρχων instead of βασιλεύς (which one might expect to be the translation of מֶלֶךְ).

Two more points need to be made about the term מלך in the Bible. The first concerns the preposition ל and the second the naming of Baʿal in Jer. A key issue to consider when designating Biblical mentions of מלך as a sacrificial term is the fact that it is preceded by the preposition ל. The form which always occurs in the Hebrew Bible is למלך. Normally, the preposition ל is translated "to" or "for" (so the majority of translations: "to Moloch" or "for Moloch"). Some have noted that the preposition כ should be used if מלך is a sacrifice and not a god. The meaning that ל would be required to have in these situations in order to signify a type of sacrifice and not a deity, however, is well within the bounds of its normal usage in the Hebrew Bible.

The particular usage of ל that my translation makes use of is actually a widespread usage labeled by Ernst Jenni as *Lamed revaluationis*. The basic meaning of this ל is translated into English with the particle "as."[52] Consider the following examples: Exod 2:10, 1 Sam 27:12, Exod 4:3, Isa 5:20, Gen 1:29, Ps 45:17, and Lev 19:18.[53]

> And the child grew and she brought him to (ל) Pharaoh's daughter and he became hers (ל) as (ל) a son, and she called his name Moses and she said, "For from the waters I drew him."

In Exod 2:10 there are three distinct uses of the preposition ל. The first ל represents the most common usage in the Hebrew Bible, it points to a dative object. This is normally signified in English with the words "to" or "for." Here the sense is "to Pharaoh's daughter." The second ל breaks from this usage, but is nevertheless common. It represents the way in which Hebrew communicates ownership. Hebrew has no verb "to have" or "to own," but signifies it with ל. The example many people learn in Introduction to Hebrew classes is: ויהי סוס לדויד. Woodenly one may say, "there is / was a horse to David." Idiomatically, this means,

[51] Mosca, "Child Sacrifice," 127.

[52] Ernst Jenni, *Die hebräischen Präpositionen*, Band 3: *Die Präposition Lamed* (Stuttgart: Kohlhammer, 2000), 26–48.

[53] For further discussion of these and similar texts, see Bruce K. Waltke and Michael P. O'Connor, *An Introduction to Biblical Hebrew Syntax* (Winona Lake, Indiana: Eisenbrauns, 1990), 209–11.

"David has / had a horse." Finally, the third use of ל in 2:10, is the *Lamed revaluationis* in Jenni's terminology. Here there is no datival or proprietary signification. Rather, the sense of the verse is that, "he became hers *as* a son." Consider the following examples of this phenomenon:

> So Achish believed (in) David, saying, "He has surely made himself odious with his people in Israel and he will be mine as (ל) an eternal servant. (1 Sam 27:12)
>
> And he said, "Cast it on the ground and he cast it on the ground and it became like (ל) a serpent and Moses fled from it. (Exod 4:3)
>
> Woe to those who declare evil (ל) good and good (ל) evil, who set (value?) darkness as (ל) light and light as (ל) darkness, who set the bitter as (ל) sweet and the sweet as (ל) bitter. (Isa 5:20)[54]
>
> It shall be yours as (ל) food. (Gen 1:29)

We need not be constrained to slavishly translate "to" or "for" for every occurrence of ל in the Hebrew Bible. The context must determine the translation.

Finally, twice in the book of Jeremiah it is clearly stated that the offering of a child sacrifice is being made to Ba'al. It is unnecessary to have any other god.[55]

> They fill this place with blood of the innocent and build high places of Ba'al to pass their children through the fire as burnt offerings (עֹלוֹת) to Ba'al, which I have not commanded nor decreed, nor did it enter into my mind. (Jer 19:4b–5)
> And they built the high places of Ba'al in the valley of Ben-Hinnom to offer their sons and their daughters as a מֹלֶךְ, though I did not command them, nor did it enter my mind that they should do this abomination causing Judah [to sin]. (Jer 32:35)

These passages from Jer should be instructive in our interpretation of the rest of the Biblical למלך passages. We have already seen that the prepositional ל should pose no problem and when we couple these Jer

---

[54] Trans. Waltke and O'Connor, 209.

[55] I will only offer a few words about these passages. There are several interpretive possibilities. For my purposes, it is important only to note that מלך is not used as a divine name. For consideration of the possible meanings of these Jer passages, see the contribution of Armin Lange in this volume.

texts with the *undisputed* usage of the term *mlk* in Phoenician / Punic colonies, a very strong case emerges for denying the existence of a god in Israel named *Molek*. The word is a sacrificial term in the Hebrew Bible in the same way it functioned in the Western Mediterranean and as our examples have shown, it makes the best sense to understand it as a causative particple of the root *hlk* in this context. Indeed, in the Bible, the word occurs only in the context of human sacrifice.

IV.

Recent archaeological finds on mainland Phoenicia certainly support reading the Biblical למלך passages in the context of Phoenician / Punic *mlk* sacrifices.[56] Perhaps even more important is an unpublished inscription from a stele that was recently discovered in Incirli, Turkey. The stele is inscribed on all four sides in standard Phoenician 8th cent. B. C. E. script. Bruce Zuckerman and Stephan Kaufman characterize it as "a commemorative boundary inscription marking the successful end of a territorial struggle between the kings of Cilicia (Que) and Kummuh and the various allied powers, presumably over the territory where the monument was originally erected."[57] The stela was later over-written in Greek, but apparently preserves the first person account of a certain King Awarikku of Que (also known from Karatepe) and the exploits of two battles that he fought. The text may discuss in some detail the use of the *mulk* sacrifice of sheep, horses, and (possibly) humans in the process of fighting wars.[58] Zuckerman and Kaufman write,

> This inscription provides that missing connection with apparent references to the *mulk* of a man, or a firstborn son. In addition, our inscription may clarify the meaning of the Biblical practice of "passing children through fire" for *molekh*. It is our belief that the Incirli inscription can provide insight into the conceptual underpinnings of a number of important ideas, narratives, and practices mentioned in the Bible, including the prohibitions against "passing children through fire" for *molekh*.[59]

---

[56] Seeden, "A Tophet in Tyre?", 39–82. Dearman, "The Tophet in Jerusalem," 59–71.

[57] See Bruce Zuckerman and Stephen Kaufman, "Recording the Stela: The First Step on the Road to Decipherment," www.humnet.ucla.edu/humnet/nelc/stelasite/stelainfo .html

[58] See ibid.

[59] Ibid.

Since the publication of these comments on their website, I have received personal communication from Steve Kaufman that in his final reading of the text (soon to be published) the word *mlk* is not certain. He did confirm, however, that there is repeated reference to the sacrifice of royal children. In so doing, the text utilizes other lexemes such as *gzr zbḥ* and *kpr*. While a clear attestation of the term *mlk* on the Incirli stela no longer seems certain, it does not appear unreasonable to place the stela in the context of a *mlk* sacrifice. Nevertheless, one clear example of the term *mlk* from the Levant does exist.

On the Mediterranean coast of the south of Tyre, a Phoenician inscription dating to the third–second cent. B. C. E. was found in the 19th cent. It contains the term *mlk*. Now known as *RES* 367, the inscription was first published in 1892.[60] The first line of the text is transcribed and translated by Gianto as follows:

> [*n*]*ṣb mlk* [xxx]
> The stela of *mulk* [xxx][61]

While several clear lines of text follow, the first (and most important line) is obscured. The text which follows, however, seems to indicate that the word being used is the term for sacrifice and not a king or god. Gianto translates the first half of the second line as follows: "which the men of 'Abdo' son of 'Abd-' is vowed—and they had paid the valuations—to their lord ʾEsmun."[62] Several things should be noted. The god Eshmun is designated as a god to whom a vow is made. In the same way that it does not make sense for *mlk* to designate a deity in Jer 19:4–5 and 32:35, it would seem unlikely that *mlk* would designate a deity in the Nebi-Yunis inscriptions. Further, the almost certain mention of a "stela of *mlk*" seems to specify that the *mlk* sacrifice is indicated. This is even more likely in light of Gianto's assertion that there are some undecipherable letters which immediately follow the term *mlk*. It is speculation, of course, that the letters could possibly be *ʾmr*, *ʾdm*, or *bʿl*. Still, the overall contents of this inscription seem very close to the language of several of the *mlk* inscriptions from the Western Mediterranean (see above).

[60] Marie-Joseph La Grange, "Une inscription phénicienne," *RB* 1 (1892): 275–81. More recently, see Colette Picard, "Monument de Nebi-Yunis," *RB* 83 (1976): 584–89 and Agustinus Gianto, "Some Notes on the Mulk Inscription from Nebi Yunis," *Bib* 68 (1987): 397–401.

[61] Gianto, "Some Notes," 398.

[62] Gianto, "Some Notes," 398.

Two more sites should be mentioned while I am discussing references to *mlk* in the Levant. Neither of these sites have produced a reference to the *mlk* sacrifice, but they should play an important role nonetheless. The first is the *tophet* found at Tyre and the second is a temple of human sacrifice in modern day Amman, Jordan.

After excavating at Ugarit and finding no evidence of a *tophet* Claude Schaeffer concluded that the there never was a *mlk* sacrifice and that the *tophet* in Carthage must have been an infant cemetery.[63] That judgment was probably premature. In late 1990, an ancient site was found by chance inside a living quarter of Tyre. The discovery of ancient pottery prompted several illegal digs in the surrounding area. By 1991, the project gained official sanction and a proper excavation (still in progress) commenced. Thus far, the analysis of the contents of twelve urns has been published. Like the urns of the Phoenician colonies, they contained the bones of animals (sheep, birds) as well as young humans.[64] Furthermore, icons of a crescent-disk on stelae at Tyre match perfectly with icons found at *every* North African *tophet*[65] While no inscription bearing a description of sacrifice has been found, the condition of the bones that were found seem to rule out other possibilities. Thus, in almost every category of comparison (except inscriptions) a Levantine site matching the *tophetim* of the Phoenician colonies (which have provided many references to the *mlk* sacrifice) has been found.

One other verifiable Levantine site of human sacrifice has been discovered. On the grounds of the modern airport at Amman, a temple site has been discovered which contains thousands of human bone fragments intermingled with (considerably less) animal bone fragments.[66] While it is possible that the site represents a "mortuary temple," the condition of the bones seems to indicate a site of human sacrifice. The

---

[63] Claude Schaeffer, Oral communication to the Académie des Inscriptions reported in CRAI, 1956, 67. Quoted in Mosca, "Child Sacrifice," 49.

[64] Helga Seeden, "A Tophet in Tyre?" 39–82. See also the note at the end of the article by Janice Conheeney and Alan Pipe, "Note on Some Cremated Bone From Tyrian Cinerary Urns," *Ber* XXXIX (1991): 83–87. Also, Dearman, "The Tophet in Jerusalem," 59–71. Dearman makes a case for offering a profile of the Jerusalem *tophet* based on the finds at Tyre, Achzib, and Nebi-Yunis. See Samuel R. Wolff, "Archaeology in Israel," *AJA* 98 (1994): 481–519.

[65] Dearman, "The Tophet in Jerusalem," 63.

[66] John Basil Hennessy, "Thirteenth Century B. C. Temple of Human Sacrifice at Amman," in *Phoenicia and its Neighbours: Proceedings of the Colloquium Held on the 9th and 10th of December 1983 at the Vrije Universiteit Brussel, in Cooperation with the Centrum voor Myceense en Archaisch-Grieske Cultuur* (ed., Eric Gubel; Leuven: Peeters, 1985), 85–104.

color of the bones (white) reflect that they were subjected to a constant, high heat and that the bodies were most likely drained of blood before they were burned.[67] The important thing to note about this site for my study is the cultic context in which it situates human sacrifice. The location of the remains in a temple precinct seems to indicate that human sacrifice, while probably carried out on city walls during times of distress, seems to have also played a role in the cultic life of some Canaanite and Canaanite-successor cultures since at least the Iron Age and possibly even the Late Bronze Age.

Finally, the Amman site may indicate that while the Classical writers who described the Phoenician / Punic rituals of human sacrifice may have been accurate in general, they also embellished some points. For example, since the bone color and condition at both Amman and Carthage (or Nora or Motya, etc.) seems to be consonant, it may be that Kleitarchos was wrong that the infants were burned alive. "When the flames fall upon the body, the limbs contract and the open mouth seems almost to be laughing, until the contracted [body] slips quietly into the brazier. Thus it is that the 'grin' is known as 'sardonic laughter' since they die laughing."[68] Indeed, it may be that the account more likely provides an additional and unsettling etymology for a certain plant that grew on Sardinia than a precise account of the human sacrifice ritual.[69]

Still, it seems that several different human sacrifice rituals must have been afoot in the ancient Mediterranean world. There is strong evidence that both the irregular sacrifice of distress (i. e., on the city wall when under attack or threat of attack) and the more regular sacrifices of the cult operated at different times, places, and geographic locations with slight variations. Further, these two practices seem to have overlapped in some instances. There is little chance of recovering the physical evidence of a sacrifice of distress on the city wall (though the Egyptian reliefs mentioned above are quite compelling). The relatively abundant evidence of the more regular cultic sacrifice seems to reflect that victims were first killed and drained of blood before being burned. Such a practice is apparently also attested from Crete during the Bronze Age.[70] A reevaluation of the bones from all presumed sites of human sacrifice in

---

[67] Henessy, "Thirteenth Century," 99. For more discussion of this site, see the contribution of Armin Lange in this volume.

[68] For the translation see Mosca, "Child Sacrifice," 22.

[69] Cf. Homer, *Od.*, 10.302.

[70] Hennessy, "Thirteenth Century," 99.

the Mediterranean may be needed to make any statements more definitive than this.

Conclusion

The Biblical term למלך is best understood as a causative participle derived from the root הלך. After briefly reviewing the largest contributions to the question of *mlk* and integrating some previously disparate evidence for the first time, I offered new translations of several Phoenician inscriptions which clarify the fact that the verb *hlk* was often used in the causative stem to signify the cultic act of "offering." I then proceeded to show how the word הלך in the *hiphil* stem was also used in cultic contexts in the Hebrew Bible. Next, I answered several specific concerns about the form of the term מלך in the Hebrew Bible: the vocalization of לַמֹּלֶךְ, the presence of the preposition ל, and the ostensible recipient of the sacrifices. Finally, I presented extra-Biblical evidence for the *mlk* sacrifice in the Eastern Mediterranean. These arguments combine to strongly indicate that the god *Molek* should once again be put to rest. He never existed in the minds of Iron Age Israelites.

Jewish Views of Human Sacrifice in the Hellenistic and Roman Period

Katell Berthelot, CNRS, Aix en Provence

How should we define the notion of "human sacrifice"? This issue is in itself problematic. For example, according to the very broad definition of sacrifice given by Hendrik S. Versnel ("a sacral act by which an object is transferred from the profane sphere into the sacral sphere or the action by which the sacral potency of beings or objects already belonging to the sacred realm is increased"),[1] the practice of חרם (*ḥerem*, ban) could be considered a kind of human sacrifice. Thomas Römer actually chooses to include it among the different categories of human sacrifices appearing in the Hebrew Bible.[2] However, the choice of the translators of the Septuaginta to translate חרם by ἀνάθημα / ἀνάθεμα shows that they did not identify it with a type of sacrifice; in Greek literature, *anathema* never means "sacrifice," but refers only to offerings. Besides the use of ἀνάθεμα or ἀναθεματίζω, the translators often chose to translate להחרים by ἐξολεθρεύω (to destroy utterly), which does not entail any religious dimension. In texts such as 2 Chr 20:23, Dan 11:44 or 1 Macc 5:5 (to pick only a few examples), there is no distinction between a religiously prescribed *ḥerem* and a great massacre as usually performed during a war, even if ἀναθεματίζω is used. The sacrificial character of these massacres is not clear at all, and, in my view, may not be found in the texts. As a result, the *ḥerem* is not among the sacrificial rites studied here. "Sacrifice" will be meant in a narrow way, as a ritual killing performed on a kind of altar (either a real altar in a temple or a mere stone performing the

---

[1] Cf. "Self-Sacrifice, Compensation and the Anonymous Gods," in *Le sacrifice dans l'Antiquité: Huit exposés suivis de discussions* (ed. Jean Rudhardt and Oliver Reverdin; Entretiens sur l'antiquité classique 27; Genève: Fondation Hardt, 1981), 135–85, 136.

[2] Cf. "Le sacrifice humain en Juda et Israël au premier millénaire avant notre ère," *Archiv für Religionsgeschichte* 1 / 1 (1999): 16–26.

function of an altar at a specific time and place), in which the victim is dedicated to a god / goddess.[3] As emphasized by Versnel, the purpose of the sacrifice is generally to obtain relief in a situation of extreme danger (a war, a famine, etc.), and sometimes to pay back the god in a situation of exceptional prosperity that might cause the jealousy of the deity.[4] In several ancient texts, be they biblical,[5] Greek,[6] or Roman,[7] human—and especially child—sacrifices are described as the ultimate solution to get out of a desperate situation. Very often, one offers to the gods that which is most precious and valuable—one's children—in order to have the deity intervene (unless it is the deity itself that requires the sacrifice, generally through an oracle).[8] Thus, the death of Jephthah's daughter is clearly a sacrifice, but the case of Isaac is more problematic, since he is not actually killed. It represents a borderline case, that nevertheless illuminates our understanding of Jewish views of human sacrifice

---

[3] In the Greek world, human victims may also be sacrificed to heroes or half-gods. See Stella Georgoudi, "À propos du sacrifice humain en Grèce ancienne: remarques critiques," *Archiv für Religionsgeschichte* 1 / 1 (1999): 61–82.

[4] Cf. "Self-Sacrifice," 164 and 177 especially.

[5] See 2 Kgs 3, in which Mesha, the king of Moab, whose territory has been laid waste by the united armies of the kings of Israel, Judah and Edom, sacrificies his eldest son, the one who was supposed to succeed his father on the throne (v. 27). This biblical scene may be compared to an Egyptian relief which has been studied by Philippe Derchain in "Les plus anciens témoignages de sacrifices d'enfants chez les Sémites occidentaux," *VT* 20 (1970): 351–55. See also Alberto R. W. Green, who concludes his book on human sacrifices in the ancient Orient with the following words: "It is also to be concluded that, aside from the early 'foundation sacrifice' and the 'ritual killing' of attendants, all evidence points to 'human sacrifice' during times of political and domestic crisis" (*The Role of Human Sacrifice in the Ancient Near East* [ASOR Diss. Ser. 441; Missoula: Scholars Press, 1975], 202).

[6] On human sacrifices in the Greek world, see Dennis D. Hughes, *Human Sacrifice in Ancient Greece* (London: Routledge, 1991); Pierre Bonnechere, *Le sacrifice humain en Grèce ancienne* (Kernos Suppl. 3; Athènes: Centre international d'étude de la religion grecque antique, 1994); Georgoudi, "À propos du sacrifice humain"; Albert Heinrich, "Human Sacrifice in Greek Religion: Three Case Studies," in *Le sacrifice dans l'Antiquité: Huit exposés suivis de discussions* (ed. Jean Rudhardt and Oliver Reverdin; Entretiens sur l'antiquité classique 27; Genève: Fondation Hardt, 1980), 195–235.

[7] See the classical work by Friedrich Schwenn, *Die Menschenopfer bei den Griechen und Römern* (Religionsgeschichtliche Versuche und Vorarbeiten 15,3; Gießen: A. Töpelmann, 1915); Arthur M. Eckstein, "Human Sacrifice and Fear of Military Disaster in Republican Rome," *AJAH* 7 (1982): 69–95; Cristiano Grottanelli, "Ideologie del sacrificio umano: Roma e Cartagine," *Archiv für Religionsgeschichte* 1 / 1 (1999): 41–59, 45–46).

[8] On the importance of youth and virginity, two aspects that make the victim particularly valuable in the eyes of the gods, see Pierre Roussel, "Le thème du sacrifice volontaire dans la tragédie d'Euripide," *Revue Belge de Philologie et d'Histoire* 1 (1922): 231; Georgoudi, "À propos du sacrifice humain," 71–72.

during the period under consideration. Another point that needs to be discussed is whether self-sacrifice may be considered a case of human sacrifice, and on what conditions. The distinction between self-sacrifice and martyrdom also needs clarification.

This article focuses on Jewish literature from the 2nd century B. C. E. till the end of the first century C. E., excluding the last biblical books as well as the first rabbinic works. Biblical or rabbinic texts are taken into consideration only with the aim of putting matters in historical perspective. Even though some targumic traditions may go back to the first century C. E., targumic literature will not be studied. Thus, the corpus I deal with includes Jewish Hellenistic literature, the Qumran library and other pseudepigraphic or apocryphal texts generally dated from the Second Temple period or shortly after (as in the case of the *Liber Antiquitatum Biblicarum*—referred to as *L. A. B.*—or of *4 Maccabees*).

Let me emphasize that during the Hellenistic and Roman period, human sacrifices were not a major topic in Jewish literature. There are relatively few texts referring to sacrifices of this kind; and one of my working hypotheses is that this rarity may be explained by the Graeco-Roman context of the Jewish writers under study. Greeks and Romans tended to present human sacrifices as a barbarian practice,[9] and to consider that they were performed by Greeks or Romans only in cases of extreme emergency and despair. Moreover, during the Hellenistic period and the beginning of the Roman period, human sacrifices are not attested as common among Greeks and Romans, if we except the polemical case of Dionysian mysteries (to which I shall return below). As a result, polemics between Jews and Greeks or Romans did not focus on human sacrifices. On the other hand, a Graeco-Roman influence might be perceived in the growing insistence on self-sacrifice (patriotic or not) that characterizes Jewish works dated from the end of the Second Temple period, even if this insistence may also be explained by historical events such as the defeat by Rome and the persecutions under Hadrian.

[9] However, in several cases (such as the famous story of Agamemnon and Iphigenia), it is a Greek god or goddess who requires the sacrifice. Thus, it would be a mistake to consider human sacrifices in Greek literature as a purely barbarian practice; see the remarks of Georgoudi, ibid., 68–69.

I. The Condemnation of Human Sacrifices, Presented as a Pagan Abomination

1. Human sacrifices as Canaanite practices

In Deut, the idolatrous rites of the Cananeans are often characterized as "abominations" (תועבות).[10] Deut 18:9–13 states that the Israelites are forbidden to imitate "the abominable practices of those nations," and specifies: "There shall not be found among you any one who makes his son or his daughter pass through the fire (לא ימצא בך מעביר בנו ובתו באש), any one who practices divination, a soothsayer, or an augur, or a sorcerer, or a charmer, or a medium, or a wizard, or a necromancer" (vv. 10–11). Last, Deut 12:31 informs the reader that God destroyed the Canaanite populations because "every abominable thing which the Lord hates they have done for their gods; for they even burn their sons and their daughters in the fire to their gods."[11] The word "even," that translates the Hebrew גם, shows that this is an extremely abominable act, the height of what is abominable to God. Note that here, the sacrifice of children is described as a regular religious practice, not as an exceptional and desperate act.

Deut is the sole book of the Pentateuch that refers to Canaanite human sacrifices; it is also the only one that prescribes the extermination or banning of the Canaanites (חרם),[12] instead of simply expelling them from the country.[13] In this context, the reference to human sacrifices—and especially, the sacrifice of children by their own parents—is not a mere chance; it is meant to present the Canaanites as utterly inhuman

---

[10] This word is used in the other books of the Pentateuch, but less frequently than in Deut, and in Gen–Num it never pertains to the deeds of the Canaanites (whereas it is the case for example in 2 Kgs 16:3).

[11] ... כל תועבת יהוה אשר שׂנא עשׂו לאלהיהם כי גם את בניהם ואת בנתיהם ישׂרפו באשׁ לאלהיהם

[12] On the *herem*, see—among many studies—Philip D. Stern, *The Biblical herem: A Window on Israel's Religious Experience* (BJS 211; Atlanta: Scholars Press, 1991); André Lemaire, "Le herem dans le monde nord-ouest sémitique," in *Guerre et conquête dans le Proche-Orient ancien: Actes de la table ronde "Etudes Sémitiques"* (ed. Laïla Nehmé et al.; Antiques Sémitiques 4; Paris: J. Maisonneuve, 1999), 79–92; Yair Hoffman, "The Deuteronomistic Concept of the Herem," *ZAW* 111 (1999): 196–210.

[13] The only exception is Lev 18:21, 24–30, according to which "the land vomited out its inhabitants" ותקא הארץ את ישביה because of their abominable practices (v. 25). These practices include devoting one's children by fire to Molech (להעביר למלך) (v. 21). On Molech, see John Day, *Molech: A God of Human Sacrifice in the Old Testament* (Cambridge: Cambridge University Press, 1989). But this passage in Lev does not prescribe the extermination of the Canaanites, it only mentions their expulsion.

and monstrous, and thus to justify their destruction at the hand of the Israelites.[14]

By describing human sacrifices as a Canaanite practice, the authors of Deut imply that the Israelite practice of children sacrifices, which is referred to in different texts of the Hebrew Bible—such as 2 Kgs 16:3, 21:6, 23:10, Jer 7:31, 19:5, 32:35, Ez 16:20–22, 36, 20:26, 31, 23:36–37—is the result of a Canaanite influence on Israel. At least, two texts are explicit about this Canaanite influence on Israel, 2 Kgs 17:15–17 and Ps 106:34–38. The latter states:

> They did not destroy the peoples, as the Lord commanded them,
> but they mingled with the nations and learned to do as they did.
> They served their idols, which became a snare to them.
> They sacrificed their sons and their daughters to the demons (ויזבחו את בניהם ואת בנותיהם לשדים),
> they poured out innocent blood, the blood of their sons and daughters, whom they sacrificed to the idols of Canaan (וישפכו דם נקי דם בניהם ובנותיהם אשר זבחו לעצבי כנען);
> and the land was polluted with blood (ותחנף הארץ בדמים).[15]

In Jewish literature from the Hellenistic and Roman period, the justification of the extermination of the Canaanites by the reference to their practice of children sacrifices is found only in a very specific context, that of Alexandria at the beginning of the first century C. E. (see below, § 2). In general, the pagan origin of human sacrifices is no longer emphasized, except in passing in *L. A. B.* 4. 16, in which one reads: "Then those who inhabited the earth began to gaze at the stars and started to prognosticate by them and to perform divination and to pass their sons and daughters through fire. But Serug and his sons did not walk in ac-

---

[14] Compare to what Bonnechere writes about Greeks and Romans vis-à-vis the Carthaginians: "À partir de la seconde moitié du Ve siècle, les Carthaginois, et les Puniques en général, qui disputaient aux Grecs les emplacements idéaux pour y implanter leurs colonies, eurent à subir les mêmes accusations. Et comme Carthage se heurta à Rome pour les mêmes raisons, Grèce et Rome sont à mettre sur le même pied en ce qui concerne leurs considérations sur le modus vivendi de leurs concurrents en Méditerranée occidentale. Et la meilleure manière de discréditer ses ennemis, c'est d'affirmer qu'ils transgressent précisément les interdits sociaux essentiels de la civilisation gréco-romaine: les Carthaginois, comme plus tard les chrétiens, sacrifient donc hommes, enfants et même vieillards, la pire atrocité à laquelle puisse se livrer un peuple soi-disant civilisé" (Le sacrifice humain en Grèce ancienne, 239).

[15] Transl. after the *New Oxford Annotated Bible*, 740.

cord with them."[16] It should be noted that, in this text, the practice of sacrificing children is not associated with the Canaanites but with the generation just after the flood, which still corresponds to the beginnings of humankind; and that the ancestors of Abraham already differentiate themselves from the rest of humankind by refusing to perform such abominable deeds.

2. The apologetic use of the reference to pagan human sacrifices[17]

In two roughly contemporaneous texts whose authors both lived in Egypt, the Wisdom of Salomon and Philo's *De specialibus legibus*, one finds a reference to Canaanite children sacrifices that has clear polemical overtones.

According to Wis 11:24, God always gives men the possibility to repent, since he loves everything that he has created. Therefore God warns his creatures before punishing them for their sins. The author illustrates his point through the example of the Canaanites:

> [3] The ancient inhabitants, too, of your holy land (καὶ γὰρ τοὺς πάλαι οἰκήτορας τῆς ἁγίας σου γῆς),
> [4] you did hate for their loathsome practices (μισήσας ἐπὶ τῷ ἔχθιςτα πράσσειν),
> acts of sorcery and unholy celebrations[18] (ἔργα φαρμακειῶν καὶ τελετὰς ἀνοσίους),
> [5] merciless slaughters of children (τέκνων τε φονὰς ἀνελεήμονας),
> banquets of human flesh and blood in which entrails were devoured (καὶ σπλαγχνοφάγον ἀνθρωπίνων σαρκῶν θοῖναν καὶ αἵματος),
> These initiates from the midst of a religious guild (ἐκ μέσου μύστας θιάσου),[19]
> [6] these parents who murder helpless souls (καὶ αὐθέντας γονεῖς

---

[16] Transl. by Howard Jacobson, *A Commentary on Pseudo-Philo's Liber Antiquitatum Biblicarum with Latin text and English Translation* (AGJU 31; Leiden: Brill, 1996), vol. 1, 95–96. Latin: (...) *et filios et filias suas traicere per ignem*. The biblical expression לעביר באש, which, according to me, refers to a sacrifical act, clearly stands at the background of the Latin text (see Jacobson, ibid., 346).

[17] For a more detailed account of this point, see Katell Berthelot, "'Ils jettent au feu leurs fils et leurs filles pour leurs dieux': Une justification humaniste du massacre des Cananéens dans les textes juifs anciens?," to be published in the *RB* in 2005.

[18] In the context of Dionysian mysteries, the word τελετή has the technical meaning of "initiation rite."

[19] David Winston translates: "initiates from the midst of a Dionysian blood revel" (*The Wisdom of Salomon: A New Translation with Introduction and Commentary* [AB 43; New York: Doubleday, 1979], 237). But θίασος could have a more general meaning.

ψυχῶν ἀβοηθήτων),
it was your will to destroy (them) at the hand of our forefathers (ἐβουλήθης ἀπολέσαι διὰ χειρῶν πατέρων ἡμῶν),
[7] so that the land most precious of all to you might receive a worthy colony of God's children (ἵνα ἀξίαν ἀποικίαν δέξηται θεοῦ παίδων ἡ παρὰ σοὶ πασῶν τιμιωτάτη γῆ).
[8] Yet these too you spared as being men (ἀλλὰ καὶ τούτων ὡς ἀνθρώπων ἐφείσω),
and sent wasps as the advance guard of your army to exterminate them gradually (ἀπέστειλάς τε προδρόμους τοῦ στρατοπέδου σου σφῆκας, ἵνα αὐτοὺς κατὰ βραχὺ ἐξολεθρεύσωσιν).[20]

God was not unaware, the author pursues, that their origin (or: nature) was evil (ὅτι πονηρὰ ἡ γένεσις αὐτῶν) and their wickedness innate (καὶ ἔμφυτος ἡ κακία αὐτῶν, v. 10), because their race (or: seed) was accursed from the beginning (σπέρμα γὰρ ἦν κατηραμένον ἀπ᾽ ἀρχῆς, v. 11), but God nevertheless gave them a chance to repent, and no one may accuse him of being unjust (see vv. 12–18).

In this passage, the author of Wisdom is concerned with the issue of God's justice—the main theme of the book.[21] Beyond the point of Noah's curse on Canaan (Gen 9:20–27), which could be considered unfair, he argues in a way similar to Deut that God's decision to destroy the Canaanites and give their land to the Israelites was just, since they had committed abominable deeds such as the murder of their own, innocent children. But the author, a Jew living in Alexandria at the beginning of the first century C. E.,[22] is also involved in a controversy with his Greek, pagan contemporaries. One of them, the famous rhetor Apion, accused the Jews of sacrificing Greeks in the Jerusalem temple.[23] This accusation is quite exceptional in Antiquity; apart from an unknown writer called Damocritus,[24] no ancient writer accuses the Jews of performing ritual killings of human beings, even when they are accused of misanthropy.

---

20 Wis 12:3–8. The translation is mine, but inspires itself from Winston's translation in *The Wisdom of Salomon*, 237 and the translation found in the *Oxford Annotated Apocrypha* (ed. Bruce M. Metzger; New York: Oxford University Press, 1977), 115–16.

21 On this issue, see Moyna McGlynn, *Divine Judgement and Divine Benevolence in the Book of Wisdom* (WUNT 2,139; Tübingen: Mohr, 2001).

22 See Winston, *The Wisdom of Solomon*, 20–25.

23 See Josephus, *C. Ap.* 2. 89–96; Menahem Stern, *Greek and Latin Authors on Jews and Judaism: With Introduction, Translation, and Commentary* (Fontes ad res Judaicas spectantes; Jerusalem: The Israel Academy of Sciences and Humanities, 1998[5]), vol. 1, 389–416; Winston, ibid., 240.

24 See Stern, *Greek and Latin Authors*, vol. 1, 530–31.

Thus, it is no surprise that Apion's slander was answered vehemently by his Jewish contemporaries. Besides the Canaanites, the author of Wisdom aims at Greeks and Hellenized Egyptians who were followers of Dionysos and members of *thiasoi*;[25] this is why he associates the murder of children and anthropophagy (Wis 12:5), a common accusation against Dionysian initiates, but an absurd one in the case of the Canaanites (no biblical text ever mentions Canaanite anthropophagy). He may have had in mind groups such as an Egyptian robber band known as the *Boukoloi*, which was associated with human sacrifice and anthropophagy.[26] In sum, the author of Wisdom attacks the enemies of the Jews and, using a well-known apologetic device, he formulates against them the very charge that some of them maliciously directed against the Jews.

The same sort of apologetic strategy is found in Philo. In the *De specialibus legibus*, concerning the offering brought to the Jerusalem temple according to Lev 23:9–10, and the necessity to thank God for the land that Jews have inherited, Philo writes:

> (...) it was no uninhabited land which they received, but one which contained a populous nation and great cities filled with stalwart citizens. Yet these cities have been stripped of their inhabitants and the whole nation, except for a small fraction, has disappeared, partly through wars, partly through heavenly visitations, a consequence of their strange and monstrous practices of iniquity and all their heinous acts of impiety aimed at the subversion of the statutes of nature (διὰ καινὰς καὶ ἐκτόπους ἐπιτηδεύσεις ἀδικημάτων καὶ ὅσα μεγαλουργοῦντες ἐπὶ καθαιρέσει τῶν τῆς φύσεως θεσμῶν ἠσέβουν).[27]

This passage reflects the Deuteronomic perspective: Canaanites were killed, not expelled, and this was due to their iniquities and impiety.

---

[25] That the author of Wisdom had Dionysian mysteries in mind while describing the Canaanites has been noted by several commentators; see for example Chrysostome Larcher, *Le Livre de la Sagesse ou la sagesse de Salomon* (EBib NS 5; Paris: Gabalda, 1985), vol. 3, 708–9. Note the following vocabulary: τέλεται, μύσται, θίασος, etc.

[26] See Winston, *The Wisdom of Solomon*, 239; Jean-Marie Bertrand, "Les Boucôloi ou le monde à l'envers," *REA* 90 / 1–2 (1988): 139–49. See also Lollianos' romance *Phoinikika* (B1 r–v); Albert Heinrich, *Die Phoinikika des Lollianos: Fragmente eines neuen griechischen Romans* (Papyrologische Texte und Abhandlungen 14; Bonn: R. Habelt, 1972), 28–79; Françoise Briquel-Chatonnet, "L'image des Phéniciens dans les romans grecs," in *Le monde du roman grec* (ed. Marie-Françoise Baslez et al.; Collection Études de littérature ancienne; Paris: Presses de l'ENS, 1992), 189–97.

[27] *Spec.* 2.170, translation by Francis H. Colson, *Philo*, vol. 7 (LCL 320; Cambridge, Mass.: Cambridge University Press, 1937), 413.

The "subversion of the statutes of nature" certainly refers to the sacrifice of one's children, not only because of the Deuteronomic influence on Philo in this specific context, but also because of the testimony of other Philonian texts. The expression "statutes of nature" refers both to the natural affection of parents for their children and to the prohibition of murder (which belongs to the ten commandments, referred to by Philo as *thesmoi*).[28] For example, in *Opif.* 171, Philo mentions among other important religious principles that: "God also exercises forethought on the world's behalf. For that the Maker should care for the thing made is required by the laws and ordinances of Nature (φύσεως νόμοις καὶ θεσμοῖς), and it is in accordance with these that parents take thought beforehand for children (καθ' οὓς καὶ γονεῖς τέκνων προμηθοῦνται)."[29] In a similar vein, Philo writes in his commentary of the Decalogue, on the subject of murder: "Let him, then, who slays another know full well that he is subverting the laws and statutes of nature (νόμους φύσεως καὶ θεσμοὺς) so excellently enacted for the well-being of all" (*Decal.* 132).[30] Thus, Canaanites, who kill their children, are guilty of a double transgression of the "statutes of nature."

Philo's condemnation of Canaanite child sacrifice, like that of Wisdom, has an apologetic dimension. Philo is concerned to refute and to confound those who accuse the Jews of *misanthrôpia*.[31] In the section of *Spec.* that deals with the prohibition of murder, after examining the case of a person causing a miscarriage to a woman (Exod 21:22–23), he writes that the lawgiver prohibits "something else more important, the exposure of infants, a sacrilegious practice (ἀσέβημα) which among many other nations, through their ingrained inhumanity (ἕνεκα τῆς φυσικῆς ἀπανθρωπίας), has come to be regarded with complacence" (3. 110).[32] In the same passage, parents who kill their children are accused of *misanthrôpia* (§ 112). Then Philo concludes with the following rhetorical question: "Men-haters too (μισάνθρωποι), for who could more deserve the name than these enemies, these merciless foes of their offspring? For

[28] See *Her.* 168–69 and above all *Congr.* 120.

[29] Translation by Colson, *Philo*, vol. 1 (LCL 226; Cambridge, Mass.: Cambridge University Press, 1929), 137.

[30] Translation by Colson, *Philo*, vol. 7, 73.

[31] On this aspect of Philo's work, see Peder Borgen, *Philo of Alexandria. An Exegete for his Time* (NovTSup 86; Leiden: Brill, 1997), 243–60; Katell Berthelot, *Philanthrôpia judaica: Le débat autour de la 'misanthropie' des lois juives dans l'Antiquité* (JSJ Suppl. 76; Leiden: Brill, 2003), 233–321.

[32] Translation by Colson, *Philo*, vol. 7, 545.

no one is so foolish as to suppose that those who have treated dishonourably their own flesh and blood will deal honourably with strangers" (§ 113).[33] Here Philo uses an argument *a minori ad maius* (from the lesser to the greater), but he also knows that for Stoicism, love towards one's fellow human beings is closely linked with love towards one's children. He cleverly underlines the contradictions of the Graeco-Roman world: a pretension to *philanthrôpia* or *humanitas* on the one hand, a practice of infanticide or abandonment of newborn children on the other. Finally, the apologetic character of the reference to Canaanite child sacrifice in *Spec.* 2. 170 becomes very clear when one reads in *Spec.* 2. 167 (a few paragraphs before): "It astonishes me to see that some people venture to accuse of inhumanity (our) nation (πῶς τολμῶσί τινες ἀπανθρωπίαν τοῦ ἔθνους κατηγορεῖν), which has shown so profound a sense of fellowship and goodwill to all men everywhere (ὃ τοσαύτῃ κέχρηται κοινωνίας καὶ εὐνοίας τῆς πρὸς [τοὺς] πανταχοῦ πάντας ὑπερβολῇ), by using its prayers and festivals and first-fruit offerings as a means of supplication for the human race in general and of making its homage to the truly existent God in its own name and in the name of those who have evaded the service which it was their duty to give" (§ 167).[34]

To conclude, there are few references to pagan human sacrifices in Jewish texts from the Hellenistic and Roman period. This is significant, because so many Jewish texts from that period criticize pagan cults and morality. The *Sibylline Oracles*, for example, have many allusions to idolatry and to homosexuality (considered a characteristic of the pagan world), but nearly none to human sacrifices. *Sib. Or.* 4. 31 evokes "monstruous murders"—maybe an allusion to Dionysian celebrations[35]—but it is uncertain whether *sacrifices* are meant. *Sib. Or.* 3. 765–66 exhorts pagans to educate their children and not to assassinate them, but these verses refer to infanticide, not to *sacrificial* practices. The condemnation of infanticide is common under the pen of Jewish Hellenistic authors, such as Philo (as we have seen above) or Josephus (see *Against Apion* 2. 202); but it should not be mistaken as raising the problem of child sacrifice. Not only do Jewish authors not refer much to contemporary pagan practices of human sacrifice—as said above, this may be

[33] Ibid., 547.

[34] Ibid., 411, slightly modified.

[35] Note that in 3 Maccabees, a book that presents the cult of Dionysos as a threat to Judaism, and in which polemical overtones are thus to be expected, no allusion can be found to human sacrifices.

explained by the Graeco-Roman context of these writers—,[36] they do not allude much to Canaanite human sacrifices, even when they deal with Deuteronomy or the conquest narrative. For example, in the *Jewish Antiquities*, Josephus rewrites Deuteronomy, Joshua and Judges and justifies the massacre of the Canaanite populations, without once referring to their "abominable practice" of human sacrifice, although this practice was heinous to a Graeco-Roman audience, too. Thus, one is led to conclude that pagan human sacrifices were not an issue any more during this period, except in the specific context of Alexandria at the beginning of the first century C. E., for the reasons described above.

II. The "Demonization" of Human Sacrifices

Whereas many texts in the Hebrew Bible characterize human sacrifices as "pagan," almost no biblical text ascribes these practices to a demonic influence on humankind. The only exception may be Ps 106:37 (see above).[37] But from the 2nd century B. C. E. onwards, the "demonization" of human sacrifices may be observed in several texts. Although "demons" are closely associated with idolatry, they do not refer simply to "foreign gods," but to evil spirits (the offspring of the watchers or the spirits of the dead giants, according to *Jubilees* and *1 Enoch*) or evil angels.[38]

---

[36] Note one very interesting remark by Philo, starting from the prohibition to imitate Canaanite practices: "(...) So if we are victorious over our enemies, let us not affect their impious ways in which they think to show their piety by burning their sons and daughters to their gods. This does not mean that all the barbarians have a custom of giving their children to the fire. They have not become so savage in nature as to bring themselves to do in peace to their nearest and dearest what they would not do in wartime to their enemies in the field or to the objects of their implacable hatred. Rather the words refer to that consuming fire in which they veritably destroy the souls of their offspring right from the cradle by failing to imprint on their still tender souls truth-giving conceptions of the one, the truly existent God" (*Spec.* 1. 312–13, translation by Colson, *Philo*, vol. 7, 281 [slightly modified]). In this context, "barbarians" should be understood as *goyim*, nations in general, including Greeks and Romans. The reference to the "cradle" has polemical overtones, probably against the Stoic conception of human natural sociability (see Jacques Brunschwig, "The Cradle Argument in Epicureanism and Stoicism," in *The Norms of Nature: Studies in Hellenistic Ethics* [ed. Malcom Schofield and Gisela Striker; Cambridge: Cambridge University Press, 1986], 113–44).

[37] If שדים is to be understood as referring to demons and not only to idols, it might imply that the final redaction or the last edition of this psalm is quite late. See also James C. VanderKam, "The Demons in the Book of Jubilees," in *Die Dämonen / Demons* (ed. Armin Lange et al.; Tübingen: Mohr Siebeck, 2003), 339–64, 353–54).

[38] See VanderKam, ibid., 343, 348–49.

In a Qumran text known as Pseudo-Daniel (4Q243–45),[39] written in Aramaic, one reads (according to the editors' reconstruction):

> (1) [ ] The Israelites chose their presence rather than [the presence of God]
> (2) [and they were sacri]ficing their children to the demons of error, and God became angry at them and sa[id] to give
> (3) them into the hand of Neb[uchadnezzar king of Ba]bylon (etc.)"[40]

Such a reference to Israelites sacrificing their children to foreign gods is not found in the biblical book of Daniel, even in Dan 9:1–20, a passage in which Daniel confesses the sins of the people and records their unfaithfulness to God and his Law. Neither is there any reference to demons. The Qumran text may be a later elaboration of the Danielic tradition that could hardly be dated prior to the middle of the second century B. C. E.

The mid-second century is also the supposed date of composition of the *Book of Jubilees*.[41] This book contains many developments involving angels and demons. In particular, different kinds of human sins and crimes are attributed to the influence of demons;[42] as James C. VanderKam writes: "(...) even the chosen line, if it lacks vigilance and fails to obey the divine will, may fall prey to the demons who lead them into idolatry and all the evils that follow from it."[43] As early as *Jub.* I. 11, God announces to Moses that the Israelites will not remain faithful to the covenant, that they will serve other gods and that "they will sacrifice their children to demons and to every product (conceived

---

39 Ed. and transl. by John J. Collins and Peter Flint, in *Parabiblical Texts Part 3* (ed. George Brooke; DJD XXII: *Qumran Cave 4*, vol. XVII; Oxford: Clarendon Press, 1996), 95–164. The fact that the text is written in Aramaic does not favour the hypothesis of a "sectarian" (or community) origin of the text, but it can not be completely excluded either.

40 4Q243 13 + 4Q244 12.Ibid., 147. The Aramaic text runs as follows (142):

1 [ ]בחרו בני ישראל אנפיהון מן [אנפי אלוהין]
2 [והוו דב]חין לבניהון לשידי טעותא ורגז עליהון אלוהין וא[מר] למנתן
3 אנון ביד נב[כדנצר מלך ב]בל (etc.)

41 See James C. VanderKam, "Jubilees, Book of," in *Encyclopedia of the Dead Sea Scrolls* (ed. Lawrence H. Schiffman and James C. VanderKam; Oxford: Oxford University Press, 2000), vol. 1, 434–38.

42 Beyond the texts quoted below, see for example 7. 27 and 11. 4–5.

43 See VanderKam, "The Demons in the Book of Jubilees," 362; idem, "The Angel of the Presence in the Book of Jubilees," *DSD* 7 / 3 (2000): 378–93.

by) their erring hearts."[44] Logically, it is Prince Mastema, the head of the demons, who is made responsible for the idea of testing Abraham by asking him to sacrifice his son. In a way reminiscent of Job (1:6–12, 2:1–6), *Jub.* 17. 15–16 reports how Mastema[45] asserted that Abraham would not remain faithful to God if asked to sacrifice Isaac, and suggested to have him tested. As in Job, God agrees to test his servant. *Jub.* 18. 1–16 consists of the account of the near-sacrifice of Isaac, and does not differ much from the biblical text (Gen 22). Still, it is noteworthy that the angel who prevents Abraham from actually sacrificing Isaac is the Angel of the Presence, who is said to stand "in front of him [Abraham] and in front of the prince of Mastema" (18. 9), and that Mastema is finally "put to shame" (18. 12).[46] The story of the near-sacrifice of Isaac becomes the story of a cosmic spiritual fight involving God and his angel on the one hand, and Prince Mastema on the other. Moreover, the responsibility for the idea of sacrificing a human being is laid on Mastema and not on God.[47]

In a Qumran text that once seemed related to the *Book of Jubilees* but is actually distinct from it,[48] entitled *Pseudo-Jubilees a* (4Q225), the description of the near-sacrifice of Isaac contains additional details. In frg. 2 col. 1 ll. 9–10, as in *Jub.* 17. 16 (but with a more concise formulation), we read:

> [9] (...) Then the Prince of the Ma[s]temah came
> [10] [to G]od, and he accused Abraham regarding Isaac. (...)[49]

---

[44] Translation by VanderKam, *The Book of Jubilees* (CSCO 510 and 511; Leuven: Peeters, 1989), vol. 2, 3 (slightly modified). The Hebrew text corresponding to this passage has been found at Qumran (in 4Q216 col. II), but unfortunately l. 11 is badly preserved and the sentence about human sacrifices can no longer be read. See VanderKam and Józef Tadeusz Milik (eds.) in *Parabiblical Texts: Part 1* (ed. Harold Attridge; DJD XIII; Qumran Cave 4. VIII; Oxford: Clarendon Press, 1994), 8.

[45] The name Mastema has the same meaning as "satan," since the root שטם is identical to the root שטן.

[46] See VanderKam, *The Book of Jubilees*, 106–7. In this case, the Hebrew original has not been found back.

[47] For a more detailed analysis of Jubilees' reworking of the biblical text, see VanderKam, "The Aqedah, Jubilees, and PseudoJubilees," in *The Quest for Context and Meaning: Studies in Biblical Intertextuality in Honor of James A. Sanders* (ed. Craig A. Evans and Shemaryahu Talmon; Biblical Interpretation Series 28; Leiden: Brill, 1997), 241–61; Leroy Andrew Huizenga, "The Battle for Isaac: Exploring the Composition and Function of the Aqedah in the Book of Jubilees," JSP 13 / 1 (2002): 33–59.

[48] See VanderKam, ibid.

[49] See VanderKam and Milik, DJD XIII, 145–47.

The text goes on with the story of Gen 22, and frg. 2 col. II provides important new information:

> [4] (. . .) Isaac said to his father "T[ie me well "]
> [5] The angels of holiness were standing weeping above [the altar]
> [6] his sons from the earth. The angels of the Ma[stemah]
> [7] being happy and saying, "Now he will perish." And [in all this the Prince of the Mastemah was testing whether]
> [8] he would be found weak, and whether A[braham] should not be found faithful [to God. He called,]
> [9] "Abraham, Abraham!" He said, "Here I am." He said "N[ow I know that]
> [10] he will not be loving." God the Lord blessed I[saac all the days of his life. He became the father of]
> [11] Jacob, and Jacob became the father of Levi, [a third] genera-[tion. *vacat* All] (. . .)[50]

Again, the responsibility for the testing of Abraham is attributed to Mastema. The difference with *Jubilees* is that there are now a multitude of angels, both good and bad, involved in the story.[51] The perspective of Isaac's death rejoices the angels of Mastema, whereas the angels of holiness cry. As underlined by Florentino García Martínez, "what Mastema hopes to achieve (. . .) is to cross God's plans and to make ineffective the promise to Abraham of a progeny numerous as the stars, the sand or the dust."[52] The goal is ultimately to destroy the holy people of God, Israel.

---

9 [. . .] ויבוא שר המ[ש]טמה
10] אל אל]והים וישטים את אברהם בישחק [. . .].

50 Ibid., 149–51.

4 לו אמר ישחק אל אביו כ[פות אותי יפה]
5 מלאכי קדש עומדים בוכים על[המזבח]
6 את בניו מן הארץ ומלאכי המ[שטמה]
7 שמחים ואומרים עכשו יאבד ו[בכול זה ינסה שר המשטמה אם]
8 ימצא כחש ואם לא ימצא נאמן א[ברהם לאלוהים ויקרא]
9 אברהם אברהם ויאמר הנני ויאמר ע[תה ידעתי כי]
10 לא יהיה אהב ויברך אל יהוה את יש[חק כל ימי חיו ויוליד את]
11 יעקוב ויעקוב הוליד את לוי דו[ר שלישי *vacat* ויהיו כול] . . .

51 According to Florentino García Martínez, 4Q225 is the oldest attestation of this element; see "The Sacrifice of Isaac in 4Q225," in *The Sacrifice of Isaac: The Aqedah (Gen 22) and Its Interpretations* (ed. E. Noort and E. J. C. Tigchelaar; Themes in Biblical Narrative 4; Leiden: Brill, 2002, 44–57), 54.

52 Ibid., 51.

The few texts quoted above are not necessarily, and not even probably sectarian—that is, stemming from the Qumran community[53]—and their understanding of human sacrifice as something diabolical must have been widespread among different Jewish circles. Still, it is consistent with the world view of the sectarian texts from Qumran (and might have influenced it). As far as the texts studied above are concerned, one should note that the issue of demons inspiring human sacrifices is generally evoked in a Jewish context, even if in *Jubilees*, demons reign over humankind apart from Israel (but Israel may nevertheless be influenced by them). Two opposite cases are referred to: 1) Israelites disobey God and sacrifice their children to demons;[54] 2) Abraham is ready to obey God and to sacrifice his son, but this is actually a test inspired by demons.[55] The lack of references to pagans incited by demons to sacrifice their children may be explained by the fact that pagan human sacrifices are not an issue any longer (as underscored in the preceding section). On the other hand, the issue of Israel's fate, and the cosmic fight in which Israel is at stake, are of great concern to the writers of the texts studied above. In this cosmic fight, the attitude of Isaac while being tied up and his willingness to be sacrificed become key elements of the victory against the forces of evil, as we shall see below. Actually, the third and last characteristic feature of Jewish perceptions of human sacrifice during the Hellenistic and Roman period is a paradoxical praise of self-sacrifice.

---

[53] Concerning 4Q225, García Martínez writes: "(...) the tetragrammaton is not written in palaeo-Hebrew but in the same script as the rest of the fragment. This detail makes a Qumran origin for the composition less likely. (...) It belongs (...) neither to the Jubilees nor to the qumranic tradition" (ibid., 56).

[54] There is another case of human sacrifices performed by Israelites in *L. A. B.* 25. 13. People from the tribe of Ephraim have sinned and they acknowledge their sin with the following words: "We desired to make our sons and daughters pass through the fire, to find out if what had been said were true" (transl. by Jacobson, *A Commentary*, vol. 1, 135; Latin: *Nos voluimus traicere filios et filias nostras per ignem* ...). In this case, no diabolical influence is mentioned. This is just a case of human wickedness and tendency to disobey God.

[55] In *L. A. B.* 32. 1–2, we read that "all the angels were jealous of [Abraham], and the serving hosts envied him" (transl. by Jacobson, ibid., 149). They are the ones responsible for the testing of Abraham, but since all the angels are concerned, they can hardly be considered to be demons. Still, the idea of a cosmic fight is present in *L. A. B.* 32, a rewriting of Deborah's song (see Bruce Norman Fisk, "Offering Isaac Again and Again: Pseudo-Philo's Use of the Aqedah as Intertext," *CBQ* 62 / 3 (2000): 481–507, 491–93.

III. From condemnation of human sacrifices to praise of self-sacrifice, as illustrated by the cases of Jephthah's daughter and of Isaac

1. A heroic virgin

Let us start with the story of Jephthah's daughter (Judg 11:29–40), which represents a more marginal tradition than Gen 22. Although some scholars have questioned the reality of the sacrifice in Judg 11,[56] it seems that it was understood as real by Jewish authors from the Second Temple period, as well as in rabbinic literature. What strikes the reader of Judg 11 is the parallel with the story of Agamemnon and Iphigenia (who was sacrificed according to some versions of the myth, and according to others was dedicated to Artemis, to be her priestess).[57] But whereas Agamemnon is compelled by the goddess to sacrifice his daughter (at least according to Euripides' version in *Iphigenia in Aulis*), no such request is addressed to Jephthah, who appears as a fool.[58] The text is thus critical and ironical. Thomas Römer emphasizes that "in Euripides as in Judges 11, the 'real hero' is the maiden, since she accepts voluntarily to be sacrificed and she pushes her father to do so."[59] According to him, the author of Judg 11 borrows from Greek tradition, and wants "to present Jephthah's daughter as the Hebrew Iphigenia."[60] Her willingness to be sacrificed may thus be explained by a Greek influence on the biblical writer, since it is a central theme in Greek literature and especially in Euripides' theatre.[61] However, as shown by Claire Nancy, Euripides is in fact very

---

[56] See the discussion in David Marcus, *Jephthah and His Vow* (Lubbock: Texas Technical Press, 1986).

[57] See Marcus, ibid., 42–43; Thomas Römer, "Why would the Deuteronomist tell about the Sacrifice of Jephtah's Daughter?," *JSOT* 77 (1998): 27–38 (and already Walter Baumgarten, "Israelitisch-Griechische Sagenbeziehungen," in *Zum Alten Testament und seiner Umwelt: Ausgewählte Aufsätze* (Leiden: Brill, 1959), 152–54).

[58] See Julie Claassens, "Theme and Function in the Jephthah Narrative," JNSL 23/2 (1997): 203–19.

[59] "Why would the Deuteronomist tell," 35.

[60] Ibid., 36.

[61] As Jan N. Bremmer writes, "a victim's voluntary participation was an important part of Greek sacrificial ideology, which stressed that the victim was pleased to go up to the altar, sometimes could even hardly wait to be sacrificed!" ("Sacrificing a Child in Ancient Greece: The Case of Iphigenia," in *The Sacrifice of Isaac: The Aqedah (Gen 22) and its Interpretations* (ed. E. Noort and E. J. C. Tigchelaar; Themes in Biblical Narrative 4; Leiden: Brill, 2002, 21–43), 30. See also P. Roussel: "Le consentement de la victime libère de toute souillure ceux qui la sacrifient" (idem, "Le thème du sacrifice volontaire," 236–38).

critical of patriotism and self-sacrifice. "Le moins qu'on puisse dire est qu'Iphigénie donne sa vie à un père, à des chefs, à un peuple qui ne la valent pas. (. . .) La leçon de tous les sacrifices renvoie le même son tragique: le meilleur y est sacrifié au pire."[62] This critical note is also found in the biblical text, but what about the rewriting of this episode in later Jewish sources?

Rabbinic sources blame Jephthah and present him as a sinner.[63] Josephus is critical too, since he writes that he "sacrificed his child as a burnt-offering—a sacrifice neither sanctionned by the Law nor well-pleasing to God; for he had not by reflection probed what might befall or in what aspect the deed would appear to them that heard of it."[64] Here Josephus is concerned with the condemnation of human sacrifices in his own time, be it among Jews, Greeks or Romans. Jephthah's act might appear barbarian. But on the other hand, Josephus also praises Jephthah's daughter: "But she without displeasure learnt her destiny, to wit that she must die in return for her father's victory and the liberation of her fellow-citizen."[65] The patriotism of Jephthah's daughter is presented as something valuable, without the slightest irony. Patriotism and self-sacrifice appear as positive values, a fact that may be understood in connection with the hopes of national restoration that endured until the revolt of 132–135 C. E.

The account of the *L. A. B.* is critical of Jephthah's foolishness too, but it is also more positive, in as much as it attributes an even greater value to the death of Jephthah's daughter, who, for the first time, receives a name (Seila) and expresses herself at length. First, Seila's patriotism is clear in § 40. 2, in which she says: "Who is there who would be sad to die, seeing the people freed?"[66] She actually admits to being sad, but explains that "I am not sad that I am going to die nor does it pain me to give back my soul, but because my father was trapped by his

---

62 "ΦΑΡΜΑΚΟΝ ΣΩΤΗΡΙΑΣ: Le mécanisme du sacrifice humain chez Euripide," in *Théâtre et spectacles dans l'Antiquité: Actes du colloque de Strasbourg 5–7/11/1981* (ed. Hubert Zehnacker; Travaux du Centre de recherches sur le Proche-Orient et la Grèce 7; Leiden: Brill, 1983), 17–30, 22.

63 See Shulamit Valler, "The Story of Jephthah's Daughter in the Midrash," in *Judges: A Feminist Companion to the Bible* (ed. Athalya Brenner; Sheffield: Sheffield Academic Press, 1999), 48–66.

64 *A.J.* 5.266, translation by Henry St. John Thackeray and Ralph Marcus, *Josephus: Books 4–6* (LCL 490; Cambridge, Mass.: Cambridge University Press, 1934), 281.

65 *A.J.* 5.265, ibid.

66 Translation by Jacobson, *A Commentary*, vol. 1, 160.

vow" (40. 3).[67] She then adds: "If I will not offer myself willingly for sacrifice, I fear that my death would not be acceptable and I would lose my life to no purpose."[68] But as she offers herself willingly, God accepts her self-sacrifice and says: "Now let her soul be given up in accord with her request, and her death will be precious before me always."[69] As noted by Cynthia M. Baker, Seila's "autonomy" is "Pseudo-Philo's own innovation."[70] This emphasis on Seila's heroism and willingness to be sacrificed sounds very Greek indeed. But it may also be explained by the events of the Jewish wars against Rome, the necessity to give a meaning to so many deaths and to encourage people to continue to resist. However, one should be aware of the fact that Seila's death is in no way a case of martyrdom. And this is true also of Isaac.

2. A willing victim in a "near-sacrifice"

The growing emphasis placed on self-sacrifice is even more striking in the case of Isaac. In the biblical narrative (Gen 22), nothing is said about Isaac's agreement to be sacrificed. He is strikingly silent and passive. In Jewish texts from the Hellenistic and Roman period, more emphasis is placed on Isaac's response to his father and on his willingness to be sacrificed,[71] even if Abraham's faith and commitment to God remain an important motif too, as the following texts show.

In *Pseudo-Jubilees b* (4Q226), frg. 7, l. II, one reads: "Abraham was found faithful to [G]o[d, and (...)]" (נמצא אברהם נאמן לאלהים);[72] this lacunary passage apparently refers to the testing of Abraham, who is declared "faithful," thus confounding Mastema and his angels.[73] In Wisdom, the accent is clearly placed on Abraham's righteousness: "Wisdom also (...) recognized the righteous man and preserved him blameless

[67] Ibid.

[68] Ibid.

[69] *L. A. B.* 40. 4, ibid., 161.

[70] "Pseudo-Philo and the Transformation of Jephthah's Daughter," in *Anti-Covenant: Counter-Reading Women's Lives in the Hebrew Bible* (ed. Mieke Bal; JSOTSup 81; Sheffield: The Almond Press, 1989), 195–209, 205.

[71] On this evolution, see Jon D. Levenson, *The Death and Resurrection of the Beloved Son: The Transformation of Child Sacrifice in Judaism and Christianity* (New Heaven: Yale University Press, 1993), 187–92.

[72] See VanderKam and Milik, DJD XIII, 165.

[73] See also *Jub.* 18. 9 "I know that he is one who fears the Lord" and 18. 16 "I have made known to everyone that you are faithful to me in everything that I have told you" (VanderKam, *The Book of Jubilees*, vol. 2, 106 and 109).

before God, and kept him strong in the face of his compassion for his child."[74] Still, the Hellenistic culture of the author may be perceived in his remark that Abraham might have had compassion on Isaac and thus failed to pass the test. Philo too is aware of the problems that arise from Gen 22. While condemning Canaanite children sacrifices, he praises Abraham for his obedience to God and his piety: "Mastered by his love for God, he mightily overcame all the fascination expressed in the fond terms of family affection [literally: the names and love-charms of kinship (συγγενεία)]" (*Abr.* 170).[75] § 174 also underscores that Abraham did not let compassion and love dissuade him to sacrifice his son. Interestingly, Philo is not so much bothered by the practice of human sacrifice itself[76] as by the argument that Abraham's deed was nothing extraordinary, since other parents and even kings sacrifice their children too (see §§ 178–83). He replies that Abraham's readiness to sacrifice his son, which goes against nature, is indeed different and worthy to be praised, since it was motivated only by his desire to obey God, and not by custom, necessity, or glory (see §§ 188–99). In §§ 200–7, Philo proceeds with his commentary by referring to an allegorical interpretation of Gen 22. But he does not condemn the literal meaning for all that. The explanation seems to be that, in this precise context, he tries to refute people who did not see in the sacrifice an abominable act, but just one more example of a common practice, thus denying the uniqueness of Abraham's deed. As a result, Philo wishes to show that it was indeed extraordinary and spends more time on the literal than on the allegorical meaning. But in *Migr.* 140, conversely, Philo rejects the literal meaning, and concerning Gen 22:3, he writes: "(. . .) he will sacrifice his only son, no human being (for the wise man is not a slayer of his offspring), but the male progeny of the rich and fertile soul, the fruit that blossomed upon it."[77] Here Philo's commentary is more congruent with his condemnation of human sacrifices in other passages of his work, as well as with the usual Jewish view of human sacrifices. Finally, the piety of Abraham

---

[74] Translation from *The Oxford Annotated Bible: The Apocrypha*, 113.

[75] Translation by Francis H. Colson, *Philo*, vol. 6 (LCL 289; Cambridge, Mass.: Cambridge University Press, 1935), 87.

[76] See also the remarks by Maren R. Niehoff in *Philo on Jewish Identity and Culture* (TSAJ 86; Tübingen: Mohr Siebeck, 2001), 171–74.

[77] Translation by Francis H. Colson and Graham H. Whitaker, *Philo*, vol. 4 (LCL 261; Cambridge, Mass.: Cambridge University Press, 1932), 211.

and his readiness to obey God are praised by Josephus too,[78] as well as by the author of the *L. A. B.*.[79]

In several texts, however, Isaac's attitude receives growing attention. In *Pseudo-Jubilees a* (4Q225), a text that has been quoted above (see § 2), the letter כ at the end of (what is left of) frg. 2 col. II l. 4 is probably the beginning of the imperative כפת, as proposed by VanderKam and agreed on by García Martínez.[80] In later (targumic or rabbinic) texts, Isaac's answer always starts with the demand to be firmly tied to the altar, in order not to move and make the sacrifice loose its value. If the reconstruction כ[פת] is accepted, 4Q225 may thus be considered our first witness to the tradition attributing to Isaac an explicit willingness to be sacrificed.[81]

In the *Jewish Antiquities*, Josephus comments on Isaac's reaction to the decision of his father to sacrifice him in the following terms:

> The son of such a father could not but be brave-hearted [or: with noble feelings, γενναῖον φρόνημα], and Isaac received these words with joy. He exclaimed that he deserved never to have been born at all, were he to reject the decision of God and of his father and not readily resign himself to what was the will of both, seeing that, were this the resolution of his father alone, it would have been impious to disobey; and with that he rushed to the altar and his doom.[82]

The adjective γενναῖος is reminiscent of the idea of "noble death," but it is a misleading association, since the death of Isaac is in no way a suicide committed in order not to surrender to an enemy. However, it may be

---

[78] See *A.J.* 1. 223 and 225, and Abraham's discourse in §§ 228–31; see Louis H. Feldman, "Hellenizations in Josephus' Jewish Antiquities: The Portrait of Abraham," in *Josephus, Judaism and Christianity* (ed. Louis H. Feldman and Gohei Hata; Detroit: Wayne State University Press, 1987), 133–53, 144 and 146–47; and above all the section "A Supreme Example of Hellenization: The 'Aqedah'," in the chapter "Abraham," in idem, *Josephus' Interpretation of the Bible* (Hellenistic Culture and Society 27; Berkeley: University of California Press, 1998), 266–85.

[79] See *L. A. B.* 18. 5, 32. 2 and 40. 2; the author goes so far as to write that Abraham was rejoicing. On the reasons why Gen 22 is referred to in these passages of the *L. A. B.*, see Fisk, "Offering Isaac."

[80] See VanderKam, DJD XIII, 149–51; García Martínez, "The Sacrifice of Isaac," 53.

[81] On the importance of this text for the history of the interpretation of Gen 22, see also Geza Vermes, "New Light on the Sacrifice of Isaac from 4Q225," *JJS* 47 (1996): 140–46 (he responds to the critiques formulated by Philip R. Davies and Bruce D. Chilton in "The Aqedah: A Revised Tradition History," *CBQ* 40 (1978): 514–46); Joseph A. Fitzmeyer, "The Sacrifice of Isaac in Qumran Literature," *Bib* 83 (2002): 211–29.

[82] *A.J.* 1 .232; translation by Thackeray, *Josephus*, 115.

that for apologetic reasons Josephus intended to present Isaac as capable of "noble death."[83]

In the *L. A. B*, the attitude of Isaac is evoked in Seila's speech, in which she remembers "the days of our fathers, when the father placed the son as a burnt offering, and he did not dispute him but gladly gave consent to him, and the one being offered was ready and the one who was offering was rejoicing."[84] The special value of Isaac's consent is set out more fully in *L. A. B.* 32. 3 (Deborah's speech), in which Isaac expresses himself as follows:

> Hear me, father. If a lamb of the flock is accepted as an offering to the Lord as an odor of sweetness and if for the sins of men animals are appointed to be killed, but man is designated to inherit the world, how is it that you do not say to me "Come and inherit a secure life and time without measure"? What if I had not been born into the world to be offered as a sacrifice to him who made me? Now my blessedness will be above that of all men, because there will be no other. Through me nations will be blessed and through me the peoples will understand that the Lord has deemed the soul of a man worthy to be a sacrifice.[85]

In spite of the awkward formulation of this speech,[86] it testifies to a noteworthy evolution in the understanding of human sacrifice. As opposed to the usual view that animals, not human beings, are to be sacrificed to God, the text states that the soul of a man too may be a sacrifice pleasing to God. But a paradoxical element remains, since Isaac will *not* be sacrificed. However, his willingness to give his own life should probably be considered the source of the blessing for the "nations." *L. A. B.* 32. 3 represents an important step towards the idea of a vicarious and expia-

---

[83] For a detailed analysis of Isaac's virtues according to Josephus, see Feldman, "Isaac," in idem, *Josephus' Interpretation of the Bible*, 290–303 (a previous version of which was published in 1993 in the *Rivista di Storia e Letteratura Religiosa* 29). He underlines the fact that Abraham is much more important to Josephus than Isaac (see 294). On Gen 22 in Josephus, see also the articles quoted above, n. 78.

[84] *L. A. B.* 40. 2; see Jacobson, *A Commentary*, 160 (Latin, 59: [. . .] *quando pater filium inponebat in holocaustum, et non contradixit ei sed epulans consensit illi, et erat qui offerebatur paratus, et qui offerebat gaudens*).

[85] Translation by Jacobson, ibid., 149.

[86] See Davies and Chilton, "The Aqedah: A Revised Tradition History," 524–25; Fisk, "Offering Isaac Again and Again," 496.

tory human sacrifice or death, even if this idea may not be considered fully developped yet in the *L. A. B.*.[87]

Finally, in no other text Isaac's near-sacrifice is so close to martyrdom as in 4 Maccabees, in which it is compared to the "near-martyrdom" of Daniel in the lions' den and of the three young men in the furnace. In the context of Antiochus' religious persecution, a mother exhorts her seven sons to follow the example of Isaac and show contempt for death (4 Macc 16,16 ff.):

> [16] My sons, noble is the contest (γενναῖος ὁ ἀγών); (...) strive zealously on behalf of the Law of our fathers. (...) [20] For His sake [i. e., *for the sake of God*] also was our father Abraham zealous to immolate his son Isaac, the father of a nation; nor did Isaac flinch when he saw his father's hand, armed with a sword, descending upon him (δι' ὃν καὶ ὁ πατὴρ ἡμῶν Αβρααμ ἔσπευδεν τὸν ἐθνοπάτορα υἱὸν σφαγιάσαι Ισαακ, καὶ τὴν πατρῴαν χεῖρα ξιφηφόρον καταφερομένην ἐπ' αὐτὸν ὁρῶν οὐκ ἔπτηξεν). [21] Moreover, Daniel the righteous was thrown to the lions; and Hananiah, Mishael, and Azariah were flung into the fiery furnace, and they endured for the sake of God. [22] Do you, too, therefore, hold the same faith in God, and be not dismayed; [23] for it would be unreasonable for you, who know religion (εἰδότας εὐσέβειαν), not to withstand suffering."[88]

Isaac is a model for the martyrs because he "endured immolation for religion's sake," according to 4 Macc 13:12. Thus, Hadas writes in a note: "Isaac as a patriarch remains the primal pattern of the willing martyr."[89] However, just as Daniel is not really to be considered a martyr (because he is ultimately saved by God), so Isaac is in no way a martyr. If one accepts Jan-Willem van Henten's definition of martyrdom,[90] it is obvious

---

87 See Geza Vermes, *Scripture and Tradition in Judaism: Haggadic Studies* (StPB 4; Leiden: Brill, 1961), 199–201; Davies and Chilton, ibid., 525–26; Fisk, ibid., 494–96.

88 Ed. and transl. by Moses Hadas, *The Third and Fourth Books of Maccabees* (JAL; New York: Harper & Brothers, 1953), 228–31. For other references to Abraham and Isaac in 4 Macc, see 14:20, 15:28, 17:6, 18:11, and especially 7:14, in which Eleazar is said to have "renewed youth in his spirit by means of reason, and by reason like Isaac's he prevailed over many-headed torture" (184–85).

89 Ibid., 211.

90 "A martyr text tells us about a specific kind of violent death, death by torture. A martyr text describes how a certain person, who is in an extremely hostile situation, prefers a violent death to compliance with a decree or demand of the (usually) Gentile authorities" ("Martyrion and Martyrdom: Some Remarks about Noble Death in Josephus," in *Internationales Josephus-Kolloquium Brüssel 1998* (ed. Folker Siegert and Jürgen U. Kalms; Münsteraner Judaistische Studien 4; Münster: Lit, 1999), 130; idem, *The Maccabean Martyrs*

that Isaac does not fit at all: he is not threatened by Gentile authorities or hostile people, and he suffers neither torture nor death. He may fairly be considered an example of a man willing to give his life to obey one of God's commands in a quite unconditional way, and from this viewpoint his attitude may be a source of inspiration for the martyrs, without his being a martyr himself. In any case, the interesting point in 4 Maccabees is that human sacrifice, if consisting in a willing self-sacrifice, becomes a positive act that may serve as a model for what will become a great religious achievement, martyrdom.[91]

Conclusion

Although human sacrifices are not a major theme in Jewish literature from the Hellenistic and Roman period, the topic is not completely missing, nor is it devoid of interest. Three points have been emphasized: the relative lack of references to pagan human sacrifices (in spite of the Biblical tradition that attributes a Canaanite origin to these practices); the tendency to present human sacrifices as inspired by demons; the reinterpretation of specific biblical human sacrifices or near-sacrifices (Jephthah's daughter, Isaac) as self-sacrifices to which a positive value is attached. Regardless of whether human sacrifices are considered a mistake inspired by demons or a valuable act of self-sacrifice, the issue of human sacrifices seems to have gained a cosmic or universal spiritual significance and may be considered an aspect of a cosmic spiritual fight, at least in some parts of Second Temple Judaism. Finally, even if condemnation of human sacrifices prevails in Jewish literature from this period, the moral judgement passed on human sacrifices remains ambivalent, as illustrated by the very notion of self-sacrifice.

---

as Saviours of the Jewish People: A Study of 2 and 4 Maccabees (JSJ Suppl. 57; Leiden: Brill, 1997), 7.

[91] On martyrdom in Judaism, see Tessa Rajak, "Dying for the Law: The Martyr's Portrait in Jewish-Greek Literature," in idem, *The Jewish Dialogue with Greece and Rome: Studies in Cultural and Social Interaction* (AGJU 48; Leiden: Brill, 2001; originally published in *Portraits: Biographical Representation in Greek and Latin Literature of the Roman Empire* [ed. Mark J. Edwards and Simon Swain; Oxford: Clarendon, 1997], 39–67), 99–133; Daniel Boyarin, *Dying for God: Martyrdom and the Making of Christianity and Judaism* (Figurae: Reading Medieval Culture 7; Stanford: Stanford University Press, 1999).

Gender Difference and the Rabbis

Bat Yiftah as Human Sacrifice

Tal Ilan, Freie Universität, Berlin

When we read today the biblical story of Yiftah sacrificing his daughter to the God of Israel we are intrigued by the problem of a human sacrifice to the God of Israel actually taking place on the pages of the Bible. How is it possible that it happened? How did the God of Israel let it happen? The usual scholarly answer to this question is that the Bible wishes to portray the time of the judges as a bad time, when the Torah was lost from Israel and righteousness faltered. The book of Judges ends with a long lament on the absence of a king who would bring order to the country. The sequel to these times is the foundation of a monarchy in the Book of Samuel.[1]

Yet scholars have also pointed out that this answer is only partial. The book of Judges is not completely negative toward its judges and is not completely pro-monarchy. For example, the first attempt to crown a king in the Book of Judges is proclaimed a failure [Jdg 9], and Yotam's parable of the trees is a strong argument against the desirability of kings [vv. 5–21]. Furthermore, in the Book of Samuel itself we find Samuel's powerful speech against monarchy and its ills [1 Sam 8:10–18]. Thus, we see that such a view of the biblical position is limited.[2]

---

[1] See e. g. Yehuda Elitzur, *The Book of Judges* (Torah, Neviim, Ketuvim im perush Daat Mikra; Jerusalem: Mosad haRav Kuk, 2nd ed. Jerusalem 1989), 9–10, 24–26 [Hebrew]; Dennis T. Olson, "The Book of Judges: Introduction, Commentary and Reflections," in *NIB*, 725–26; 731–32. In this article only a sample bibliography on the Book of Judges will be cited. My main interest is the reworking of the story of Yiftah's daughter in rabbinic literature. The only earlier discussion of these texts that I am aware of is found in Leila Leah Bronner, *From Eve to Esther: Rabbinic Reconstructions of Biblical Women* (Gender and Biblical Tradition 1; Louisville, Ky: Westminster, 1994), 129–34, where she discusses many of the texts cited here.

[2] E. g. J. Alberto Soggin, *Judges: A Commentary* (OTL; Philadelphia: Westminster, 1981), 176–77.

This view is modified by those who would argue that only the last chapters of the Book of Judges are pro-monarchic. These tell of a foundation of an illegitimate temple in Dan (Judg 17–18) and of the rape of the Levite's concubine by the Benjaminites of Gibeah (Judg 19–21). The leitmotif of these chapters is the repeated verse: "In those days there was no king in Israel. Every person did as was right in his eyes" (17:6; 19:1; 21:25).[3] Those who make this limited argument, however, cannot use the story of Yiftah's daughter as an example to demonstrate the evils of monarch-less times, since it is found far earlier in the book, after the first failed attempt by Abimelech to crown himself king (Judg 9) and before the Samson cycle (Judg 13–16).

Thus, another, revolutionary suggestion has been put forward recently, namely that human sacrifice is not so anomalous or outrageous in the eyes of the God of Israel.[4]

A further scholarly suggestion for explaining the human sacrifice story is that some chapters of the Book of Judges have parallels in Genesis, but with a negative outcome in the former. Both the populace of Sodom demand that the messengers (angels) who have come to Lot be handed over to them to be raped (Gen 19:5), and the Benjaminites of Gibeah make a similar claim toward the Levite and his concubine (Judg 19:22). But while the messengers of Sodom are saved by a miracle (Gen 19:10–11), the concubine is handed over, raped and murdered (Judg 19:25–27). Similarly, Abraham is commanded to sacrifice his son, but Isaac is saved at the last moment (Gen 22:11–12). Yiftah's daughter, on the other hand, is sacrificed by her father (Judg 11:39). No divine intervention is reserved for her.[5] This is an exciting literary observation, but not a real answer to the question, why would these parallel stories be told with contradictory conclusions.

This is where gender studies have brought useful insights into play. It has rightly been claimed that these bad things don't just happen in Judges where they did not happen in Genesis. They also happen to women but not to men. Women are raped but not men. Daughters are sacrificed, but not sons. Gender scholars have argued that this is because

---

[3] E. g. Olson, "Judges," 864–65.

[4] Jon D. Levenson, *The Death and Resurrection of the Beloved Son: The Transformation of Child Sacrifice in Judaism and Christianity* (New Haven: Yale University Press, 1993); Carol L. Delaney, *Abraham on Trial: The Social Legacy of Biblical Myth* (Princeton: Princeton University Press, 1998).

[5] E. g. Soggin, *Judges*, 215; 282.

biblical texts use women to imagine the unimaginable for men. They use women because they take less pity on them.[6]

The Early Rabbis

This study is about the reflection of the story of Yiftah's daughter in rabbinic literature. It appears that the rabbis were interested in questions similar to the ones we raised above. Their first observations on the story of Yiftah's daughter make it abundantly clear that they do not believe that the God of Israel ever required human sacrifice and they think he was displeased with such offerings. In doing so, they, like us associated the sacrifice of Yiftah's daughter with the near-sacrifice of Isaac. In the earliest Tannaitic layer of rabbinic literature (dating to the 2nd–3rd cent. C. E.) we find them grouping together various stories associated with human sacrifice found in the Bible one with the other and with God's displeasure. Their argument is formulated as follows: The Hinom Valley in Jerusalem is identified in the Bible as the site of human sacrifice to the Canaanite god Molech or Baal (2 Kgs 23:10; Jer 7:31; 19:5; 32:35; 2 Chr 28:3; 33:6). Three times the prophet Jeremiah accuses the Israelites of sacrificing children to foreign gods at that location and then states emphatically: "They [i. e. the children of Israel] built the high places of Baal in the Tophet in the Hinom Valley to burn their sons and daughters in fire as burnt offerings which I did not command or decree, nor did it come into my mind" (e. g. Jer 19:5). It is this verse that the rabbis use to connect the story of Yiftah's daughter with that of Isaac. They state:

> Rabbi Yosi said: My son Eleazar says three things [in connection with this verse]: "I did not command," in my Torah "or decree" in the Ten Commandments "nor had it come into my mind" that a person should sacrifice his son on the alter. Others say: "I did not command," Yifatah "or decree" Mesha King of Moab [who also sacrificed his son, cf. 2 Kings 3:27] "nor did it come into my mind" that Abraham should sacrifice his son to me on the alter. (*Sifre Deut* 148)

[6] The most important studies for these arguments are Phylis Trible, *Texts of Terror: Literary-Feminist Readings of Biblical Narratives* (OBT 13; Philadelphia: Fortress, 1984), 65–116; Mike Bal, *Death and Dissymmetry: The Politics of Coherence in the Book of Judges* (CSJH; Chicago: University of Chicago Press, 1988).

This midrash associates a prophetic diatribe against human sacrifice with three actual events mentioned in the Bible where human sacrifice took place. By associating the actual sacrifice of Yiftah's daughter with the trail of Abraham, the rabbis indicate that they are aware of the similarity between the case of Abraham, who was willing to sacrifice his son to his God, but was prevented from doing so at the last moment, and the case of Yiftah who was also willing to sacrifice his daughter to his God, an act that was not prevented and thus took place. Yet at this point they were not willing to go beyond condemning both cases as going against the will of God.

The other observation about Yiftah and his generation of judges displaying a time of lax law and order, which we saw in modern scholarship, we also find in the earliest Tannaitic stratum of rabbinic literature. This observation is made in association with the only other verse in the Bible found outside the Book of Judges were Yiftah is mentioned. In 1 Sam 12 the prophet Samuel relates to the people a concise history of Israel up to his time, mentioning the Exodus, where Moses and Aaron had been prominent, and then the time of the judges, mentioning three by name—Yerubaal, Bedan and Yiftah. At least one of the judges that is mentioned in this list (Bedan) is unknown from the Book of Judges. On this verse the early rabbis of the *Tosefta* make the following observation:

> It is written: "The Lord who appointed Moses and Aaron" [1 Sam 12:6] and it is also written: "And the Lord sent Yerubaal and Bedan and Yiftah and Samuel" [1 Sam 12:11]. "Yerubaal" is Gideon [as in Judg 7:1]; "Bedan" is Samson and "Yiftah" is Yiftah. Elsewhere in scripture it is written "Moses and Aaron were among his priests and Samuel also was among those who called his name" [Ps 99:6]. Thus scripture [in 1 Sam 12] has placed three lightweights of the world among three of the world's greatest. This is to teach you that the court of Yerubaal was in the eyes of God as great as the court of Moses and the court of Yiftah was as great in his eyes as that of Samuel. You are thus informed that whoever is nominated leader of the people, even if he is the lightest of weight, is considered equal to the greatest of the great. It is also stated "If any case arises requiring decision between one kind of bloodshed and another; one kind of legal right or another; one kind of assault or another; any case within

> your town that is too difficult for you, then you shall arise and go up to the place which the Lord your God will choose and coming to the Levitical priests and to the judge who is in office in those days, you shall consult them and they shall declare to you the decision. Then you shall do according to what they declare to you" [Deut 17:8–10]. You have no other judge than the one of your generation. And scripture also says: "Say not: Why were the former days better than these?" [Qoh 7:10]. (*t. Roš Haš* 1:18)

The purpose of this text is to observe that some generations produce men of better quality and some do not, but that every generation needs to rely on the judges and courts of its day, as they are God's representatives on earth. The rabbis' critical view of the time of the judges as being inferior in the quality of the leaders and law-courts it produced is demonstrated by suggesting that the courts of Gideon, Samson and Yiftah produced inferior verdicts compared to the courts of Moses, Aaron and Samuel. Thus the observation of modern scholars that the time of the judges was a time of turmoil and unrest, which needed correcting, is seconded by the rabbinic judgement.

This early tradition does not suggest in any detail how the court of Yiftah had produced impaired justice. However it certainly served as a departure point for later midrashim precisely on the issue raised above, namely how could it have happened that God allowed a case of human sacrifice to ever take place in Israel at this time. The following midrash is from the *Genesis Rabbah*, an early Aggadic midrash from the Land of Israel, probably dating to the 4th–5th cent. C. E.:

> And was Phinehas the Priest not present there to annul [Yiftah's] vow? Yet Phinehas said [to himself]: He needs me, so why should I go to him? Furthermore, I am a high-priest, son of a high-priest, why should I go to this ignoramus? Yiftah, on the other hand, said [to himself]: I am the head of all the officers of Israel. Should I be going to Phinehas? Between this one and this one the girl was lost. (*Gen. Rab.* 60)

This tradition suggests how the justice system of Yiftah's days failed to function properly. Honor was at stake. Yiftah had taken a vow to sacrifice his daughter. But according to rabbinic legal development, a competent priest or judge may release Israelites from their vows (*m.Ned.* 9).

Because they believe that the Torah is eternal, the rabbis assume that biblical heroes should act according to rabbinic legal fictions. This tradition thus nicely illustrates the rabbinic principle, often at work in their composition, that "there is no early or late in the Torah" (e.g. *b. Pesaḥ* 6b). Phinehas was certainly a competent priest who could annul vows. However, guarding his honor against the infringement of the likes of an upstart like Yiftah prevented him from saving the girl. Similarly, honor considerations also prevented Yiftah from consuling Phinehas. He jealously guarded his newly won honor, gained in war and victory over Israel's enemies, and he refused to bow to Phinehas' authority. Both were equally responsible for the girl's death. The tradition thus continues to show how God eventually punished both for failing to cooperate:

> And both were punished for her bloodshed. Yiftah died by his limbs falling off. Everywhere he went he lost a limb and it was buried there, as it is written "And Yiftah of Gilead died and was buried in the *towns* of Gilead" [Judg 12:7]. It is not written "the town of Gilead" but the "towns of Gilead." Phinehas lost his divine inspiration, as it is written "Phinehas son of Eleazar son of Aaron the priest was ruler over them in time past. God had been with him" [1 Chr 9:20]. It is not written "is ruler over them" but rather "*was* ruler over them in time past." (ibid.)

This text is a beautiful example of a close and precise reading of the text, in which the rabbis pay attention to textual details. They observe the plural form mentioned in the biblical text for the place of Yiftah's burial; they also note the past tense used in the Book of Chronicles with regard to Phineas' divine inspiration. This is done in order to produce a historical reconstruction, which shows God's justice at work in Israel. Bickering over honor caused Yiftah's daughter to die, and those who were guilty of this injustice were duly punished. The issue, which this tradition seems to ignore, however, is the unnecessary bloodshed that had taken place and which in turn required the punishment of Yiftah and Phinehas. If God could punish the latter, he could certainly have saved the former.

The rabbis of *Genesis Rabbah* also note this difficulty. They, being Torah scholars, are on the lookout for other halakhic solutions to Yiftah's difficulty. Obviously going to Phinehas to annul his vow would have been one such outlet. But with their knowledge of Torah, they suggest other solutions as well. With relation to it, they make the following halakhic observations:

> Rabbi Yohanan and Resh Laqish. Rabbi Yohanan Said: He should have dedicated her to God [הקדש דמים, literally blood dedication, or monetary dedication] instead of sacrificing her. Resh Laqish said: He should not even have dedicated her, since the rabbis teach: "If a person said about an unclean or crippled animal: These are a burnt offering, he has said nothing. [If he said] these are *for* a burnt offering, they should be sold, and a sacrifice should be bought and sacrificed for their price. (ibid.)

This halakhic discussion is rather complicated. The sacrifice that Yiftah offered to bring to God if he arrive victorious was a "burnt offering" (עולה Judg 11:31). However, according to rabbinic ruling (*m. Tem* 3:3), for this sort of sacrifice, one should only bring male beasts. A Tannaitic tradition quoted only in the *Yerushalmi* further observes that if a person chose a female for the burnt offering sacrifice, it should be dedicated to God instead of being sacrificed. This means that it should not be used for labor or slaughtered for food, but should eventually die of old age (*y. Pesaḥ* 9:6, 37 a). Rabbi Yohanan compares Yiftah's daughter to a female chosen for a burnt offering, which is valid only for males. However, Resh Laqish suggests another analogy. He compares Yiftah's daughter not to a female but to an unclean beast. Another rabbinic dictum, which he then quotes (*m. Tem* 5:6), states that when such a promise had been made, depending on the language of the promise, one either has not made a promise at all, or should sell the unclean animal and buy a pure one with the money and sacrifice the latter as a burnt offering. The difference in terminology is based on whether the sacrificer had used the word עולה or לעולה. Since the biblical text about Yiftah clearly uses the first of these two formulations, Resh Laqish maintains that his vow was invalid, and he should have done nothing. Both Rabbi Yohanan and Resh Laqish think Yiftah should not have sacrificed his daughter and had acted foolishly because he did not know the law. Like Phinehas, the priest of his day, they view him as an ignoramus. Note that Rabbi Yohanan and Resh Laqish also think it possible for Yiftah to have known not just the written Torah, handed down in Sinai, but also rabbinic dicta added to it at a later stage.

So we see that like modern scholarly observation, the rabbis, too, considered the times of the judges as bad times. It is thus of interest to inquire whether the rabbis, like modern scholars, also noted the gender discrimination between the story of a male human sacrifice and the story about a female one. The tradition just cited from *Gen. Rab.* actually begins with an observation which may be thus considered:

> "Behold, I am standing by the spring of water and the daughters of the men of the city are coming out to draw water. Let the maiden to whom I shall say: Pray let down your jar that I may drink, who shall say: Drink and I will water your camels, let her be the one whom thou has appointed for thy servant Isaac" [Gen 24:13–14]. Four asked indecently. Three were answered decently and one was answered indecently. And these are Eliezer, Caleb, Saul and Yiftah. Eliezer said: "Let the maiden etc." And what if she had been a maidservant? The Holy One blessed be He presented Rebecca to him. Caleb said: "Whoever smites Kiryat Sefer and takes it, to him will I give Akhsah, my daughter as wife" [Josh 15:16]. And what if he had been a slave? The Holy One blessed be He presented Othniel to him. Saul said: "The man who kills [Goliath] the king will enrich with great riches and will give him his daughter" [1 Sam 17:25]. And what if he had been a slave? God presented David to him. Yiftah asked indecently and Holy One blessed be He answered him indecently. Asked indecently, as it is written: "And Yiftah made a vow to the Lord and said: If thou wilt give the Ammonites into my hand, then whoever comes forth from the doors of my house to meet me when I return victorious from the Ammonites, shall be the Lord's and I will offer him up as a burnt offering" [Judg 11:30]. Said the Holy One blessed be He to him: and what if it had been a camel or a donkey or a dog? Would you have sacrificed [an unclean animal] to me? What did the Holy One blessed be He do? Presented his daughter to him, as it is written "And Yiftah came to his home in Mitzpah and behold, his daughter came out to meet him with timbrels and dance" [Judg 11:34]. (ibid.)

This midrash makes a clear distinction between all the cases were a vow was produced putting God on trial and to which he responded favorably and the case of Yifah's daughter, where he responded vindictively. The rabbis seem to suggest that this happened because in all other cases the vow uttered involves marital obligations between humans, and the worst that could have happened was the production of a match between persons of unequal social status. In the case of Yiftah's vow sacrilege may have occurred. Yiftah may have offered God an unclean animal as sacrifice. To this God reacted mercilessly by sending out Yiftah's daughter. Unlike the second part of this midrash, where the daughter is lost in a struggle over honor between her father and a priest, in this part of the midrash she is lost in a struggle between God and his faithless servant. God sends out the daughter as punishment for the father.

Yet, we may also observe here another disparity between the three cases, which are favorably answered, and this one, which is answered negatively. In all three other cases we find biblical male heroes about to be married—Isaac, Othniel the first Judge, and David. God seems disinclined to punish his male heroes and so the vows they (or someone on their behalf) made produce the right match. The case of Yiftah's daughter is not similar. No one is about to get married here. In fact we hear at the end of the story that the daughter dies tragically as an unmarried virgin. As opposed to his male heroes, on whom God takes pity, he has no such compassion for his female ones. By putting all these biblical texts one next to the other, the rabbis have come close to revealing to us the gender prejudice present in the composition of the Bible. In this their observations come close to those of modern feminist scholars.[7]

The Tanhuma

A late, post-Talmudic rabbinic composition (7th–9th cent.) collects all these materials together and creates a completely new composition regarding Yiftah's daughter. We may view this long text as a late retelling of the biblical story, and a culmination of all rabbinic considerations, woven into one common thread. In addition, however, it is surprising to note that this text makes Yiftah's daughter into its heroine, giving her a voice and allowing her to speak for herself, against her father and against the entire establishment which conspires to kill her. I shall

---

[7] For a modern comparison of Akhsah and Yiftah's daughter see Bal, *Death and Dissymmetry*, 43–44, 49.

present the text in the order in which it appears in the midrash *Tanhuma*, commenting on it as I go along.

> Another idea. "When a man makes a special vow of persons to the Lord at your valuation. Then your valuation of a male from twenty years up to sixty years old shall be fifty shekel of silver, according to the shekel of the sanctuary. If the person is a female your valuation should be thirty shekel" [Lev 27:2–3]. (*Tanhuma* [Buber], *Behuqotai* 7).

The discussion in *Tanḥ.* begins with a biblical verse from the legal section of the Torah, which discusses the case of a vow a person makes to God to present to him a living soul, whether his own or someone else's. The text continues by explaining that such a vow entails monitory payment. A person who makes such a vow is required to lay out money instead of dying or killing someone. This is the verse that the *Tanḥ.* chooses in order to raise the issue of Yiftah's daughter. We may assume that like Rabbi Yohanan and Resh Laqish in *Gen. Rab.* the editors of the *Tanḥ.* will claim that had Yiftah read this biblical verse, he would have known that the sacrifice of his daughter was unnecessary. This midrash will, however, be less complicated, because it does not require Yiftah to be acquainted with late rabbinic legislation. What it suggests is that the Torah is full of legal loopholes, which would have made Yiftah's vow null and void.

As is usual in *Tanḥ.* discourse, a counter verse from the later books of the Bible will now be presented as an intertext, which highlights and explains the verse at hand:

> This is what is meant by the verse "The fruit of the righteous is a tree of life, [and he who takes souls is wise]" [Prov 11:30]. This refers to the Torah, since whoever is a Torah scholar learns how to take souls, as you read "he who takes souls is wise." Thus you also find with Yiftah of Gilead that because he was no Torah scholar he lost his daughter. (ibid.)

The intertext the rabbis have chosen comes from Proverbs, where it is claimed that only a wise person should be allowed to take souls. What the original meaning of this verse was is now hard to decide.[8] The rabbis connect "taking souls" with making a vow for a living soul. They

[8] E. g. see the translation of this verse in RSV.

use the association of taking souls in Prov with a wise person in order to demonstrate that Yiftah had made such a vow, but since he was not learned in Torah (i. e. not wise), he lost. Thus we have a legal ruling from the Torah, an extension of this pronouncement from wisdom literature, and a biblical story—that of Yiftah and his daughter—which demonstrates the connection between the two verses. The text continues by demonstrating these claims:

> When did this happen? When he was fighting the Ammonites he made a vow, as it is written: "And Yiftah made a vow to the Lord and said: If thou wilt give the Ammonites into my hand, then whoever comes forth from the doors of my house to meet me when I return victorious from the Ammonites, shall be the Lord's and I will offer him up as a burnt offering" [Judg 11:31]. At that moment the Holy One blessed be He became angry with him. The Holy One blessed be He said: If a dog or a pig or a camel confronts him when he comes home, would he sacrifice it to me? Thus he presented his daughter to him, as it is written "and behold, his daughter came out to meet him with timbrels and dance and when he saw her he rent his clothes" [Judg 11:34–35]. (ibid.)

Here we see how the *Tanḥ.* editor isolated God's argument against Yiftah from the broader context of the *Gen. Rab.* midrash on biblical heroes who made indecent vows making it part of the extended story of Yiftah's daughter. Having done so, the storyteller now uses another part of the *Gen. Rab.* text:

> But Phinehas was there, and yet he said: "I cannot take back my vow" [Judg 11:35]. This is because Phinehas said: Should I, a high-priest, son of a high-priest, degrade myself and go to this ignoramus? And Yiftah said: Should I, the head of the tribes of Israel, head of its officers, degrade myself and go to that private citizen? Between the two the poor soul was lost. And both were punished for her bloodshed. The Holy Spirit departed from Phinehas, and the bones of Yiftah became scattered, as it is written "and he was buried in the towns of Gilead" [Judg 12:7]. (ibid.)

This of course is an almost verbatim insertion of the *Gen. Rab.* tradition we have just encountered. But now the story shifts. Since these two men refused to use their power to save the girl, she is hence allowed to take the initiative. The *Tanḥ.* continues:

> His daughter said to him: My father, is it written in the Torah that [the Israelites] should sacrifice the souls of their children on the alter? On the contrary, it is written: "When any one of you brings an offering to the Lord, you shall bring your offering of cattle from the herd or from the flock" [Lev 1:2] "of cattle" and not of people. He said to her: My daughter, I have vowed "whoever comes forth from the doors of my house" [Judg 11:31]. She said to him: Our father Jacob had vowed "And of all that that thou givest me I will give the tenth to thee" [Gen 28:22]. And the Holy One blessed be He gave him twelve tribes. Did he sacrifice one of them? And furthermore, Hannah vowed, saying "I will give him to the Lord all the days of his life" [1 Sam 1:11]. Did she sacrifice her son to the Holy One blessed be He? All this she said to him but he did not heed her. She thus said to him: Leave me and I shall go to the law court, perhaps one of them will find a let-out for you, as it is written: "Let me alone for two months that I may go down to the mountains" [Judg 11:37]. Said Rabbi Levi ben Berachiah: Is there a man who goes down to the mountains? One goes up to the mountains. What does "go down to the mountains" mean? These are the Sanhedrin, as it said "Hear you mountains the controversy of the Lord" [Mic 6:2].

The failure of the men in the story to find compassion in their hearts to save the girl, and the despair of the *Tanḥ.* editor from his predecessors' disinterest in the fate of the daughter, leads him to place in her mouth the strongest arguments he can muster against her sacrifice. She quotes scripture in order to prove that the God of Israel did not institute human sacrifice. She brings biblical examples, which show that other vows made by Israelites were not taken literally. Jacob had not sacrificed a son. Neither did Hannah actually sacrifice Samuel. The rabbinic principle we saw at work in the *Gen. Rab.* tradition that "there is no early or late in the Torah" allows the rabbis to have Yiftah's daughter bring

Hannah as an example although the latter had supposedly lived quite a while after Yiftah's daughter.

Yiftah's daughter's plea to her father, and afterwards to the court of law of her days shows that the *Tanḥ.* editor finds it hard to believe that she went silently to her death. According to this version the daughter did not want to die, and since no one did anything for her, she had to take the initiative. However, as the biblical story continues, and as the *Tanḥ.* is ultimately dependent on the biblical story, we find that all her attempts fail. The text continues:

> She went to them but they did not find an outlet for his vow. About them scripture remarks: "A poor man who oppresses the needy is a downpour with no bread" [Prov 28:3]. "A poor man" is Yiftah who was poor in Torah. He was an offshoot of a sycamore. "Who oppresses the needy" that he oppressed the needy when he said [to the people of the tribe of Ephraim] "say Shibolet and he said Sibolet" [Judg 12:6] and he would slaughter him. Thus "a downpour with no bread," since there was someone to annul his vow but "no bread," since the Holy One blessed be He hid the halakhah from them, so that they will find no outlet to annul his vow. Since they found no outlet he went up and slaughtered her before the Holy One blessed be He.

This part of the text is also an original *Tanḥ.* composition. The editors interpret another biblical verse, also from Prov, as referring to Yiftah, in order to illustrate the principle we had seen at play further up in this discussion, that the justice distributed in the days of Yiftah was of a lower quality than that of other historical times. They do so by referring to another biblical event which involves Yiftah and which has not yet been associated in any midrash with the story of Yiftah's daughter. It is the story of his relations with members of the neighbor tribe—Ephraim. Yiftah had proved himself an unjust and bloody man not just with relation to his daughter but also with relation to his co-Israelites. Thus, when the rabbis of the *Tanḥ.* finally describe Yiftah's action against his daughter, they do not use sacrifice language, but rather the language of murder and bloodshed—slaughter (שחט).

The *Tanḥ.* discussion continues with reference to the earliest Tannaitic Yiftah tradition, which links him negatively to Jeremiah's anti-human-sacrifice diatribe.

> And the Holy Spirit calls out: Did I ask for souls to be sacrificed to me "which I did not command, or decree nor did it come into my mind" [Jer 19:5]. "That I did not command" Abraham to slaughter his son, but rather said to him: "Do not lay your hand on the lad" [Gen 22:12]. I did this to show how Abraham would do my bidding, because the nations of the world were inquiring why does the Holy One blessed be He love Abraham so. So he said to him: "Take your son" [Gen 22:2], thus, "I did not command" Abraham to slaughter his son "or decree" to Yiftah to sacrifice his daughter "nor did it come into my mind" that the King of Moab should fall into the hands of the King of Israel and that he would sacrifice his firstborn to me, as it is written: "Then he took his eldest son who was to reign in his stead and offered him for a burnt offering upon the wall" [2 Kgs 3:27].

Having faithfully reproduced this early tradition, the *Tanḥ.* ends its discussion in the normal circular way of the rabbinic proem, returning to the question raised at the beginning of the text, namely the tragic results of not being a Torah scholar. Had Yiftah known the Torah, he would not have needed to abide by his vow to sacrifice his daughter. Here the *Tanḥ.* returns to the biblical verses from Lev and Prov with which it had began its long midrash.

> What caused Yiftah to lose his daughter? The fact that he did not read the Torah. For had he read the Torah he would not have lost his daughter, as it is written "When a man makes a special vow etc." [Lev 27:3] "if the person is a female etc." [v. 4]. Thus "The fruit of the righteous is a tree of life" [Prov 11:30].

If the text of the *Tanḥ.* indeed sums up and represents faithfully rabbinic reflections about the sacrifice of Yiftah's daughter, we may observe that their concerns had not been far removed from ours when reading the story. They noted with horror Yiftah's actions and interpreted them as impious. They explained them against their historiographic understanding of the time of the Judges as a time of injustice, and raised several legal objections that would have been used in better times to prevent such an event from taking place. In the *Tanḥ.*, in the absence of other Torah scholars to teach the law and make legal deductions from legal precedents, it becomes the daughter's obligation to speak up and teach us all Torah. Thus the *Tanḥ.* is employing here an important principle taken from feminist reading strategies of placing the woman at the center and giving the marginalized a voice. That she is not heard is, in their opinion, a strong indictment of a system that ignores the words of a wise woman.

Human Sacrifice and Pauline Christology

PETER LAMPE, University of Heidelberg

Struggling with image problems, the early Christians had to defend themselves against allegations that they were celebrating Thyestean feasts (Θυέστεια δεῖπνα), sacrificing and eating human flesh (of children) during their Eucharist (Athenagoras, *Supplic.* 3; 31). They vehemently rejected these allegations. Was there, however, some truth to the accusations, at least some symbolic truth? Did not God, for example, sacrifice his own child, letting his sadism run free, as one modern writer put it?[1] We will explore early Christian Christology, particularly Paul's Christological thinking (I.), before we analyze its application in the eucharistic ritual (II.). The source texts are seldom exegetically uncomplicated.

I. Christology

Jesus of Nazareth died on a Roman cross as a criminal. In a limited time span after this death, Peter and other apostles had visions of the deceased Jesus. Instead of interpreting these visual experiences as apparitions of a ghost, they understood them within the framework of the Jewish category of "resurrection" (Dan 12; etc.), believing that God had raised Jesus from the dead and enthroned him as Lord (κύριος) at God's right hand (e. g., 1 Cor 15:3–8; Rom 1:4). For them, in the light of this resurrection, the senseless and shameful death of Jesus suddenly took on a positive meaning: Jesus died "for our sins" (ὑπὲρ τῶν ἁμαρτιῶν ἡμῶν 1 Cor 15:3; the expression is part of a pre-Pauline formula). There is "deliverance in Christ Jesus, whom God put forward as a *place of atonement because of his blood . . .* " (χάρις διὰ τῆς ἀπολυτρώσεως τῆς ἐν Χριστῷ Ἰησοῦ ὃν προέθετο ὁ θεὸς ἱλαστήριον διὰ πίστεως ἐν τῷ αὐτοῦ αἵματι

[1] Tilmann Moser, *Gottesvergiftung* (Frankfurt/Main: Suhrkamp, 1980), 20: "Bei deinem eigenen Sohn warst du dann ungeniert und hast deinem Sadismus freien Lauf gelassen."

Rom 3:24 f.). He was "sacrificed" as "our paschal lamb" (τὸ πάσχα ἡμῶν ἐτύθη Χριστός 1 Cor 5:7). His blood makes possible a "new covenant" (τοῦτο τὸ ποτήριον ἡ καινὴ διαθήκη ἐστὶν ἐν τῷ ἐμῷ αἵματι 1 Cor 11:25, which is another pre-Pauline formula).

Particularly the Old Testament category "*place of atonement*" (ἱλαστήριον) needs explanation. Does it mean that Christ's crucifixion was understood as a human "sacrifice," a "sacrifice of atonement" (*"Sühnopfer"*)? In a further step, we will need to explore whether sacrificial categories other than "atonement" were applied to the Christ event. Finally, we will need to ask how prominent the sacrificial categories were in Pauline Christological thinking. Are the numerous ὑπέρ formulations ("for us" 1 Cor 11:24; "for our sins" 15:3; etc.) to be interpreted within the framework of the ἱλαστήριον idea or of other sacrificial categories?

The result will be differentiated. In Paul, Christ's death on a Roman cross can be seen in analogy to the offering of a Passover lamb, and in analogy to the covenant "burnt offerings" and "peace offerings" of Exod 24 (the latter always were connected with a festive communal meal). Contrary to widespread opinion, however, Paul did *not* interpret Christ's death as a "sacrifice of atonement" for sins (Lev 4 f.; 16), and he did *not* see an analogy to the attempted offering of Isaac in Gen 22. The ὑπέρ formulations do *not* represent a sacrificial category.

1. Leviticus 4 f.; 16: Sacrifice of atonement (כפר) for sin / offence (אשם / חטאת)

According to Old Testament tradition, rituals of atonement broke the connection between wrong doing and its damaging consequences, between sin and resulting disaster. One of these rituals was the animal sacrifice of atonement (Lev 4 f.; 4:20: כפר). By slaughtering an animal and sprinkling the altar with its blood, i. e., by offering the animal's life and vitality to God (17:11), the sacrificing person eliminated the imminent disastrous consequences of sinful behavior.

This sacrifice of atonement only wiped out sins that were committed ignorantly (4:2, 13, 22, 27; 5:2–4, 15, 17 f.), not transgressions deliberately done. Therefore, the older scholarly opinion, according to which the sacrificial animal died *on behalf of* the sinner, needs to be discarded.[2]

[2] Cf. the discussion in, e. g., Manfred Oeming, "'Fürwahr, er trug unsere Schuld': Die Bedeutung der alttestamentlichen Vorstellungen von Sünde und Sündenvergebung für das Verständnis der neutestamentlichen Abendmahlstraditionen," in: *Sühne, Opfer,*

If it had died "on behalf of" the sinner, *representing* the sinner's entire existence, the deliberate sins also would have been eliminated by this death. But they were not.[3]

Furthermore, sins committed in ignorance did not deserve death. Therefore, there was no need for a death *in lieu of* that of the sinner. Thirdly, if the sacrificial animal had been perceived as representative of and identical to the sinful existence of the sacrificing person, the animal would have been construed as ritually unclean. On the contrary, however, it was perceived as extremely holy.[4] Fourth, by laying the hand on the head of the sacrificial animal, the sacrificing sinner did not express that the animal *represented* the sinner. Laying the hand on the animal's head was not an act of *identification*.[5] It was less complicated: This gesture made sure that the sacrifice was given in the name of this person, that is, that the resulting atonement was an atonement for exactly this person who laid a hand on the animal's head—and for nobody else (Lev 1:4; 4:4, 15, 24, 29, 33). Since the person, who performed the atoning ritual, a priest, was not identical with the person(s) who needed atonement (4:15 f., 24 f., 29 f., 33 f.), a ritual gesture was needed to identify the person(s) for whom the atonement ritual was celebrated. By laying a hand on the animal, the sacrificing person also expressed the wish that God would accept the offering: "He shall lay his hand upon the head of the burnt offering, and it shall be accepted" (Lev 1:4).

In Lev 4, the only act of identification or representation was that the elders of the congregation of Israel could represent the entire congregation when laying their hands on the sacrificial animal. If Gese[6] were right, we would have to assume a complicated process of double identification: The congregation was represented by the elders, who in turn would have been represented by the sacrificial animal. The latter would have died in place of the elders, who in turn symbolically would have died in place of the whole congregation. Things do not need to be made more complicated than they were.

A second misunderstanding would be to assume that the animal took over the burden of sin and eliminated it by dying.[7] It was rather the sprinkling of blood at the altar that constituted the center of the atoning ritual and that brought about the atonement. God, as creator, gave the animal's blood, i. e., the animal's life, to the sacrificing person, who

---

Abendmahl: Vier Zugänge zum Verständnis des Abendmahls (ed. idem and Andreas Wagner; Neukirchen: Neukirchener, 1999), 1–36, and Siegrid Brandt, *Opfer als Gedächtnis: Auf dem Weg zu einer befreienden theologischen Rede von Opfer* (Altes Testament und Moderne 2; Münster: Lit, 2001), 133–40.

[3] Cf., e. g., Num 15:30 f.; 35:6–34. The only exceptions from this rule were formulated in Lev 5:1, 20–26. Lev 5 lists special cases.

[4] See Brandt, *Opfer*, 133. For additional reasons against the identification / representation theory, which are not repeated here, see 134–36.

[5] Contra Hartmut Gese, "Die Sühne," in: *Zur biblischen Theologie: Alttestamentliche Vorträge* (ed. idem; BEvT 78; München: Kaiser, 1977), 85–106, 96 f. Cf. the discussion in, e. g., Brandt, *Opfer*, 126 f., 134–36.

[6] Previous note.

[7] This was true for the eliminating scape-goat ritual (Lev 16:10, 21 f.), which is not to be confused with the sacrifice of atonement that concerns us.

in return gave this life and energy back to God (instead of consuming it, which was forbidden).[8] The effect was that the sinner was reconciled with God (e.g., Lev 4:20). The sprinkling of blood/life was like "sowing seed" for a new beginning in life.[9] Sins that had accumulated before God's presence at the altar were cleansed away by the force of the blood/life.

The ἱλαστήριον that Paul's Christological text uses as a metaphor (Rom 3:25) refers to a special case of the Israelite animal sacrifice of atonement. On Yom Kippur, Israel's great Day of Atonement (Lev 16; cf. 23:27 f.; 25,9), the high priest approached the *kapporet* (כפרת = ἱλαστήριον), the "place of atonement," which was located in the most inner part of the sanctuary, in the Holy of Holies. He sprinkled the *kapporet* with the animal's blood (16:14 f.). In this way, all of Israel was reconciled with God (16:16).

What was this "place of atonement" where sins were forgiven? And how could it metaphorically be applied to Christ? According to Exod 25:17 ff. (cf. Heb 9:5), the golden ark in which the tablets of the covenant were kept was covered with the golden *kapporet*/ἱλαστήριον.[10] Two cherubim of gold were at the two ends of the *kapporet*, overshadowing it. God was perceived as using the *kapporet* as his throne, "appearing in a cloud upon it" (Lev 16:2). By sprinkling the *kapporet* with animal blood (life), the high priest offered this blood to God. The "place of atonement" represented God: there, God reached out, receiving this

---

[8] Lev 17:14. Verse 11 reads: "The life of the flesh is in the blood; and I (God) have given it to you for making atonement for your lives on the altar; for, as life, it is the blood that makes atonement."—Some scholars still adhere to the misleading idea that in this ritual the sacrificed animal represented the sacrificing person and that the animal was used on behalf of this person (see above). They therefore interpret the offering of an animal's blood/life in this way: This offering of life symbolically showed that the sinner turned over his or her own life to God, and therefore God forgave (e.g., Bernd Janowski, "Sühne II," in *RGG* 7 [ed. Hans Dieter Betz et al.; 4th edition; Tübingen: Mohr, 2004], 1844), or this offering of life at the altar showed that the sacrificing person symbolically reunited his or her own life, which was ruined by sin, with God, and therefore it was healed (e.g., Gese, "Sühne," 85–106). These interpretations seem to be reading too much Christian thought into an archaic ritual. Early Christians indeed were ready to formulate metaphorically that they turned themselves and their lives over as a "living sacrifice" to God (cf. Rom 12:3; 15:16; Phil 2:17; 4:18; 1 Pet 2:5). However, these formulations do not occur in the context of atonement categories. The whole idea of representation, according to which the animal in the Israelite sacrificial ritual of atonement was used in lieu of the sinner, needs to be dropped for lack of evidence (see above).

[9] Cf. Brandt, *Opfer*, 136–40.

[10] English Bible translations traditionally render it as "mercy seat."

offering; there, Israel came into close contact with God; there, heaven and earth met; there, Israel's relationship to God, which was troubled by sin, was healed.

Christ as, metaphorically speaking, ἱλαστήριον, thus was construed as representative of the enthroned God, as mediator between God and the human race. In him, God was present. He was the "place" where atonement and reconciliation between God and humans took place. However, this does not imply that Christ's death was interpreted as "sacrifice." Nowhere does the text metaphorically equate Christ's blood with the sacrificial animal blood with which the *kapporet* was sprinkled. On the contrary, Christ himself was the *kapporet*.

The misunderstanding that Paul in Rom 3:25 construed Christ as a "sacrifice of atonement"[11] could arise because this verse *does* talk about Christ's blood, but in a different way. There are two alternative readings of Rom 3:25: "God put Christ forward as a place of atonement, effective through faith / trust *in*[12] his blood (i.e., in his death on the cross as a saving event)." Or, "God put Christ forward as a place of atonement because of his blood (i.e., because of his death on the cross), effective through faith / trust." Both readings are possible. Christ's cross was the reason for his becoming the *kapporet*, but this does not imply that his cross was interpreted as a "sacrifice of atonement."[13]

The same is true for Rom 8:3; 4:25, and 2 Cor 5:21. Especially Peter Stuhlmacher[14] saw these verses as permeated by sacrificial terminology and used them as evidence that Paul interpreted Christ's death as a "sacrifice of atonement" or as a "guilt offering." He was

---

[11] English Bible translations such as the NRSV falsely translate Rom 3:25: "Christ Jesus, whom God put forward as a sacrifice of atonement by his blood." Rudolf Bultmann, among other scholars, also wanted to interpret ἱλαστήριον in this way (*Theologie des Neuen Testaments* [8th edition; Tübingen: Mohr, 1980], 295). However, the text itself does not say this.

[12] For πίστις ἐν = "faith / trust in," see Gal 3:26; Eph 1:15; Col 1:4; etc.

[13] One of the alternatives would be, e.g., to interpret the cross as a non-sacrificial representation (see below 6.1.) in analogy to Isa 53: Christ died in place of the sinners, taking over their punishment, and therefore he became the *kapporet* between God and the sinners.—The intricate scholarly debate about Rom 3:25 cannot be picked up and unfolded here. For a summary, see, e.g., Brandt, *Opfer*, 204–14.

[14] "Zur neueren Exegese von Röm 3,24–26," in *Versöhnung, Gesetz und Gerechtigkeit: Aufsätze zur biblischen Theologie* (ed. idem; Göttingen: Vandenhoeck & Ruprecht, 1981, 117–35); idem, "Sühne oder Versöhnung," in *Die Mitte des Neuen Testaments: Einheit und Vielfalt neutestamentlicher Theologie* (Festschrift Eduard Schweizer; ed. Ulrich Luz and Hans Weder; Göttingen: Vandenhoeck & Ruprecht, 1983), 291–316, 308 f.

convincingly refuted by Cilliers Breytenbach and others.[15] Their arguments do not need to be repeated here.

2. Passover Lamb

Paul twice clearly understood Christ's death as a symbolic "sacrifice." In an ethical context, he formulates: "Our paschal lamb, Christ, has been sacrificed" (τὸ πάσχα ἡμῶν ἐτύθη Χριστός 1 Cor 5:7). The Passover image refers to liberation (from Egypt), in Paul's context to liberation*liberation* from the power of sin. The Christian congregation, therefore, is challenged to start an *exodus* from sinful behavior (1 Cor 5).

At first glance, Christ is also referred to as a *Passover* lamb in John 1:29, 36 ("Here is the Lamb of God who takes away the sin of the world"). However, the function of a Passover lamb offering was not to "take away sin." More likely, John's lamb metaphor was an echo of Isa 53:7, 12: The Suffering Servant "was afflicted, yet he did not open his mouth, like a lamb that is led to the slaughter ... he bore the sin of many" (53:7f. is quoted in Acts 8:32). A third alternative would be to connect John's metaphor with the daily Jewish *tamid* offering of a lamb. In the morning, it took away the sins of the night; in the evening, it cancelled the sins of the day.[16] In 1 Pet 1:19, the exegesis likewise has to decide between the Passover lamb and the Isa 53 lamb (cf. 1 Pet 2:23).[17]

Interestingly enough, where we clearly find a sacrificial image as a symbol for Christ's death, the idea of *human* sacrifice is suppressed in favor of an explicit animal metaphor.

3. Exodus 24

The second text that clearly uses sacrificial categories is the pre-Pauline eucharistic formula: "This cup signifies the new covenant because of my blood" (τοῦτο τὸ ποτήριον ἡ καινὴ διαθήκη ἐστὶν ἐν τῷ ἐμῷ αἵματι

---

[15] Cilliers Breytenbach, "Versöhnung, Stellvertretung und Sühne: Semantische und traditionsgeschichtliche Bemerkungen am Beispiel der Paulinischen Briefe," *NTS* 39 (1993), 59–79, 73; idem, *Versöhnung: Eine Studie zur paulinischen Soteriologie* (WMANT 60; Neukirchen: Neukirchener, 1989), 159–66, 203. For 2 Cor 5:21, see also Otfried Hofius, "Sühne und Versöhnung: Zum paulinischen Verständnis des Kreuzestodes Jesu," in *Paulusstudien: Band 1* (ed. idem; WUNT 51; Tübingen: Mohr, 1989), 33–49. For Rom 4:25, see, e.g., Brandt, *Opfer*, 220f.

[16] Cf., e.g., Gerhard Friedrich, *Die Verkündigung des Todes Jesu im Neuen Testament* (Biblisch-theologische Studien 6; Neukirchen: Neukirchener, 1982), 50f.

[17] For a third alternative (the Jewish sacrifice of a lamb that integrated pagan proselytes into the people of Israel), cf., e.g., Norbert Brox, *Der erste Petrusbrief* (EKKNT 21; Zürich: Benzinger, 1979, 82 n. 281.

1 Cor 11:25).[18] The Old Testament background can be found in Exod 24, especially 24:8. At a feast at the Sinai, animals were slaughtered for "burnt offerings" (עלת) and "peace offerings / offerings of well-being" (זבחים שלמים). The flesh of the animals slaughtered for the "offerings of well-being" (24:5) was eaten by the congregation, and God was perceived as sharing in this communal meal by receiving the blood and fat pieces. However, Moses deviated from the rule that usually *all* blood was given to God.[19] He only used half of the blood to sprinkle the altar. After having read the rulings of the covenant between God and Israel, he dashed the other half of blood on the people of Israel and said: "See the blood of the covenant that the Lord makes with you" (23:8). In this exceptional scene, a new relationship between God and Israel was established, the Sinai covenant. God and Israel shared in the blood (life) of the sacrificed animals, and this communal act constituted their new covenant—not unlike a blood brotherhood. "Because of this blood" (cf. the eucharistic formula), the new covenant was established.

The Exod 24 background of the eucharistic ritual has both elements: (1) the blood of slaughtered and sacrificed creatures makes possible a new covenant, and (2) the feast that is connected to the founding of the new covenant is connected with a communal meal of the congregation.[20] In other words, Christ's giving up of himself and his life for others, his death, is seen in analogy to the slaughtered animals of Exod 24. This sacrificial death constituted a new relationship / covenant (1) between God and the believers and (2) between the believers themselves, who were supposed to be united in a sharing community. The atonement category does not play a role at all in this world of images evoked by Exod 24.[21]

---

[18] See also 1 Pet 1:2 for the same set of ideas.

[19] Cf. Deut 12:24.

[20] The flesh of a sacrifice of atonement, in contrast, was never eaten by the congregation. It was taboo and excluded from the fellowship of the congregation (Lev 4:3–21; 16:23–28). It is therefore not surprising that the Old Testament sacrifice of atonement category cannot be found behind the early Christian eucharistic theory. Contra, e.g., Gerd Theißen, "Ritualdynamik und Tabuverletzung im urchristlichen Abendmahl," in *Ritualdynamik: Kulturübergreifende Studien zur Theorie und Geschichte rituellen Handelns* (ed. Dietrich Harth; Heidelberg: Synchron, 2004), 275–90, who uses this asocial taboo feature of the Israelite sacrifice of atonement as a building block for his theory of the eucharistic ritual.

[21] Thus correctly also Brandt, *Opfer*, 249.

4. Genesis 22

Some authors such as Jon D. Levenson[22] have tried to interpret Christ's crucifixion as the new *akeda*, the father's sacrifice of his own son. In *Gen 22,* Abraham almost offered Isaac as a burnt offering. Can the sacrifice of an only child be an expression of divine love? Can salvation and life result from such a cruel constellation? The question needs to be put in an exegetical-historical way: Did the writers of the New Testament anywhere perceive Christ's death as a sacrifice that his divine father had enacted? Did the New Testament authors anywhere pick up Gen 22 in order to interpret Christ's crucifixion? Sigrid Brandt[23] recently dedicated a thorough analysis to this question—with the result that explicit references to Gen 22 never connect Jesus' death and the binding of Isaac. These references do not occur in Christological, but rather in soteriological-ethical contexts (Heb 11:17–19; Jas 2:21–23). Perhaps Rom 8:32 ("he did not withhold—οὐκ ἐφείσατο—his own Son, but handed him over—παρέδωκεν—for all of us," cf. also 4:25) comes close to an allusion to Gen 22. However, φείδομαι in Gen 22:12, 16 has a meaning quite different from Rom 8:32. In Genesis, Abraham did not withhold his son from *God*; in Romans, God did not withhold his son from the *world* and from becoming a human being. This difference makes it more difficult to assume that Paul alludes to Gen 22. Φείδομαι belongs to the apostle's own active vocabulary (Rom 11:21; 1 Cor 7:28; 2 Cor 1:23; 12:6; 13:2); its usage did not need to be motivated by tradition. Furthermore, in Paul's context παρέδωκεν (Rom 8:32; cf. 4:25) does not exclusively or even primarily refer to Christ's death, but more generally to his being handed over to human existence, which is marked by the undoing and the curse of sin (cf. ὁ θεὸς παρέδωκεν in Rom 1:24, 26, 28)—a curse that Christ broke by not being caught in the vortex of sin. If there is any Old Testament background to Rom 8:32, it is not to be found in Gen 22, but in the Greek text of Isa 53:6 (παρέδωκεν αὐτὸν ταῖς ἁμαρτίαις ἡμῶν "the Lord handed him [i. e., the Suffering Servant] over to our sins"). Last but not least, according to Gal 1:4, not the father, but Christ himself "gave himself for our sins." And in his Abraham texts of Rom 4 and Gal 3, Paul even avoided Gen 22 by only referring to Gen 12:3; 15:5 f.; 17:5, 10 f. Within the framework of Paul's doctrine of justification by faith, it was not Abraham's ἔργα that mattered, not his obedient acting and *akeda*, but Abraham's πίστις in God's promises. It is improbable that Gen 22 ever played a role in Paul's Christological thinking. An allusion to Gen 22 would have been counterproductive to his doctrine of justification by πίστις. Also, no support for a "new *akeda*" theory can be found in the Gospel of John (3:16 τὸν υἱὸν τὸν μονογενῆ ἔδωκεν): God's "giving" of his son refers to God's sending him as revealer. The goal of this sending is not the obliteration of the revealer, but the successful revelation and proclamation of the "father."

5. Additional post-Pauline texts with sacrificial imagery

In the deutero-Pauline Letter to the Ephesians (5:2; cf. LXX Ps 39:7) and the Letter to the Hebrews (7:27; 9:28), Christ's death was interpreted as a "sacrifice" (θυσία; ἑαυτὸν ἀνενέγκας), even as a sacrifice of atonement (μίαν ὑπὲρ ἁμαρτιῶν θυσίαν 10:12). Less clear are 1 John 2:2 and 4:10: Christ is labelled "expiation—ἱλασμός—for our sins." However,

---

[22] *The Death and Resurrection of the Beloved Son: The Transformation of Child Sacrifice in Judaism and Christianity* (New Haven: Yale University Press, 1993.

[23] *Opfer,* 146–73.

1 John 4:10 shows that Christ's entire mission (ἀπέστειλεν) was seen as "expiation," not just his death on a cross. And ἱλασμός, "a means of appeasing," does not automatically imply a cultic sacrificial aspect.

6. Paul's ὑπέρ formulations

In a recent study, building on the previous scholarly discussion and its arguments, Breytenbach[24] refuted the idea that the Pauline Χριστὸς ὑπὲρ ... (a person) ἀπέθανεν formulations[25] are to be understood within the framework of sacrificial categories. But how then are they to be understood? There are two alternative interpretations.

6. 1. The ὑπέρ formulations are based on the idea of *representation* ("Stellvertretung"; ὑπέρ = "on behalf of," "in place of"), which is *not* a sacrificial category, as we saw above, contrary to a widespread misunderstanding.[26] Paul, in 2 Cor 5:20, illustrates the category of representation: "We are representatives / ambassadors for (ὑπέρ) Christ, God making his appeal through us. We beseech you in place of / on behalf of (ὑπέρ) Christ." Accordingly, the Pauline ὑπὲρ ἡμῶν formulations and their equivalents imply that Christ took our place and died instead of us—in analogy to the Suffering Servant of Isa 53:4 ff.[27] Similarly, Deut 24:16 reads: "The fathers shall not be put to death *in lieu of* their children (ὑπὲρ τέκνων), nor shall the children be put to death *in lieu of* the fathers (ὑπὲρ πατέρων); every man shall be put to death because of his own sin (τῇ ἑαυτοῦ ἁμαρτίᾳ)." According to Paul, human beings as sinners deserve nothing but eternal death (e. g., Rom 5:12, 17, 21), but Christ steps in on

---

24 " 'Christus starb für uns': Zur Tradition und paulinischen Rezeption der sogenannten 'Sterbeformeln,' *NTS* 49 (2003), 447–75.

25 E. g., 1 Thess 5:10; 2 Cor 5:14 f., 21; Rom 5:6–8; 14:15.

26 See above 1.

27 See, e. g., 53:4 f. and 12: "He has borne our infirmities and carried our diseases ... upon him was the punishment that made us whole, and by his bruises we are healed ... he poured out himself to death, and was numbered with the transgressors; yet he bore the sin of many, and made intercession for the transgressors." In Isa 53, the category of representation is not connected with cultic, sacrificial ideas. As, e. g., Bernd Janowski has shown, Isa 53:10 does not refer to a guilt offering or a sacrifice of atonement, although some translations suggest this (e. g., NRSV: "an offering for sin"). אשם in v. 10 has its pre-cultic meaning ("abolition of culpability and responsibility"). See convincingly Janowski, "Er trug unsere Sünden: Jesaja 53 und die Dramatik der Stellvertretung," in *Gottes Gegenwart in Israel: Beiträge zur Theologie des Alten Testaments* (Festschrift Hans-Walter Wolff; ed. idem; Neukirchen: Neukirchener, 1993), 303–26. The idea of representation (dying on behalf of) is also conveyed by 4 Macc 6:29 (ἀντίψυχον), but without an ὑπέρ formulation.

their behalf and takes over this curse and deadly fate, so that his human followers may live (e. g., 6:6–8). He went under the "curse in lieu of us" (Gal 3:13; cf. 2 Cor 5:21).[28]

Besides Isa 53, the Greek world offers analogies for this category of representation. Although Alcestis did not need to die herself (παρόν μοι μὴ θανεῖν),[29] she, as a loving spouse, happily died in place of (ὑπέρ = ἀντί) her husband in order to rescue him from death (θέλουσ' ὑπερθανεῖν; θνῄσκω ὑπὲρ σέθεν; σὺ δ' ἀντιδοῦσα τῆς ἐμῆς τὰ φίλτατα ψυχῆς ἔσωσας; ἀντὶ σοῦ γε κατθανεῖν).[30] Herakles' daughter, Makaria, was ready to die in place of her siblings (ἀντὶ τῶνδε κατθανουμένην and θνῄσκειν ἀδελφῶν τῶνδε κἀμαυτῆς ὕπερ).[31]

6. 2. A second cluster of possibilities is ὑπέρ = (1) "in the interest of," "in favor of," "for the benefit of," "for the protection of" ("zugunsten," etc.), or simply (2) "because of" ("wegen").[32] The parallelism between verses 1 Cor 8:11 (ἀπόλλυται ὁ ἀσθενῶν ἐν τῇ σῇ γνώσει, ὁ ἀδελφὸς δι' ὃν Χριστὸς ἀπέθανεν) and Rom 14:15 (ὁ ἀδελφός σου λυπεῖται . . . , μὴ ἐκεῖνον ἀπόλλυε ὑπὲρ οὗ Χριστὸς ἀπέθανεν) helps support this second cluster of possibilities. Both texts treat the same ethical problem, the eating of idol meat. They establish the equation δι' ὃν ἀπέθανεν ("he died on account of whom," "for the sake of whom," "because of whom") = ὑπὲρ οὗ ἀπέθανεν.

In the Greek world, King Kreon's son, Menoikeus, deliberately died for the benefit of his fatherland, liberating it in this way (ὑπερθανὼν

[28] Of course, one could state that this rescuing death in lieu of somebody else was a voluntary "self-sacrifice." However, this would be a figurative expression, which blurs the categories. "Representation" lacks the cultic setting and therefore needs to be distinguished from clearly cultic sacrificial categories.

[29] Euripides, *Alc.* 284.

[30] Euripides, *Alc.* 155; 284; 340 f.; 524. Cf. also προύθανε 620; 698; 1002. Plato, *Symp* 179 b: ὑπὲρ τοῦ αὑτῆς ἀνδρὸς ἀποθανεῖν and ὑπεραποθνῄσκειν. *Anthologia Graeca* (7. 691) and Pseudo-Apollodorus (*Bibliotheca* 1. 106) also use ὑπέρ in respect to Alcestis' death. *IG* XIV 607 e, f, i = *CIL* X 7567: ὑπὲρ γαμέτου Πώμπτιλλα τὴν ζωὴν ἀντέλαβεν θανάτου; *IG* XIV 607 q = *CIL* X 7578: θανεῖν Πώμπτιλλαν λύτρον ὑπὲρ γαμέτου. Like Alcestis, this Pomptilla died as a price of release (as a ransom) in lieu of her spouse. Here the categories of ransom and representation are combined. For the non-cultic, non-sacrificial category of ransom, see 1 Cor 1:30; Gal 3:13 below.

[31] Euripides, *Heracl.* 580; 532.

[32] All references, listed in n. 25, could be repeated here. Ὑπέρ indicates the reason ("because of") in, e. g., Isocrates, *Evag.* 60:1: ὑπὲρ τῶν γεγενημένων ὀργιζόμενος. "For the protection of" = e. g., Plutarch, *Comp. Ages. Pomp.* 4:3: μαχόμενον ὑπὲρ τῆς πατρίδος. "In the interest of" = e. g., Demosthenes, *Chers.* 66: λέγειν ὑπὲρ Φιλίππου.

χθονός and Κρέοντος παῖς ὁ γῆς ὑπερθανών).[33] The Maccabean patriots died for the benefit of their country and for the benefit and protection of the covenant and of the laws (δότε τὰς ψυχὰς ὑμῶν ὑπὲρ διαθήκης πατέρων and ὑπὲρ τῶν νόμων καὶ τῆς πατρίδος ἀποθνήσκειν).[34]

Logically, the second cluster of semantic possibilities (6. 2.) is automatically implied in the first semantic possibility (6. 1.)—like concentric circles. Whenever a rescuer like Christ steps in and takes the place of somebody else, voluntarily taking over this person's punishment and fate (6. 1.), this happens "for the benefit" and thus also "because of" this person (6. 2.).

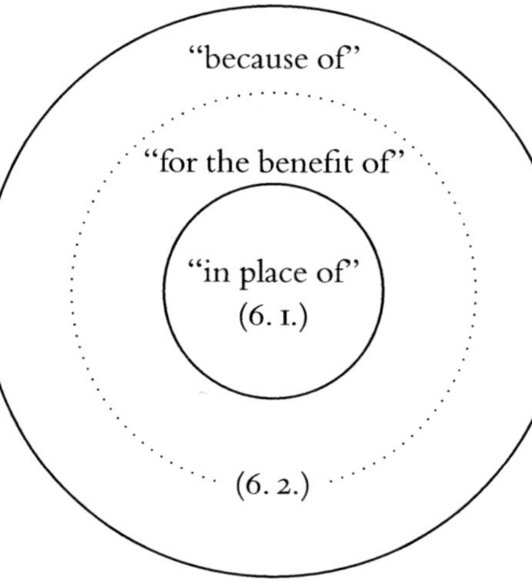

[33] Euripides, *Phoen.* 998 and 1090.—See further Plutarch, *Pel.* 21. 3 (in battle, the Spartan king, Leonidas, died ὑπὲρ τῆς Ἑλλάδος) or Euripides, *Iph. aul.* 1375: Agamenon's daughter, Iphigenia, voluntarily died for the benefit of Hellas in order to liberate it from a hopeless situation. An explicit ὑπέρ formulation, however, is missing here. For Iphigenia, see Sam K. Williams, *Jesus' Death as Saving Event: The Background and Origin of a Concept* (HDR 2; Missoula, Mont.: Scholars, 1975), 155 f.

[34] 1 Macc 2:50 (cf. 6:44); 2 Macc 8:21; 6:28; 7:9; 4 Macc 1:8, 10 and 10:20 (ὑπὲρ τοῦ θεοῦ "because of," "for the sake of," "in the interest of God"). For ὑπέρ = περί, see 2 Macc 7:37; 13:9. For ὑπέρ = διά, see 4 Macc 6:27.—For the Greek parallels and for the parallels in the Maccabean Books, see further, e. g., Hendrik S. Versnel, "Quid Athenis et Hierosolymis? Bemerkungen über die Herkunft von Aspekten des 'effective death,'" in: *Die Entstehung der jüdschen Märtyrologie:* Originally presented as Papers at a Workshop held in Leiden 1985 (ed. Jan W. van Henten; StPB 38; Leiden: Brill, 1989), 162–93; Marinus de Jonge, "Jesus' Death for Others and the Maccabean Martyrs," in: *Text and Testimony: Essays on New Testament and Apocryphal Literature in Honour of A. F. J. Klijn* (ed. Tjitze Baarda and Albertus F. J. Klein; Kampen: Kok, 1988), 142–51.

6.3. If the semantic field of 6.2. is the larger of the two concentric circles, what happens to the area not covered by 6.1.? Does Paul use this semantic area, too? Besides the ὑπὲρ ... (a person) ἀπέθανεν formulations, Paul picks up the pre-Pauline formula ἀπέθανεν ὑπὲρ τῶν ἁμαρτιῶν in 1 Cor 15:3. Similarly, he writes δόντος ἑαυτὸν ὑπὲρ τῶν ἁμαρτιῶν in Gal 1:4. Does this imply a cultic, sacrificial idea? There is no evidence for this. A simple "because of" suffices: He died because of (ὑπέρ) our sins. Rom 4:25 conveys the same idea in the expression παρεδόθη διὰ (*because of*) τὰ παραπτώματα ἡμῶν. The universal power of sin made Christ's coming necessary, as Paul elaborates in several chapters of Rom (1–3; esp. 3:9, 23–24). Later, the post-Pauline 1 Peter (3:18) formulates: Χριστὸς περὶ ἁμαρτιῶν ὑπὲρ ὑμῶν ἀπέθανεν: "*because of* sins he died in place of us / for the benefit of us." And Isa 53:5 describes the Suffering Servant, who represents the sinners: "He was wounded *because of* our transgressions, crushed *because of* our iniquities (two times διά + accusative); upon him was the punishment that made us whole."[35] A direct philological parallel is 1 Kgs 16:19: "Zimri ... died *because of* the sins that he committed" (ἀπέθανεν ὑπὲρ τῶν ἁμαρτιῶν αὐτοῦ ὧν ἐποίησεν).[36] And Ps 37:19 LXX reads: "I am troubled *because of* my sins" (μεριμνήσω ὑπὲρ τῆς ἁμαρτίας μου). Again in the Septuagint, Odes 12:10 reads "to refuse me *because of* my sins" (ἀνανεῦσαί με ὑπὲρ ἁμαρτιῶν μου). To be able to load a little preposition (ὑπέρ) with heavy sacrificial associations, we would need clear evidence from the context. Paul does not give this evidence. The pre-Pauline expression "he died because of our sins" (1 Cor 15:3) can be easily understood within the framework of non-

[35] Breytenbach, "Christus starb," 469 f., denies that Isa 53 is in the background of 1 Cor 15:3. However, his proposal lacks philological soundness. He interprets ἀπέθανεν ὑπὲρ τῶν ἁμαρτιῶν as a septuagintism, allegedly meaning "he died, in order to eliminate the consequences of sins" ("um die Auswirkungen ihrer Sünden zu tilgen"). The Septuagint references that he quotes do not support this unusual translation at all; most of them do not even offer ὑπέρ.

[36] See also 1 Esd 7:8: "They offered ... twelve male goats because of the sin (ὑπὲρ ἁμαρτίας) of all Israel." Here we do have a sacrificial context, but it is conveyed exclusively by the rest of the sentence, not by the ὑπέρ itself. The same needs to be said about Mic 6:7 (ὑπὲρ ἁμαρτίας), Ezek 43:22, 25; 45:22 f. and 40:39; 44:29; 45:17, 25; 46:20 LXX. The latter verses translate "sin offering" and "guilt offering" as τὰ ὑπὲρ ἁμαρτίας καὶ ὑπὲρ ἀγνοίας, which is unusual (cf. LXX Lev 4:3 et al..; Ezek 42:13: τὰ περὶ ἁμαρτίας; περί and ὑπέρ were equivalents in this respect; see also 1 Pet 3:18 above). However, the literal translation even here would be "the (offerings) because of sin and because of mistaken conduct." Heb 5:1 and 10:12 need to be taken in the same way (θυσία ὑπὲρ ἁμαρτιῶν).

cultic, non-sacrificial representation in analogy to Isa 53; very easily, the expression κατὰ τὰς γραφάς in 1 Cor 15:3 refers to Isa 53.

7. Plurality of soteriological concepts

Paul's ὑπέρ formulations are placed in the immediate context of other soteriological concepts, as Rom 5:6–8, for example, shows. In 5:9, the forensic category of *justification* is used (δικαιωθέντες), in 5:10 the originally political category of *reconciliation* (κατηλλάγημεν; also 2 Cor 5:14 ff.). We already discussed the category of *representation*, which is not cultic. Rom 8:23, 1 Cor 1:30, and Gal 3:13 mention deliverance by payment of *ransom* (ἀπολύτρωσις, ἐξηγόρασεν). The point being made is that cultic sacrificial categories are by no means the only, and not even the central, soteriological categories in Paul's work. Paul approaches the same Christ event from *different* angles, picking up *different* traditional terms and ideas, since he knows that no traditional category by itself can plumb the depths of the soteriological μυστήριον.

II. Eucharist

Early Christian Christology molded ritual acts, particularly the eucharistic ritual. The early Christians interpreted the Eucharist as a ritual that makes Jesus' death present for the participants. After quoting the eucharistic tradition in 1 Cor 11:23–25, Paul, in v. 26, summarizes this tradition in his own words: "As often as you eat this bread and drink the cup, you *proclaim the Lord's death* until he comes" (ὁσάκις γὰρ ἐὰν ἐσθίητε τὸν ἄρτον τοῦτον καὶ τὸ ποτήριον πίνητε, τὸν θάνατον τοῦ κυρίου καταγγέλλετε).

Several questions arise for the interpreter. How is Christ's death made present in the eucharistic ritual? Is it only through "proclaiming"—a proclaiming through words and / or ritual acts such as breaking bread that symbolize Christ's death? Or is Christ (realistically or symbolically) sacrificed over and over again in the eucharistic ritual? More dramatically, is his sacrificed body (realistically or symbolically) even eaten during this ritual, in a taboo-breaking manner? How is the risen Lord perceived to be present at the meal? The apostle Paul's answers are mainly to be found in 1 Cor 10–11.

1. Christ's presence as host

There is no doubt that, for Paul and the Corinthians, the risen Christ, with his saving power, was *personally present*[37] at the Eucharist *as the host*[38] *of the ritual*. In this aspect, the Eucharist did not differ, for example, from a sacrifical meal of the Sarapis cult. Sarapis was considered present at the table both as guest and host. The participants at the sacrificial meal contributed food; Sarapis received these contributions and served them out to all who were present (Aelius Aristides, *Sarapis* 54. 20–28[39]). Paul himself does not shrink from drawing a parallel between the Lord's Supper and pagan cultic sacrificial meals (1 Cor 10:18–22). The risen Lord is present as the host;[40] his saving power is inherent in the sacramental act (15:29; 10:1–13).[41]

2. Is Christ present *in the elements* of bread and wine?
Is his self-sacrificing death therefore *repeated* in the ritual?

2. 1. Whether Paul and the Corinthians also believed in a real presence of the Lord *in the elements* of bread and wine (cf. John 6:52–58) is another and exegetically controversial question. In any case, such an assumption cannot be based on 1 Cor 11:23–25.

The cup or the wine is *not* equated with Christ's blood. The cup signifies the new *covenant* that was established *because* of Christ's blood on the cross (τὸ ποτήριον ἡ καινὴ διαθήκη ἐστὶν ἐν τῷ ἐμῷ αἵματι 11:25, see above).

---

[37] Cf. ὁ δὲ κύριος τὸ πνεῦμά ἐστιν (2 Cor 3:17), and τὸ πνεῦμα τοῦ θεοῦ οἰκεῖ ἐν ὑμῖν (1 Cor 3:16).

[38] Cf. the expressions ποτήριον κυρίου πίνειν ... τραπέζης κυρίου μετέχειν as opposed to τραπέζης δαιμονίων (1 Cor 10:21). Furthermore, by quoting the Jesus sayings of 1 Cor 11:24 f. during the eucharistic ritual, the liturgical leader of the eucharistic meal necessarily gave the impression that Christ himself was handing out the bread and serving the cup.

[39] *Aristides* (ed. Wilhelm Dindorf; Leipzig: Weidmann, 1829).

[40] This kind of "real presence" (Realpräsenz) is labeled "prinzipale Realpräsenz" in the framework of categories developed by Hans-Josef Klauck, *Herrenmahl und hellenistischer Kult: Eine religionsgeschichtliche Untersuchung zum ersten Korintherbrief* (Neutestamentliche Abhandlungen NS 15; Münster: Aschendorff, 1982), 373 f.: "Der erhöhte Kyrios ist personal zugegen ... als Princeps, das heißt als Tischherr und Gastgeber." For the parallel to the Sarapis cult, see Peter Lampe, "Das korinthische Herrenmahl im Schnittpunkt hellenistisch-römischer Mahlpraxis und paulinischer Theologia Crucis (1 Kor 11,17–34)," *ZNW* 82 (1991), 183–213, 196 f., 199, 206.

[41] Cf. also Paul's formulations that "spiritual food" and "spiritual drink" are consumed at the Eucharist (10:3–4), i. e., "food belonging to and given by the Spirit."

In a similar way, the expression "this is my body for you" (τοῦτό μού ἐστιν τὸ σῶμα τὸ ὑπὲρ ὑμῶν 11:24) does not necessarily refer to the bread. It is also possible that the demonstrative pronoun "this" picks up on the liturgical act of blessing and breaking the bread (11:24): This act of breaking blessed bread symbolizes "my body (broken) for you;"[42] this act points to Jesus' body on the cross and to his death on the cross. The formulation "*do* this (τοῦτο ποιεῖτε) in remembrance of me" (11:24) supports the reading that, not the element of the bread, but the entire liturgical *act* of blessing and breaking the bread is what is interpreted in 11:24.

Thus, the pre-Pauline eucharistic tradition in 1 Cor 11:23–25 does not prove that Christ was present *in the elements* and that pre-Pauline or Pauline Christians thought they were, at least symbolically,[43] eating the body of Christ and drinking his blood when eating eucharistic bread and drinking wine.

2. 2. Without any solid evidence that Christ was considered present *in the elements*, these verses also do not prove that Christ's sacrifice on the cross was *repeated* in the ritual. Christ's death happened "once for all" (ἐφάπαξ Rom 6:10). The sacramental ritual only "proclaims" (καταγγέλλειν 1 Cor 11:26) Christ's unique sacrifice; the ritual makes it present for Christians and allows the power (δύναμις) of Christ's death to affect the existence of participating Christians. In a similar way, Paul's missionary *preaching* makes Christ's crucifixion present with its saving and condemning power (ὁ λόγος ὁ τοῦ σταυροῦ ... δύναμις θεοῦ ἐστιν ... 1 Cor 1:18–2:5).

2. 3. However, there are still other Pauline texts.[44] Is the idea of a real presence of Christ *in the elements* implied in 1 Cor 10:16f. (cf. 11:27)? In these verses, cup / blood and bread / body are made parallel. Does this parallelism mean that Christ's body was considered to be consumed

---

[42] "This is" (τοῦτό ἐστιν) can be interpreted as "this means / signifies / symbolizes." In the immediate context, see 11:25 τὸ ποτήριον ἡ καινὴ διαθήκη ἐστὶν κτλ. See also the allegorical equations of Gal 4:24; Mark 4:15–16, 18.

[43] "Symbolically," they would eat the body of Christ if 11:24 were to be understood as "this (bread) signifies my body" (see previous note). "Realistically," they would eat the body of Christ if 11:24 were to be understood as "this (bread) is my body." Both readings are possible, but both readings are not the only possible ones (see above). Therefore, none of these readings can be used as proof of anything.

[44] For the discussion of 1 Corinthians 10–11, see Peter Lampe, "The Eucharist: Identifying with Christ on the Cross," *Int* 48 (1994), 36–49.

in the eucharistic elements? These texts, too, are open to alternative readings, and their ambiguity should alert us to the fact that the New Testament Christians concentrated on questions other than the ones we are asking here. For Paul, the *ethical implications* of the Eucharist (11:17–34) were far more vital than the intricate speculative discussion of *how* Christ might be present in the Lord's Supper. The fact *that* Christ was present mattered for Paul; the *function* in which Christ was present (saving and judging; cf. 11:29–32) was of importance.

In 10:16, the expression κοινωνία τινος can be rendered as either "community with" or "sharing in" the Lord's body and blood. Can the context help us make the choice? In 10:20, κοινωνία τινος denotes "people who are *in community with* the demons" as their partners, because they participate in the sacrifices offered to the demons. Analogously, 10:16 seems to suggest that the participants in the Eucharist are put into a close "community with" Christ's body and blood, that is, with the dying Christ on the cross: In the sacrament, they die with him (Rom 6:3–8). Christ's presence *in the elements* is not indicated by this understanding. Also, it cannot be gleaned from the expression "partaking of" (μετέχω 1 Cor 10:17, 21): Paul speaks of "partaking of the one bread" and "of the table of the Lord"; he does not signal that Christ's body is eaten in the eucharistic elements. It is significant that 10:16 does *not* read: "The cup, is it not the blood of Christ? The bread, is it not the body of Christ?"

2. 4. In summary, there is no solid evidence that the pre-Pauline or Pauline Christians interpreted the eucharistic ritual as a "sacrifice." Yes, through "remembrance" (ἀνάμνησις 1 Cor 11:24 f.) and "proclaiming" (καταγγέλλειν 11:26), through liturgical words and symbolizing[45] sacramental acts, the ritual made Christ's unique death on the cross *present*. And yes, this death could also be construed as a "sacrifice" (see above I.)—among other interpretations. However, all this does not mean that the "sacrifice," which once took place in Jerusalem in the 30's C. E., was *repeated* in the eucharistic ritual.

2. 5. In the subsequent tradition after Paul, things changed. Mark 14:22 reads: "this (bread) is / signifies[46] my body ... this (cup) is / signifies my

[45] Breaking bread symbolized (but did not repeat) the breaking of Christ's body on the cross. Drinking from *one* cup symbolized the covenant founded by this death on the cross.

[46] Both readings are possible. See above n. 43.

blood."[47] Now we are getting closer to the idea that Christ is present *in the elements*—or that at least the elements symbolize Christ's crucified body. John 6:52–58 finally presupposes the idea that the participants in the Eucharist "chew" (τρώγων 6:54, 56, 57) Christ's flesh and drink his blood, although the author of the Gospel of John distances himself from this scandalous (6:52) materialistic idea by spiritualizing it.[48]

III. Christology and the Eucharist

The different New Testament interpretations of the Eucharist share the understanding that this ritual referred back to Jesus' death—a death that could be interpreted as a "sacrifice" (among other soteriological concepts). This contributed a profound and fascinating tension to the ritual.[49] On the one hand, the meal of bread and wine was unspectacular, non-aggressive and peaceful; no animal was slaughtered, no blood seen. The ritual was intended to facilitate communion and fellowship, strengthening the social ties among the participants. It was intended to fortify the cooperative and social skills of the Christians (see especially 1 Cor 11:17–34). On the other hand, the Christological point of reference of this ritual was dramatic, brutally violent and broke a taboo: A man had been slaughtered for the benefit of others. On the one hand, the ritual was progressive by leaving behind bloody animal sacrifices practiced in the Jewish and pagan cults, nurtured social qualities and conveyed the idea that sharing and fellowship enable life. On the other hand, it represented a regression by alluding to an archaic and brutal human self-sacrifice. A life had been taken so that others could live. The lives of the Christians existed at the expense of somebody else's life.

---

47 Καὶ ἔδωκεν αὐτοῖς and λάβετε exclude that "this is / signifies..." refers to the liturgical acts; clearly, reference is made to the elements of bread and wine. Not surprisingly, Paul's τοῦτο ποιεῖτε is missing. For the Lukan version of the eucharistic tradition, which still can be read along the lines of Paul's understanding, see Lampe, "Das korinthische Herrenmahl," 207.

48 "It is the spirit that gives life; the flesh is useless. The words (about chewing Christ's flesh, etc.) that I have spoken to you are spirit and life" (6:63). In other words, these words need to be understood metaphorically, not literally. Their symbolic understanding, however, would not be possible without the materialistic idea in the heads of people whom the Gospel of John addresses. In the second century C.E., Justin, for example, seems to have adopted this materialistic idea (*Apol.* 1.66.2).

49 See Gerd Theißen and Anette Merz, *Der historische Jesus: Ein Lehrbuch* (2nd ed.; Göttingen: Vandenhoeck & Ruprecht, 1997), 384–85; more detailed Theißen, "Ritualdynamik" (see above n. 20), 275–90.

The tension could only be tolerated and overcome because Christ's "sacrifice" led to a *resurrection* of the sacrificed—which exploded all Old Testament sacrificial logic. For the pre-Pauline and Pauline Christians, a pneumatic, risen Christ was present in the eucharistic ritual as host of the meal (see above), not as the meal itself. And this host, who once sacrificed himself in order to share his life with his followers, invited a congregation to a communal meal and to sharing.

The interpretative category of "sacrifice" was picked up by the early Christians in order to explain the saving power of Christ's death, and therefore they necessarily ended up talking about a "*human* sacrifice"—which seems like an archaic regression to a level even lower than that of the *animal* sacrifices of the Old Testament cult. The early Christians sensed the scandal of this regression and tried to soften it by using the animal metaphor of "lamb" when talking about Christ (e.g., Rev 5:12 τὸ ἀρνίον τὸ ἐσφαγμένον). Moreover, they even burst open the category of "human sacrifice" by confessing the resurrection of the victim. The victim became Lord (κύριος) with power (ἐν δυνάμει Rom 1:4). The dead sacrificial creature became the living center of communion and community.

Picking up the category of human sacrifice as an interpretive tool and at the same time transcending and breaking it apart, the early Christians played with fire without getting burned.

Religious rituals often play with the *fascinum* of the taboo and the scandalous, but at the same time stay at a safe distance from it. This is not unlike modern spectators of the recent Mel Gibson movie, *The Passion of Christ*. The movie brutally showed blood and torture beyond historical authenticity. However, since the movie was a religious Jesus movie, created by a conservative and pious Catholic, this kind of demonstration of violence was socially accepted. Children were admitted to this display of atrocious violence, although the same display would have been X-rated in another movie. For some church communities, seeing the movie as a group was a sort of religious ritual.[50]

Religious rituals often toy with the taboo and atrocious. They allow us once in a while to break the rules in a socially accepted manner. In

---

[50] In order to avoid misunderstandings: This "sort of ritual" with its voyeurism cannot really be compared with a ritual such as the Eucharist. The one and only tertium comparationis is that they both break taboos in a socially accepted manner. In case of the Eucharist, a taboo is broken in even a socially constructive manner. Whether this can be said about the Mel Gibson movie voyeurism is doubtful.

this way, the rules are not nullified. On the contrary, in this way, the acceptance of the rules often is stabilized.[51]

[51] See the Roman Saturnalia, as one of many examples. Once a year, the slave and the master changed roles, the slave bossed his master. The ritual of breaking the rules made it easier for the slave to return to everyday life in which masters bossed their slaves.

Human Sacrifice in Medieval and Modern Judeo-Christian Traditions

The Collective Suicides in the Persecutions of 1096 as Sacrificial Acts[1]

Rainer Walz, University of Bochum

I.

The distinguishing attribute of the martyrdom of Ashkenazic Jewry (*qiddush hashem*) during the first crusade in 1096 is that it was often performed as suicide, or more exactly: killing one's relatives with suicide following. Quite often the male Jews when threatened by the crusaders killed the members of their families—among them the children—before they committed suicide. The usual explanation of these acts is that they wanted to prevent falling into the hands of the Christians who would either baptize them—above all the children—by force or kill them. Some years ago these suicides have attracted new attention when Israel Yuval suggested that they can be seen in a causal relation to the development of the legend of ritual murder.[2] His hypothesis is that the Jews killed their children as a kind of sacrifice in order to exert pressure on God to accelerate the course of history and bring about messianic revenge and that the Christians, shocked by such a behaviour, consequently brought up the tale that the Jews killed Christian children for ritual purposes. This provocative hypothesis has caused some sensation and indignation.[3]

Before discussing the events in 1096 we will describe the structure of Jewish martyrdom in comparison with that of the Christians. This will show that the Jewish martyrdom of 1096 has rather a complicated

[1] This is an abridged version of the article: "Die Verfolgungen von 1096 und die Ritualmordlegende. Die Debatte über die Thesen Israel J. Yuvals." *Aschkenas* 9 (1999): 189–232. New literature could only be used exceptionally.

[2] Israel Jacob Yuval, "Vengeance and Damnation, Blood and Defamation: From Jewish Martyrdom to Blood Libel Accusations," *Zion* 58 (1993): 31–90 [Hebrew].

[3] The answers to Yuval in this polemic are to be found in *Zion* 59 (1994).

structure, because four elements are combined in the events of that year: 1. the idea of sacrifice, 2. the idea of martyrdom, connected with hope for eternal life, 3. the killing of co-believers and suicide, 4. the idea of revenge. In the sacrificial theory in the time of the Temple the dominant concept was, as with probably all sacrifices in early religions, that God should be given a gift. This gift should make up for something given by God beforehand (*zebakh shelamim* "peace offering"; *zebakh hatodah* "thank offering") or for a crime which had to be expiated (*khatta'ʾt* "trespass offering" and *ʾasham* "offering for sin"). The suffering of the animal which was sacrificed was certainly not central to the act. Nevertheless at some point of history the idea of the sacrificial gift was explicitly combined with that of meritorious and representative suffering. This becomes clear in the suffering of God's Servant in Deutero-Isaiah who is called an offering for sin (*ʾasham*, Isa 53:10). One might suppose that the origin of this idea (the 'Sitz im Leben') was oriental despotism, which often showed the divergence of power and justice.[4] This is confirmed by the observation that in Greece the tortured philospher-martyr was also suffering from the tyrant.[5] We find the idea of the suffering just man again in Christ: his death is a sacrifice, and it is above all suffering. This presupposes that suffering in itself is considered good and should not be avoided. This concept, in itself highly strange, can also be found in rather different contexts: in torture for the purpose of initiation in primitive cultures, in war, but also, more related to martyrdom, in the behaviour of the ascetic. The strange combination is also made plausible by the fact that the criminal who expiates his crime with death is also suffering. All this might lead to the idea that the suffering of someone who is pure is valued higher by God than the death of a guilty person. So the death of innocent children may be seen as a representative suffering for the sins of others.[6]

The next idea is that of dying for one's belief. It requires the willingness to be killed by a persecutor for an idea or a dogma. This in itself is strange, too, because other reactions seem to be much more plausible: 1. resistance to, even killing the persecutor, in order to avoid death,

---

[4] A different case is Job where it is not a tyrant who decrees the suffering.

[5] Steffen Diefenbach, "Jenseits der ‚Sorge um sich': Zur Folter von Philosophen und Märtyrern in der römischen Kaiserzeit," in *Das Quälen des Körpers: Eine historische Anthropologie der Folter* (ed. P. Burschel; Cologne: Böhlau 2000), 99–112.

[6] Solomon Schechter, *Aspects of Rabbinic Theology: Major Concepts of the Talmud* (Schocken paperbacks 15; New York: Schocken 1961), 310 f. Cf. *b. Šhabb.* 32 b.

2. renunciation of one's idea / belief for the same purpose (the attitude of Nicodemism, according to John 3:1 ff.).[7] In martyrdom suffering is central from the beginning. The idea that martyrdom is decreed by God because of the martyr's own sins certainly existed, but was not the most important aspect. Much more important was the concept of the innocent martyr. Just as with God's Servant in Isa 53 the combination of suffering with moral superiority in the same person requires justification. It is often stressed that the innocent martyr dies in order to expiate the sins of others or even out of pure love for God. The prescription that the sacrificial animal in the Temple service had to be without blemish may have helped to connect the image of the innocent martyr's death with the sacrificial lamb. This connection had some plausibility in the following history of religion. The baptists very early saw their martyrs as lambs led to the slaughter like God's Servant (Isa 53:7).[8] Even Luther, the theologian of grace who exasperately fought against the understanding of the mass as a sacrifice, saw the early martyrs of the Reformation in the sacrificial context![9]

The third element is that of collective killing and suicide. Suicide was basically forbidden in Jewish and in Christian religion. Christians who committed suicide or even killed their family in persecution were certainly not regarded as martyrs. The Christian martyrs willingly suffered death from the hands of others. The Jewish martyrs of 1096, on the other hand, often combined military response with death by their own hands. Sometimes they fought the Christian aggressors as long as they could, and only when there was no longer any hope they killed themselves.[10]

The fourth element of the structure to be dealt with here, that a religious sacrifice wants revenge, needs explanation, too. The animal killed in the ritual in the Temple did not need any revenge.[11] The combination of sacrifice with revenge was only possible because innocent men

---

[7] This was a widespread attitude from the 16 th century onward in Protestant Christianity. It was theoretically justified by the famous botanist Otto Brunfels. Cf. Carlo Ginzburg, *Il nicodemismo: Simulazione e dissimulazione religiosa nell'Europa del cinquecento* (Biblioteca di cultura storica; Turin: Einaudi 1970). The parallel with the behaviour of the Marranos is striking.

[8] Rainer Walz, "Die Inszenierung des Martyriums bei den Täufern," in *Die Inszenierung des Todes* (ed. M. Oberweis and L.-M. Günther; Sources of Europe 3; Berlin: Europäischer Universitätsverlag, 2006; in print.

[9] Martin Luther, *Werke*, Weimar Edition 35, 413; Weimar Edition 8, 224.

[10] See footnote 84 below.

[11] Expiatory rituals for the death of animals do exist in shamanist cultures. Cf. Karl Meuli, "Griechische Opferbräuche," in: *Phyllobolia: FS Peter von der Mühll* (Basel:

were killed or killed themselves. But the paradoxical structure remains. Christ's death as sacrifice was wholesome for mankind, but nevertheless required revenge. The Jews as his murderers, so the Christian view for a long time, were punished by God and had to be punished by men as 'deicidae,' though Christ's death in itself was good for all mankind! This combination of martyrdom with revenge can often be found. Innumerable times the baptists stressed that the persecutors were punished by God.[12] Only the Munster baptists and some related groups performed this revenge themselves.[13]

We will have to examine how these four elements of Jewish martyrdom are interrelated in the events of 1096.

II.

But first we will show how Jewish martyrdom developed from ancient times to the crusades. The Jewish tradition of martyrdom is based on some central Old Testament narratives: the *ʿaqedah* of Isaac (Gen 22), the report of the men in the fiery furnace (Dan 3), Eleasar who refused to eat pork (2 Macc 6), the mother and her seven sons who were killed most cruelly by the oppressors (2 Macc 7). Also important for the idea of martyrdom in Jewish culture was the martyrdom of rabbi Aqiba (died 135 CE) during the Bar-Kochba insurrection, who was executed because he did not obey the command not to study the Torah.[14] In the first century of the Christian era or even earlier, when the Hebrew version of the *Ascensio Isaiae* was written we find the idea that the prophet was killed in a most cruel way.[15] The tradition was formed that Abraham was killed in the furnace of Nimrod.[16] All this led to the characterization of

Schwabe, 1946), 185–288; repr. in *Gesammelte Schriften* 2; (ed. Th. Gelzer; Basel: Schwabe, 1975), 907–1021, 948 ff.

[12] Walz, *Inszenierung*.

[13] Gary K. Waite, "From Apocalyptic Crusaders to Anabaptist Terrorists: Anabaptist Radicalism after Münster, 1535–1545," *ARG* 80 (1981): 180–91.

[14] Theofried Baumeister, *Die Anfänge der Theologie des Martyriums* (Münsterische Beiträge zur Theologie 45; Münster: Aschendorff 1980), 64; Hans Werner Surkau, *Martyrien in jüdischer und frühchristlicher Zeit* (FRLANT 54; Göttingen: Vandenhoeck & Ruprecht 1938), 36 ff.

[15] Baumeister, Anfänge, 60. Cf. *OTP* (ed. J. H. Charlesworth; London: Darton, Longman, and Todd, 1983–85), vol. 2, 163.

[16] Louis Ginzberg, *The Legends of the Jews* 1 (trans. H. Szold; Philaldelphia: The Jewish Publication Society of America, 1961), 198–203.

Jewish religion as the religion of martyrdom.[17] But the usual kind of martyrdom must be distinguished, as already shown, from two further forms:

1. killing oneself in order to avoid an act forbidden by the religious law or to escape being killed by the persecutors—a kind of death considered as defilement. In between 'true' martyrdom and self-killing we find the provocation that causes the persecutor to kill his victim.
2. the killing of a fellow-believer for the same reasons.

These two forms of martyrdom were realized after the Roman conquest of Jerusalem. They are reported for the final phase in Massadah.[18] From Massadah to the crusades only few suicides of this kind are reported. Abraham Grossman has found some suicides before the crusades: the suicide of three rabbis in Otranto in the middle of the 10th century,[19] the suicide of pious Jewish women under the persecutions of Robert II (987/996–1031): "Some honorable dignified women came and encouraged each other and said: let us go to the river and drown ourselves, so that the name of God be not defiled, for it is sacred to heaven, and the fire-sacrifice is good for us, and it is better for us to die than to live".[20] Death by provoking the persecutor to killing also occurred. The chronicle tells us that in 1007 the Christians persecuted a Jew in order to convert him. But he "insulted their belief in their presence, scoffed at their abominations and reviled their pictures" and was killed by them.[21]

What were the motives of people acting in this way or what motives were imputed to them?

Eleasar, mentioned above, preferred obeying the law and dying in honour to living in shame (2 Macc 6:19–23). He also was afraid of the bad effect of hypocrisy on the youth (v. 24) and also of punishment by God (v. 26). There was also the idea that martyrdom wipes out sin—the sins

[17] Wilhelm Bousset, *Die Religion des Judentums im späthellenistischen Zeitalter* (ed. H. Gressmann; HNT 21; 4th ed.; Tübingen: J. C. B. Mohr, 1966), 374.

[18] The sources are given below.

[19] Abraham Grossman, "Roots of Qiddush Hashem in Early Aschkenaz" [Hebrew], in *Sanctity of Life and Martyrdom: Studies in Memory of Amir Yekutiel* [Hebrew] (ed. I. M. Gafni and A. Ravitzky; Jerusalem: Merkaz Zalman Shazar, 1992), 109 f.

[20] *Book of Persecutions in Germany and France: Memoirs of Contemporaries of the Epoch of Crusades and Selected Poetry* [Hebrew] (ed. A. M. Habermann; Jerusalem: Sifre Tarshish, 1945), 19.

[21] Loc. cit., 20.

of the martyr himself or the sins of the people, so that the martyr changes the fate of the Jewish people for the better.[22] Two further motives can be found: the hope for a life in heaven, but above all we can observe a change in the perception of suffering. Very early, already in the martyrdom of Aqiba, we find the idea that not the atonement for one's own sins or those of others is the point, but that martyrdom is the perfect expression of the love of God—in both directions! As described above, a theology of suffering developed: not the sinner is punished by God with martyrdom, but suffering is sent to the just![23] The motive of revenge can also be found early. It is clearly to be seen in the *Assumptio Mosis* which was written about the time of Jesus Christ.[24] Its author does not represent the quietist passive kind of martyrdom, but hopes to influence history and to move God to messianic revenge: "Nunc ergo, filii, audite me! Videte enim, et scite quia numquam temptan<te>s Deum nec parentes nec proavi eorum, ut praetereant mandata illius. Scitis enim, quia haec sunt vires nobis. Et hoc faciemus: ieiunemus triduo, et quarto die intremus in spelunca quae in agro est, et moriamur potius quam praetereamus mandata Domini dominorum, Dei parentum nostrorum. Hoc enim, si faciemus et moriemur, sanguis noster vindicabitur coram Domino. Et tunc parebit regnum illius in omni creatura illius."[25]

A precondition for this is that the martyr does not suffer death for his own sins or those of his forefathers. Only then God's revenge is required to achieve a moral balance. In the *Assumptio Mosis* the affliction of God's people is very serious, the suffering of the Jews is worse than that of godless peoples. Since the fathers did not transgress the commandments the present generation cannot suffer for their sins. This conveys an es-

---

22 Jan Willem van Henten, Das jüdische Selbstverständnis in den ältesten Martyrien, in *Die Entstehung der jüdischen Martyrologie* (ed. J. W. van Henten; StPB 38; Leiden: Brill 1989), 127–61, 135.

23 Ephraim E. Urbach, *The Sages: Their Concepts and Beliefs*, vol. 1 (Publications of the Perry Foundation in the Hebrew University of Jerusalem; Jerusalem: Magnes Press 1975), 445; *b. Ber.* 61.

24 Johannes Tromp, *The Assumption of Moses: A Critical Edition with Commentary* (SVTP 10; Leiden: Brill, 1993), 116 f.

25 Loc. cit., 18 (9,4–10,1): "Now then, my sons, hear me! See then, and know that neither our parents, nor their ancestors have tempted God by transgressing his commandments. Surely you know that here lies our strength. And this we shall do: Let us fast for three days, and on the fourth day let us enter into the cave which is in the field, and let us die rather than transgress the commandments of the Lord of lords, the God of our fathers. For as we shall do this and die, our bood will be avenged before the Lord. And then his kingdom will appear in his entire creation." Cf. *OTP* 1, 920 f.

chatological meaning to the persecutions. The martyrdom accelerates the eschatological process because it forces God to interfere. The end is coming because revenge is caused by the martyr. This means that the problem of theodicy gets a temporal solution: the future will make good for the unjust suffering. So revenge gets a messianic aspect.[26] This idea was obviously not unusual in those days. In the Revelation of St. John we find a similar passage. Those killed on behalf of God's word "cried with a loud voice, saying, How long, O Lord, holy and true, dost thou not judge and avenge our blood on them that dwell on the earth?" They are told that they have to wait for a short time: "that they should rest yet for a little season, until their fellowservants also and their brethren, that should be killed as they were, should be fulfilled" (Rev 6:10 f.). Here the quest for revenge is expressed by the martyrs already in heaven, it is not the hope of those still alive to influence God's acts.[27]

The sources on the Massadah events offer a valuable insight into the ideas of those killing themselves or, more exactly, the ideas of those reporting about the events. We give the interpretation of the report which was well known to Ashkenazic Jewry in the time of the first crusade. This is the description in the *Sefer Josippon*, a Jewish chronicle composed in the tenth century in southern Italy which gave the Jews information about the *khurban*, the destruction of the second Temple.[28] This work was based on the five books of *Histories* by Pseudo-Hegesippus, a Latin adaptation of Josephus' *Bellum Iudaicum*. The author of the *Sefer Josippon* depends on Hegesippus' book.

In two passages the *Sefer Josippon* raises the question of self-killing: 1. when Josephus goes over into the Romans' camp, 2. during the suicides in Massadah. When Josephus is asked by the Romans to desert the Jewish front and cooperate with them those around him implore him

[26] The foundation for this is Deut 32:43. Cf. Jacob Licht, "Taxo, or the Apocalyptic Doctrine of Vengeance," in *JJS* 12 (1961): 95–103; Paul Volz, *Die Eschatologie der jüdischen Gemeinde im neutestamentlichen Zeitalter: Nach den Quellen der rabbinischen, apokalyptischen und apokryphen Literatur* (Tübingen: Mohr, 1934), 201; Cuthbert Lattey, "The Messianic Expectation in The Assumption of Moses," in *CBQ* 4 (1942): 9–21; Martin Hengel, *Die Zeloten: Untersuchungen zur jüdischen Freiheitsbewegung in der Zeit von Herodes I bis 70 n. Chr.* (AGJU 1; Leiden: Brill 1961), 272: Martyrs as the seed for the coming reign of God.

[27] The idea that the blood of the martyrs rises to God's throne can be found in later Christian sources, too, compare the Baptists's song in: Clarence Bauman, *Gewaltlosigkeit im Täufertum: Eine Untersuchung zur theologischen Ethik des oberdeutschen Täufertums der Reformationszeit* (Studies in the History of Christian Thought 3; Leiden: Brill 1968), 77 f.

[28] *The Josippon (Josephus Gorionides)* [Hebrew] (ed. D. Flusser; 2 vols.; Jerusalem: Bialik, 1980–1981).

to prefer death instead. They argue that this is better than seeing the shame of his people, that it is better to die through one's own sword than through that of the enemies. After all they expostulate with him that he cannot trust the Romans' promises and remind him of Saul's and Jonathan's deaths (1 Sam 31). Josephus himself, they say, had taught them that every Jew killed in action will share life in heaven.[29] Josephus answers that God has given life and that he only can take it and that he will be enraged, if it is thrown away,[30] that it is good to die through the hands of the enemies and that nobody is allowed to kill his brother. "If we kill each other now we will be regarded as murderers, for we have murdered each other."[31] Josephus denounces Saul's suicide as a fearful act.[32] He even argues with the nature of animals who have their teeth and their claws and who fight to their death or their salvation. Finally he offers the example of the responsible captain who does not leave his ship in danger.[33]

The collective suicide in Massadah is described in the following way by the *Sefer Josippon*: Eleazar calls the chiefs of the Jews in Massadah and reminds them of Abraham who was prepared to sacrifice Isaac, and King Josiah who preferred eternal life to life in this world.[34] He refers to the reward in heaven which they cannot get in this world. There they will have rest, here only trouble, here the soul is imprisoned in the body, in the garden of Eden it will be liberated from its prison.[35] This argument is followed by the request to commit suicide. Those killed are described as sacrifices.[36] Platonic ideas are clearly used to justify this kind of logic.[37]

---

29 The great light (*ha'or hagadol*) is used in the crusade chronicles for heaven (cf. no. 77) just as well as in the *Josippon*, loc. cit., vol. 1, 313, 424, 426. The 'great light' can be found in Hegesippus as follows: "[...] revolare ad superna, ad illam regionem paradisi, ubi pias animas deus sacravit?", *Hegesippi qui dicitur historiae libri v*, CSEL 66 (Wien: Hoelder, Pichler, and Tempsky, 1932–1960), III 16 (p. 212); "[...] in illum purum et splendidum superiorem revolat locum [...]," loc. cit., V 53 (p. 410). Here as in other passages we have a free adaptation of the original: The expression 'great light' can be found already in Isa 9:1.

30 For life as a pawn: *piqqadon*, cf. Flusser, *The Josippon*, vol. 1, 314.

31 Loc. cit., 315. Compare Hegesippus III 17, 214.

32 Flusser, *The Josippon*, vol. 1, 316.

33 Loc. cit., 317.

34 Loc. cit., 424.

35 Loc. cit., 425 f.

36 Loc. cit., 430.

37 For the interpretation of the events in Massadah see Menachem Stern, "The Suicide of Eleazar ben Jair and his Men at Masadah, and the 'Fourth Philosophy'" [Hebrew], *Zion* 47 (1982): 367–98. Stern compares the suicides after the Roman conquest with the suicides in Greek and Roman culture. He stresses that Eleazar's ideas are based on the

The *Sefer Josippon* had a great authority in Ashkenaz. Isaak Fritz Baer states that it influenced the generation of the first crusade[38] and Abraham Grossman says that rabbi Gershom of Mayence, 'the light of exile,' copied the book with his own hands as he did with the Talmud and the Mishnah. With this act he gave the book great authority.[39] So *Sefer Josippon* was regarded as part of the old holy literature. In it Josephus is regarded as an important writer and he ranges directly behind the 24 books of the bible and the books of wisdom by Salomo and the sages of Israel.[40] This means it somehow set the model for the events of the year 1096. The events were not absolutely new, as Abraham Grossman has stressed in the article mentioned.

III.

In spite of these precedents several passages in the Hebrew chronicles describing the crusades emphasize that the acts of the Jews in 1096 were something extraordinary[41] and they picture the collective suicides of the Jews much more vividly than the murders committed by the Christians. In order to give some impression of what happened, two such killings shall be described here.[42] We use the editions of the chronicles by

'fourth philosophy,' according to which one was not allowed to subject oneself to foreign domination. Stern also compares the events in Massadah with the suicides of medieval Jews and shows that already medieval Christian chroniclers compared them to the report in Josephus, loc. cit., 392 f.

[38] Isaak Fritz Baer, "Preface" to Habermann, *Persecutions*, 4. See also Steven Bowman, " 'Josippon' and Jewish Nationalism," in *PAAJR* 61 (1995): 23–51, 32 ff.

[39] Grossman, "Roots," 117. Cf. Abraham Grossman, "The Cultural and Social Background of Jewish Martyrdom in Germany in 1096," in *Juden und Christen zur Zeit der Kreuzzüge* (ed. A. Haferkamp; Vorträge und Forschungen 47; Sigmaringen: Jan Thorbecke, 1999), 73–86, 81 ff.

[40] Flusser, *The Josippon*, vol. 1, 143 f.

[41] *Hebräische Berichte über die Judenverfolgungen während der Kreuzzüge* (ed. A. Neubauer and M. Stern; Breslau 1892; repr. Darmstadt: Wissenschaftliche Buchgesellschaft, 1977), 9 [Hebrew text with translations, but with omissions]: "Who has ever seen, who has heard [...]"; Habermann, *Persecutions*, 32: "Who has heard and seen anything like that. Ask and see, whether there was such an ʿaqedah in the times and generations since the first man!" *Chronicle of Eliezer bar Nathan* (Neubauer and Stern, *Berichte*, 41): "Who could hear this and would not be astonished?"

[42] For a critical analysis of both stories see Jeremy Cohen, *Sanctifying the Name of God: Jewish Martyrs and Jewish Memories of the First Crusade* (Jewish Culture and Contexts; Philadelphia: University of Pennsylvania Press 2004), 91 ff. and 106 ff. We are not concerned with the reliability and the general interpretation of the reports, but only with the sacrificial aspects.

Neubauer / Stern and Habermann.[43] Probably the killing of children by their own mother illustrates the case best. Rahel, wife of rabbi Jehudah in Mayence, had two daughters, Bella and Matrona, and two sons, Isaac and Aaron. Before the Christans came she asked her woman-friends, not to spare her children, in order to avoid their capture and baptism. When one of the friends came with her slaughtering-knife to kill Isaac, the mother began to lament and asked her not to do this in his brother's presence. He should not see his brother's death. Now Aaron fled and Isaac was killed. The mother spread her sleeves, in order to gather the blood as in a basin. Aaron, seeing how his brother was killed, cried: "Do not slaughter me!" and hid under a chest. The two daughters, however, whetted the knife themselves, their mother bent their necks and killed them. Then she took her son by his feet from under the chest and killed him. The verb *zabakh* (to sacrifice) is used for the killing. She laid the still quivering bodies beside herself in her sleeves[44] and lamented over them. When the crusaders came and saw the slaughtered children they killed the mother. The father of the children committed suicide when he realized what had happened.[45]

Another act of this kind mentioned in the chronicles is just as significant. Mar Isaac bar David, son of the chief (*parnas*) of the Jewish community in Mayence, whose wife had been killed by the crusaders, was baptized with other Jews against his will. A priest was willing to receive him in his own house, so that he might recover his health. His mother had survived the pogrom and had been able to avoid baptism, but had been injured and was in bed. Her baptized son had saved her. When Mar Isaac returned to his house and saw that the crusaders had not touched his assets in the cellar, he said to himself that all his money was no longer of any value to him now that he had betrayed his faith. He planned to expiate his sin. Through the grace of God he hoped to get to heaven to his friends who had already been killed. He justified his plan with his intention to save his children who could not yet choose between good and evil from the hands of the enemies. At first he prob-

43 Neubauer and Stern, *Berichte*; Habermann, *Persecutions*. There is an English translation of these chronicles in: Shlomo Eidelberg, *The Jews and the Crusaders: The Hebrew Chronicles of the First and Second Crusades* (Madison: University of Wisconsin Press 1977).

44 Cf. the description in Josephus, *De bello judaico: Der jüdische Krieg* (ed. O. Michel and O. Bauernfeind; vol. 2; Darmstadt: Wissenschaftliche Buchgesellschaft, 1969), VII 9, 146. This is not mentioned in the *Sefer Josippon*, where the dead are thrown into a hole, Flusser, *The Josippon*, vol. 1, 430 f.

45 Neubauer / Stern, *Berichte*, 9 f.

ably had believed to secretly educate them as Jews. He took in workers who should repair the doors of his house which had been knocked in during the pogrom. On the day before Sabbath—the work had not yet been finished—he told his mother that he wanted to give God an expiatory sacrifice, in order to find reconciliation. She implored him not to do it, but he locked the house and asked his children whether they were willing to be sacrificed. They answered: "Do what you want to be done."[46] He took his son and his daughter to the synagogue about midnight, killed them in front of the arc, sprinkled their blood on the columns of the arc, and said: "This blood shall be for the expiation of my sins." Then he returned home and set his house on fire on all four corners, burning his mother. Now he went back to the synagogue, set it on fire, too, and went from corner to corner with lifted arms, praying. Christians held out a stick in order to get him out of the fire, but he declined.[47]

We have chosen these examples out of the great number of impressive events. The killing of the children by their parents in which the ritual aspects of sacrifice are clear even without a detailed analysis brings up difficult questions. How did Ashkenazic Jews explain that God allowed these crimes, how did they judge the behaviour of the parents involved? How did they interpret the events and what aims were connected with the killings?

Not only in the examples mentioned above, but in numerous other passages it is said that the martyrs performed their suicide or the killing of their co-believers as a sacrifice. The killings were regarded as an "expiation (*kapparah*) for all our sins" and as sin offerings and trespass offerings (*khatta'ot*, *'aschamot*).[48] This can be seen from details concerning the ritual: the knife with which the killing was done was not to be notched,[49] as the case of Rachel and her children shows. Such a notched knife made the sacrifice legally null and void.[50] So we find the call to everybody possessing a knife to examine it before the killing.[51] The martyrs are called *temimim* (without blemish) and thus they fulfill the re-

---

46 Loc. cit., 12.

47 Loc. cit., 12 f.

48 Loc. cit., 32.

49 Loc. cit., 7 and 9.

50 For the Hebrew term *pagum* cf. *Complete Dictionary of Ancient and Modern Hebrew* (ed. E. Ben Yehuda; vol. 6, Schöneberg: Langenscheidt, 1951), 4811 with an explanation.

51 Neubauer and Stern, *Berichte*, 7. The servant (*shammash*) of the synagogue in Cologne is asked to examine the sword, 19 f.

quirements of the animal to be sacrificed.[52] In the case of Mar Isaac this category of sacrifice becomes especially clear. He performs his martyrdom as an expiation for his conversion to the Christian belief and sprinkles the blood of his children on the arc of the synagogue in Mayence (as the altar!), in order to visualize the sacrificial meaning. In the Old Testament ritual the blood had to be sprinkled on the altar or before the veil of the sanctuary.[53] The chronicler sees the monstrosity of the events in the fact that 1096 parents and children were sacrificed on one and the same day—against the prescriptions in the Old Testament, according to which a ewe is not be slaughtered on the same day as its lamb.[54]

But there also existed the strange interpretation of the killing as a wedding ceremony, which is interesting, because we find it so often in the martyrology of the baptists. When Sarith, a young bride, observed the killing and wanted to flee her father-in-law took her, kissed her on her mouth and cried: "Look all of you at the wedding (*khuppah*) I make for my daughter, my daugher-in-law, today."[55] Then he killed her in the lap of her fiancé, killing his son afterwards.

Salomo bar Simon is doubtful about why God admitted all this. There are many hints that he understood the pogroms as a punishment for the sins of the people.[56] Very often he talks about these sins and stresses that the heavenly law-court is just.[57] He even reports that most of the rabbis of all communities died a year before the events. This he interpreted in the light of Isa 57:1 ("the righteous is taken away from the evil to come"). The righteous were saved before the catastrophy, from which the reader might draw the conclusion: the sinners had to live through it. Salomo bar Simon also says that no prophet can find out, why the sins were weighed by God in such a way that the holy community was punished with death, as if they had shed blood. But God is a just judge, "and the guilt is ours."[58] The same interpretation is shown in the ex-

[52] Loc. cit., 17. The martyrs are called burnt offerings (*'olah kalil*), 22. Cf. the numerous passages with *tamim* in Leviticus.

[53] Lev 1–4 passim.

[54] "And [whether it be] cow or ewe, ye shall not kill it and her young both in one day," Lev 22:28; Neubauer and Stern, *Berichte*, 17.

[55] Neubauer and Stern, *Berichte*, 20.

[56] Loc. cit., 3: "the sin of the community [...] as if they had shed blood."

[57] Cf. *gezirah*, loc. cit., 1; "our sins caused the victory of the enemies [...] the hand of God lay heavily on his people," 6; *din shamayim*, 8.

[58] Loc. cit., 3.

pression that God has left his people and has given it in the hands of wicked Edom.[59]

But this is not the only reason given by the chronicler. Apart from sin we find other interpretations already mentioned above. Salomo bar Simon also says: "It was a heavenly decree, to examine those who adore him whether they will bear the yoke of the pure fear of God."[60] That the killings of the martyrs were understood as examinations is also made clear by the comparison with Abraham's willingness to sacrifice Isaac. This is the great model for martyrdom in the chronicles. Salomo bar Simon says that the community of Mayence was visited with ten temptations (*nissayonot*) like Abraham, Hananiah, Mishael, and Azariah.[61] The last three were in the fiery furnace in Dan 3. He stresses the martyrs' obedience towards God. But Abraham's sacrifice is even surpassed: in Mayence it was not only one sacrifice as with the patriarch, but there were 1100 sacrifices.[62] The strength of a son is shown in the fact that he is slaughtered by his father without being bound, different from Isaac in the Old Testament![63]

Salomo bar Simon also expresses very often the idea that those killed were an elite which God had found worthy of martyrdom.[64] They are called the crown of Israel, the honour of the Torah and the scholars. Innocent babies and innocent souls were killed. They are called the glory of Israel, the sin-fearing men, the men of action, the splendour of wisdom, purity and segregation and of the priesthood.[65] The blood of the killed is a merit which serves for the expiation of the sins of the coming

59 Loc. cit., 2. Similar: "bad troubles"; "for we have sinned against God," 4. "We were not even respected as much as Sodom and Amora" 5; "the heavenly judgment," 8.

60 Loc. cit., 4. The same idea: "in order to examine our generation, God came to show their love [for God] to all," 21.

61 Loc. cit., 7.

62 Loc. cit., 8; Shalom Spiegel, *The Last Trial: On the Legends and Lore of the Command to Abraham to Offer Isaac as a Sacrifice* (New York: Jewish Publication Society of America 1967), 17 ff.

63 Neubauer and Stern, *Berichte*, 41.

64 He writes on the community of Mayence: "they were found holy, all together to go up to God," loc. cit., 6: "In one place were united: torah, greatness, riches, honour, wisdom, humility and benevolence [. . .]" "Yea, since the day of the destruction of the second temple there have not been their equals in Israel, and after them none will be like them," 8. "Their merits, justice, piety, innocence and sacrifice (*ʿaqedah*) may be our just mediator and advocate before the High One, that he may lead us out of the exile in Edom soon in our days, and our just Messiah may come in our days, amen," 17.

65 Loc. cit., 8.

generations.[66] The martyrs are supposed to be intercessors with God for the surviving so that they would be led from the exile and the Messiah would come.[67] Above all the community in Mayence was regarded as an elite.[68] A further argument was that their acts would make a great impression on the Christians.[69]

The search for an explanation led to the desire for punishment of and revenge against the persecutors. Salomo bar Simon states that the crusaders sought revenge for the death of Christ.[70] So revenge was a strong motivation on both sides! He tells us that where they could the Jews took revenge themselves. So they killed a Christian who was among them by stoning him.[71] Rabbi Kalonymos of Mayence tried to murder the bishop.[72] But above all, Salomo bar Simon hopes for revenge from God. He is the lord of revenge, and his coming is implored. He is asked to pour his wrath on the peoples. Psalm 79:12 is quoted: "And render unto our neighbours sevenfold [...]"[73] In some passages God is even put under pressure. The chronicler asks God in a reproachful tone in the words of Isa 64:12: "Wilt thou refrain thyself for these things, O Lord? Wilt thou hold thy peace, and afflict us very sore?"[74] The chronicler stresses that revenge may come in their days and that they may see it with their own eyes. But the events get an eschatological meaning.[75] God's revenge shall become known among the peoples and the Messiah shall come soon.[76]

Those killed go to eternal bliss. The chronicler uses the same expressions as the *Sefer Josippon*: the martyrs see the great light (*ʾor gadol*).[77]

---

66 Loc. cit., 17. Cf. the same idea: "And the lord of revenge may revenge in our days and before our eyes the shed blood of his servants, and their merit and their justice may stand for us as a merit and may defend us in bad days," 28.

67 Loc. cit., 7.

68 "[...] for God chose this good generation for himself, in order to justify through them the generations coming after them," loc. cit., 25. Cf. no. 52.

69 Loc. cit. , 41. Cf. Jacob Katz, *Exclusiveness and Tolerance: Studies in Jewish–Gentile Relations in Medieval and Modern Times* (Scripta Judaica 3; Oxford: Oxford University Press 1961), 91. Cf. Habermann, *Persecutions*, 73, 77 f. The Christians should see the truth of Jewish belief. At the same time there was the hope that the Christians would realize their errors, loc. cit., 43.

70 Neubauer and Stern, *Berichte*, 1.

71 Loc. cit., 10.

72 Loc. cit., 15 f.

73 Loc. cit., 17.

74 Loc. cit., 20.

75 Loc. cit., 17. There is a messianic allusion: redemption from the exile in Edom, 23.

76 Loc. cit., 17.

77 Loc. cit., 12 (instead of *ʾor meʾir*).

They will be in the world where there will be always daylight, in the garden Eden. They will see God in his greatness (*kabod, godel*) and will get a golden crown with gems and pearls in it and will have their meals in the society of rabbi Aqiba.[78] It will be an everlasting world of light and bliss, which is opposed to the world of darkness, need and decay.[79] The soul will find rest in paradise in the light of life.[80] It is interesting that the hour of martyrdom is also the hour of proselytes and similar persons. Mar Jacob bar Sulam, whose mother had not been a Jewess and whose family had not been honoured, cried: "Up to now you despised me, now see what I am going to do." Then he took his knife and cut his throat.[81] There was also a true proselyte (*ger tsedeq*) who asked the rabbi: "If I slaughter myself for the sanctifying of his great name, what will happen to me?" The rabbi answered: "You will be with us in our camp, because you are a true proselyte and you will be with the other just proselytes in their camp and you will be with Abraham, our father, who was the first true proselyte (*ger tsedeq*)."[82] This does not only show how strong his hope was to have a share in the coming world, but also that men with a somehow ambiguous status could make sure by the *qiddush hashem* that they were full members of the Jewish community.

But in spite of all this praise of martyrdom, in spite of all the languishing for it[83] we find a clear appreciation of life in the acts of those prepared for the *qiddush hashem*. The chronicles tell that the Jews did everything to save their lives: through flight, through fighting the aggressors, through negotiations with them, through bribery and through tricks.[84] Sacrifice was only the last way out! The baptized Jews were not condemned, they were even praised (*beshebakh*), because they tried to observe the ritual law, because they went to the churches because they were forced only and out of fear. The heathens knew that their conversion was not sincere (*beleb shalem*) and they observed the shabbat in the presence of the Christians! "And who calumniates them behaves like

---

78 Loc. cit., 22.

79 Loc. cit., 7. Cf. Katz, *Exclusiveness*, 86.

80 Loc. cit., 11.

81 Loc. cit., 10.

82 Loc. cit., 22.

83 *Das Buch der Frommen: Nach der Rezension in Codex de Rossi 1133*, (ed. J. Wistinetzki; Frankfurt a. M.: Wahrmann, 1924), no. 251, 83. For examples for blasphemy in order to provoke martyrdom, cf. above.

84 Neubauer and Stern, *Berichte*, 5f., 26. Cf. Peter Browe, "Die Judenbekämpfung im Mittelalter," in: *ZKT* 62 (1938): 378.

one who calumniates God (*medabber pene hashekhinah*)."[85] So there was a balanced judgment which we will discuss below.

But facing the terrible events Salomo bar Simon is in confusion. The explanations given do not satisfy him. So he asks why the heaven which darkened during Isaac's sacrifice by Abraham on Mount Moriah does not darken now. "Ask and see whether from the time of the first man there was such a sacrifice (*ʿaqedah*)?"[86] Obviously the fate of Job is of significance in his reflections. Since the evils are in no relation to the sins committed he cannot understand that God allowed what happened. The same point is made in poetry. In a *selikhah* on the events of 1096 it is said: "Our God, why have you left us, far away from help for us?"[87]

So we find a mixture of contradictory and complementary explanations. Obviously an unequivocal interpretation was not possible. The knowledge of human sinfulness, but also the idea that the martyrs, and above all those who had committed suicide, were an elite, led to interpretations which connected the events with the course of history. Most important, of course, in our context, is that the martyrs were compared with the sacrifices in the Temple. This was not new. Already the *Sefer Josippon* emphasized that the collective suicide in Massadah was a sacrifice.[88] As we have seen, the chronicler represents Mar Isaac as a man who brings an expiatory sacrifice.[89] The idea that an elite was killed fits in well with the regulations for the sacrifices in the Old Testament according to which the animal should be without blemish.[90] Rabbi Kalonymos was described as an excellent man of his age, as a God-fearing man, dignified to be sacrificed on the innermost altar.[91] The expression 'innermost altar' refers to the idea of an altar in heaven, on which the souls of the pure are sacrificed to God.[92]

---

85 Loc. cit., 29.

86 Loc. cit., 8.

87 Habermann, *Persecutions*, 87.

88 Flusser, *Josippon*, vol. 1, 430: *qorban ʿolah*!

89 Neubauer and Stern, *Berichte*, 12.

90 Lev 1 ff.

91 Neubauer and Stern, *Berichte*: "bound (*ʿaqud*) on the innermost altar," 3. In the *b. Menaḥ* 110 a the altar in the height is mentioned.

92 Avigdor Aptovitzer, "The Temple in the Height in the Haggaddah" [Hebrew], *Tarbiz* 2 (1930): 137–53; Isaac Fritz Baer, "The Persecutions of 1096" [Hebrew], in *Sefer Assaf: Collected articles in Honour of Prof. Simchah Assaf* (ed. M. D. Cassuto, J. G. Klausner, and J. Gutmann; Jerusalem: Mosad Harav Kuk 1953), 126 ff.; Gerson D. Cohen, "Messianic Postures of Ashkenazim and Sephardim," in *Studies of the Leo Baeck Institute* (ed. M. Kreutzberger; New York: Leo Baeck Institute 1967), 117–56. Ashkenazic Jews were

Besides the chronicles a further genre of sources shows the intellectual reflection of and the emotional participation in the events. Religious lyric was of great importance in those days. Jewish scholars did not only write commentaries on the biblical books, but also on the post-biblical poetry. In poetry the parallels between martyrdom on the one hand and the *ʿaqedah* of Isaac and the sacrifice in the temple on the other hand are drawn out even more clearly than in the chronicles.[93] The lamentations (*qinot*) express the feelings of the surviving and try to give significance to the events. Some of these lamentations clearly expect that God will take revenge.[94] The poem "God, do not pass over our blood in silence" by the rabbi David bar Meshullam may be given as an example. David bar Meshullam was one of the *shtadlans* of Speyer who had been sent to Henry IV in 1090.[95] His poem shows the sacrificial symbolism in all its details. It is said that women and children performed the sacrifice, that they were chosen sheep, one year old and without blemish. The poet mentions the great order (of sacrifice) which they fulfilled, he mentions the slaughtering of children and babies, tells us the parts of the 'victims' (according to Lev 1 ff.), describes the ritual waving of the shoulder or other parts[96] and the sprinkling of the altar with blood. He calls the Shema the martyrs had on their lips when they were dying the sacrificial blessing. He also compares the killing with the *ʿaqedah* on Mount Moriah.[97]

It seems that the lamentations stress much more than the chronicles the idea that this martyrdom is the merit of an elite, not a sin offering. Much more than the chronicles they ask for revenge.[98] For this purpose the monstrous character of the events is shown. David bar Meshullam

---

not emotionally passive. Martyrdom was not only a punishment for their own sins, but a proof of election. The victims died because of their perfection. The elect were penitential sacrifices for the others. Cf. for this George F. Moore, *Judaism in the First Centuries of the Christian Era: vol. 1 The Age of the Tannaim* (Cambridge Mass.: Harvard University Press 1927), 546 ff.

93 Important poems in Habermann, *Persecutions*; *Prayer-Book for the Festival Days: According to the Ashkenazic Tradition* [Hebrew] (ed. D. Sh. Goldschmidt; 2 vols.; Jerusalem: Leo Baeck Institute, 1970).

94 Cf. the poem "Give them to shame," Habermann, *Persecutions*, 105 f.

95 Loc. cit., 69.

96 *Tenufah*, ritual of wave offering, see e. g. Lev 9:21.

97 Habermann, *Persecutions*, 69–71.

98 Neubauer and Stern, *Berichte*: "Revenge in our days,", 14; "Revenge the blood of your servants shed in our days and before our eyes soon, amen"; "When shall come the robber so that we can take the heavenly judgment on us? We have already prepared the sacrifices (*ʿaqedot*) and made the altars for his name," 8; "they were both gathered into the

tells in his poem how the "slaughtering and the slaughtered" are lying on each other, how the blood of fathers and sons flows together, how children ask their parents to kill them and how they are bathed in their blood. Naked, the daughters are lying under women with their bellies slit open, out of which new-born babies are coming. The cruel character of the events justifies the prayer for revenge. One even finds the image of the purple dress of God, on which the blood of those killed is sprinkled, calling God to revenge.[99]

IV.

Killing one's own children in persecution is certainly a monstrous act and needs further explanation. One important question is why killings of this kind and suicide as mass events did not occur before the crusades (apart from Massadah) and why only Ashkenazic Jewry took this path. In order to clarify this we will first consider the regulations of Jewish law for martyrdom. As Josephus' speech already shows human life ranges high in Jewish law—contrary to the characterization of Jewish religion as a religion of martyrdom mentioned above. Martyrdom was not—as with some early Christians—an aim in itself. In the Talmud this question is discussed, but we cannot go into details here. According to some passages of the Babylonian Talmud Jews have to accept death when forced by a non-Jew to commit *ʿabodah zarah*, i. e., the act of idolatry, a sexual crime or murder.[100] Never are they allowed to perform such acts even if the consequence of their refusal is death. But if Jews are forced to commit other transgressions of the law they are supposed to yield to the pressure in order to save their lives.

The glorification of the victims, among them the father who does not show mercy to his son,[101] contradicts the usual understanding of the law. Whereas in the tradition of Massadah, obviously continued in the *Sefer Josippon*,[102] killing oneself is allowed or even recommended, the

treasure of his perfection till the revenge of the shed blood of his servants. Then he will judge the heathens for the many corpses," 16. Cf. Ps 10:6, Deut 32:43.

99 Habermann, *Persecutions*, 87.

100 Cf. *b. Sanh.* 74 a–b; *b. ʿAbod. Zar.* 27 b, 54 a. There is also the important difference whether the violation of law is committed in public or in private places, cf. Alyssa M. Gray: "A Contribution to the Study of Martyrdom and Identity in the Palestinian Talmud," in: *JJS* 54 (2003): 242–72.

101 Neubauer and Stern, *Berichte*, 41.

102 G. D. Cohen is of a different opinion, cf. no. 112 and Grossman, "Background," 81 ff.

more restrictive regulations are also continued. This can be shown in the *Mishneh Torah* written by Maimonides in the 12 th century which sums up the talmudic regulations and does not give any hint that killing oneself is allowed, if a Jew is forced to commit idolatrous acts, sexual crimes or murder. In Maimonides' work it is quite clear that the Jew has to be killed through the hand of the persecutor.[103] This is the view of Sefardic Jewry.

But there is also another tradition. Whereas the halakhic sources of the Talmud only speak about death through the hand of the persecutor and never suggest killing oneself in such a situation, this is done in the haggadic parts of the Talmud. In *b. Giṭ.* 57 b the story of Jewish boys and girls is told who drown themselves on a voyage in order to avoid sexual abuse by a non-Jew. It is expressly mentioned that the boys chose death because they wanted to avoid homosexual acts. Ashkenazic Jewry seems to have stressed this haggadic tradition which appreciated those who had committed suicide. If you assume that those acting in 1096 did not transgress the commands of their teachers in law, which means that the suicide and the killing of others was lawful in their eyes, we must ask the question why and how this special Ashkenazic view developed. In a widely received article Gerson D. Cohen deals with the Sefardic and the Ashkenazic cultures. These two cultures differ in their messianic expectations.[104] According to Cohen Ashkenazic Jewry was rather passive in their messianism whereas Sefarad was active in this regard. This is due to the fact that Ashkenaz had close relations to Palestine in the early and high Middle Ages and shared its messianic restraint, whereas Sefarad was oriented towards Babylon and was influenced by its messianic excitement. According to Cohen there was not a single pseudo-Messiah in Ashkenaz down to the beginning of the 16 th century (about 1500: Asher Lemmlein who shows traces of Sefardic influence).[105] The great messianic movements, among them those of the 16 th and 17 th centuries of David Reubeni and Shelomo Molkho and of Sabbatai Zevi, were formed by Sefardic Jews. In their eschatological speculations the two cultures also differed.[106]

---

[103] Maimonides, *Mischneh Torah: Sefer Hamadda, Hilchot Jesodei Tora*, V, 1 ff.

[104] Gerson D. Cohen, "Messianic Postures."

[105] Loc. cit., 123. In Ashkenaz there was no "original messianic literature whatever," loc. cit., 125.

[106] Loc. cit., 128 ff. In Ashkenaz there were only few eschatological speculations, but there were such calculations with the Hasidim and the Tosafists in the 12 th and 13 th centuries. But they differed from those of the Sefardim. The first were more prophetic in

On the other hand the Sefardic Jews had a deep interest in the worldly culture of their environment, in philosophy and science which resulted in a different reaction on persecutions from that in Ashkenaz.[107] Their rationalistic skepticism led many of them to giving up their own world-view, on the other hand they were prepared for apostasy since they expected the messianic age in the near future, so that living in a non-Jewish belief-system for a short span of time did not seem unbearable to them.[108] Cohen says that there was no immediate connection between persecution and messianic movements. This was not the religion of the suppressed.[109] Not even one of the pogroms caused a messianic movement. These were flourishing in regions of relative stability: the Near East, North Africa, the Iberian peninsula. Active messianism was not fostered by economic or social circumstances. On the other hand quiescence and passivity had so much penetrated the Ashkenazic communities that there was no longer any outward aggressive behaviour.[110] Cohen goes even back to the Bar-Kochba-insurrection. He says that since then Palestine had been rather quiet. Qietism had even developed in apocalyptic literature. The visionary who implores God's revenge on the heathens waits for this to come and does not act himself. He satisfies himself with "violent and bloody fantasies that will one day become a reality."[111] Apocalyptic literature had the function of suppressing and sublimating aggressive emotions. This attitude spread in all regions of the diaspora where the schools of Palestine, the holy land, were influential. Here there were mystical speculations. The *Sefer Josippon*, so Cohen, confirmed this quietism because it condemned the insurrection against the Romans.[112] Cohen mentions four examples of the difference. In Ashkenaz the persecutions of 1096 and 1648 (Chmielnitzki-insurrection) were characterized by the *qiddush hashem*. On the contrary,

---

nature, the last were more 'rational' calculations. The Ashkenazim found new speculations in the gematria, whereas the Sefardic Jews stuck to the traditional calculations. There was a mystical mystery in Ashkenaz and rational calculation in Sefarad, which did not contradict mathematics, logic and astromy, loc. cit., 137.

[107] Isaac Fritz Baer, *A History of the Jews in Christian Spain: 2. From the 14 th Century to the Expulsion* (Philadelphia: Jewish Publication Society of America, 1966), 253 ff. and 273 ff.

[108] Cohen, "Messianic Postures," 153. Cf. Grossman, "Background," 85.

[109] Loc. cit., 143. Cf. Gershom Scholem, *Sabbatai Sevi: The Mystical Messiah 1626–1676* (London: Routledge & Kegan Paul, 1973), 88 ff. on the connection between Sabbatianism and the Chmielnitzki-insurrection.

[110] Cohen, Messianic Postures, 143.

[111] Loc. cit., 144 f.

[112] Loc. cit., 145. This evaluation contradicts that of Grossman, s. below.

in Sefarad the persecutions of 1147 (by the Almohads) and 1391 (in Castile and Aragon) were characterized by apostasy and the rise of the Marranos. There was no relation between messianism and persecutions, but one between the belief-system and the attitude towards persecutions. Jews in Ashkenaz, not in the least harassed by religious doubt, saw the only solution in the *qiddush hashem* and considered forced conversion as a failure, a failure for which the circumstances accounted and which therefore was pardonable.

These combinations by Cohen have been expanded by Hayim Soloveitchik. He says that before 1096 there was not one example that suicide in persecution was permitted in order to avoid forced conversion. So he states the following characteristics of Ashkenazic Jewry:

1. In the Ashkenazic communities of Germany and France there was a deep religious feeling,[113] whereas a laxist attitude dominated in Spain.

2. In Ashkenaz there were no religious alternatives. The Tosafists did not see any danger in the forced conversions and did not doubt the basic faithfulness of the Jewish people. The chronicles described martyrdom in a fashion which recommended imitation. Forced conversions were put up with and provisions were made for return to the Jewish belief, circumstances permitting. Insults of those baptized by force were forbidden.[114]

3. In Ashkenaz the willingness to fulfill the law increased in spite of all tribulations and persecutions. Suffering from a yoke which was always harder to bear the Jewish people did not try to get a maximum of relief. The consequent attitude towards the *qiddush hashem* typical of Ashkenaz was paralleled in the fact that the burden of the religious law became always heavier, the regulations stricter. For instance the famous question concerning the use of

[113] Cf. Alan Mintz, *Hurban: Responses to Catastrophe in Hebrew Literature* (New York: Columbia University Press 1984), 84 ff.

[114] Habermann, *Persecutions*, 56 f. Cf. above p. 227 f. and Abraham Grossman, *The Early Sages of Ashkenaz: Their Lifes, Leadership, and Works* [Hebrew] (Jerusalem: Magnes Press, 1981), 122. In the chronicle of Salomo bar Simon we also find the appreciation of those converted by force, Neubauer and Stern, *Berichte*, 29.

non-Jewish wine (*yayin nesekh*) Ashkenazic teachers did not compromise whereas a certain laxism could be observed in Sefarad.[115]

Soloveitchik's and Cohen's articles find the causes for the different attitudes towards martyrdom in the cultural conditions. Grossman emphasizes other connections. He also stresses the close relation between Ashkenaz and Palestine. The fact that also expert teachers of law like Rabbenu Tam justified the suicides and the killing of 1096 results, in his eyes, from the specific view of the religious law.[116] Whereas in other centres of Jewish culture haggadah and halaka were separated strictly and there was the principle that no command of the law was to be derived from haggadic sources, these were much more positively valued in Ashkenaz. The haggadah was used for halakic statements, the haggadic parts of the Talmud were used integrally.[117] According to the haggadic sources, also in the Babylonian Talmud, self-killing was possible and even recommended as a model.[118] According to Grossman Ashkenazic Jewry has to be judged according to these sources, not those of other Jewish centres. Grossman relates—just as Cohen—this specific attitude of Ashkenaz to its close relations with the Jewish culture in Palestine. This was passed over to Germany above all through the Italian Jewry. So he argues that the *Sefer Josippon* which had been written in Italy was decisive for the understanding of *qiddush hashem* among the Ashkenazic Jewry. Therefore the events of Massadah, communicated on this way deeply influenced conditions in Germany. But different form Soloveitchik and Cohen, Grossman thinks that the Ashkenazic rabbis could not be sure about their followers. Many sources show that Ashkenazic Jewry was in a deep crisis in those days, because Christian propaganda had its effect, as is documented by many surprising interpretations of the Bible.[119] Apostasy occurred to a much higher degree than assumed up to now. The chroniclers were alarmed and feared that the Jews would not sustain the pressure from the Christians. This is

---

115 Haym Soloveitchik, "Religious Law and Change: The Medieval Ashkenazic Example," in *AJSR* 12 (1987): 216 („It is in the tosafist period that the Jewish kitchen was fettered").

116 Grossman, "Roots," 108.

117 Cf. p. 231 above; Grossman, *The Early Sages*, 429–32.

118 Cf. *b. Giṭ* 57 b.

119 Abraham Grossman, "The Jewish-Christian Polemic and Jewish Biblical Exegesis in Twelfth Century France: On the Attitude of R. Joseph Qara to the Polemic" [Hebrew], *Zion* 51 (1986): 29–60 with impressive examples.

why they made the imitation of the heroic deeds of former days an obligation. The appreciation of the *qiddush hashem* was a reaction on the temptations of apostasy. The nearly complete repression of the conversions to the Christian belief is good evidence of the crisis and of the success of Christian propaganda.

It is obvious that the authors mentioned contradict each other partly, so when Grossman states a great danger for Jewish culture in Ashkenaz through apostasy, whereas Cohen stresses the faithfulness and confidence of this group. But the central statement is important for all of them: In Ashkenaz the attitude towards martyrdom and self-killing differed from that in Sefarad. Soloveitchik and Cohen say that the reason for this is the different attitude towards messianism and rationalism; Grossman argues that the two contradicting attitudes to martyrdom result from the fact that the role of the haggadah for the religious law was judged differently in the two religious cultures.

A further qualification has to be made. Ram Ben-Shalom and Abraham Gross have shown that the *qiddush hashem* in Spain and Portugal was performed quite often in 1391 and after 1492. But because this is rather late compared with the first crusade the basic distinctions between the two cultures can be maintained.[120]

We need not go into details about Yuval's hypotheses. In our context it is important that he sees two kinds of reaction. Revenge is characteristic of Ashkenazic Jews. They closely connect, in Yuval's eyes, eschatological / messianic redemption with revenge and the destruction of Christianity, whereas the Sefardic Jews favoured the concept of redemption and conversion. The Ashkenazic concept has precursors whom Yuval finds in poetry and in the midrash. The most important point in Yuval's argument, however, is that the Jews believed that they could accelerate revenge by killing innocent children. The blood of a child, Yuval says, had the power of a lamb, i. e. it was a sacrifice that enforced God's intervention.[121] As already said, Yuval's theses met violent opposition. This thesis is, of course, not necessary to show the sacrificial character of this kind of martyrdom, it only stresses the moment of revenge in it.

[120] Abraham Gross, "On the Ashkenazi Syndrome of Jewish Martyrdom in Portugal" [Hebrew], *Tarbiz* 64 (1994 / 95): 83–114; Ram Ben-Shalom, "Kidush ha-Shem and Jewish Martyrdom in Aragon and Castile in 1391," *Tarbiz* 70 (2000 / 01): 227–82.

[121] Yuval, "Vengeance and Damnation," 70.

V.

The details have confirmed the complex structure of the events of 1096. We can see that ideas originally well separated were combined here. Some of these combinations had a long history and can be observed in Jewish and Christian martyrdom, above all the connection between sacrifice and martyrdom which showed its plausibility from ancient Jewish history down to early modern times. The Jews could of course draw these parallels much better, because they had the tradition of actual sacrifices kept alive for every Jew in the Mishnah and the Talmud. One might even say that the interpretation of martyrdom as sacrifice stressed the continuity of Jewish religion after the interruption of the Temple sacrifices. But Jewish martyrdom was also more complicated than its Christian counterpart. It differed from the mainstream of Christian martyrdom by the inclusion of suicide and even active killing of the persecuted co-believers, by the combination of willingness to suffer with aggression against the persecutors, even killing them, if the circumstances allow for it, so that sanctifying the name was not an aim in itself as with many Christian martyrs. If death was provoked by some of the persecuted this only happened, when no way out was left. In clear opposition to this is the mitigation of the idea of martyrdom in so far as renunciation and conversion were allowed in some circumstances or were at least not regarded as complete failure as it was the case in the mainstream of Christian doctrine. The explicit praise of those who gave in to pressure and converted will probably not be found in the documents of Christian religion. That this praise was expressed by Salomo bar Simon, the Ashkenazic chronicler of the pogroms of 1096, forms a bridge between the two Jewish cultures, the Sefardic and the Ashkenazic, with their different attitudes towards martyrdom, so much stressed by the scholars. It is remarkable that the two contradicting attitudes, mildness towards the baptized and the cult of those sanctifying the name, could go so closely together in one and the same person.

God's Sacrifice of Himself as a Man

Anselm of Canterbury's *Cur deus homo*[1]

Jasper Hopkins, University of Minnesota

1. *Uniqueness and Paradoxicality*: As the present volume attests, there are in the history of religion many stories of human beings offering to the gods both human and non-human sacrifices. These practices are usually meant either to placate and appease a wrathful, jealous deity or to ingratiate oneself into divine favor through this act of sacrificial devotion. More rarely, the sacrifice is an expression of thanksgiving to a particular deity for aid that has been rendered or for prayers that have been answered. Many of the deities who were importuned and worshiped by the ancient Greeks were believed to be mortal. For example, in one version of the legend, the god Dionysus was, as a child, sacramentally killed by the Titans, who dismembered him, boiled his members, and feasted ritually upon them. Zeus is said to have retrieved his uncooked heart, to have swallowed it, and to have produced a new Dionysus from this ingested organ.

The Christian story differs significantly from such Grecian and other sagas; for the Christian God cannot, qua God, either die or be put to death. Thus, Nietzsche is speaking contrary to Christian theology when in his work *Joyful Wisdom* he fictionalizes about the madman who comes to the marketplace one morning carrying in broad daylight a lit lantern. "I am looking for God," he proclaims. Where has He gone? "*Wir haben ihn getötet*—ihr und ich":[2] "*We have killed Him*—you and I," he answers. Thus, for Nietzsche, God is dead. In other words, the Judeo-Christian

[1] English: *Why God Became a* [*God*]*-man*. Anselm completed the *Cur deus homo* in 1098. The text of the *Cur deus homo* is available in English translation in Anselm of Canterbury, *Complete Philosophical and Theological Treatises* (trans. Jasper Hopkins and Herbert W. Richardson; Minneapolis: Banning, 2000). The translation is also found at www.cla.umn.edu/jhopkins/.

[2] Friedrich Nietzsche, *Die fröhliche Wissenschaft* III, 125 (in *Werke in drei Bänden* II, ed. Karl Schlechta (Munich: Hanser, 1966). My translation.

idea of God is a decadent idea; and the God who is implored by Christians and Jews is as good as dead, for He remains silent and *absconditus*, never responding to His followers' worshipful entreaties. Nietzsche is perturbed, furthermore, by the seeming paradoxes at the core of the Christian story. One such putative paradox—not singled out explicitly by Nietzsche—is the following: the Christian religion forbids human sacrifice; and yet, this very religion began with, and is founded upon, the self-sacrifice of the man Jesus, understood to be the Christ, to be the dying and rising Savior of those who trust in Him.

If we are to believe Jonathan Smith, the Christian conception of such a Savior is unique in the history of religion. For in the history of religion, outside of Christianity, "there is no unambiguous instance ... of a dying and rising deity."

> All the deities that have been identified as belonging to the class of dying and rising deities can be subsumed under the two larger classes of disappearing deities or dying deities. In the first case, the deities return but have not died; in the second case, the gods die but do not return.[3]

To be sure, there *is* something both unique and initially paradoxical about the Christian story. Already in the eleventh century Anselm of Canterbury recognized this fact and wrote his *Cur deus homo* in order to elucidate it. That is, he recognized that the Gospels are unique insofar as their central account does not depict the sacrifice-of-a-human-being that is made along the lines of, say, Aeschylus's Iphigenia—i. e., a sacrifice made in order to placate, or to win the favor of, What-is-supernatural. Rather, the sacrifice on the Cross is meant to serve as an *example* of righteousness and is understood to be required by *justice*. There is no thought of favoritism or of appeasement. On the other hand, Anselm had to deal with the paradoxical-like question of how God, who alone has immortality[4] and cannot die, can intelligibly be thought, qua incarnate, to make a sacrifice of Himself to Himself—a sacrifice that has redemptive value for mankind.

2. *Fundamental Issues*: *Cur deus homo* is written in the form of a dialogue, with the simple monk Boso asking questions and the more learn-

---

[3] Jonathan Z. Smith, "Dying and Rising Gods," *The Encyclopedia of Religion* (ed. Mircea Eliade), vol. IV, 522[a].

[4] 1 Tim 6:16.

ed monk Anselm replying; in an ancillary way, Anselm likewise poses questions to Boso. Of these mutual queries eight stand out as more pivotal than the others; and, thus, they constitute the architectonic of the dialogue: (1) Why could not God, out of mercy alone, simply have forgiven sinful human beings, without His having had to become incarnate and to die? (2) Why did not God create angels and human beings such that from the beginning they were unable to sin—as in the future life redeemed human beings will be unable to sin and as the good angels are now unable to sin? (3) How does sin dishonor God? (4) How grave is sin? (5) What payment needs to be made to God for having dishonored Him? (6) How does Christ's death suffice to return honor to God and to blot out all men's sins—past, present, and future? (7) Was Christ's death compelled? (8) How is the meaning of Christ's death to be elucidated theologically?[5]

2. 1. Anselm goes to great lengths to show that God could not simply, out of mercy, overlook man's sin.[6] (a) For were He to do so, something disordered would be forgiven. Sin results in a disordered relationship between intellect and will; furthermore, it is something disordered because it mars the beauty of the universe and tends to undermine the principles of moral justice that govern the universe. It would be unfitting for God simply to accept such a disordering. (b) Moreover, were God simply to forgive the sinner, He would be dealing with the sinner and the non-sinner in the same way. For He would be treating both as blameless, whereas only the latter is so. Consequently, such treatment would be unfitting. (c) Furthermore, were sin to go unpunished or unatoned for, it would be subject to no law. In this respect injustice would resemble God, who holds the prerogative of being subject to no law. This resemblance would be unfitting. (d) In another vein, redeemed men (Anselm says) are supposed to replace the angels who fell—replace them in order to complete the foreordained perfect number of inhabitants of the Heavenly City; in addition, redeemed men are supposed to be *equal to* the good angels, who have never sinned. Now, clearly, if human beings entered the Heavenly City stained by sin, they would not be equal to the good angels and, therefore, would not be replacements for the fallen angels. Accordingly, it would be unfitting for God simply

---

[5] The ordering of these questions does not reflect the order in which they are raised within the dialogue.

[6] *Cur deus homo* I, 12 and I, 19.

to overlook man's sin. (e) Finally, the overlooking would be unfitting because it would be unwise. Anselm asks us to suppose that a rich man owned, and were holding in his hand, a pearl of great value and of great purity, which he permitted some envious person to knock out of his hand, with the result that it fell into the mire. It would be foolish for the rich man to pick up the unclean, unwashed pearl and to place it in its clean and costly receptacle. Similarly, it would be unwise of God to situate unpurified human beings in Heaven.

In the case of God, notes Anselm, "even the slightest unfittingness is impossible,"[7] just as "necessity accompanies any degree of reasonableness, however small, provided it is not overridden by some other more weighty reason."[8]

2.2. But, thinks Boso, it would seem that God in His wisdom and omnipotence could have created angels and human beings such that from the beginning they were unable to sin—even as the good angels have already been thus confirmed in righteousness and as redeemed human beings will, in the resurrection state, be thus confirmed.[9] Anselm expresses mild consternation at Boso's confusion; and he deals frontally with it: It is impossible, he says, that any creature should be identical with God. But only God is such that by nature He cannot sin. Hence, whoever by nature cannot sin would be identical with God—something which no creature can be. For no creature can be its own Creator; no being can bring itself into being, for it would have to have existed before it existed.

2.3. Now, sin dishonors God. For

> when a rational nature wills what it ought to, it honors God—not because it confers anything on Him but because it willingly submits itself to His will and governance. And, as best it can, it stays in its proper place in the universe and preserves the beauty of the universe. But when it does not will what it ought, then it dishonors God from its own point of view. For it does not willingly submit itself to His governance; and it disturbs (as much as lies in its power to do so) the order and the beauty of the universe—even though it does not at all injure or tarnish God's power or dignity [in and of itself].[10]

---

7 *Cur deus homo* I, 20.
8 *Cur deus homo* I, 10.
9 *Cur deus homo* II, 10.
10 *Cur deus homo* I, 15.

In itself, notes Anselm, God's honor cannot be violated. Yet, were He to permit disobedience and wickedness to go unrequited, His doing so would seem to detract from His nature as Goodness and Righteousness—something unfitting.

2.4. In fact, sin is so grave, teaches Anselm, that any disobedience to God, who is Truth itself and Justice itself, ought not to be committed, even if by committing it, this very world and an infinitely multiple number of other such worlds could be preserved from destruction.[11] From a purely human point of view, such a sin might seem trifling—as Lot's wife's looking back at emblazoned Sodom and Gomorrha seems trifling.[12] But from the point of view of Supreme Justice, any deviation from justice is tantamount to endorsing the untruth that one's own greater good resides in injustice and self-will. It is tantamount to believing that God's decrees are arbitrary and capricious and that God does not have man's best interest at heart, so to speak, so that He is being despotic. Such a belief is, in its objective intent, rebellious: man steals himself from God's governance, rebelliously believing His governance to be in some respects unwise and unfair.

Anselm rejects the so-called Devil-ransom theory, fostered by Augustine in his *De trinitate* XIII, 12–15 and XV, 25, his *De libero arbitrio* III, 10, and his *Enchiridion* XLIX. According to this theory Adam's believing the Devil and yielding to his temptation resulted in his delivering himself and his descendants into the Devil's possession. The Devil continued to exercise this dominion until mankind was ransomed by God. This ransom came about through the Devil's unjustly acting against a perfectly just man—viz., Jesus—thereby forfeiting his claim against the human race. Thus, when He ascended, Jesus "led captivity captive" (Eph 4:8); i.e., He delivered the human race from the hands of the Devil, so that whoever chooses to follow Him will ultimately altogether escape from the Devil's control and influence. Accordingly, God dealt with Satan by way of justice rather than by way of force.

To this theory Boso objects in *Cur deus homo* I, 7. Man, he says, was never in the Devil's possession; rather, both the Devil and man were always in God's power. Furthermore, he says, the theory does not explain the need for the Incarnation. For God could have dealt with Satan by justly punishing him for having induced Adam into willing evilly.

---

[11] *Cur deus homo* I, 21.

[12] Gen 19:15–17 and 24–26.

That is, it would not have been wrong for God to deal with Satan by using force, since Satan was not really justly in possession of man. Thus, God would be just—not unjust—in forcefully freeing man from Satan's unjust possession. Through the words of Boso, then, Anselm is maintaining that Augustine's Devil-ransom theory does not explain *cur deus homo fieri oporteret*—why God had to become a [God]-man—in order to effect the salvation of fallen human beings.

2.5. So then, what payment must be made to God in order to repair the apparent dishonor done to Him by a wayward and disordered act of self-will? According to Anselm, two things must occur in order that the debt incurred by sinning be satisfied: first of all, obedience to God must be resumed; and, secondly, amends must be made for the injury inflicted. In general, one who steals must repay more than he has stolen—because of the fact that he must not only return the stolen property but must also make amends for the inflicted grievance. Similarly, since Adam through stealing himself, as it were, from God's possession did an injustice to God, thereby dishonoring Him, (1) he must give himself back to God through repentance, (2) he must resume his acts of obedience, and (3) he must make amends for having transgressed against his Lord, who had given him life and health and safety and nourishment and companionship and happiness—in short, who had given him all that he was and had.[13]

But if any act of willful disobedience to God is so grave that it ought not to be committed even in order to spare an infinity of worlds, and if the payment must be proportional to the gravity of the wrong-doing, then the payment will need to be such that it is something greater in value than the value of an infinite number of beautiful, orderly, life-fostering, and life-sustaining worlds. No human being can make such a payment—the payment of something that is greater than every existing thing besides God.[14] Indeed, only God *can* make such a payment; but only man *ought to* make the payment. Therefore, if payment is to be made, it will have to be made by a God-man. Here Anselm invokes the tenets of orthodox Christian theology: the triune God will, in the person of the Son, assume a human nature, thereby becoming incarnate as the God-man, identified by Anselm at the end of the *Cur deus homo* as the historical Jesus, the Son of God, who is two natures in one person.

[13] 1 Cor 4:7.

[14] *Cur deus homo* II, 6.

And the human nature is an Adamic human nature, having come from Mary, who was a descendant of Adam, i. e., was a member of the Adamic race, as are we all.

2. 6. But how will Christ's death serve to satisfy the debt incurred by sin, and why must the one who makes payment be of Adam's race? On Anselm's view one who makes satisfaction of the incurred debt must be of Adam's race because otherwise the Adamic human race would not be restored to its full dignity, and thus God's original plan in creating man would seem to be a failure—something unfitting.[15] Anselm is conceiving of the race as like a family; indeed, we ourselves sometimes use the expression "the family of man." Thus, only a family-member can redress the wrong done by another family member and can thereby not only restore honor to the aggrieved party but also restore honor and dignity to the family as such.

In accordance with the following rationale, thinks Anselm, the God-man's death suffices to more than outweigh the gravity of all sins; for the God-man will offer to God something that is of more value than everything that is not God: viz., He will offer up Himself, His human life, for the glory of God the Father. In effect, God offers Himself to Himself for man's sake. The God-man is fully divine, even as He is fully human. Insofar as He is God, He cannot die; and insofar as He is human, He is not condemned to die, since His human nature is sinless and since only sinful human beings are under the sentence of mortality. Thus, when the God-man allows Himself to be killed rather than to tell a lie, He honors God, who is Truth itself. To speak now historically rather than abstractly: Jesus, the God-man, could have saved His life by denying that He was Messiah, by denying that He was the Son of God, by repudiating His statements "I and the Father are one"[16] and "Before Abraham was, I am."[17] Instead of making such a repudiation, He stood by the truth (according to Anselm's orthodox theology) and refused to tell the lie; and He foresaw that His doing so would occasion His death, which He freely accepted. Now, since any aggression against the Person of God is incomparably grave, i. e., is graver than all other sins that are not against the Person of God, and since *the good of Jesus's life is as good as the putting Him to death is evil*,[18] His giving up His life—

[15] *Cur deus homo* II, 8.
[16] John 10:30.
[17] John 8:58.
[18] *Cur deus homo* II, 14.

i. e., His acceptance of death, His voluntary self-sacrifice—is infinitely meritorious. Such merit deserves to be rewarded. But since Jesus, qua God, is in need of nothing, He may rightly and fittingly ask the Father to transfer the reward to whomever He Himself chooses.[19] He asks that it be transferred to those human beings who penitently beseech Him to do so. In summary, the merit of Christ's voluntary surrender of His life for the sake of the truth is of more worth than is an infinity of worlds such as our own.

2. 7. But Boso sees a further problem. Even if we grant that only through the death of a God-man could God rightly have arranged for man's salvation, still it seems that the God-man, Jesus, did not voluntarily accept death but rather had to die, whether or not He chose to. For suppose we grant, with Anselm, that the reason Jesus was born free of original sin is twofold: (1) because of Mary's having become purified, prior to His birth, through her faith in His future death and (2) because His conception was free of all concupiscence, since Mary was impregnated by the Holy Spirit rather than through sexual intercourse. It follows that Jesus could have been born free of sin only if He was actually going to die. And so, once having been born, He had to die. Otherwise, Mary's faith would not have been true faith and Jesus would not have been born without the guilt of original sin.[20] Anselm goes on to argue that Jesus did not die against His will but died voluntarily because—as Son of God, i. e., as God the Son—He accepts, *from eternity*, this earthly mission. And *in the order of time* His self-surrender of His life for the honoring of God, and of God's justice, serves to defeat the Devil, to whose temptation-to-escape-suffering He did not yield. ("O my Father, if it be possible, let this cup pass from me: nevertheless not as I will but as Thou wilt."[21])

2. 8. Theologically, Jesus's death poses certain conceptual difficulties. Anselm writes of Jesus: "Since He Himself is God—viz., the Son of God—He offered Himself to Himself (just as also to the Father and the Holy Spirit) for His own honor. That is, [He offered] His humanity to His divinity, which is one and the same divinity common to the three

[19] *Cur deus homo* II, 19.

[20] *Cur deus homo* II, 16. In his *De conceptu virginali* Anselm offers an alternative explanation for how it is that Christ was born without the guilt of original sin.

[21] Matt 26:39.

persons."[22] So, on the one hand, the Son can be said to have offered up Himself to the Father; but, on the other hand, God can be said to have offered up Himself to God. But in neither case is the divinity being offered up but only the life of the humanity, which is able to die, although it is not under any necessity of dying. But if Jesus died as a man and not insofar as He is God (for the divine nature is impassible and immutable), how can it rightly be said that *God sacrificed Himself* on the Cross? Here, then, we must speak more carefully and must take the foregoing expression to mean that the Incarnate Second Member of the Trinity (God the Son) offered up His human nature to His divinity—i. e., to God as a whole (viz., Father, Son, and Holy Spirit). Indeed, we must speak still more carefully; for it is not the whole of His *human nature* that dies and that is resurrected: it is only His *human body*, not also His *human soul*, that dies. (The whole of human nature consists of both a body and a rational soul.) In the end, then, Jesus, the God-man, sacrifices His human life by letting His human body be put to death for the sake of righteousness and truth. His soul and His divine nature and His divine person continue on and are reunited with the body at His resurrection. Yet, since any harm done to Christ's body is also an assault on His person, the sin of putting Him to death is, in and of itself, incomparably more sinful than is any other conceivable sin that is not against His person, declares Anselm. This declaration allows Anselm to proceed to assess the merit of Christ's self-surrender of His bodily life as infinitely meritorious. In any event, the consistency and the intelligibility of Anselm's reasoning depend upon one's presupposing his orthodox Trinitarianism and Christology.

In conclusion, then, Anselm holds that the death of Christ is sufficient to atone for all the sins of all mankind. And in dying, the Incarnate God, in the person of the Son, offers up His humanity to His divinity in order to procure the salvation of His fellow-human beings.

3. *Six Misunderstandings of Anselm's Theory of Atonement*: A number of misconstruals of Anselm's position have gained currency and must be set straight.

3. 1. *Infinite Sin*: To begin with, interpreters have misunderstood Anselm's doctrine that any sin—no matter how trivial it may seem to us to be—is so serious that it ought not to be committed even in order to

---

[22] *Cur deus homo* II, 18.

save from destruction our entire world and an infinite number of other such worlds. This conception of Anselm's is combined by interpreters with Anselm's further claim that a sin against the person of God (such as occurred in the crucifying of Christ) is the greatest conceivable sin. Thereupon it is concluded by these same interpreters that the Jews—who instigated Christ's death, who rejected Pilate's offer to release Jesus, and who cried out "His blood be upon us and upon our children"[23]—bear infinite guilt. Yet, nothing could be more out of line with Anselm's teaching. For in *Cur deus homo* II, 15 Anselm explicitly states:

> A sin done knowingly and a sin done in ignorance are so different from each other that the evil which these men could never have done knowingly, because of its enormity, is *venial* [my italics] because it was done in ignorance. For no man could ever will, at least knowingly, to kill God; and so those who killed Him in ignorance did not rush forth into that infinite sin with which no other sins are comparable. Indeed, in order to ascertain how good His life was, we considered the magnitude of this sin not with respect to the fact that it was done in ignorance but as if it were done knowingly—something which no one ever did or ever could have done.

At times, interpreters take Anselm to be teaching that *any* sin against God is an infinite sin. Walter Kasper, for example, in re-iterating Anselm's position, writes: "Sin is directed against the infinite God and therefore is itself infinite."[24] This statement, however, embodies a misunderstanding, since, for Anselm, no actual sinful act is infinitely sinful, incurring infinite guilt—even though the payment for sin must be an infinite payment, as Anselm explains.

3. 2. *Use of the Word "homo"*: A second misconception relates to Anselm's use of the Latin word "*homo*," translatable into English variously as "man," "a man," "the man," "mankind," "human nature," "a human nature," "the human nature," "human being," and so on. (Latin has neither a definite nor an indefinite article, though it can use various substitutes, when needed.) The title "*Cur deus homo*" is often translated as "*Why God Became Man*." And this translation is unobjectionable as long as it is understood as the equivalent of "*Why God Became a Human Being*," "*Why God Assumed a Human Nature*." But too often it is construed as indicating that God assumed not a particular human nature—

[23] Matt 27:25.

[24] Walter Kasper, *Jesus the Christ* (trans. V. Green; New York: Paulist Press, 1976), 219.

though, to be sure, a perfect one—but universal human nature, thereby becoming man as such, rather than a particular man, a particular human being with a particular human nature. Ferdinand Christian Baur, for example, in his *Die christliche Gnosis*, states that "Christus als Mensch, als Gottmensch, ist der Mensch in seiner Allgemeinheit, nicht ein einzelnes Individuum, sondern das allgemeine Individuum."[25] Anselm, however, does not hold a view such as Baur's. In order to make this point clear, I have translated the title "*Cur deus homo*" as "*Why God Became a* [*God*]-*man*," for this is the topic that Anselm addresses, and this is the meaning that he intends to convey.[26]

Furthermore, we should keep in mind that when Anselm speaks of God's becoming a [God]-man, he always means "man" in the sense of "human being" and not in the sense of "male" (*vir* in Latin). God the Son assumed a human nature (*homo*), thereby becoming a human being (i. e., a man [*homo*]). Nonetheless, it is true that Anselm also holds the view that it was more appropriate for God the Son to become incarnate as a male rather than as a female. God the Son becomes the Son (not the Daughter) of the Virgin. But the question can be raised—and Anselm raises it in *Monologion* 42, as well as at the end of *De incarnatione verbi* 17—as to why the first two members of the Trinity are referred to as Father and Son, rather than as Mother and Daughter. While acknowledging that the Supreme Being is without sexual distinction, Anselm nonetheless reasons that *Father* and *Son* are the preferable symbols:

> Is it [preferable to call them father and son] because among those natures which have a difference of sex it is characteristic of the better sex to be father or son and of the inferior sex to be mother or daughter? Now, although this is by nature the case for many [beings], for others the reverse holds true. For example, in some species of birds the female sex is always larger and stronger, the male sex smaller and weaker.
>
> But, surely, the Supreme Spirit is more suitably called father than mother because the first and principal cause of offspring is always the father. For if the paternal [cause] always in some way pre-

[25] "Christ as man, as God-man, is man in his universality; He is not a particular individual but is the Universal Individual" (my translation). Ferdinand Christian Baur, *Die christliche Gnosis oder die christliche Religionsphilosophie in ihrer geschichtlichen Entwicklung* (Tübingen: Osiander, 1835; repr., Darmstadt: Wissenschaftliche Buchgesellschaft, 1967), 715.

[26] Cf. Anselm's *De incarnatione verbi* 11.

> cedes the maternal cause, then it is exceedingly inappropriate for the name "mother" to be applied to that parent whom no other cause either joins or precedes for the begetting of offspring.[27]

So although Anselm prefers the masculine symbols *father* and *son*, and although he uses the words "man" (*homo*) and "men" (*homines*) generically when he speaks of man's fall and redemption, he is not doing so in a way that nowadays some people would regard as sexist. And we must remember, too, that Anselm, in his *Oratio ad Sanctum Paulum* (*Prayer to St. Paul*), refers to Jesus as our Mother, who—like a mother hen—gathers Her chicks under Her wings: "Sed et tu IESU, bone domine, nonne et tu mater? An non est mater, qui tamquam gallina congregat sub alas pullos suos? Vere, domine, et tu mater."[28]

3.3. *A Feminist Critique.* Some Feminists, nevertheless, seek to fault Anselm's reasoning in the *Cur deus homo* on the grounds that it makes God into a sadistic Overlord.[29] For in the name of justice Anselm is led to make the following claim: "It is impossible for God [in and of Himself] to lose honor. Either the sinner freely repays what he owes or else God takes it from him against his will. For either a man willingly exhibits due subjection to God (be it by not sinning or be it by making payment for his sins), or else God subjects him to Himself against his will *by tormenting him* [my italics] and in this way demonstrates that He is his master—a fact which the man refuses to acknowledge voluntarily."[30] Certain Feminists object to depicting the Divine Being as directly causing suffering—as tormenting someone. As Dorothee Sölle writes: "Each attempt to view suffering as immediately or mediately caused by God is in danger of thinking sadistically about God."[31] And Elga Sorge objects to viewing *as a loving act* God the Father's delivering His Son over to death on the Cross: "To be able to interpret—of all things!—*killing*

---

[27] *Monologion* 42.

[28] *Sancti Anselmi Cantuariensis archiepiscopi Opera Omnia: ad fidem codicum rec.* (ed. Franciscus Salesius Schmitt; Seckau 1938–61; repr. Stuttgart-Bad Cannstatt: Frommann, 1968), vol. III, 40. [Vol. III is contained in tome II.]

[29] See Regula Strobel, "Feministische Kritik an traditionellen Kreuzestheologien," in *Vom Verlangen nach Heilwerden: Christologie in feministisch-theologischer Sicht* (ed. Doris Strahm and Regula Strobel; 2nd ed.; Fribourg: Edition Exodus, 1993), 52–64. Strobel refers to Dorothee Sölle, Elga Sorge, and Christa Mulack, among others.

[30] *Cur deus homo* I, 14.

[31] Quoted from Regula Strobel, op. cit., 52 (my translation).

as an act of love is probably something reserved for men, or, certainly, for persons blinded patriarchally."[32]

Contrary to the foregoing opinions, we may say that God the Father's arranging for human salvation by means of His allowing His Son to be put to death is not a sadistic conception either for Anselm or for any orthodox Christian theologian or even apart from all theology. Anselm takes great pains to exhibit the divine rationale and to argue that human salvation is possible only through the compassionate self-sacrifice of a God-man. But even leaving aside his necessary appeal to orthodox theology, it is wrong to suppose either (1) that an act of self-sacrifice, and the commissioning thereof, is, necessarily, sadistic or (2) that all punishment administered by an omnipotent being is, necessarily, sadistic. And why need our envisioning of such punishment be, necessarily, from the perspective of the patriarchally blinded? Indeed, the beauty of the *Cur deus homo* lies in the fact that Anselm succeeds in presenting a theory that balances divine justice with divine mercy—a view that sees God as taking suffering (including suffering of soul) upon His incarnate human nature so as to be able to spare man from eternal suffering. In short, one might, perhaps, with arguable plausibility suggest that the doctrine of Hell is a sadistic doctrine.[33] But to claim that self-sacrifice cannot be done out of love is altogether implausible and tendentious. Even in secular literature, such as Charles Dickens' *Tale of Two Cities*, self-sacrifice is deemed an act of fellow-feeling and of goodness. For in that novel Sydney Carton, through the use of a drug and a disguise, changes places with Charles Darnay and is guillotined in his stead. And Carton experiences something edifying in his self-sacrifice: "It is a far, far better thing that I do than I have ever done; it is a far, far better rest that I go to than I have ever known."[34]

Contrary to Elga Sorge's previous judgment, Anselm, and orthodox Christian theology generally, do not judge the act of *killing* Jesus to be an act of love. Rather, they judge Jesus's *undergoing of death* (in obedience to the Father's command) to be an act of love. The difference between

---

[32] Quoted from Regula Strobel, op. cit., 53 (my translation).

[33] E. g., note Marilyn M. Adams's line of reasoning in her *Horrendous Evils and the Goodness of God* (Ithaca, NY: Cornell University Press, 1999), 41–43. Some points critical of Adams are made by Katherin A. Rogers in her article "A Defense of Anselm's *Cur Deus Homo* Argument," in *Proceedings of the American Catholic Philosophical Association* 74 (2000): 187–200.

[34] Last sentence of the novel.

the active and the passive voices here is a difference that makes all the difference, so to speak.

3. 4. *The Parallel with the Abraham-Isaac Story*: Occasionally, the death of Christ is likened to the Old Testament account of Abraham and Isaac. As it is said, both Abraham and God the Father were willing to sacrifice their respective only-begotten son. And in both cases, it is presumed, the sons were willing to be sacrificed. In the former case the sacrifice was not actually made, whereas in the latter case it was. Let it be said, however, that these similarities are dwarfed by the differences of the two cases, so that any parallelism becomes relatively insignificant. To mention only one consideration: the sacrifice made by God the Father was made in order to accomplish the salvation of mankind—something not the case with the intended sacrifice of Isaac. But, if we care to note a second thing, Isaac did not foreknow that he was to be the intended victim, and he did not go to Mount Moriah in order to die. By contrast, on Anselm's theory, Jesus foresaw His death and was born into the world in order to sacrifice His life. Finally, Jesus's death can intelligibly be regarded by Anselm as a self-sacrifice, whereas in no sense could Isaac's intended death be considered to be a self-sacrifice.

3. 5. *Relationship between* rationes convenientes *and* rationes necessariae: Confusion has arisen about Anselm's distinction between "fitting reasons" (*rationes convenientes*) and "compelling reasons" (*rationes necessariae*). The confusion results from Anselm's having spoken of certain fitting reasons as also compelling and from his having envisioned certain compelling reasons as also fitting. Thus, he can sometimes refer to fitting reasons as necessary and to necessary reasons as fitting; and his doing so has tended to blur that very distinction. And yet, not unsurprisingly, the distinction is really very clear, once we explore Anselm's terminology more fully. We have already seen (in 2. 1. above) that, according to Anselm, the slightest unfittingness is impossible in the case of God and that in our reasoning about God even a small degree of detectible fittingness amounts to rational necessity, provided our conclusion is not outweighed by stronger reasons on the other side. In other words, *rationes convenientes* are conditionally necessary, whereas *rationes necessariae* are "unconditionally" necessary, inasmuch as there cannot be had (Anselm believes) any over-riding weightier reasons.

A clarifying example of Anselm's distinction occurs in *Cur deus homo* II, 16, where Anselm is attempting to draw from Scripture a theological conclusion that is not found explicitly in Scripture. He poses the question of whether or not Adam and Eve, whose sin precipitated the Fall, will be among the redeemed. And he reasons that they will be. For at no time in the history of the human race could there have been a period when no human being was saved—lest it seem that God's purpose in creating the human race would have been thwarted:

> We must not believe that there was any time—from the point of man's creation—in which this present world with the creatures created for men's use was so empty that in it there was no member of the human race who shared in the end for which man was created. For it seems unfitting that God would even for a moment have permitted the human race ... to have existed in vain, so to speak. For to some extent these men would seem to exist in vain as long as they did not seem to exist for that end for which they were especially created.

Accordingly, Boso agreeingly asserts: "We can conclude that this view is not only fitting but also necessary." Boso does, however, place conditions upon this rational necessity: "For if this view is more fitting and more reasonable than the view that at some time there was no one concerning whom God's purpose in creating man was being accomplished, and if nothing opposes this reasoning, then necessarily there was always someone who shared in the aforementioned reconciliation. Hence, we must not doubt that Adam and Eve shared in that redemption, even though Divine Authority does not openly state this." Although Boso uses the conditional word "if" (*si* in Latin), Anselm goes on to reason that it would indeed be incredible (*incredibile*) that God would exclude Adam and Eve from His original plan. Thus, Anselm is making the strong claim that the opposite view about Adam and Eve could not be more reasonable than is the inference that Adam and Eve are among the redeemed. So, in the end, Anselm implicitly removes the conditions from the rational necessity, so that the conclusion about Adam and Eve is not only fitting but also (absolutely) necessary to believe. And the necessity in question is theological, not logical, necessity. For it is a necessity that holds in the light of certain theological presuppositions. Yet, although this kind of necessity may be said to be *conditional* upon the presuppositions, nonetheless it is properly referred to as *unconditional* necessity because the theological presuppositions are *absolute* presuppositions, so that the inferences supported by them are as theologically necessary as theological inferences ever get.

Finally, let it be clear that the necessity is rational necessity, that it is the kind of necessity that governs our inferences. It is not a necessity that constrains God to act. Although God never acts without a reason,[35] it would be bizarre to state that He is compelled to act reasonably.

3.6. *Not a Real Sacrifice*: Occasionally, one encounters the claim that the God-man's sacrifice of Himself on the Cross was not a real sacrifice—or at least, not a sacrifice effective in showing love[36]—because it involved suffering only with respect to His human nature. That is, since the divine nature is impassible (according to Augustine, Anselm, Aquinas, et al.), God qua God experiences no suffering, so that the prospect of, and the event of, crucifixion and death presented no divine anguish, no divine distress. Hence, God cannot be said to have suffered with us either in the circumstances surrounding His death or at any moment whatsoever during his earthly life. Now, someone who cannot dread death (whether a painful death or not) and cannot *grievingly* foresee that his plans, aspirations, memories, loving-relationships, etc., will be terminated by his death cannot rightly be thought of as sacrificing himself; for he is giving up nothing whose anticipation brings with it a sense of loss. Moreover, as Anselm's theory is interpreted as teaching, the God-man can never be unhappy—not even in the face of death. So in giving His life (in the sense of letting it be taken from Him), He makes no *sacrifice*. At most, it is said, Anselm can assert that Jesus lets Himself be *martyred* for the truth, rather than saving His life by denying, untruly, that He is God. And martyrdom, it is said, is not the same thing as sacrifice.

The foregoing misunderstanding serves to bring out, once again, the fact that Anselm's orthodox Christology is a necessary condition of the viability of his theory of Atonement; for the foregoing observations derive from an impugning of that orthodoxy. Anselm does maintain that although Christ shares some of our misfortunes, He is not unhappy.[37] But, at the same time, Anselm takes seriously the New Testament's presentation of Jesus as groaning in spirit (John 11:33) and as saying, "My

---

35 *Cur deus homo* I, 8 and II, 10.

36 See Adams's exploratory discussion in *Horendous Evils*, 121, 168–70, and 174. On p. 174 she writes: "I prefer a version of my Christological hypothesis according to which God the Son suffers in *both* natures—in the Divine nature ... and in the human nature ... ." (On p. 121 the reference in footnote 30 needs to be corrected to read: "*Cur Deus Homo*, bk 2, chap. 12 ... .")

37 *Cur deus homo* II, 12.

soul is sorrowful even unto death" (Matt 26:38). He reconciles the apparent discrepancy between the passage in *Cur deus homo* and the passages in Scripture by recourse to the doctrine of the hypostatic union of Jesus's two natures—i. e., the doctrine of the intimate union of the divine nature with the human nature in the Person of God the Son. This union is so close that it allows for Jesus to be said to suffer with respect to His human nature (though not with respect to His divine nature). Yet, it is the God-man, Jesus, who suffers in and through the human nature: the human will, the human intellect, the human body. And it is the God-man who is not unhappy, in and because of the divine nature. (A person, not a nature, is rightly said to be happy.) According to Anselm the reason that the God-man is not unhappy is that He willingly accepts this human condition and willingly undergoes the sacrifice of His life. The fact that He does not grieve over this sacrifice-as-such does not render it less a sacrifice and more an instance of martyrdom. He accepts being made a curse; for it is written "Cursed is every one that hangeth on a tree" (Gal 3:13; Deut 21:23). Thus, Anselm can both concede that Jesus dreads death (as witnessed by His agony in Gethsemene) and is not unhappy; for "as something-beneficial which someone possesses against his will does not conduce to his happiness, so to experience something-detrimental wisely and willingly, without being compelled to, is not [a cause of] unhappiness."[38] Happiness, after all, is a state of being, whereas sorrow and distress are transient feelings.

So, in last analysis, Anselm can be seen as insisting upon the real nature of Christ's sacrifice—i. e., as insisting upon the intelligibility of our speaking of Christ as willingly and obediently sacrificing Himself. However, this intelligibility is dependent upon the intelligibility of the theological doctrine of the hypostatic union of Christ's two natures and upon the following theological concession: Just as the soul apart from the body cannot experience the pain of a material fire, so God the Son—in and of Himself—cannot, apart from incarnation, experience pain and suffering. Yet, God-incarnate can be said to experience both physical pain and psychological distress—in and through His human nature.

Finally, there is a sense in which self-sacrifice and martyrdom are not mutually exclusive. If one let's himself be slain because of his belief in a putative noble-truth that he chooses to continue affirming rather than choosing to renounce, then he is appropriately said to be a martyr

---

[38] Loc. cit.

for the truth. However, if he foresees that his entering into a given situation (such as entering into Jerusalem, for example) will force upon him the making of such a choice, and if he could avoid that situation but chooses not to do so, in order thereby to die in witness of the truth: his martyrdom just is a self-sacrifice.

4. *The Key Problem Facing Anselm's Account*: As brilliant as Anselm's *Cur deus homo* is in the history of Western spirituality, its reasoning nonetheless embeds an ineliminable fallacious inference—one pointed out by Wolfgang Gombocz and others.[39] Put concisely, Anselm's basic argument, as we have seen, is that only an Adamic man *ought* to make satisfaction on behalf of his race; but only God *can* make satisfaction; therefore, satisfaction must be made by a God-man, if it is to be made at all.[40] Now, this argument (as I pointed out many years ago and as Gombocz accentuates and expands upon) is invalid by virtue of its equivocating on both the word "ought" and the word "can." Let us consider these briefly. With respect to human beings Anselm uses the word "ought" (*debere*) in the sense of "to owe": only an Adamic man *owes* . . . . However, with respect to Christ, Anselm uses "ought" in the sense of "should if He chooses to." For Christ, although He is a man, is a sinless man. Unlike all other Adamic human beings, He does not owe to God a debt that has resulted from His sinning. Nor is He under obligation to make restitution on behalf of His fellow-human beings. Nor is He under the sentence of death, as are all other human beings. Accordingly, qua God-man, He does not owe to God any payment (other than obedience); it is not true to say of Him that He ought (*debere*) to make satisfaction (i. e., that he *owes* [*debere*] the making of satisfaction). But, in another sense, He *ought* to make satisfaction inasmuch as He wills to redeem His fellow human beings; and this redemption can be accomplished only by His freely yielding up His life.

---

[39] Wolfgang L. Gombocz, "Anselm von Aosta als Schrecken der 'europäischen' Anthropologie? Anmeldung der philosophischen Pflicht 'Cur Deus Homo' zu durchkreuzen," in *Entwicklungslinien mittelalterlicher Philosophie. Vorträge des V. Kongresses der Österreichischen Gesellschaft für Philosophie* (ed. Gerhard Leibold and Winfried Löffler; Vienna: Hölder-Pichler-Tempsky, 1999), part 2, 73–86. Idem, "*Cur Deus homo* als 'europäische' Last: Einwände vor allem gegen den Theologen Anselm," in *Cur Deus Homo* (ed. Paul Gilbert et al.; Rome: Pontificio Ateneo S. Anselmo, 1999), 453–70. Jasper Hopkins, *A Companion to the Study of St. Anselm* (Minneapolis: University of Minnesota Press, 1972), 195–97.

[40] *Cur deus homo* II, 6.

Likewise, an equivocation occurs with respect to the modal word "*can*." As I earlier wrote:[41]

> When Anselm says "Only man ought to," he is also tacitly saying "Only man can"; and this sense of "can" is different from the sense of "can" in the statement "Only God can." Only God can—in the sense that only God has the power to make satisfaction; only man can—in the sense that only man can consistently be thought to make satisfaction. That is, only God *can effectively*; only man *can acceptably*. For it is theologically unacceptable (i. e., inconsistent with other theological tenets) for man to be forgiven immediately, apart from any satisfaction's having been made; and it is theologically unacceptable (inconsistent) for anyone who is not a man (of Adam's race) to make payment for ... [Adam's] and his descendants' debts.

This equivocation on "can" is significant because Anselm states that a sinless non-Adamic man *cannot* make satisfaction for the Adamic human race because he would not be of that race. But this sense of "cannot" is different from the sense in which he cannot make satisfaction because he lacks the power to do so. To be sure, a non-Adamic human being would lack the power. Yet, there is a second reason why he cannot make satisfaction: viz., he *cannot* because he *ought not*. But this "ought not" is not meant in the sense that he does not *owe* (though, indeed, he would not owe anything except continued obedience) but in the sense that his sacrifice is not *appropriately* transferable.

We may re-state the entire matter more pointedly:[42]

> Only Adam and his natural descendants $ought_1$ in that only they owe; but Jesus $ought_2$ in that He wills to. Only God can_1 in that He has the power to; but only man can_2 in that no other alternative is theologically admissible. Anselm's confusion occurs when he infers, invalidly, that because only man $ought_1$ and only God can_1, only a God-man $ought_2$ and can_1.

The foregoing line of reasoning evidences Anselm's main fallacy. However, following upon this fallacious inference of his there come subsidiary confusions. For he implies

> that only Adamic man can_2 because only Adamic man $ought_1$—that is, that non-Adamic man can_2not because he $ought_1$ not. But

[41] Hopkins, *Companion*, 196–97.

[42] Ibid., 197.

> if Jesus both ought$_1$ not and can$_2$, why should the case be different for a non-Adamic man? Why, in other words should we predicate "can$_2$not" rather than simply "can$_1$not" of a non-Adamic man? Clearly, a non-Adamic man who was not also God could$_1$ not render satisfaction, for he would not have the power to make a payment greater than everything which is other than God. But why could$_2$ not God have become incarnate by assuming a non-Adamic human nature in order for a non-Adamic God-man to render satisfaction?[43]

Anselm's only answer to the last question is that a non-Adamic man's sacrifice would not restore the honor and dignity of the Adamic human race—restore it by virtue of a *member of that race's* making satisfaction and defeating the Devil on behalf of the entire race.

In the end, then, Anselm must discard His simple argument to the effect that only a man *ought*; only God *can*; and, therefore, only a God-man both *ought* and *can*. For the conclusion is a non-sequitur and, as such, requires additional premises in order for it to be derived. And it now, too, becomes clear that Anselm's theory of divine sacrifice is plausible mostly in the combined contexts (1) of feudal honor (including family honor) and (2) of the ecclesiastical penitential system. The former context promotes the idea that honor is due to an individual in proportion to his rank or social position or ontological degree of perfection. The latter context fosters the notion that penance must be done for each sin and that the penance must be proportional to the gravity of the sinful act. Nowadays, however, in Western societies, class distinctions tend to be minimized, the spirit of political egalitarianism tends to prevail ("one man, one vote"), and paradigms related to kings and royalty—paradigms such as that of *lèse majesté*—no longer hold sway. Similarly, the idea of there having to be a strict proportion between penance and pardon is less widely accepted. Accordingly, Anselm's theory—as insightful as it was in the medieval context—will hold less appeal to many in the twenty-first century. But were the notions of honor and of rank to be restored, Anselm's theory of Atonement might once again become more widely embraced. And *a fortiori* this acceptance might well become still more broadly based were there to be a renewed appreciation of the notion of holiness.

---

[43] Ibid., 197.

5. *Concluding Recapitulation*: We have seen, then, that in his *Cur deus homo* Anselm teaches that incarnation and death were the only means whereby God could accomplish the reconciliation of human beings with Himself, once the human race had fallen. In and through Jesus—who is the God-man, two natures in one person—God lovingly effects the supreme sacrifice of Himself qua human to Himself qua divine. This salvific sacrifice *of* a human being *by* the Divine Being, *to* the Divine Being, *on behalf of* all human beings who will avail themselves of it—this sacrifice is unique and unrepeatable.[44] And the account of it—whether the simple presentation in the Pauline epistles or the more elaborate theological expansion in Anselm's *Cur deus homo*—is unparalleled in the history of religion.

For Further Reading in addition to the items in the footnotes:

Adams, Marilyn M., "Satisfying Mercy: St. Anselm's Cur Deus Homo Reconsidered," *The Modern Schoolman* 72 (January / March, 1995): 91–108.

Eckardt Jr., Burnell F., *Anselm and Luther on the Atonement: Was It "Necessary"?* San Francisco: Mellen, 1992.

Gilbert, Paul, Helmut Kohlenberger, and Elmar Salmann, ed., *Cur Deus Homo*. Rome: Pontificio Ateneo S. Anselmo, 1999.

Heyer, George S., "Anselm concerning the Human Role in Salvation," in *Texts and Testaments: Critical Essays on the Bible and Early Church Fathers* (ed. W. Eugene March; San Antonio: Trinity University Press, 1980), 163–72.

Keshgegian, Flora A., "The Scandal of the Cross: Revisiting Anselm and His Feminist Critics," *AThR* 82 (summer 2000): 475–92.

Kienzler, Klaus, "Die Erlösungslehre Anselms von Canterbury: Aus der Sicht des mittelalterlichen jüdisch-christlichen Religionsgesprächs," in *Versöhnung in der jüdischen und christlichen Liturgie* (Hanspeter Heinz et al., ed.; Vienna: Herder, 1990), 88–116.

MacIntyre, John, *St. Anselm and His Critics: A Reinterpretation of the Cur Deus Homo*. London: Oliver and Boyd, 1954.

Nellas, Panayiotis, "Redemption or Deification? Nicholas Kavasilas and Anselm's Question 'Why did God become Man?'" *Sourozh* 66 (December 1996): 10–30.

---

[44] Heb 9:25–28.

Kierkegaard's "Fear and Trembling," the Sacrifice of Isaac, and the Critique of Christendom

Christopher Roberts, University of North Carolina, Chapel Hill

Considering the prevalence of religious violence in the world today, there is some justification for naming Kierkegaard's *Frygt og Baeven* (1843; *Fear and Trembling*) the most portentous religious polemic of the nineteenth century. One might further argue that the text owes its contemporary relevance, paradoxically, to its archaic topic, the narrative known in Hebrew as the *Aqedah*, the "Binding of Isaac." By way of the *Aqedah* Kierkegaard investigates topics such as the meaning of worship, the nature of faith, and the relation between communal norms and religious obligations. Kierkegaard's choice of the *Aqedah* was savvy because the opportunity to confront this range of issues stems from the provocative practice it depicts—namely, human sacrifice. Through a strategic defamiliarization of this narrative, Kierkegaard explores Abraham's exemplary travail in the face of human sacrifice[1] in order to challenge what he sees as the religious complacency of contemporary Christendom.[2]

---

[1] Attentive readers of Gen 22 will note that during the narrative the very notion of the ritual depicted undergoes transformation. That is, what sets out to be a human sacrifice, becomes, through divine intervention, an animal sacrifice. Nonetheless, *Fear and Trembling* never diminishes Abraham's suffering by focusing upon this intervention, in that this would read the text backwards and not forwards. Such a focus on Abraham's intention to sacrifice Isaac, and the faith this putatively demonstrates, places this text firmly in an exegetical tradition the most prominent figures of which are Paul and Luther. For a decisive articulation in this tradition, see Martin Luther, "The Example of Abraham," in *A Commentary on St. Paul's Epistel to the Galatians: Based on Lectures Delivered by Martin Luther at the University of Wittenberg in the Year 1531 and First Published in 1535* (trans. Ph. S. Watson; Grand Rapids, Mich.: Fleming H. Revell, 1998), 143–72.

[2] One might argue here that "Christendom" is a concept without a referent, since by Kierkegaard's time the Holy Roman Empire no longer existed, and whatever unity the term might once have denoted was irreparably fractured with the Reformation. This usage, then, is both ironic and indicative of an emergent phenomenon—namely, the

The present essay begins with the premise that *Fear and Trembling* is the opening salvo of a polemic against Christendom that will continue for the rest of Kierkegaard's life. Since he explicitly targets "Christendom" only after the 1848–49 constitutional reforms transformed the State Church into the "Danish People's Church" (*Folke Kirken*), what social or explicitly Christian practices does Kierkegaard critique in the early 1840s? As a first response, one might note the prominent role played in this text by the "teleological suspension of the ethical." Is the "ethical," then, the stumbling block of aspiring Christians?[3] Because in this text the "ethical" is virtually synonymous with the "universal," their correlation both underscores the normative claims immanent to the social sphere, and obscures the text's specific point of departure.[4] By examining some of the *Aqedah* variants nested within *Fear and Trembling*, this paper will bring the "ethical" into sharper focus, and thereby clarify the object of Kierkegaard's critique.

In examining the formal aspects of narrative in *Fear and Trembling*, this essay will not address its more theological themes. If one focuses upon its homiletic passages the problem becomes one of clarifying the existential nature of the religious transformation extolled. However, the use of a pseudonym in Kierkegaard's strategy of indirect communication leaves the reader in doubt whether this in fact amounts to a positive account of faith. Thus, this paper will attend less to the goal or nature of the movement of faith than to what the text insists such a movement must sacrifice or leave behind. In particular, we will discuss how the *Aqedah* variants delineate strata of worldliness which help Kierkegaard transform the sacrificial object: no longer does Abraham sacrifice a human being, he sacrifices his "humanity."

---

melding of religious and social boundaries into the semblance of homogeneity. For more on this topic, see Per Lonning, "Christendom (Christenhed)," in *Theolological Concepts in Kierkegaard* (ed. N. Thulstrup and M. M. Thulstrup; Bibliotheca Kierkegaardiana 5; Copenhagen: C. A. Reitzels, 1980), 257–62.

[3] For an intriguing exploration of this concept in relation to Kierkegaard's stages of existence, see Merold Westphal, "The Teleological Suspension of Religiousness B," in *Foundations of Kierkegaard's Vision of Community: Religion, Ethics, and Politics in Kierkegaard* (ed. G. B. Connell and C. St. Evans; Atlantic Highlands, N.J.: Humanities Press, 1991).

[4] Although this text has a pseudonymous narrator, Johannes de silentio, for brevity's sake I will speak of Kierkegaard as the author. Nevertheless, the issue of pseudonymity and the charged distance Kierkegaard maintains between different perspectives (between Kierkegaard and Johannes as well as between Johannes and Abraham) are vital to the text's architecture. For more on this topic, see Mark C. Taylor's *Kierkegaard's Pseudonymous Authorship: A Study of Time and the Self* (Princeton: Princeton University Press, 1975).

This agenda draws upon much recent work in Kierkegaard studies, which have departed from "existentialist" readings[5] in order to understand his oeuvre in relation to its social, historical and cultural setting. Hence, after a half-century of examining Kierkegaard as an isolated and idiosyncratic individual, the exploration of Kierkegaard's socio-cultural context has become a vital prerequisite for interpreting his texts. [6]

Since the present essay took form under the influence of "this new sensitivity to the social and political aspects of Kierkegaard's thought,"[7] our guiding question is, how does Kierkegaard employ the *Aqedah* to articulate his nascent critique of Christendom? To answer this, we will briefly turn to Kierkegaard's social and historical context in order to specify the object of his critique, the compromised and costless worship Kierkegaard believed was characteristic of "Golden Age" Denmark. Next, we will turn to *Fear and Trembling* and examine some of its rhetorical strategies. Finally, we will focus on the "Attunement" section that consists of four variations on the central scenario of the *Aqedah*, which each anticipate in highly compressed form the themes that Kierkegaard will proceed to develop. Through explicating these variations, I will show how Kierkegaard's interpretation of human sacrifice posits costly or sacrificial worship as essential to religious life. In conclusion, I will examine Kierkegaard's reification of "humanity" as a sacrificial object, and some of the difficulties that attend this maneuver.

[5] The extent of such works is immense, owing in part to Heidegger's predominance in twentieth century philosophy. Because Kierkegaard is one of the only philosophers cited without criticism in *Being and Time*, Heidegger's construction of an existentialist tradition has greatly affected Kierkegaard's historical reception. For a small sample of the existentialist readings of Kierkegaard, see: Hermann Diem, *Kierkegaard's Dialectic of Existence* (trans. H. Knight; Edinburgh: Oliver & Boyd, 1959); Louis K. Dupre, *Kierkegaard as Theologian: The Dialectic of Christian Existence* (New York: Sheed & Ward, 1963); Helmut Fahrenbach, *Kierkegaards existenzdialektische Ethik* (Philosophische Abhandlungen 29; Frankfurt am Main: V. Klostermann, 1968); Friedrich Carl Fischer, *Existenz und Innerlichkeit: Eine Einführung in die Gedankenwelt Søren Kierkegaards* (Munich: C. H. Beck, 1969); Jean Andre Wahl, *Philosophies of Existence: An Introduction of the Basic Thoughts of Kierkegaard, Heidegger, Jaspers, Marcel, Sartre* (trans. F. M. Lory; New York: Schocken, 1969).

[6] Although Kierkegaard's theological and philosophical context has long been a topic of concern, the recent turn towards the historical context of his life, as opposed to more "eternal" questions, is surely a welcome one. Exemplary among such works are Bruce H. Kirmmse, *Kierkegaard in Golden Age Denmark* (The Indiana Series in Philosophy of Religion; Bloomington: Indiana University Press, 1990); Jon Bartley Stewart, *Kierkegaard and His Contemporaries: The Culture of Golden Age Denmark* (Berlin: W. de Gruyter, 2003), and George Pattison, *Kierkegaard, Religion and the Nineteenth-Century Crisis of Culture* (Cambridge: Cambridge University Press, 2002).

[7] George B. Connell and C. Stephen Evans, "Introduction," in *Foundations*, ix.

The Problem of Christendom

To establish a polemical continuity between this early text and Kierkegaard's later attack on "Christendom,"[8] we must ask, under what guise does the term appear in *Fear and Trembling*? This question will also help us distinguish Kierkegaard's position from similar critiques of established religion, for *Fear and Trembling* does not champion a laity oppressed by religious elites. Instead, the substance of this critique is that the mutual accommodation of church and state fails to foster true religious elites at all. In Kierkegaard's opinion, these elites are utterly incapable of understanding a figure like Abraham.[9] Furthermore, in contrast to his later texts, which focus on the social status of the priesthood, here the problem is more cultural than social, in the sense that, through faulty sermons concerning Abraham, Kierkegaard discerns a general flaw in Danish acculturation. With the clichés that issue from contemporary pulpits as evidence, Kierkegaard claims that the elites of Christendom are in fact cultured mediocrities.

The cause of this mal-acculturation, Kierkegaard argues, is the tendency to blend spheres that should be kept distinct, for these religious elites fall short precisely because they fail to distinguish worldly from spiritual laws. Far from being the failure of a few individuals, moreover, their worldly success requires them to equate the two spheres. Kierkegaard, by contrast, insists that the "external and visible world" is arbitrary and unjust, but "the world of spirit" is a true meritocracy, for there, "only the one who works gets bread," and "only the one who draws the knife gets Isaac."[10] Thus, in the world of spirit, without the risk and cost of spiritual expenditures, one can expect no spiritual returns at all.

---

[8] One of the earliest texts in which the problem of Christendom appears centerstage is the 1851 publication, *On My Work as an Author*, collected in *The Point of View: On My Work as an Author, the Point of View for My Work as an Author, Armed Neutrality* (ed. and trans. by H. V. Hong and E. H. Hong; Princeton: Princeton University Press, 1998). Kirmme calls attention to "Kierkegaard's post-1848 radicalism," which he argues is a consequence of Denmark's constitution in 1849 and the emergence of a "Danish People's Church." On this, see Bruce Kirmmse, " 'But I Am Almost Never Understood ...' Or, Who Killed Søren Kierkegaard?" in *Kierkegaard: The Self in Society* (ed. G. Pattison and S. Shakespeare; New York: St. Martin's, 1998), 181.

[9] Søren Kierkegaard, *Fear and Trembling*, and *Repetition* (ed., trans. and introd. by H. V. Hong and E. H. Hong; Kierkegaard's Writings 6; Princeton: Princeton University Press, 1983), 28–30.

[10] Kierkegaard, *Fear and Trembling*, and *Repetition*, 27.

In his social history of early-to-mid-nineteenth-century Denmark, Kirmmse argues that Kierkegaard's understanding of the relation between religion and politics cannot be separated from "the great social groupings and religious tendencies ... of Golden Age Denmark."[11] Since space will not allow coverage of all these phenomena, for the sake of brevity we can focus on a successful clergyman, J. P. Mynster. Not only a regular guest of Kierkegaard's father, he was, according to Kirmmse, young Kierkegaard's "exemplar in religious matters" whose position and prestige had much to do with the fact that he was "overwhelmingly on the side of the absolutist government, of hierarchy, public order, and good taste."[12] Nevertheless, after the constitutional reforms Mynster enthusiastically embraced the "People's Church," a vacillation he could rationalize because, according to the historian Olesen Larsen, "[I]n Mynster we do not encounter anything ... other than bourgeois humanism which has been united with a faith in Providence and dressed in orthodox expressions."[13] After witnessing Mynster's opportunism, Kierkegaard came to see in him the very worst of Christendom.

As his problems with Mynster's version of Christianity began to take shape in the early 1840s, Kierkegaard does not follow the logic that makes his enemy's enemy his friend. That is, Kierkegaard does not turn to liberalism or populism as an antidote to a cultured authoritarianism. Rather than side with one of the factions contending for power on the terrain of religion, Kierkegaard transforms the struggle altogether by shifting attention away from its social, political, and cultural stakes, in order to insist upon its religious significance.

With the questions of "Problema I" ("Is there a teleological suspension of the ethical?") and "Problema II" ("Is there an absolute duty to God?"),[14] Kierkegaard attempts to pry the religious away from the social. This sets Kierkegaard against Denmark's historical détente between the church and the crown that led to the formation of the Danish State Church. To argue this point, instead of divesting the church of its social elements, Kierkegaard insists, "The idea of the Church is not

---

[11] Kirmmse, *Golden Age Denmark*, 39.

[12] Kirmmse, *Golden Age Denmark*, 50.

[13] Kristoffer Olsen Larsen, *Søren Kierkegaard læst af K. Olesen Larsen* [*Søren Kierkegaard Read by K. Olesen Larsen*] (Kirkehistoriske Studier [Studies in Church History] 1; Copenhagen: G. E. C. Gad, 1966), 117, cited in Kirmmse, *Golden Age Denmark*, 103.

[14] Kierkegaard, *Fear and Trembling*, and *Repetition*, 54, 68.

qualitatively different from the idea of the state."[15] This is so because both share an existence in *det Almene*.[16] For Kierkegaard, *det Almene* is the realm of language, discourse, and universally valid ethical rules—in short, the tissue of norms that functionaries like Mynster and social institutions such as church, state, and family inculcate and uphold. *Det Almene* thus refers to what Kirmmse calls "Mynster's Golden Age view of society . . . , with no strict boundary between . . . social . . . and . . . spiritual conditions."[17] With this term, then, Kierkegaard objectifies all the elements that separate Christendom from Christianity.

The concept of *det Almene* allows Kierkegaard to treat the cultural elitism of the conservatives, the modernizing humanism of the liberals, and the pietistic populism of the peasants as fundamentally equivalent phenomena. Thus, *det Almene* encompasses every given ideological position and frees the "religious" from all worldly contaminants. In search of a religious position distinct from the sectarian formations of his day, perhaps it was inevitable that Kierkegaard would turn away from social movements and enthusiastic sentiments in order to return, in true Protestant fashion, to the tradition of scriptural exegesis.

Kierkegaard's Variations on the *Akedah*

Early in the text Kierkegaard speaks of those "assistant professors [whose] life task is to judge the great . . . according to the result."[18] Like these people, because "we are curious about the result, . . . we do not want to know anything about the anxiety, the distress, the paradox. We

---

[15] Kierkegaard, *Fear and Trembling*, and *Repetition*, 74.

[16] *Det Almene*, "the universal" or "the general," was the standard Danish term used to translate Hegel's *Sittlichkeit*. While a literal English translation produces "customariness," *Sittlichkeit* is often rendered into English as "customary morality." The term retains its more technical sense with Miller's translation, "ethical order." For the pivotal development of this notion, see Hegel's sections on "The Ethical Order" (§§446–76) in *Phenomenology of Spirit* (trans. A. V. Miller, with a foreword by J. N. Findlay; Oxford: Oxford University Press, 1977). The translation of *det Almene* in *Fear and Trembling* as "the universal" is thus highly misleading, as noted by Klaus-M. Kodalle, "The Utilitarian Self and the 'Useless' Passion of Faith," in *Cambridge Companion to Kierkegaard* (ed. A. Hannay and G. D. Marino; Cambridge Companion Series; Cambridge: Cambridge University Press, 1998), 399. Although "the general" does provide the sense of publicity and suffusion that we find in Hegel, it ignores the historical diversity of "ethical orders." In order to avoid further confusion, in this essay I will leave *det Almene* untranslated, thus foregrounding its status as a technical term the semantic domain of which must be elaborated textually.

[17] Kirmmse, *Golden Age Denmark*, 129.

[18] Kierkegaard, *Fear and Trembling*, and *Repetition*, 62–63.

carry on an esthetic flirtation with the result. It arrives just as unexpectedly but also just as effortlessly as a prize in a lottery."[19] In other words, with a narrative like the *Aqedah*, the very fiber of which is suffused with distress, it is all too easy to read every word with a view determined by the happy transformation of a human sacrifice into that of an animal. This is precisely the flawed reading that Kierkegaard hopes to correct. Insisting that "the result ... is finitude's response to the infinite question,"[20] Kierkegaard rereads the story through the lens of the infinite questions that it raises, the most prominent of which is the religious status of that costliest form of worship, human sacrifice.

Kierkegaard's approach to the *Aqedah* thus consists of various strategies for keeping the story unresolved. The first of these is his use of a pseudonymous narrator, "Johannes de silentio." Because this narrator explicitly denies any truly religious insight into Abraham, one can read this name in a way that makes the text into an extended *aporia*, the rhetorical figure of speaking about the inability to speak. In other words, with such a narrator producing a discourse on the inadequacy of discourse to approach an understanding of Abraham, the latter is projected outside of the linguistic realm, thereby sundering the religious from the discursive.

Another strategy for resisting resolution, and the one that most concerns us here, is the repetition of the *Aqedah* with significant changes. In the "Attunement" section early in the text, Kierkegaard challenges simplistic readings of the *Aqedah* by tuning the reader's ear with several narrative variations that defamiliarize Abraham.[21] Since different actions entail different stories, and thus different Abrahams, Kierkegaard can compare several such personae, some of whom one might more easily understand. The chief benefit of this method is that, although the endings differ, it enables Kierkegaard to repeat the beginning of the narrative anew several times. This works in consonance with his overall

---

[19] Kierkegaard, *Fear and Trembling*, and *Repetition*, 63.

[20] Kierkegaard, *Fear and Trembling*, and *Repetition*, 63.

[21] The aesthetic theory developed by Victor Shklovsky and the other "Russian Formalists" relies upon "defamiliarization" as a technique to such an extent that for them it serves as the criterion of the aesthetic object. Kierkegaard's employment of the technique strips Abraham's behavior of its "givenness," and makes the reader aware of the narrative's uncanny aspects. In this way, defamiliarization through repetition serves purposes congruent to the aporetic structure of the text as a whole. For the pioneering work on this topic, see Victor Shklovsky, "Art as Technique," in *Russian Formalist Criticism: Four Essays* (trans. L. T. Lemon and M. J. Reis; Lincoln, Nebr.: University of Nebraska Press, 1965).

agenda since, in contrast to the assistant professors who would focus on the result, Kierkegaard argues that "since the creation of the world it has been customary for the result to come last and ... if one is truly going to learn something from greatness one must be particularly aware of the beginning."[22]

Before delving into the four variations, it should be noted that each is followed by an interlude that discusses the *Aqedah* in relation to weaning. Kierkegaard uses weaning, an irreversible break in the life of the individual, to underscore the disjunctive relation between the realms of *det Almene* and religion, *det Almene* reducing individuals to relative particulars within its totality, and religion singularizing each individual in relation to the Absolute.[23] Thus, by an analogical transposition of the father-son relationship to that of the mother and the child, Kierkegaard foregrounds the movement of faith the individual must make beyond the worn platitudes and warm pieties of *det Almene*. The richness of the "weaning" metaphor, then, allows Kierkegaard to speak of both continuity and discontinuity, of the movement of faith as the culminating step in the development of the autonomous individual, as well as a radical break from nature, an irrevocable and costly alienation. As we will see, this metaphor's implications for acculturation complicate Kierkegaard's highly schematic argument.

Abraham as Philosopher

The sequence of the variations in the "Attunement" section seems calculated to avoid the appearance of an ordering principle, either that of progressively worsening failures or ever more successful approximations. For purposes of exposition, then, I will address the variations in order from the crudest to the subtlest failure. Hence, the first variation we will discuss[24] tells the story of an Abraham who cannot take God's command at face value. In fact, he rejects God's command as a temptation to sin against communal norms. When the journey begins, Kierkegaard writes that "Abraham rode thoughtfully down the road."[25] If the Abraham of the *Aqedah* is the faithful believer, this Abraham is the thoughtful philosopher who conceives his God in terms similar to Kant's rational

---

[22] Kierkegaard, *Fear and Trembling*, and *Repetition*, 63.
[23] Kierkegaard, *Fear and Trembling*, and *Repetition*, 56.
[24] In the text the order is Abraham as Confessor, Ascetic, Philosopher, and Faithless.
[25] Kierkegaard, *Fear and Trembling*, and *Repetition*, 13.

and moral deity, a God stripped of divine will and spontaneity to become the guarantor of the moral law. This Enlightenment project of rationalizing religion, undertaken by a string of philosophers culminating with Kant and Hegel, was but one aspect of the larger process that, beginning with the Peace of Augsburg in 1555, gradually mitigated religious conflict in modern Europe and validated the secular state. The religious cost of this social benefit, however, was that it empowered the state to accept or reject religious practices according to their compatibility with the ethical precepts of society as a whole. This set in motion a process of mutual accommodation between church and state that, as Kierkegaard reads the situation in Denmark, led to the compromise of Christendom.

The philosophical Abraham believes that a just and good God could not contradict the all-inclusive sanctions of *det Almene*; thus, unable to reconcile the contradiction between God's command and *det Almene*, he treats God's command as a temptation, and chooses allegiance to *det Almene* as the default position a believer should take. Nevertheless, the contradiction continues to trouble him. By treating God's command as a temptation, the philosophical Abraham must conclude that his prior willingness to obey God had been a sin, all the while recognizing that God's command and the imperative nature of *det Almene* are equally intractable. If to that which is highest and best one rightly sacrifices the next best, this leads at last to an impasse: "He [Abraham] could not comprehend that it was a sin that he had been willing to sacrifice to God the best that he had . . . ; and if it was a sin, . . . he could not understand that it could be forgiven, for what more terrible sin was there?"[26]

This least achieved Abraham, farthest from the knight of faith, does not even reach the intermediary status of the tragic hero.[27] The tragedy of tragic heroes consists in the fact that, as every tragic plot reveals, *det Almene*, the customary ethical order, is not self-consistent.[28] By enjoin-

---

[26] Kierkegaard, *Fear and Trembling*, and *Repetition*, 13.

[27] Another intermediary figure, the knight of infinite resignation, is a romanticized variant of the tragic hero, and will not concern us here.

[28] As Hegel interprets the classical Greek polis, the ethical order is split into "Spirit as government, . . . openly accepted and manifest to all" versus "a *natural* ethical community," which is "the Family, as the *unconscious*, still inner Notion [of the ethical order]." These two cannot find resolution into a higher synthesis, because at the historical stage of the polis "each of the opposites in which the ethical substance exists contains the entire substance, and all the moments of its contents" (*Phenomenology of Spirit*, 268). Thus, with the advent of the nation-state as a mediating institution, tragic contradictions such as

ing conflicting allegiances to the family and to the state, to the matriarchal order of kin and to the patriarchal order of alliance, *det Almene* itself brings tragic heroes to tragic ends.

While not ignorantly rejecting the conflict like the philosophical Abraham, what makes tragic heroes such as Agamemnon, Jephthah, and Brutus inferior to knights of faith is that they do not transcend *det Almene*. As Kierkegaard puts it, the tragic hero "allows an expression of the ethical to have its *telos* in a higher expression of the ethical; he scales down the ethical relation between father and son or daughter and father."[29] Although his actions impose rank upon the conflicting imperatives, this figure remains contained within the ethical, never accessing the religious plane at all. Nonetheless, an incremental advance has taken place: tragic heroes face *det Almene*'s contradictions and suffer for it in a way that brings knowledge, unlike the philosophical Abraham whose inability to comprehend such contradictions leaves him ignorant.

Abraham as Confessor

The previous narrative illustrated an Abraham who chose communal norms over religious demands. The next narrative shows an Abraham who wants to obey, but also wants to share the burden by speaking about his predicament. We read, "Abraham said to himself, 'I will not hide from Isaac where this walk is taking him.'"[30] We are not told why Abraham does this: perhaps to let Isaac participate as a willing victim in the sacrifice, perhaps because Abraham wanted Isaac's understanding,

those that embroiled Antigone and Creon are safely relegated to a past historical stage. A central strategy in Derrida's influential reading of *Fear and Trembling* in *The Gift of Death* (trans. D. Wills; Religion and Postmodernism; Chicago: University of Chicago Press, 1995), however, is to strip the *Aqedah* of its exceptional character and claim that the conflict of non-negotiable ethical claims depicted there is always taking place, for "one is unable to be responsible at the same time before the other and before others, before the others of the other. If God is completely other, the figure or name of the wholly other, then every other (one) is very (bit) other. *Tout autre est tout autre* .... [W]hat can be said about Abraham's relation to God can be said about my relation without relation to *every other (one) as every (bit) other* [*tout autre comme tout autre*], in particular my relation to my neighbor or my loved ones who are as inaccessible to me, as secret and transcendent as Jahweh" (*The Gift of Death*, 77–78). Such a statement, while revising Kierkegaard's reading, also rejects Hegel's position that Antigone's conflict with Creon can no longer take place because the state as intermediary offers the resources to mediate such conflicting claims without violence. As history since Hegel has made painfully apparent, we have little reason to be so sanguine.

[29] Kierkegaard, *Fear and Trembling*, and *Repetition*, 59.

[30] Kierkegaard, *Fear and Trembling*, and *Repetition*, 10.

which would be tantamount to his forgiveness. Whatever the reason for this disclosure, Isaac does not understand, and begs for his life.

The pathos of this scene is the most tragic of all the variations because Isaac's response is the direct consequence of Abraham's failure. The ability to maintain silence, to sacrifice one's desire for the other's understanding, to risk misrecognition—to Kierkegaard these are necessary conditions for becoming a knight of faith. Silence exiles one from *det Almene* because the latter is the realm of ethics, language and social reciprocity, as well as subsidiary functions like explanation, justification and recognition. In silence one foregoes the possibility of justifying one's actions, a recourse open even to the tragic hero. Thus, again, the tragic hero remains within *det Almene*, and now in a second sense: although singled out for suffering, the tragic hero is able to explain his or her actions and claim the community's understanding. As Kierkegaard observes, "When in the crucial ... moment Agamemnon, Jephthah, and Brutus ... heroically have lost the beloved," everyone will shed "tears of compassion for their agony, of admiration for their deed."[31] Since on the tragic stage the plot hinges upon the revelation of truth and the banishment of ignorance, tragic heroes communicate and the community recognizes them *as* tragic heroes.

What distinguishes the Abraham of the *Aqedah* from the merely tragic hero is that Abraham's act "transgressed the ethical altogether and had a higher *telos* outside it, in relation to which he suspended it [the ethical]."[32] To suspend the ethical completely, then, one must do so in silence, but this Abraham is "unable to endure the martyrdom of misunderstanding."[33] Indeed, perversely, because of his desire to speak the truth Abraham is ultimately forced to lie to Isaac.[34] In turn, this drives Isaac to a God who is an all too familiar source of protection and consolation, for Isaac cries aloud, "[I]f I have no father on earth, then you [God] be my father!"[35] Read against the weaning metaphor, it appears that, because Abraham could not wean himself from the loquacity of *det Almene*, Isaac could not wean himself from a God conceived as a paternal protector.

---

[31] Kierkegaard, *Fear and Trembling*, and *Repetition*, 58.

[32] Kierkegaard, *Fear and Trembling*, and *Repetition*, 59.

[33] Kierkegaard, *Fear and Trembling*, and *Repetition*, 80.

[34] "Then Abraham ... said, 'Stupid boy, do you think I am your father? I am an idolater. Do you think it is God's command? No, it is my desire'" (*Fear and Trembling*, and *Repetition*, 10).

[35] Kierkegaard, *Fear and Trembling*, and *Repetition*, 10.

Abraham as Ascetic

The next narrative shows an Abraham who, in obeying God's command, rejects the world so entirely that he is left devoid of the love that makes his sacrifice a truly costly gesture. This Abraham rode to the mountain in silence, and when he reached it, "Silently he arranged the firewood and bound Isaac; silently he drew the knife."[36] The reiterated emphasis on silence reveals that this Abraham obeys God's command with the grimness of a condemned man. His ascetic demeanor resembles that of the tragic hero, but unlike the latter, this Abraham does not attempt to make himself understood. Here Abraham has renounced all enjoyment in the world, as well as the possibility of communal recognition that follows from the expression of motives, intentions, and reasons in general.

Because the ascetic Abraham externally complies with God's command, Kierkegaard shifts the idea of sacrifice away from the simple destruction of a valued object.[37] Kierkegaard's God is not anthropomorphic in the sense that he *desires* or *needs* the offerings. Instead, for Kierkegaard sacrifice enacts a transformation *in the sacrificer* that prepares the ground for faith, the two being concomitant but without one causing the other. Hence, the point is not to destroy a particular object, but, here, to break one's relation to *det Almene*, which entails sacrificing all that is recognizably human in oneself. To do this, renunciation and silence are essential. To make worship truly costly, then, one must reject explanations, justifications, and other prestigious displays of one's religiosity—that is, the cultural returns of religious expenditure.

The ascetic Abraham has achieved these two sacrifices. Therefore, we must clarify why this Abraham is not yet a knight of faith. This ascetic Abraham not only accedes to God's command by valuing it above the claims of *det Almene*, he exceeds it by renouncing all affective relations to the world as a whole, for after this renunciation the sacrifice of Isaac, a single being in the world, becomes superfluous. In his rush to renounce

[36] Kierkegaard, *Fear and Trembling*, and *Repetition*, 12.

[37] In *Sacrifice: Its Nature and Function* (trans. W. D. Halls, with a foreword by E. E. Evans-Pritchard; Chicago: The University of Chicago Press, 1964), 9, Henri Hubert and Marcel Mauss define sacrifice as a species of consecration, but one whose effects "extend beyond the thing consecrated; among other objects, it touches the moral person who bears the expenses of the ceremony." Such a shift as Kierkegaard's, then, is not incongruent with this development in anthropology.

he has numbed himself to the trial. With no hold in the world at all, there is nothing left at stake, no beloved to put at risk.

Instead of this, the knight of faith must lovingly lead to the altar Isaac, *det Almene*, indeed the world as a whole. Thus, the paradox Abraham lives is that he does not extinguish all worldly love in preparation for the sacrifice, but continues to love Isaac *even as* he sacrifices him. As Kierkegaard puts it, "Since God claims Isaac, he [Abraham] must, if possible, love him even more, and only then can he *sacrifice* him .... Only in the moment when his act is in absolute contradiction to his feelings, only then does he sacrifice Isaac."[38] Hence, faith must be radically distinguished from renunciation, for an Abraham ascetically shorn of connections to the world might kill Isaac, but one cannot say that he sacrifices him.

Abraham as Faithless

Now we reach the final variation. Because this Abraham's actions most closely resemble those of the *Aqedah*, Kierkegaard shows here how subtly he calibrated his criteria of Abraham's achievement. Briefly, then, let us review the preceding variations. First, Abraham could not understand how God could contravene *det Almene*, and, rejecting this contradiction, rejected God's command itself as a temptation. Next, rejecting the inevitable misunderstanding, Abraham confessed his intentions to Isaac instead of proceeding in silence. Finally, Abraham ascetically performed the rite that God commanded, but renounced the love and hope he needed to distinguish the sacrifice from mere killing.

In the fourth and final variation, we see an Abraham who avoids the others' pitfalls. Thus, the stage is set, but at the moment of the sacrifice "Isaac saw that Abraham's left hand was clenched in despair, that a shudder went through his whole body."[39] Again, Abraham fails, but the reason is not immediately clear. Having insisted that "to exist as the single individual is the most terrible [existence] of all,"[40] why does this shudder in the face of terror count for Kierkegaard as a failure?

Although this Abraham performs the finite movements of the journey and the preparations with near perfection, he is unable to integrate them with the movement of faith or infinitude. The "left hand was clenched

---

[38] Kierkegaard, *Fear and Trembling*, and *Repetition*, 74.
[39] Kierkegaard, *Fear and Trembling*, and *Repetition*, 14.
[40] Kierkegaard, *Fear and Trembling*, and *Repetition*, 75.

in despair" while the right hand clenched the knife: this schism in Abraham's soul, a literal schizophrenia, manifests itself as a shudder. The external piety of Abraham falls like a veil, revealing nothing to support it but despair. The weaning interlude that follows shows that this Abraham, though in external conformity with God's command, has not met the final, internal criterion—that is, constant, unwavering faith. The interlude reads, "When the child is to be weaned, the mother has stronger sustenance at hand so that the child does not perish."[41] According to this metaphor, then, Abraham's faith fails to bridge the transition between worldly and spiritual sustenance.[42]

As we have seen, Kierkegaard experiments with variations of the *Aqedah*, breaking with Gen 22 at different points in order to isolate components of Abraham's sacrifice. Because of the importance Kierkegaard attributes here to Abraham's ritual manner, binding his son on the altar becomes a necessary but not sufficient condition of Abraham's success. By delineating the felicity conditions of a proper sacrifice, Kierkegaard presents his case against Christendom, in particular the compromises between church and state that reduce religion to the generalized norms of *det Almene*. As the sphere of language, ethics, and social relationships in general, *det Almene* includes essential aspects of what makes a being recognizably human. Thus, Kierkegaard argues that we must sacrifice in silence, uncomprehending, and alone, all that is truly human, even as we continue to love what we sacrifice to the utmost possible degree. With *det Almene* as our Isaac, Kierkegaard challenges Christendom to perform this movement of paradoxical passion that he calls faith.

Conclusion

Although no authority predominates in *Fear and Trembling* aside from the example of Abraham, through the heritage of the pivotal term *det Almene* the text engages the epoch's philosophical disputes. Kierkegaard inherited an Enlightenment sense of discursive production where, instead of the exegete returning to authoritative texts that define the goals

---

41 Kierkegaard, *Fear and Trembling*, and *Repetition*, 14.

42 This theme concords with the analysis in Hubert and Mauss as well: "this outward continuity of the rites is not enough .... In short, a religious act must be accomplished in a religious frame of mind: the inward attitude must correspond to the external one. We see how, from the very outset, sacrifice demanded a *credo* (*shraddha* is the equivalent of *credo*, even philologically), and how the act carried faith with it" (*Sacrifice: Its Nature and Function*, 28).

and parameters of the exegesis, as one finds with the early Christian fathers, the Enlightenment author combines the work of exegete with that of the critic in order to open the text as a site of epistemological disclosure. To effect such a disclosure, Kierkegaard's maneuver of totalizing all human phenomena extraneous to the religious sphere plays a key role. Through a combination of, first, the Pauline thematic of the *Aqedah* (the sacrifice of Isaac as an index of Abraham's faith in Rom 4), and, second, the totalizing reification of *det Almene*, Kierkegaard tightens the tension of the trial to the point that Abraham transcends every possible calculation of quotidian expenditure and return. In this way Kierkegaard acknowledges scriptural authority at the same time that he vertiginously escalates the stakes of the narrative. A consequence of this strategy is that, in order to demonstrate the insuperably radical nature of the *Aqedah*, Kierkegaard keeps the attention focused away from the object and on the agent of sacrifice—that is, away from Isaac as victim and on Abraham's relation to socio-cultural imperatives in the universal realm of ethics.

This nearly exclusive attention on Abraham results from a variety of maneuvers. First, the analysis deals only with Gen 22, in which Abraham is the primary earthly agent. Furthermore, in contrast to what the "weaning" anecdotes might suggest, no longer is it the natural relation between father and son that provides the narrative's pathos; instead, in reading the *Aqedah* as the sacrifice, not of Isaac, but of Abraham's love for Isaac, this love becomes, not one emotion among others, but the overcoded metonym of the sum total of all human relations and values. In short, Abraham's love for Isaac comes to stand for Abraham's affective relations to the mundane sphere as a whole. The question then becomes, just as the weaning anecdotes metonymically figure all mother-child relations as mere modes of nourishment, can one reduce *det Almene*'s vast repertoire of values and relationships to an "object" of sacrifice?

For the scholar of religion and—and *as*—culture, Kierkegaard offers a compelling case study of an author mobilizing the resources of one sphere against the other. But can one marshal the practice of sacrifice, which has cultural currency outside of specifically religious domains, against culture itself? While it is true that in *Fear and Trembling* Kierkegaard's employment of religious themes takes his contemporaries to task, it is equally true that Kierkegaard draws upon a wealth of Danish culture, including such elements as folk songs and tales, popular novels, and the plays and operas of the contemporary stage. This double game of employing cultural resources in the service of a religious critique of culture helps to account for the astonishing richness of his texts, as well as their exasperating paradoxes. In fact, much like the *Bildern* of possible and historical subject-object formations in that great text of philosophical *Bildung*, Hegel's *Phenomenology of Spirit*, Kierkegaard's text functions as a form of aesthetic *Bildung* or acculturation, "attuning" the reader to hear the shuddersome music of Abraham's ordeal.

Since Kierkegaard saw Hegelianism at the root of contemporary malacculturation, he does not adopt Hegel's strategy and intervene in the process of Danish acculturation through a single privileged mode of discourse, the philosophical. Instead, Kierkegaard's intervention utilizes multiple cultural media in a polyvocal strategy that relies heavily upon this public culture. Furthermore, Kierkegaard seeks to recalibrate the acculturated sensibility of his contemporaries in order to encompass the passionate extremities of a figure like Abraham, and to do this the text employs numerous rhetorical strategies to project the reader into his perspective. For this reason, the weaning metaphor works against some of the text's more overt arguments, for the mother provides not only nourishment to the child, but also access to such cultural fundamentals as language and the affective gestures of aesthetics, which are not left behind.[43]

If *Fear and Trembling* indeed operates on an aesthetic level as a valorization of a religious movement, I remain skeptical whether the clean distinction between the religious and the cultural is at all possible.[44] This difficulty emerges in another context when Kierkegaard asks, "What,

---

43 This is not to essentialize the reproductive power of women in cultural terms, but merely to elaborate Kierkegaard's weaning metaphor along the lines that he laid down.

44 Such attempts to isolate a primeval and / or pure essence of religion free of merely cultural contaminants are legion. In fact, one might read Kant as attempting such a transfiguration in the way that he distills religion to a moral core, and then proposes this moral framework as holding for any "rational agent." For an excellent treatment of this topic, see Allen W. Wood, *Kant's Moral Religion* (Ithaca, N. Y.: Cornell University Press, 1970). In regard to this pure form of religion, we can borrow from Hegel's critique of Kant: a universal reason abstracted from specific socio-cultural contexts is in fact ideal, but in the negative sense of "shorn of reality." In this light, it is highly ironic that Kierkegaard uses a Hegelian term (the Danish equivalent of *Sittlichkeit*) in a pre-Hegelian sense, to speak of universal social norms in a way that ignores historically specific contexts. But in this we have learned from Kierkegaard: although all children are eventually weaned, it matters a great deal how this takes place, and though the variant Abrahams were willing to sacrifice Isaac, not all of them were able to do so in the correct manner. In the same way, then,

then, is education? I believed it is the course the individual goes through in order to catch up with himself, and the person who will not go through this course is not much helped by being born in the most enlightened age."[45] If Kierkegaard argues convincingly that the individual cannot borrow an educational impetus from her age on the cheap, it is also true that her age marks that individual in ways too deep for reflection. Thus, when attacking Hegel in favor of the pathos of the individual, Kierkegaard is never more dialectically entangled with his age and its Hegelianism than in the very instant that he attempts to extricate the individual decisively from his or her socio-cultural context. It is for this reason that the struggles that take place in Kierkegaard's texts contest without transgressing the limits of post-Hegelian philosophy.

Through limning these contradictions, we return at last to the central affective paradox, which is that, although Abraham must sacrifice his humanity, he must also continue to love humankind as represented in the person of Isaac. Kierkegaard thus reads the *Aqedah* against its construal as a historical event demarcating two sacrificial regimes, the human and the animal, for according to the Pauline thematic, the change of the ritual object serving as currency in the sacrificial economy is inessential compared to Abraham's subjective ordeal and achievement. With love (the metonym or synechdoche of one's "humanity") as the *subjective sacrificial object*, and *det Almene* (the total set of affective relations to the world) as the *objective sacrificial object*, such a situation constitutes a paradox in the positive sense that the "double movement" of faith[46] becomes a sacrifice that never stops taking place.

As I have argued, in constructing his own faith-based reading of the *Aqedah*, love plays at least two roles in Kierkegaard's telling: it is both the object of sacrifice and the emotional bearing that determines how one sacrifices. In other words, to sacrifice one's love lovingly requires a love that plays an active role throughout the rite, so that love takes a position on both sides of the knife. This love is no putatively "natural" or given emotion,[47] moreover, but remains imbricated in the accultur-

---

the fact *that* the norms of *det Almene* apply universally is a tautological claim; questions concerning *how* they might vary in application cross-culturally are ones that Kierkegaard does not address.

[45] Kierkegaard, *Fear and Trembling*, and *Repetition*, 46.

[46] On this and the "infinite movement" of faith in particular, see *Fear and Trembling*, and *Repetition*, 35, 36, 38, 40–46.

[47] In arguing for a comparative and interpretive approach to emotion that acknowledges the role played by culture, Lutz and White suggest the need for a "basic reconceptualiza-

ated framework of communal affectivity. Since the emotions provide a clear case in which one cannot divorce the individual from the cultural, and a cold, heartless sacrifice is no sacrifice at all, all this is to say that *det Almene* is not a discreet object, and culture is not totalizable. Should we further conclude, then, that one's humanity is in fact unsacrificeable?

Such a conclusion would be inevitable only if we retained the traditional sense of sacrifice as a delimited spatio-temporal act. However, for Kierkegaard's text the public motions of the ritual were merely the conditions of possibility for demonstrating the criterial characteristic of the knight of faith. In this way, for Kierkegaard the whole of Gen 22, wherein the protagonist "resigned everything infinitely, and then he grasped everything again by virtue of the absurd,"[48] takes place all at once and without cessation, for the knight of faith "has made and at every moment is making the movement of infinity."[49] With the focus no longer on sacrifice as a specific kind of act but rather on faith as a unique mode of being, Derrida's observation that "this land of Moriah ... is our habitat every second of every day"[50] derives directly from Kierkegaard's insistent claim that Abraham's trial is not safely relegated to a past historical stage, but stands as a challenge to would-be Christians down to the present day.

If *det Almene* proved too broad a term for Kierkegaard's critique of Hegel, and if its sacrifice does not afford the clear and distinct separation between religious and mundane spheres that *Fear and Trembling* seeks to effect, at least, perhaps, it indicates a gap between the religious and the cultural, an incongruence that resists any foreclosure of critique and opens the possibility of each subjecting the other to perpetual interrogation.

---

tion that will give renewed emphasis to the public, social and cognitive dimensions of emotional experience" and at the same time forge links "between the often dichotomized worlds of the rational and irrational, public and private, individual and social" (Catherine Lutz and Geoffrey M. White, "The Anthropology of Emotions," *Annual Review of Anthropology* 15 [1986]: 429).

48 Kierkegaard, *Fear and Trembling*, and *Repetition*, 40.

49 Kierkegaard, *Fear and Trembling*, and *Repetition*, 40.

50 Derrida, *The Gift of Death*, 69.

Viktor von Weizsäcker: " 'Euthanasia' and Experiments on Human Beings" [Part I: "Euthanasia"] (1947)

With an Introduction by[1]
Udo Benzenhöfer and Wilhelm Rimpau,
University of Frankfurt / Main and University of Berlin

Introduction

(Udo Benzenhöfer and Wilhelm Rimpau)

In 1947 Professor Viktor von Weizsäcker published " 'Euthanasie' und Menschenversuche" (" 'Euthanasia' and Experiments on Human Beings"), in which one of the themes considered was human sacrifice and medicine.

Weizsäcker[2], born in 1886, a doctor with a marked interest in philosophy, was from 1922 Associate Professor, from 1930 Professor, of Neurology at the University of Heidelberg. In the 1920s Weizsäcker wrote numerous revolutionary neuro-physiological and neurological-clinical papers. Moreover, he advocated a co-operation of psychoanalysis and clin-

---

[1] We want to thank Maria Urban (Bonn) for the translation of the introduction.

[2] For his life and work see: Viktor von Weizsäcker, *Natur und Geist: Begegnungen und Entscheidungen* (Gesammelte Schriften 1, Frankfurt / Main: Suhrkamp, 1986); Thomas Henkelmann, *Viktor von Weizsäcker (1886–1957): Materialien zu Leben und Werk* (Berlin: Springer, 1986); Martin Wein, "Viktor von Weizsäcker 1886–1957: Auf neuen Wegen in der Medizin", in *Die Weizsäckers: Geschichte einer deutschen Familie* (ed. Martin Wein, München: Knaur, 1991), 341–410; Wilhelm Rimpau, "Wege zur anthropologischen Medizin: Viktor von Weizsäcker," *Jahrbuch für Kritische Medizin* 12 (1987): 54–67; Udo Benzenhöfer, ed., *Anthropologische Medizin und Sozialmedizin im Werk Viktor von Weizsäckers* (Frankfurt am Main: Lang, 1994); Rainer-M. E. Jacobi, "Gegenseitigkeit und Verantwortung: Viktor von Weizsäckers Beitrag zur medizinischen Ethik", in *Medizingeschichte und Medizinethik* (eds. Andreas Frewer and Joseph N. Neumann, Frankfurt / Main: Campus, 2001), 276–310.

ical medicine and during the 1920s and 1930s wrote important contributions to social medicine. In 1926 Weizsäcker, together with the Jewish philosopher Martin Buber and the Catholic priest Josef Wittig, created the—albeit short-lived—inter-confessional periodical "Die Kreatur." Here Weizsäcker published fundamental contributions to medical anthropology. In "The Doctor and the Patient" he wrote: "We (the doctors) learnt the structure of the human body as tissue, that of the tissue as chemical substances. We learnt that all of this is altered by disease (...). We can now make the judgement: this is sick.—But the patient can say: I am sick."[3] This marked nothing less than the "introduction of the subject into medicine." In this publication Weizsäcker also pointed out the importance of the "biographical method" for clarification of the origin of the illness. In his opinion, illness was to be understood as something which the patient "not only has, but also does" (as Weizsäcker later formulated it). At all events, Weizsäcker tried to understand the illness as a crisis and therefore also as an opportunity for the subject. In 1941 Weizsäcker became Professor of Neurology at the University of Breslau. One of the main fields of interest here was research on the "Theory of the Unity of Movement and Perception." A comprehensive monograph was published in 1940 entitled "Der Gestaltkreis" ("The Circle of Form"). In Breslau Weizsäcker was also director of the Neurological Research Institute attached to the University. One of the Institute's departments conducted research on pathology of the brain. This department, directed by Dr. J. Scherer, profited from the so-called "euthanasia of children."[4] In 1942 a "Children's Department" ("Kinderfachabteilung") was established in the Psychiatric State Hospital in Lubliniec.[5] Here handicapped children were killed. Medical records of the murdered children have been preserved. According to re-

[3] von Weizsäcker: "Der Arzt und der Kranke," in *Der Arzt und der Kranke: Stücke einer medizinischen Anthropologie* (vol. 5 of *Gesammelte Schriften*, 1926, Frankfurt / Main: Suhrkamp 1987), 9–26, 18.

[4] This only became known to the broader German public in the 1980s; see Karl Heinz Roth, "Psychosomatische Medizin und 'Euthanasie'," *1999. Zeitschrift für Sozialgeschichte des 20. und 21. Jahrhunderts* 1 (1986): 65–99, 84. However, this study contains numerous errors. By the way: Already in 1975 Dionizy Moska (*Przeglad Lekarski* vol. 32, 114)—as discovered by Rimpau in early 2004—had referred to Weizsäcker's Institute in the Lubliniec context.

[5] For the subject "euthanasia of children" see the survey by Benzenhöfer, "Genese und Struktur der NS-Kindereuthanasie," MONATSSCHRIFT FÜR KINDERHEILKUNDE 151 (2003): 1012–19. Lubliniec was not the only children's department. Between 1940 and 1945 about 30 such departments were established.

search by Viktor von Weizsäcker's daughter, Cora Penselin, 209 of 294 existing records contain a post-mortem report from the Neurological Research Institute in Breslau.[6] Brain and spinal cord of the 209 children were without doubt examined in Breslau. All of the reports are signed by Dr. Scherer. The medical records also contain carbon copies of a standard letter from Lubiniec addressed to "the Neurological Research Institute Professor von Weizsäcker, Breslau," which states, "Enclosed I am sending you in accordance with your letter of 25. 3. 42 fixed samples of brain and spinal cord (the patient's name follows) with the request that it be examined pathologically. I enclose a summary of the medical records." However, this letter is not proof that Weizsäcker himself knew of and profited from the "euthanasia of children." Nevertheless, his institute was definitely involved. Further clarification of this point is needed. Weizsäcker left Breslau in January 1945. Following a short period as prisoner of war, he came to Heidelberg, where he was Deputy Head of the Physiological Institute, and then in 1946 Professor of General Clinical Medicine. From 1951 he suffered from symptoms of Parkinson's disease and retired in 1952. He died on 8. 1. 1957 in Heidelberg.

"'Euthanasia' and Experiments on Human Beings" was published in 1947 in the newly-founded periodical *Psyche* (co-publisher was the university lecturer Dr. Alexander Mitscherlich) and almost simultaneously as a separate edition.[7] In a way, Weizsäcker had a "direct line" to Nürnberg, as Mitscherlich, his collaborator in Heidelberg, was in 1946 a member of a German medical commission[8] attending the Nürn-

[6] For more comprehensive information see Cora Penselin, "Bemerkungen zu den Vorwürfen, Viktor von Weizsäcker sei in die nationalsozialistische Vernichtungspolitik verstrickt gewesen," in *Anthropologische Medizin und Sozialmedizin im Werk Viktor von Weizsäckers* (ed. Benzenhöfer, Frankfurt/Main: P. Lang, 1994), 123–37. See also Rimpau, "Viktor von Weizsäcker im Nationalsozialismus," in *Von der Heilkunde zur Massentötung: Medizin im Nationalsozialismus* (eds. Gerrit Hohendorf and Achim Magull-Seltenreich, Heidelberg: Wunderhorn, 1990), 113–30 and Benzenhöfer, "Viktor von Weizsäcker und Breslau," *Jahrbuch der Schlesischen Friedrich-Wilhelms-Universität zu Breslau* 26/27 (1997): 454–65.

[7] See *Psyche* 1 (1947): 68–102 and as separate publication *'Euthanasie' und Menschenversuche* (Heidelberg: Schneider, 1947). See also von Weizsäcker, "'Euthanasie' und Menschenversuche," in *Allgemeine Medizin: Grundfragen medizinischer Anthropologie* (vol. 7 of *Gesammelte Schriften*, (Frankfurt/Main: Suhrkamp, 1987), 91–134.

[8] The commission comprised originally: (1.) Privatdozent Dr. med. Alexander Mitscherlich; (2.) Fred Mielke (medical student from Heidelberg; he came from a lecture course of Mitscherlich), (3.) Dr. med. Wolfgang Benstz (Heidelberg; he had written his thesis under Weizsäcker in 1939); (4.) Dr. med. Friedrich Jensen (Frankfurt/Main; he was recommended by Dr. med. Carl Oelemann); (5.) Dr. med. Alice Gräfin von Platen (intern under Weizsäcker in Heidelberg; she published in 1948 "Die Tötung Geisteskranker in

berg medical trial. The charges of the American military tribunal included "euthanasia"-crimes and experiments on humans in concentration camps. Mitscherlich and the medical student Fred Mielke published a documentation in March 1947 (that is during the trial, which lasted from 9. 12. 1946 until 19. 7. 1947).[9] Possibly, although this has not been completely determined, Weizsäcker wanted to make his study available to the military court as an "expert opinion."[10]

For the theme "human sacrifice," Section 1 d is of most importance.[11] Here Weizsäcker explored the possible "motives of a destruction of life ('euthanasia') from the medical point of view." In his opinion there were three "medical" motives for such a destruction: worthlessness of life, compassion and sacrifice.

Weizsäcker's arguments on the theme of worthlessness of life[12] were complex. What must in any case be recorded is that his analysis brought him to the view that medicine oriented *solely* to the scientific-biological standpoint must almost inevitably come to a devaluation of (incurable) diseased life: "If the doctor assumes a value of this temporal life without regard for its eternal value, then indeed this temporal life may be so worthless that it deserves destruction" (p. 11). What arguments did Weizsäcker offer against this? His comments were brief. However, it is clear that for him only "anthropological medicine" which understands the transcendence of life, could prevent the otherwise almost inevitable killing of the sick. According to Weizsäcker such anthropological medicine must have solidarity and mutuality of doctor and patient as the key ideas.

Deutschland"); (6.) Dr. med. Wolfgang Spamer (in private practice in Neckarsteinach near Heidelberg; former co-worker of Weizsäcker); see Jürgen Peter, *Der Nürnberger Ärzteprozeß im Spiegel seiner Aufarbeitung anhand der drei Dokumentensammlungen von Alexander Mitscherlich und Fred Mielke* (Münster: Lit, 1994), 39 f. The Commission was—so to speak—Weizsäcker-weighted.

[9] See Alexander Mitscherlich and Fred Mielke, *Das Diktat der Menschenverachtung* (Heidelberg: Schneider, 1947).

[10] In Section 3 a) Weizsäcker writes of an "expert called as a consultant [Gutachter] in a lawsuit" (p. 42 f.).

[11] For a short introduction see also Fritz Hartmann, "Opfer in der Medizin und der Naturwissenschaft," in *Zur Theorie des Opfers: Ein interdisziplinäres Gespräch* (ed. Richard Schenk, Collegium Philosophicum 1, Stuttgart: Frommann-Holzboog, 1995), 105–18.

[12] Weizsäcker was here directly or indirectly referring to the much-discussed book by Karl Binding and Alfred Hoche, *Die Freigabe der Vernichtung lebensunwerten Lebens: Ihr Maß und ihre Form* (Leipzig: F. Meiner, 1920).

Compassion or sympathy with the sick, whom one wished to spare further suffering, Weizsäcker rejected as a legitimate medical motive for the "destruction" (better: extermination) of life. His argument was summarized thus: "A pity which is directed only towards a biological or psychological reality prevents the effective sympathy which must transcend both the biological fact and the psychological phenomenon" (p. 14).

Concerning sacrifice Weizsäcker first of all commented that it is a particularly effective motive.[13] "The idea of sacrifice implies a special dialectic which transforms a mere motive into a law, a 'should,' a duty, an unescapable compulsion and a moral action." He proceeded from the idea of a "modern form" of human sacrifice: "Its active modern form appears to me to be the principle of solidarity, the precursors of which were human sacrifices and their substitutes, animal and food sacrifices. The argument based on solidarity may be formulated somewhat as follows: if the whole people is in danger of life and can be saved only by the elimination of a few single individuals, then they must be sacrificed—even though they do not appreciate this necessity. Those who are informed and able to grasp the causal connections have then not only the right but the duty to enforce this sacrifice, in other words, to kill" (p. 14). How can this idea obtain a medical connotation? Weizsäcker's answer was: "By assuming that the term 'sick' refers now not only to individuals, but to a solitary community, a collectivity, a people or to humanity as a whole. There would exist then a social disease from which a people or humanity is suffering. This need not be merely a sum of individual diseases, as in an epidemic like typhus or malaria. A collectivity might be sick as such, in a new and peculiar way. We are then confronted with disease in an enlarged sense of the word. Comparable to the amputation of a gangrenous foot which saves this whole organism, the eradication of diseased components of the people would save the latter. Considered as a sacrifice both cases would be legitimate, logical and necessary

[13] This "argument" also appeared (suggested) in the book by Binding and Hoche, *Freigabe*, 56: "Wir haben es [...] verlernt, in dieser Beziehung den staatlichen Organismus im selben Sinne wie ein Ganzes [...] zu betrachten, wie ihn etwa ein in sich geschlossener Organismus darstellt, der, wie wir Ärzte wissen, im Interesse der Wohlfahrt des Ganzen auch einzelne wertlos gewordene oder schädliche Teile oder Teilchen preisgibt und abstößt." Translation: "We have forgotten [...] to view the state organism in this respect as a whole [...], like for example a self-contained organism, which, as we doctors know, in the interest of the whole sacrifices or disposes of single parts that have become worthless or harmful".

as a medical intervention" (p. 14 f.). According to Weizsäcker this (possible) medical motive should not be underestimated, not least because it fulfilled a particular form, to which almost all sacrifices conformed: "Consider then the historical forms of sacrifice and notice that there occurs a frequent change in the object and in the selection of sacrifice; Abraham sacrifices his son, Agamemnon his daughter, Christian theology God's son, the church in the sacrifice of mass the host and the wine; in war, however, the sons of the country and in revolutions the carriers of a social idea are sacrificed. And yet the form of sacrifice, viz. [original: fiz.] liberty through death, has remained the same throughout" (p. 16). Weizsäcker rejected the accusation that this was "mere quibbling." It was not as simple with the NS-"euthanasia" as many people claimed, namely: "There have been people in politics who, by terror or seduction, have made some doctors behave in an unmedical way; these doctors have thereupon transgressed the boundaries of medicine; that, however, is no real concern of medicine itself" (p. 17). In Weizsäcker's opinion this argument was "fallacious": "For what kind of medicine was it which could be terrorized or seduced to such a degree? There must have been some foundation for it in medicine itself" (p. 17). To Weizsäcker it seemed possible, "that medicine itself participates essentially in the spirit of sacrifice, but that it had lost consciousness of this fact. And it could also be that the politicians have forced medicine to perform a sacrifice without knowing what a genuine sacrifice is. Thus this meeting between politics and medicine was not external and haphazard, but on the contrary inherently probable. But in that case the state of affairs is exactly the contrary from the one implied in the statement which says that the doctors have transgressed their boundaries. Medicine had become restricted to a scientific technique which treated man only as an object instead of considering him as an individual who transcends itself in and into a society. Therefore medicine had lost the idea and the practice of sacrifice and thus it became susceptible when this idea was forced upon it from outside in a degenerate and mendacious form. I therefore emphatically deny that it is correct to say that those doctors have merely transgressed their proper limits. One should say rather that they have transgressed them in a wrong direction. In my opinion this was due as well to a personal inadequacy as to a mistaken idea of medicine in general. A solidarity could not be established nor could a real sacrifice be realized by the way in which a policy of extermination under the guise of euthanasia and in the name of a sacrifice was carried out" (p. 18 f.). Certainly, Weizsäcker did not define what a permissible sacrifice would be, but in conclusion he indicated the most important characteristic: "A doctor who would invoke a medical motive would have to show that his attitude is 'fair,' i. e. based on mutuality and not authoritarian, i. e. based on a feeling of superiority. One can say that any appeal to the prevalent right of a majority, of the healthy, the efficient or the racially preferred, does not create a solidarity, for this can be based only on mutuality. This means that the 'sacrifice' of another is never a real sacrifice and that the latter can be demonstrated only in the sacrifice of one's self" (p. 24).

Finally, a short comment on the long unpublished translation, which is part of Viktor von Weizsäcker's estate.[14] The translator, Dr. Edgar Taschdjian, was a biologist with special interest in ethical questions. His son, Martin Taschdjian, provided the following information on his father's biography: "Born in Vienna, he grew up in Constantinople during the Armenia massacres of the early 1920s. He returned to Vienna where he received his Ph. D. and worked initially as an agronomist in Abyssinia and Brazil in the 1920s and the early 1930s. He wound up in China in the late 1930s, teaching biology at Fu Jen University, which was a Catholic institution in Peking. There he associated with Franz Weidenreich and Teilhard de Chardin, and married. Because (for reasons too complicated to go into) he had Italian citizenship, he was not interned under the Japanese occupation. In mid-1948 he was hired at Loyola University of Chicago to teach Biology and was joined at the end of that year by his family (including my brother and me). In 1952 we moved to New York where he taught Biology at St. Francis College (Brooklyn) and retired as Chairman of the Department. Perhaps due to his Chinese associations his interests had expanded from genetics into philosophy, and this led him into general systems theory and cybernetics. He also had an interest in semantics and the use of language. He was a member of the General Systems Society and I often heard him mention Bertalanffy. He wrote and published extensively, though many of his papers are unpublished. He died in 1988."[15] It has not been explained how Taschdjian came into possession of Weizsäcker's article in "Psyche" or the separate publication. In his "Translator's Preface" he wrote of

[14] Cora Penselin, Viktor von Weizsäcker's daughter, kindly made it available for this publication.

[15] E-mail of 15. 4. 2003 to Wilhelm Rimpau.

his reasons for the translation: "The present treatise by Professor Viktor v. Weizsäcker of Heidelberg University deals with a subject which ought to be of interest to any doctor or prospective doctor as well as to anybody interested in the ethical standards of the medical profession. The arguments advanced by Dr. v. Weizsäcker are not only inspired by a deeply Christian feeling for the rights and the individuality of the patient but they also consider necessities of medical practice with which teachers of ethics are usually not familiar. Whilst the article may not conform strictly to any religious dogma or canon, it seemed to this translator that the arguments advanced ought to be known, thought over and discussed by teachers and students both in the medical and ethical field. As a basis for such thought and discussion it is hoped that this translation will help to stimulate interest in the problems of medical ethics. Chicago, December 1949. Dr. Edgar Taschdjian" [not paginated].

The translation itself can clearly not be termed "philological," but it conveys an acceptable impression of the text. In order to keep the text readable, the editors stepped in only seldom. These few comments are indicated by square brackets. It should be made clear that only the first part of the text is printed here.[16]

[16] A reprint of the second part on the experiments on human beings and the third part of "mutuality and solidarity as a guide for medical action" would have exceeded the bounds of this volume. The script of the translation comprises 53 pages (plus one page with the Translator's Introduction).

[p. 1]

"Euthanasia" and Experiments on Human Beings.

By Viktor [original: Victor] von Weizsäcker

I realize, that the present treatise is not exhaustive and may only serve as a stimulus for the reformulation of the problem. It will be evident that my analysis originated from the trial of doctors at Nuremberg, though it proceeds on somewhat more rationalized lines. During its preparation, a collection of documents made by A. Mitscherlich and F. Mielke (Das Diktat der Menschenverachtung) appeared under the auspices of the same publisher. This publication has widened the public's understanding of the trial and has enabled it to judge it more adequately. Here, however, I am not concerned to define my position and attitude toward the Nuremberg trial, but rather to analyze the spirit of medicine. There is not only one [in the German text in italics] spirit of medicine or in the medical profession; but there is one spirit [in the German text in italics] of medicine which could prove at the trial neither its innocence nor its lack of contribution to these crimes which are abhorred by every honest man. The spirit, which was the real, though invisible defendant on the Nuremberg bench—a spirit which considers man only as an object—is not restricted to Nuremberg but permeates the whole world to some extent and appears in euthanasia and experiments on humans only in a specially crude and repulsive form. This may make us liable to a new error of judgment and reasoning; one is liable to say (and some do so already): the atrocities of Dachau show what is prohibited and not permissible, but therefore they show also quite clearly what is permissible and advisable. In other words: "Euthanasia" and human experiments are "as such" medically legitimate provided one keeps within moral limits. What exactly is meant by [p. 2] "as such" remains undefined and vague. I confess that it was only in the course of my investigation that I obtained sufficient clarity to realize that there is no "as such justification" for such measures and that this can be proved with the help of the principle of solidarity which enables one also to define the essence of destructive and of experimental practices. If this proposition should be correct, the next step would be to test in every morally doubtful case, whether it complies with the law of mutuality or not. This should be done throughout the realm of medicine, not only at or beyond its [original: it] borders. The discussion of any further consequences lies outside the scope of the present treatise. Of greater importance for us, however, is the problem of man in medicine, of man as an object, a subject, a natural object or a subject of values. It is appalling and challenging that such events seem to have been necessary in order that the danger be realized and that the meaning of an objective science be questioned and re-evaluated. The following is intended to contribute to the solution of this important task.

1. Can the artificial shortening of life (so-called euthanasia) of incurable insanes be justified from the medical point of view?

a) What is meant by "medical point of view"?

This terms seems to presuppose that there is a general moral norm or morality, the application of which to medicine requires special professional knowledge and experience in certain particular situations. As if somebody has to be a trained medical man in order to be able to judge which actions in medicine should be considered moral or unmoral. But even then the opinion of a single doctor would not be sufficient if it does not coincide with the generally valid opinion of the total medical profession; which would seem to mean that there is such a thing as a professional ethics by which the individual doctor must govern himself.

[p. 3] But this presupposition, that there is an undisputed medical point of view which only demands application, is not valid. The opinions are divided, so that a certain action may be judged either permissible, desirable or necessary or bad, punishable and avoidable. If then there is no self-evident and generally accepted medical ethics, we must look for the reason for this deficiency. The reason is that the concept of medicine is not uniform; historically it is subject to change and development and for the individual practitioner it is insofar subject to his own discretion as it is nowhere determined by state laws, nor is it contained in medical examinations or in the licence to practice. The conceptual idea of medicine and thus the professional ethics exist only individually and subjectively. As a consequence religious, philosophical, political and personal points of view contribute to the ethical principles which an individual has or to the manner in which he acts practically if he lacks such principles. A further consequence of this state of affairs is, however, that

I too am obliged to speak here for my own medical point of view and on the basis of my personal attitude, in other words, as an individual. I am unable to foresee which and how many of my colleagues will agree with me. Nevertheless I shall try not to speak "authoritatively" but in accordance with the ethical convictions of my profession and by taking into account the time in which we live and its actual conditions. I believe, furthermore, that the concept of a medical point of view presupposes two things: first an obedience to some kind of laws, even though unwritten ones, and secondly a personal liberty for decision without which no morality is possible.

Finally I hold that medical action is indeed so specific that it would be senseless and useless to maintain that morality is the same everywhere and that medical morality is the same as that in every other situation. [p. 4] In so far I accept the concept of a "medical point of view" and do not try to sidestep or avoid the question which confronts us.

b) What is meant by "Incurable insanity"?

One must not cling here to the literal meaning of "mental disease." A congenital idiocy or an arteriosclerotic or traumatic one are not really mental diseases. On the other hand a great many lesser mental abnormalities are incurable and the classification of a case will depend thus upon the degree or intensity of the disease, i. e. upon the line which the doctor subjectively considers as delimiting a mere abnormality from a psychopathic disease [translation error; mental disease]. It can be seen that here already a judgment of values is involved and not only a determination of facts. Of course the assumption of incurability is uncertain in a great many cases. Diagnostical errors, exceptions from the rule or therapeutical improvements may transform an incurable case into one which can be cured. Furthermore, the concept of cure is a relative concept. A man may be incurably sick and yet be socially adjusted and even useful: on the other hand, there are social and destructive psychopaths who are not mentally sick. If therefore, the concept of an "incurable mental disease" should be the criterion or motive for the elimination of such persons, it must be admitted that this expression is so chosen that it is either inadequate to express the real meaning viz. worthless life, or else that this meaning is intentionally obscured by its use [translation incomplete; either cannot express or is intended to obscure]. Nevertheless, its relative subjectivity, the existence of fluid transitions between sick, abnormal and healthy and finally the ratio of errors which is necessarily connected with all human and even scientific knowledge, all these limitations are not sufficient to declare that the verdict of incurability is generally and absolutely impossible. A great many cases can and must be designated by the well-informed doctor as incurable—of course within the limits of all human judgments.

[p. 5] c) The factors which enter into a decision involving a medical destruction.

First of all it must be clearly understood that numerous medical actions are intentionally or unavoidably connected with destructive measures. One may therefore legitimately speak of a medical order or scale of destructibility and it is to be regretted that such an order has not been formulated expressly at an earlier date in any country and exists so far only in fragments(*).
1. An intentional destruction may affect in the first place a certain part of the body. An amputation, as well as any surgical operation destroys tissues in order to help the rest of the organism.
2. The destruction of a whole living organism must be carried out in the case of pathological births, where one is obliged to choose between the life of the mother and that of the child and where one chooses that of the mother in order to preserve the one which is more "valuable" or essential. A similar case is that of the so-called medical indication for an artificial abortion or interruption of pregnancy. The same applies also to a medical indication for sterilization or castration, with the difference, that here unconceived, i. e. potential life, is destroyed.
3. Another, not intentional, but still unavoidable kind of destruction is involved in the so-called medical risk. Examples are e. g. narcosis or [original: of] smallpox vaccination, the risks of which may be accurately determined by statistical methods. There is a continual intergrading series from here down to single cases and events the risks of which cannot be estimated statistically.
4. A special case is that of the doctor who is trying to introduce for the first time a new treatment. Here there is also a risk; but the [p. 6] doctor is not protected by the common opinion held by other doctors or by

(*) See v. Weizsäcker, Medical Problems, Thieme Leipzig 1934, pp. 72–73. Also: A. Mitscherlich, Freedom and bondage in disease, Classen and Geverts [recte: Claaszen & Goverts], Hamburg 1946, p. 121.

the public. And yet, it would be tantamount to a suppression of almost every important medical progress if such risks could not be taken voluntarily and intentionally. But for the same reason, the factors entering into the decision must be investigated here with special care. Famous examples, some of which have involved the loss of life, are the development of stomach resection by Billroth or the testing of tuberculin by Robert Koch. Numerous similar examples can be found throughout the history of modern medicine.

5. Damages and casualties due to technical mistakes [better: malpractice] imply that a doctor has carried out a destruction by negligence or in ignorance of accepted rules of medical art. The content of these rules is determined usually in a court of law by the opinion of an expert authority. This shows that an authoritative decision is unavoidable even where the juridical or political constitution is not authoritarian but democratic.

These five preliminary remarks were necessary to clarify and prepare an objective discussion of the factors which enter into a decision involving a medical destruction. We shall limit ourselves here first to such measures which produce death. I shall base this discussion therefore on the following two assumptions: 1) that there is no "medical point of view" which is self-evident and which can be applied here; 2) that there is no medical system in which measures of destruction are not already and necessarily contained.

Since, as mentioned above, a "medical order of destructibility" in the form of a law or of a formulated professional prescription does not exist so far, but since, on the other hand, destructions are a necessary part of medical practise everywhere, the problem of how a decision is arrived at may perhaps be clarified by a comparison with destructions outside the realm of medicine. We find there legal, permitted and [p. 7] prohibited destructions of human life.

Legal destructions are executions according to criminal law and war according to international law. Only in the first case is the decision arrived at by a legal procedure, by a judge and an executioner. In case of war, the individual soldier is protected by international law, whilst the initiation of war is determined by a political decision. In both cases, however, the will which makes the decision is that of an organ which is itself derived from the common will of individuals and peoples living together in political assocation. The present attempts to modify international law interest us here only in so far as here also an evolution and a status nascendi is necessary; such an initial [translation error; no "initial" in German text] condition should be possible also for the medical power of destruction. It may well be that this power must be reformed from time to time and that we are confronted at present with such a task.

Permitted destructions of life are those which can, but need not be performed [translation error: War leads over to permitted destruction of life; it can, but need not be used]. Here belong destructions in self-defense and in suicide. In both cases the decision is arrived at individually, i. e. without a legal organization. These cases are in so far akin to medical destruction, as the doctor, in many cases, is obliged to make the decision by himself: e. g. if the patient is an embryo, a minor, or an unconscious or insane person; also if his action does not suffer any delay, so that he is unable to consult other persons. These cases are analogous to the case of self-defense.

Suicide is not punishable in Germany and most other countries, whilst it is punishable in England if it is unsuccessful. It is true that in Germany also punishments for attempted suicides are said to have occurred in the case of soldiers which were considered to have committed self-mutilation. In those countries where suicide is permitted, the aiding and [p. 8] abetting of this act is likewise permitted. We have here thus a decision arrived at jointly by two persons and the same applies to the case where one person kills another upon demand of the latter; this type of killing is punishable according to paragraph 216 of criminal law. It is of special importance in the case of double suicides of lovers or married couples in which one of the two persons happens to survive.

This survey shows that two points must be considered in a decision involving the taking of life for medical reasons, viz. the legality of the action and the agreement of all persons concerned. It can be foreseen that the permissibility of the so-called euthanasia will have some connection with these two points. I shall now discuss the way in which, in my opinion, a decision for euthanasia *should* be arrived at.

If a patient suffers from an incurable disease causing unbearable pains, and sufferings, the law does not permit the doctor to terminate the patient's life, whether with or without the latter's consent. In this case many doctors nevertheless illegally and at their own risk induce death or accelerate it by the omission of excitants or stimulants. I agree with these doctors as well if it is done with as without the patient's request. But I would reserve myself the right to examine in detail each individual case as well as the moral personality of the doctor. For it may happen that the accelerated demise may be recommended by several motives, some of which may be unmoral, e. g. interests of inheritance, prevention of influence on a testament, etc.—This is a case of a formally illegal and yet materially i. e. ethically permitted euthanasia.

Euthanasia without the above conditions, i. e. the killing of "incurable psychopaths" [translation error; incurable mentally ill people] and of "worthless life" has been legalized only in the national-socialist state. Here, therefore, such actions can be considered as legal, provided one considers the relative administrative orders as laws. [p. 9] This would mean that the permissibility or prohibition is completely transferred to the juridical and political realm and falls outside the scope of medical judgment. In that case, however, it remains to decide whether these orders and laws, if such existed, are medically justified. Only after we have settled this can we return to the factors which go into the making of a decision. For the kind of decision will depend upon the kind of efficient motives which enter into it.

d) The [original: the] motives of a destruction of life ("Euthanasia") from the medical point of view.

There are three motives for such a destruction: Worthlessness of life, compassion and sacrifice.

The destruction of worthless life can be motivated only if one has positively determined the value of a certain life in particular or of life in general. Is there a medical evaluation of life? Of course: a healthy life, from the doctor's point of view, is more valuable than a sick life. Apparently then, the only possible indication for the production of disease would be that by the production of a restricted artificial disease another and graver disease can be cured or prevented. Examples are the malaria therapy of paralysis, therapies involving fever and shock, the temporal aggravation of a neurosis during psychotherapy, etc.

But how about incurable diseases? Killing because of worthlessness can in *no case* be motivated by medical reasons, since the destruction is carried out not for the sake of healing, but because of worthlessness. If, in an animal epidemic, the sick animals are killed, this is done in order to prevent the extension of the epidemic. If, however, a sick animal is killed because it has no longer any economic value, then the animal is not treated as an animal but as an economic object. Here we are confronted by the question whether medicine, in any sense whatsoever, considers man as a valuable *object*, and this question requires a detailed investiga- [p. 11! Number 10 was omitted] tion, which will be carried out below.

Apart from this, the question of the medical killing of men because of the worthlessness of their life can be answered only if one knows *who* determines *what* life as more diseased than death or lifelessness. This is possible if men consider death in general as an improvement, e. g. from a religious point of view. If then a religious patient and a religious doctor agree that death is healthier than life, then a destruction of worthless life would have to be considered. This view, however, makes sense only if temporal life as such has no value at all, but derives its value only from eternal life, for which it is a preparation. This preparation is then the proper aim and purpose of medicine and the task of medicine would be then not so much the destruction of temporal life but rather the preparation for eternal life by means of the temporal. Thus euthanasia would obtain a completely different meaning: medicine as a whole would have the purpose of euthanasia, viz. the good and correct preparation for a death which initiates eternal life.

Therefore one can say: the destruction of *worthless* life is the task of medicine as a whole, but the destruction of worthless *life* is a murder like any other, since only temporal life can be killed and since this destruction shortens or prevents the preparation for the eternal life.

On the other hand, one may say: a medicine which tries to preserve temporal life for its own sake, cannot further the preparation for eternal life and may even prevent this preparation. If the doctor assumes a value of this temporal life without regard for its eternal value(*), then indeed this temporal life may be so worthless that it deserves destruction. The attribution of values to purely biological life has therefore as to its immediate consequence its possible biological devaluation and constitutes [p. 12] thus the spiritual prerequisite for a destruction of this biological disvalue or worthlessness. Thus the purely biological concept of vital values has for its consequence the biological condemnation (in the case of an incurable disease). A purely biological concept of medicine is therefore the spiritual premise for the killing of certain patients.

We can express this also by saying that a definition of life which does not comprise a transcendental concept, a purpose or value, must lack any

(*) Procreation does not create an eternal value, e. g. a race may die out. It is therefore not permissible to assume that the procreation of a species is equivalent to the creation of eternal life.

inherent safeguards against a concept of worthless [original: worthess] life in the biological sense. Thus the door would be opened to a policy of destruction of worthless life. If, on the other hand, life is considered as essentially transcendental, then all valuations must be made exclusively with this aim in view, viz. the realization of this transcendence and the same applies to medical valuations. A medical action, therefore, should be qualified ethically as truly medical only if it is performed for the purpose of transcending the purely biological realm.

There is, however, a second quality of medical action, which likewise seems to confer upon it an ethical character: the sympathy with the patient's suffering. Medical compassion seems to satisfy the condition of transcendence which we have postulated above. For in compassion the doctor transcends the biological fact exactly in the same way and in the same sense as the patient himself. Psychical suffering is no biological value, but it transcends the fact of physical existence. On this basis one might say that by killing a patient out of compassion for his suffering one shortens the latter and thereby one transcends also his physical existence.

Others again say that the objective lack of dignity of an idiot and the sight of such a worthless life causes the spectator such torment that [p. 13] he feels the duty to remove its cause.—It is not evident how all the above can be presumed to be medical motives. Besides, in many cases, pains, nausea, vomiting and diarrhoea are sufferings useful for rendering the patient conscious of his disease and for initiating the defense against it. The doctor's compassion is of no use to the patient: his unemotional objectivity is of much greater value to the latter. If I am sick, another person's pity or compassion is for me an ambivalent or ambiguous phenomenon: it may console or insult, it may calm or excite. One feels sometimes more or less distinctly that the pity of a healthy man may be for him either a partial payment, a satisfaction, a masochistic enjoyment of pain or a pious raising of his eyes towards Heaven. The patient's suffering is not the cause but the effect of the disease and considered as a symptom, its treatment is always inferior to an aetiological [original: aethiological] therapy. There is a fundamental divergence between the aim of the patient and that of the doctor for while the former wants to be treated, the latter wants to help. This divergence cannot be removed by pity of compassion; on the contrary, it may thereby be increased and fixed; we are not there to suffer with the patient but to collaborate in his recovery. Therefore the patient may draw greater advantage from a doctor who wants to enrich himself than from one who feels pity with him. Compassion in the medical sense affects the patient only if it affects him in his innermost essential aim, i. e. as a *subject*. It is not evident at all that this subjective aim is always the removal of the objective phenomena which we call symptoms. Symptomatic treatment, as has been emphasized above, is always inferior to causal treatment. [The following sentence in the German text was not translated: Thus it can reach the point where the feelings of compassion touching the symptoms alone displace the discovery of the subject and the cause, thus preventing the individuation of the patient, thereby also preventing the cure.] It may even happen that feelings are mere sentimentality, they pave the way for a pseudo-ethics and are unsuitable to become the basis for a solidarity of and between individuals which could be the true aim of sympathy and of an ethical [p. 14] compassion. The general conclusion at which we arrive thus is this: A pity which is directed only towards a biological or psychological reality prevents the effective sympathy which must transcend both the biological fact and the psychological phenomenon.

We come thus to the third possible motive of a medical destruction of life, viz. to sacrifice. Here the motives of worthlessness and of pity are combined into one, but only the idea of sacrifice has a force sufficient to bring about an action which resembles a murder as closely as does euthanasia. The idea of sacrifice implies a special dialectic which transforms a mere motive into a law, a "should," a duty, an unescapable compulsion and a moral action. I do not wish to discuss here the religious and cultural history of sacrifice. Its active modern form appears to me to be the principle of solidarity, the precursors of which were human sacrifices and their substitutes, animal and food sacrifices. The argument based on solidarity may be formulated somewhat as follows: if the whole people is in danger of life and can be saved only by the elimination of a few single individuals, then they must be sacrificed—even though they do not appreciate this necessity. Those who are informed and able to grasp the causal connections have then not only the right but the duty to enforce this sacrifice, in other words, to kill.—How can this idea obtain a medical connotation? By assuming that the term "sick" refers now not only to individuals, but to a solidary community, a collectivity, a people or to humanity as a whole. There would exist then a social disease from which a people or humanity is suffering. This need not be merely a sum of individual diseases, as in an epidemic like typhus or malaria. A collectivity might be sick as such, in a new and peculiar way. We are then confronted with disease in an enlarged sense of the word. Comparable to the amputation of a gangrenous foot which saves this whole [p. 15] organism, the eradication of diseased components of the people would save the latter. Considered as a sacrifice both cases would be legitimate, logical and necessary as a medical intervention.

He who does not like this argument and its consequences cannot get rid of it by pathetical rhetorics or by an appeal to revealed religion and its texts, by an appeal to the idea of humanity or human rights, demanding that the task of medicine be restricted to the healing of single individuals and objecting to the transition from an individual to a collective therapy(*). We know that such a pure individualism has never existed in medicine and cannot exist there. Furthermore, the assumption of such an individualistic standpoint is nothing but a partisan vote; it may even give the impression of an attempt at authoritarian dictation. Evidently, here as in politics, the difficulty can be overcome only if we do not attempt to settle once and for all the alternative between individualism and collectivism, but try rather to combine the requirements of the individual [translation error; individuation] with that of society and thus to realize solidarity.

It is not sufficient to prove that a restriction of medicine to individual therapy is actually unfeasible and ideologically too one-sided. He who attempts this forgets, that the idea of medicine receives an enormous impetus from the prospect of its extension to human affairs in general. "To serve humanity"—that is an exalting hope which, even though it were an illusion, should not be rejected without very careful examination. It would be still more narrow-minded to underestimate the power inherent in the idea of sacrifice and I maintain that the use of this idea by national socialism has [p. 16] been of utmost importance for its power over many minds. I maintain, moreover, that the idea of sacrifice inherent in the national-socialist measures of liquidation constituted their more dangerous aspect. These events must not be judged only by looking at those who were merely thoughtless and vain tools, and they must be judged not only on the basis of their conscious but rather on the basis of their unconscious motives. It should be realized that the idea of sacrifice combines and fuses into one the ideas of killing and of salvation! It should also be realized that this fusion cannot be carried out at all in an alert, logical and rational consciousness, but *must* be performed unconsciously and irrationally. Consider then the historical forms of

(*) Compare e. g. Thure v. Uexkuell in "Zeit".

sacrifice and notice that there occurs a frequent change in the object and in the selection of sacrifice; Abraham sacrifices his son, Agamemnon his daughter, Christian theology God's son, the church in the sacrifice of mass the host and the wine; in war, however, the sons of the country and in revolutions the carriers of a social idea are sacrificed. And yet the form of sacrifice, viz. [original: fiz.] liberty through death, has remained the same throughout. It is evident that even those who see themselves condemned unjustly to death, think of themselves as sacrificial victims. Sacrifice is the only possibility by which right and wrong can be combined and neutralized. That is why in the modern world war has remained the most common and persistent application of the idea of sacrifice and he who wishes to abolish war must realize that he must either abolish the idea of sacrifice or else create a new form and outlet for it.

These considerations were necessary in order to clarify completely the problem of medical destruction. For it is conceivable that we are confronted not so much with a phenomenon beyond the scope [p. 17] of medicine, a heterogeneous intrusion from without, but rather [omitted: an alienation,] a degeneration of medicine itself. This might seem to some to be mere quibbling, but it really is not. I have heard it said: there have been people in politics who, by terror or seduction, have made some doctors behave in an unmedical way; these doctors have thereupon transgressed the boundaries of medicine; that, however, is no real concern of medicine itself. This argument, however, is fallacious. For what kind of medicine was it which could be terrorized or seduced to such a degree? There must have been some foundation for it in medicine itself. It could be that medicine itself participates essentially in the spirit of sacrifice, but that it had lost consciousness of this fact. And it could also be that the politicians have forced medicine to perform a sacrifice without knowing what a genuine sacrifice is. Thus this meeting between politics and medicine was not external and haphazard, but on the contrary inherently probable. But in that case the state of affairs is exactly the contrary from the one implied in the statement which says that the doctors have transgressed their boundaries. Medicine had become restricted to a scientific technique which treated man only as an object instead of considering him as an individual who transcends itself in and into a society. Therefore medicine had lost the idea and the practice of sacrifice and thus it became susceptible when this idea was forced upon it from outside in a degenerate and mendacious form.

I therefore emphatically deny that it is correct to say that those doctors have merely transgressed their proper limits. One should say rather that they have transgressed them in a wrong direction. In my opinion this was due as well to a personal inadequacy as to a mis- [p. 18] taken idea of medicine in general. A solidarity could not be established nor could a real sacrifice be realized by the way in which a policy of extermination under the guise of euthanasia and in the name of a sacrifice was carried out. Neither the worthlessness of life, nor compassion nor the idea of sacrifice in the form in which it was applied are therefore capable of justifying from the medical point of view the so-called euthanasia of the national-socialist regime. But it appears that the effectiveness of the idea of sacrifice does belong into the realm of medicine and that it is incumbent upon modern medicine to develop it.

e) Individuality and Totality.

The question which is most important for the necessary and moral development of the idea of sacrifice in medicine is this: who sacrifices whom? When we have demanded above that a sacrifice has to be performed in a spirit [original: spirity] of solidarity, this implied already that the sacrifice must be conceived as a common undertaking. But since individual death is indivisible in so far as it is a physical death, there arises immediately the problem: who is sacrificed? There is one who kills and one who is killed and thus all the problems of murder, capital punishment, law, morality, religion, and metaphysics are involved. It is not wrong to attempt a solution of these problems on the basis of the spirit of medicine, but it would be wrong on the part of medicine to leave them to other sciences or disciplines and to consider them as extraneous to medicine. That this is correct can be seen from the fact that when non-medical viewpoints were adopted in medical actions of destruction [p. 19] they frequently produced medically unjustifiable actions. The problem is evidently to harmonize the claims of the individual and those of a community in their totality and the method chosen for this purpose, the way in which the decision is arrived at, will be determined by those values which are intended to survive in the final count.

Since most men voluntarily do not like to die, the application of some kind of *superiority*, the application of force against the will or without the will of those to be killed enters into any definition of "euthanasia." It is true that suicide has not infrequently been committed as a sacrifice for others; e. g. when somebody who is doomed politically kills himself in order to save his family from the burden of prosecution, punishment, etc. But the killing of incurable psychopaths [translation error; incurable mentally ill people] recommended by doctors, especially psychiatrists (and not only national socialist ones) is based on an application of force by superior power. I have explained already that worthlessness of life and pity cannot justify a medical killing and that only the idea of sacrifice, though in a form which we have yet to determine, *might* contain a medical motivation. If now a superior force is required, it is evident, as experience shows, that this force which attempts an equilibrium between an individual and a group must originate outside of medicine.

The initial use of force is made already by the internment of a psychopath [translation error: mentally ill person], by the interference with his liberty. It would be wrong to see in the diagnosis "psychopathological" [translation error: mentally ill] nothing but a majority vote. The internment is motivated by the danger which the insane constitutes for other persons as well as for himself. But besides and above this, there is the expert authority which decides whether the case is psychopathological or purely criminal. If an insane is to be killed, [p. 20] he is confronted not merely by a majority, but by an authority which, besides, possesses a superior power. In order to determine what kind of an authority this is, one must know how it has obtained its authority and its power. Since we are concerned here only with a medical indication for the killing, it would seem that a medical killing is inherently impossible. But the situation is not as simple as that. Imagine a case in which some persons may only become or remain healthy if a certain other person dies, then this would perhaps constitute a medical indication for his death. Such an indication would exist also if without his death a number of others would have to die. This is the justification for the internment of a psychopathic mass murderer or in general of a socially dangerous psychopath [translation error: mentally ill person]: but this example shows also that internment is sufficient and killing superfluous.

The above cases show already that the problem of harmonization between the individual and society is a problem of mutuality. Society may demand that a psychopath be rendered harmless, but not that he be killed; those who advocate killing are obliged to rely on other motives than the prevention of danger. They are obliged to invoke other motives because they do not want to accept mutuality in their relations with the insane and refuse to renounce their own authoritarian superiority. This avoidance of mutuality is a self-assertion which tries to mask itself by a devaluation of the patient, rationalized by appeals to science, truth or a feeling of human dignity. Science says: the psychopath [translation error: mentally ill person] is abnormal; truth says: he is mentally confused (i. e. insane); dignity says: he is no man, but subhuman. These devaluations, whether legitimate or not, have in any case not been obtained in mutual relations with the patient. The verdict is not derived from dialectic contact with [p. 21] this individual patient but from other sources.

It is now time to define what is meant here by mutuality and by dialectic contact. We mean thereby something which does not presuppose a superiority but only tries to find one. There can be found in social life innumerable conditions in which an authoritarian decision is inevitable and even a democratic or communistic society does not attempt to avoid them. The reason why such an authoritarian decision becomes questionable when life and death are in the balance, is that here mutuality no longer exists: one is killed, the other lives and therefore this decision is always: you or me, in their utmost totality. Killing can therefore never be based on mutuality. The question arises whether this case should be made the starting-point for other, milder ones, or whether, on the contrary, it should be considered as a rare and abnormal border case of social life. I am of the opinion that this case is fundamental for the understanding of life as a whole, that every life is both individual and social and that only on this basis a moral critique of human actions and motives can be achieved. Medicine in no way makes an exception and this means that its authority is justifiable only under but not above the relation of mutuality between doctor and patient.

Once this is accepted, the prospects of a medical justification of so-called "euthanasia" become very unfavourable. It is evident that all those who have recommended, ordered or performed it, have not asked the patient whether or not he wants to die and to die *thus*. It is moreover evident that they have not conceded to him or that they have not believed him capable of a decision of equal value. It is also evident that the opinion of the people has not been asked. Neither has a majority been determined by vote, nor has an elected parliament been [p. 22] heard, nor has one attempted to determine the attitude of the doctors or of their duly authorized representatives. The primary intention was that of eradication and selection of advisers was secondary and adapted to this primary aim.—A totally different question, however, is whether such means would have made possible at all a harmonization between individual and society. [In the translation a dittography follows: I even concede as a harmonization between individual and society.] I even concede as a hypothesis, that this intention could have existed and that it would have been commendable if it had existed. Dr. Mitscherlich is perfectly right when he says that events have shown what a bad form of society a dictatorship really is. But even then one may ask whether a hypothetical good dictatorship would have been capable of solving the problem of harmonization. For we have said above that the question "you or me" is unavoidable in any society. The question which we must answer then is, what form a medical decision, which also is unavoidable, should assume.

The answer to this question may be given as follows: If the alternative is between life and death, the question cannot at all refer to medicine as it is, but as it *should* become. At least a number of those who gave orders to medicine and of those who carried them out were conscious of this fact. They felt the immanence of a great new epoch and therefrom derived the courage [omitted: from a long-term perspective] to undertake such hazardous deeds. This is the reason why they now—clumsily enough—call themselves idealists. Paradoxically they are as well victims and collaborators of an inhuman medicine which they have learned as protestants against it [translation error: which they have learned as well as those who were protestants against such a medicine]. They are both.

In other words: the equilibrium or harmony between individual and human society as a whole cannot be achieved forcibly by one individual [p. 23] who arrogantly claims to represent the community. The same applies when a doctor, without mutuality, ventures to decide as an authority about life or death or even lesser values, in the name of medicine, science, truth or human dignity. It is true that Schiller says: Life is not the highest of all values. But he forgets to mention that also innocence—according to him a higher value—may decide the alternative between life or death. In simpler words: Superiority cannot produce solidarity in the medical realm. It always has been and is presumptuous to attempt a solution of this problem by an appeal to some superior court. Every judge must decide for himself what punishment should correspond to such presumption; but whatever the decision, it will be a decision concerning presumptiousness.

I believe that once we have got to this point, all other difficulties are only of secondary importance. For instance, the question of free will. It may happen that a man volunteers to sacrifice himself; he may volunteer on the front for a patrol, for an attacking group or for a rearguard action. In the case of insanity, suicide may be interpreted as a voluntary sacrifice. The one who survives will then, in all honesty, have only a feeling of guilt, for it is evident that the other man's sacrifice confers upon him a rank which was beyond the survivor. Here solidarity has failed and any praise given to the other's sacrifice is simultaneously a confession of one's own flight from self-sacrifice. Considered rationally, euthanasia, from the point of view of those who practiced and who passively permitted it, is a complete failure. It can be said that euthanasia is an attempt at solution of a real problem, but that to solve it wrongly is a guilt and that to avoid any attempt at a solution is participation in a guilt. Considered from [p. 24] the point of view of sacrifice, every man who does not sacrifice himself deserves death and even the judge must decide whether and how he may estimate the guilt of the accused as greater than his own. In this, he need not consider a medical justification for euthanasia; for, in my view, there is none. A doctor who would invoke a medical motive would have to show that his attitude is "fair," i. e. based on mutuality and not authoritarian, i. e. based on a feeling of superiority. One can say that any appeal to the prevalent right of a majority, of the healthy, the efficient or the racially preferred, does not create a solidarity, for this can be based only on mutuality. This means that the "sacrifice" of another is never a real sacrifice and that the latter can be demonstrated only in the sacrifice of one's self.

f) The inviolability of life (The concept of "habeas corpus" in medicine).

It is impossible to speak with any clarity of a medical indication for euthanasia without stating who the man is whom it refers to. It is therefore confusing to speak of an "inviolability of life" as if the commandment "thou shalt not kill" referred to man's life and not to the man himself. It is just as misleading to consider a physical destruction as prohibited but a psychical one as permissible or as unnoticeable and indemonstrable [translation error: optional or not determinable]. If one holds correctly that certain interventions are unmoral in general or from the medical point of view, this conviction is not based on any law concerning only the physical integrity, but rather on the legitimate feeling that man *as man* has an inviolability which must not be infringed. Man, however, can be determined only as a man amongst men, i. e. socially, on the basis of mutuality. There is thus no abstract inviolability of [p. 25] life, but if one accepts a risk of life or if a life is destroyed, this should only be done on the basis of mutuality. It is maintained that an insane is unable to participate in this mutuality and that the doctor, therefore, must dispose of him somewhat in the manner of a trustee. Assuming that this be correct, the trustee would have to arrive at his decision on the basis of an optimal and not of an inferior kind of solidarity. Hence the indignation of the relatives against nazi euthanasia; they were ignored. If a doctor believed that Hitler incorporated the highest or best solidarity, then he would have been right from his point of view. One cannot accuse him of an infringement of any law of inviolability; for there is only an inviolability of man and all arguments for an individual, familial or democratic solidarity are already invalidated by his belief in the Fuehrer.

It is thus evident that in national socialism there cannot exist any medical indication for euthanasia, for the medical idea is absorbed there by the idea of leadership and is unconditionally subservient to the latter. Hitler was not only the political commander in chief but he was also the chief doctor. Some of those doctors were in this situation or at least believed so.

We can speak of a medical indication only if the medical idea is present [omitted: *at all*]. This idea, in my opinion, is a prescription to help sick persons. The inviolability of man, however, must be preserved in spite of any medical intervention in the function of body or soul. Usually this is achieved by the freedom in the choice of a doctor, by the confidence which the patient has in him, etc. If an insane were no longer capable of this mutuality, then a trusteeship would be necessary and a violation of his life would be permissible, since he is no longer a man.

[p. 26] It can be concluded that under all circumstances the doctor must preserve the inviolability of man, but this still leaves open the question whether an incurable insane is a man or can no longer become one.

g) Is an incurable insane a man?

If one puts this question to a number of normal, healthy persons one will hear the most conflicting opinions. What decision shall we take? I am of the opinion that also the insane still is, in a larger sense of the word, a man (see under 1 b), but I do not propose this view as an authoritarian decision. I would, however, be inclined to analyze the motives of all those who declare an insane as a non-human and am prepared to show that they are acting from non-medical and non-human motives. The decisive argument is this, that anybody who denies human essence to an insane thereby shows himself to be inhuman. And this implies that his verdict is no longer medical.

I do not presuppose here that every doctor is clear in his mind about this point. But if the question of guilt is raised and if one condemns a treatment which takes the patient for a mere object, then the accused is not a certain doctor, but rather a certain type of medicine; and the degree and scope of the guilt must be determined on this basis. The demonstration, that an incurable insane is a man can be made inductively and approximately on the basis of a great many single observations, which will be sufficiently convincing for most doctors and laymen. Then there would remain only a distinction between human and unhuman insanes. But who should make such a distinction and is science capable of making it? It would be not only impossible, but even unnecessary.

The conclusion at which we thus arrive is, that an insane is also [p. 27] a man and that a medical euthanasia under the pretext that he is not, is illegitimate.

h) Summary: A medical indication of so-called euthanasia is impossible.

I was able to find only a single case in which the shortening of life through a medical action or its omission can be recognized as ethical: the case of a person dying painfully from carcinoma. Only this case merits the use of the term euthanasia in its original meaning. The law does not permit it even here and yet I could not vote in favor of the cancellation or modification of paragraph 216 of criminal law. The doctor, by doing something legally prohibited and thus exposing himself to danger, demonstrates thereby that mutuality which has been shown to be the prerequisite of every ethical action. This is a type of human action for which, so far at least, a legal formulation has been impossible. Such an action would be more akin to the commandment: Love thy neighbor as thyself. The so-called euthanasia which we have discussed so far does not deserve the name and cannot be justified medically. Its restriction to the incurably insane does not make sense since the diagnosis of incurability and the motives of worthlessness, of pity and of sacrifice apply equally or even more distinctly to other diseases. The killing of all such cases would then be perfectly consistent and has, as a matter of fact, been carried out.

The grounds on which we have rejected the so-called euthanasia were of two kinds: First, its motives, viz. worthlessness, pity [original: ptiy] and sacrifice were shown to be unmedical and unethical. Secondly, the ways and means by which the decision is arrived at has been shown likewise to be unmedical and unethical. Both of these arguments, however, do not yet [p. 28] exclude the possibility that a different motivation and a better way of determination might still justify a euthanasia. But such a possibility is excluded by our refusal to subscribe to a type of medicine which ascribes a value to biological life as such and for its own sake. Only a medicine which values not the mere fact of life, but man as a person, is a healing medicine; it must transcend the purely biological facts. Now it is true that death is such a transcendence. In this sense, medicine as a whole and every single medical action should transcend the biological realm. But they must be oriented not towards death as such, but towards the transcendation. Otherwise the aim of medicine would be to kill, which is an evident absurdity.

On the other hand, we have seen that the idea of sacrifice is not extraneous to medicine and will continue to remain one of its constitutive elements throughout its further development. The question arises then, what consequences this would have for a medicine whose therapy is directed towards the support of biological life. We shall discuss this in the following section.

[. . .]

Still Ransoming the First-Born Sons?

Pidyon Haben and Its Survival in the Jewish Tradition

YAAKOV ARIEL, University of North Carolina

Introduction: The Survival of an "Unlikely" Ritual

Observers of contemporary religious practices are intrigued when encountering a rather unexpected Jewish ritual: ransoming of the first-born sons. *Pidyon Haben*, ransoming of the first-born sons, who, theoretically, would otherwise become servants of God, or more precisely, the priestly class, has survived since, at least, the Roman period to the present. Examining the roots of the ritual, its purpose, the actual manner in which it has been practiced, and the changes it has undergone throughout the centuries, can shed light on some key institutions within the Jewish tradition. These include: popular beliefs in the need to protect newborns, the shifting position of the priesthood after the destruction of the Temple, and the relationship that has existed in post-Temple Judaism between the ancient priestly claims to mediate between God and his people and the actual lack of any significant role for priests after the Temple was gone. The ritual also illuminates the position of women in the Jewish tradition in relation to that of men, as evidenced by matrilineal descent versus patrilineal descent. It offers a window into the competing definitions of who qualifies to be recognized as a "Jewish child," and the differences in the performance of the ritual among different communities of Jews. Most importantly, the ritual serves as an example of "irrational," beliefs and practics that have survived the impact of the Enlightenment on the Jewish tradition. Such rituals are rooted in concepts of "purity and danger" that have a strong hold on the Jewish religious community, even centuries after the cultural milieus and social structures that gave rise to the rituals have disappeared.

The Roots of the Ritual

One can only speculate on the historical roots of the ritual for the ransoming of the first-born. Medieval and modern Jews have offered a number of explanations for the origin of *Pidyon Haben*.[1] However, there are no historical documents that can offer any definite picture of the origins of the ritual.[2] A number of short biblical passages state the need to dedicate to God the first-borns among agricultural produce, animals, and humans. Other biblical passages order the Israelites to ransom their sons. Both Numbers and Deuteronomy contain statements to the effect that all first-borns in cattle and humans belong to God. Deut 15:19–20, for example, states that one must consecrate to God all first-born sheep and cattle. One should bring these first-born animals to the only Temple, sacrifice, and then eat them there, thus fulfilling one's duty to God and enjoying the meat at the same time. Biblical passages in Leviticus, Exodus, and Numbers do not, however, offer consistent rationale for the ransoming of the first-born sons, leaving readers to wonder as to its origin and significance. At what exact moment in Israelite history the "ransoming" began remains a mystery. Did it come to replace actual sacrifices of first-borns to the Lord? Did it come to replace an offering of sons to the service of the God of Israel? Did it come to offer an alternative to cults that the Israelites were tempted to join in spite of their God's warning that He "has not conceived or imagined such practices"?

In establishing the origins of the ritual of the ransoming of the first-born, one cannot disregard the reality that the sacrifice of children was practiced in the ancient Mediterranean world, for example, among such groups as the Phoenicians, until the Roman Empire put an end to it. The Israelites were well aware of that practice, if not directly influenced by it. Deut 11:30, for example, condemns the worshiping of other gods,

---

[1] For example, Israel Meir Lau, *Practical Judaism* (Tel Aviv: Masada, 1978), 324–27; Burt Kagan, "The Redemption of the First Born Son," www.jewishmag.com/51mag/pidyanhaben/pidyanhaben.htm; Shraga Simmons, "Pidyon Ha'Ben: Explaining the Jewish Ceremony of Buying a Baby Boy for Five Silver Coins," www.aish.com/literacy/lifecycle/pidon_haben.asp.

[2] On child sacrifice in biblical times, see Hermann Leberecht Strack, *The Jew and Human Sacrifice: Human Blood and Jewish Ritual* (trans. H. Blanchamp; New York: Bloch, 1909); Roland De Vaux, *Studies in Old Testament Sacrifice* (Cardiff: University of Wales Press, 1964), 63–90; Robert J. Thompson, *Penitence and Sacrifice in Early Israel Outside the Levitical Law: An Examination of the Fellowship Theory of Early Israelite Sacrifice* (Leiden: E.J. Brill, 1963).

emphasizing that their worship includes the sacrifice of children, a custom that made the Lord, the true God of Israel, angry. This statement offers information on the culture in which the Israelites of the First Commonwealth lived, which included practices that the authors of biblical compilations, such as Numbers, Deuteronomy, Isaiah, and Jeremiah, militated against. There are more than hints that the Israelites sacrificed children to "foreign" gods. Jeremiah laments over such practices, pointing to them as the worst sin (Jer 7:31). There is no such mention in Amos, a prophet who preceded Jeremiah, and who, no less emphatically than Jeremiah, criticized the Israelites in both the Northern and Southern kingdoms for their disloyalty to their true God and for their insensitivity to social injustice. Yet Deut 14:1 demands that the Israelites follow God's commandments in a straight-forward manner, neither adding nor detracting anything. One detects more than a hint here of discouraging the Israelites from establishing or performing the sacrifice of children.

The first Book of Samuel tells the story of Hanna, a woman from Ramatayim-Tsofim. Happily married, she was nonetheless unable to bear children. Hanna pleads and prays, asking for a child, whom she promises to offer to God. She offers her son, before she even conceives him, on the basis of a *neder*, a promise contingent upon God's favorable action. After giving birth to her son, Samuel, and allowing for a few years of upbringing, Hanna presents her son to the high priest, Eli, and leaves Samuel with him. According to the biblical tale, Samuel became a member of Eli's household, close to him as a son, but there is no mention of other servant-children, offered by other parents, to the service of God, who might have worked in the Tabernacle side-by-side with Samuel. In fact, the Hebrew Bible (Josh 9) offers an explanation for the existence of a permanent class of Temple servants, the Gibeonites, an ethnic group, who, according to the biblical story, were destined to perform perpetually the menial tasks in the Temple. In addition to the Gibeonites, about whom one hears little more in the biblical text, Deuteronomy makes the claim that the Levites, an entire Israelite tribe, had turned into a priestly class, assigned to the service of God, in lieu of each Israelite family dedicating its first-born sons to God.

In sum, how does one make sense of the contradictory biblical statements and try to determine when and how the ritual of the ransoming of the first-born son evolved? Child sacrifices, or offerings of children to temple services existed among Mediterranean cultures in biblical times, and such practices influenced the Israelites. While the actual sacrifice of infants stirred strong opposition, and was conceived by the writers of the Hebrew sacred texts to be an "alien" practice, exercised in contrast to the wishes of the Israelite God, it seemed reasonable to the Israelites that first-borns, like first fruits and first-born animals, should be dedicated to God, at least symbolically. One can speculate that the ransoming of the first-borns had been introduced by the priestly class in Jerusalem as part of a larger agenda, namely one that came to give the Temple in Jerusalem and its custodians, the priests, more power, as well as additional sources of income.[3] The ritual of the ransoming of the first-born sons in pre-Mishnaic times may have served two purposes at the same time, reflecting a wish to offer an alternative to the sacrifice of children while benefiting the priestly class and adding to the prestige of the priests and the wealth of the Temple.

The amazing thing about the ransoming of the first-borns is not that such a ritual developed in biblical times, when child sacrifice, or offering of children to gods, were practiced by a number of neighboring communities, if not by the Israelites themselves, and were part of the era's cultural framework. What is remarkable about the procedure is that it survived beyond biblical times, long after the Temple was destroyed and its priestly class dispersed, and continued during eras in which Jews had no recollection, not to mention inclination, of offering their first-borns to God. Indeed, Jewish self-perception has developed into viewing the Jewish tradition as a culture that had distanced itself early on from human sacrifice, and later on, gave up on the sacrifice of animals, as well.[4] One would have expected Jews to erase all traces of the offering of children to God and give up on a ritual that came to exempt first-borns from being offered, even if only symbolically, to the service of God. Yet, the ritual has survived, and so has the role of priests in performing it and accepting the ransom. How can one explain the persistence of such an archaic ritual with "savage" and "irrational" elements? And how can one explain the persistent role of priests, whose other duties had become redundant?

---

3 Cf. Moshe Weinfeld, *Deuteronomy and the Deuteronomistic School* (Oxford: Clarendon Press, 1972).

4 Moshe Ben Maimon (Maimonides), *Mishne Tora* (Berlin: Horev, 1926), book 7, chapter 11, 122–23.

Jewish Priesthood and *Pidyon Haben*

The ransoming of the first-born sons has remained the only ritual in which a *kohen*, a priest, has to officiate. The destruction of the Temple in 70 C. E. brought about a sharp decline in the status of the *kohanim*, the ancient priestly class, their function disappeared, and whatever priestly duties and privileges remained, they became mainly symbolic. The rabbis took over as the custodians of the tradition and its official interpreters, constructing a text-oriented, non-priestly, post-Temple tradition. Judaism has maintained a polite nod towards the priestly class, and priests have not been completely banished. *Kohanim* have been careful to retain their priestly identity. They adopted names that have pointed to their priestly origins. They, as well as rabbinical sages and Jewish laypersons, in general, might have assumed that one day the Temple would be rebuilt and the priests would be called again to fulfill their ancient duties. The laws governing priests as a separate, superior, caste of pure beings have remained in effect. These include special laws of purity, as befits a caste of Brahmins, the ancient mediators between God and his people. Priests, for example, are forbidden to touch bodies of dead humans or to enter cemeteries. But such laws of priestly purity do not reflect the *kohanim*'s very limited position in the post-Temple Jewish tradition.

As a special courtesy, symbolic in nature, toward this ancient order, *kohanim* are the first to be "called to the Torah" during weekly Torah readings, and are thus asked to read the first paragraph of the weekly Torah portion. On occasion, *kohanim* bless the congregation with the priestly blessing. But these duties can also be performed by non priests, and synagogue services can take place without *kohanim*. In essence, priests have no authority and no real function, as they do not perform any more priestly sacramental duties. Post-Temple Judaism has turned all Jewish adult males into priests who can, indeed are commanded, to perform sacraments. Regular, non-priest, Israelites consecrate wine and bread, bring in the Sabbath, differentiate between the sacred and the profane when the Sabbath and the holidays come and go, preside over the celebration of holidays, and bless their children with a paternal blessing on their own. Synagogue services are designed in a manner that allows regular members of the community, to perform all duties, including reading the Torah, preaching, and presiding over services. Jews conduct even major life-cycle events and rites of passage, such as *Berit Milah*, *Bar Mitzvah,* weddings, and divorces, funerals, burials, and memorials on their own, without the aid of priests. Indeed, the priestly performance of *Pidyon Haben* is the only sacrament that priests still perform, and that regular Israelites cannot perform in a priest's stead. It is the one and only function, albeit mostly symbolic, for which a priest needs to be present. The explanation lies in the nature of the ritual.

The Nature of the Ritual

Pidyon Haben is by no means a central ritual, and it has probably never been one. In fact, only a minority of Jews, whether observant, traditionalist, or secular, have the opportunity to perform the *mitzvah*, for the simple fact that the ritual has been interpreted in a manner that limits its scope to only a fraction of the overall population of Jewish children.[5]

Ransoming of the first-born is reserved for boys, excluding all girls, yet it relates only to those boys who are the first ever to come out of their mother's womb.[6] Boys born after the birth of an elder sibling are excluded from that category. Likewise, even first-born boys born to mothers who have had miscarriages or given birth to still-borns are not considered first-borns, in the sense that they do not need to be ransomed. Boys born after the birth of girls, or after the birth of babies who died in infancy, or after unsuccessful pregnancies, are not in need of "ransoming." This points to the popular rationale that has sustained the ritual and kept it alive. It is about protecting babies from unfortunate occurrences, and families that had already suffered and paid their sad tribute are in lesser need of protection. The evil spirits who are waiting to spoil the good fortune of a family have already caused their damage. First-born sons are particularly precious, and therefore more vulnerable, and need more protection than girls or sons who are not first-borns. Modern or post-modern people might see no difference between first- or second-borns, or between boys and girls, and in fact adore and spoil their young females. But pre-modern Jews, as well as other nations, took a different approach. In a charming moment in the movie version of *The Good Earth*, the heroes, remembering that the evil spirits are out there to get healthy first-born boys, turned around and declared loudly that the child is "merely a girl," and an ugly one, too.

---

[5] Cf. Bekhor Ha'adam, *Encyclopedia Talmudit* 3 (ed. Shlomo Zivan; Jerusalem: Mosad Harav Cook, 1951), 286–93.

[6] "Tractate Bekhorot," *The Mishna* (trans. Jacob Neusner; New Haven and London: Yale University Press, 1988), 803.

In a traditional society in which sons inherited their fathers' professions and reputations, they were the pride of their parents and the rock on which parents hoped to rely for support and comfort in old age. In eras long before the invention of Social Security, pension funds, retirement plans, and savings accounts, parents expected their elder boys to work with their fathers and gradually take their place. Daughters, on the other hand, had lesser long-range value. Parents had to provide them with a dowry, gaining little in return. They would go away, joining their husbands' families, and would see to their in-laws' comfort. Neither the family's pride, nor its well-being, depended on daughters as much as on sons, with first-borns serving as their families' flagships. They needed extra protection. The evil spirits were about to attack them first.

Jewish lore is fully informed about evil spirits and their danger. There has always been Samael, an arch-demon and co-conspirator of Lilith, the chief female demon. Lilith is of particular danger to mothers and their newly born babies. Lilith, by way of introduction, was Adam's first wife, whom he rejected, and who has not missed an opportunity ever since to harm the descendants of Eve, Adam's preferred, established wife who became the mother of all humans.[7] Lilith had established her own chthonic dynasty. Unwittingly, Adam and his male descendants have provided Lilith and other female spirits with the means to multiply and fill the shadow earth. Every time that men have sexual pleasure other than with their legitimate female partners, they procreate negatively, fertilizing unseen female demons, and providing them with the means to produce offspring.[8] The jealous and revengeful Lilith is not alone. Agrat bat Mahlat, for example, is also a shrewd and dangerous attacker, leading men astray. Jews were not alone in their understanding that evil spirits are around and can hurt mothers and children. Likewise, Jewish sages were certain that women had means to protect themselves that men do not possess.[9]

With the kind of medical treatment available to women and children until the twentieth century, one should not wonder that Jews have been afraid of demons and blamed them for bringing death or disability in

[7] Cf. Hayyim Nahman Bialik and Yehoshua Hana Rawnitzky, *Sefer Ha'aggadah: Mivhar Ha'aggadot Shebatalmud Ubamidrashim* (Tel Aviv: Devir, 1960), vol. 1, part 1.

[8] Gershom G. Scholem, *Elements of the Kabbalah and its Symbolism* (Jerusalem: Bialik Press, 1977), 148–52.

[9] Rebecca M. Lesses, "Exe(o)rcising Power: Women as Sorceresses, Exorcists, and Demonesses in Babylonian Jewish Society of Late Antiquity," *JAAR* 69 no. 2 (June 2001): 343–76.

numbers that, in relative terms, are unimaginable today. It was prudent for women giving birth, whether in Germany or in Yemen, to protect themselves with reassuring amulets, calling upon God and his supportive angels to defend them and their children. "Milefanai Michael, Ahorai Raphael uLetzidi Shehinat El," reads a popular amulet, which is still in use. ("Michael is in front of me, Raphael behind me, and on my side the presence of God.")[10] Other measures could also help: a red string, preferably one that has measured the tombstone of a saint, could be attached to a delivering woman's bed, or to that of the newly born. Garlic held in a small cloth over the bed can offer additional protection. Like the fictional Chinese couple in *The Good Earth*, Jews are careful to take protective measures when talking about their children. One should never compliment one's kids, or, for that matter, any other kids one wishes well. A good means of protection would be to add "kein ein hore" (with no evil eye, or with no evil intention) to any positive description of good health, intelligence, beauty, or success. "A beautiful baby, kein ein hore," would be a good way to describe a pretty baby. Another option would be to spit, symbolically, as if to erase the said word. "A beautiful baby, tfu, tfu, tfu."

Such measures, intended to protect mothers and babies, were in wide use, until Jewish proponents of the Enlightenment decided that they represented a superstitious and anachronistic stage in the development of Judaism, and actively militated against such practices, pushing them under the Jewish rug. The author would like to recommend, however, that persons interested in the history of Jewish lore and customs visit Jewish museums, where religious objects, including amulets, are exhibited. Exhibitions in the Jewish museum in Berlin, or the Jewish museum in Prague provide ample evidence as to how wide-spread such practices were among European Jewry in pre-Enlightenment times. Such measures have had a strong hold in other Jewish diasporas, such as Morocco or Yemen, as well. When rabbinical scholars in Yemen in the nineteenth century, influenced by the European Enlightenment, and perhaps also by the neighboring Moslem Wahabi movement, attempted to "re-educate" Yemenite Jews and fight "superstitious," kabbalist beliefs, they caused bitter resentment and a split in the community.[11] Such old-

[10] The author last saw such an amulet on the door of a family with a newly born baby in Chapel Hill in 2000.

[11] Haim Shabazi, "The Dor-Dea Controversy in Yemen," in *The Jews of Yemen in Modern Times* (ed. Josef Tobi; Jerusalem: Zalamn Shazar Center, 1984), 123–36.

time practices as carrying protective amulets, visiting holy shrines, as well as other *segulot*, means of protection, have persisted as before.

The Procedure of Ransoming

Many of the rules and regulations governing the ritual of *Pidyon Haben* are stated in the Talmud in *Tractate Bekhorot*, whose compilation began in the first century, B. C. E. The rules of approaching a *kohen*, any *kohen*, for ransoming one's son seems unmistakably designed for an exilic community spread around the globe, with no priestly center to which Jews could make a pilgrimage to redeem their sons. While all other payments and presents to *kohanim* were abolished with the destruction of the Temple, medieval rabbinical authorities declared *Pidyon Haben* an exception, a rite practiced in all times, all over the glove, thus accommodating it to the exilic reality of Jewish life.[12] Medieval rabbinical commentators, notably Maimonides, reaffirmed the regulations and simplified the rules, which found their way into the *Shulkhan Arukh*, the commonly acknowledged compilation of Jewish law, which came about at the end of the Middle Ages. Talmudic and Medieval compilations turned what was probably a custom into an obligation, *mitzvah*,[13] and setting rules and regulations for the celebration.

While the first-borns in need of ransoming are defined as live boys who have come first from their mother's womb, it is the duty of the father to ransom his son. In fact, the interplay between matriarchal and patriarchal status and duties reaches a peak in the performance of the ritual. While it is her first-born son, the mother is not obliged to be present at the execution of the ritual, and the ritual, at least theoretically, is a patriarchal scene, in the sense that the actual ransoming is a discussion between the father and the *kohen*, the priest. At the same time, the ritual is reserved to the mother's first-born son, even if the father already has another son from a previous wife who has already been ransomed, or if the designated father is not even the actual biological father. If a father died or moved away, the guardian or stepfather should ransom the mother's first-born son. As a last resort, a first-born son may ransom himself when he has reached adolesence. As mentioned earlier, the ritual takes place in the presence of a *kohen*, a priest who needs to officiate

[12] Cf. Shlomo Gantzfried, *Kitzur Shulkhan Arukh* (New York: Hebrew Publication, 1926), 45–46.

[13] *Mishne Tora*, book 7, chapter 11, 122–23.

in the ceremony. In the Ashkenazi, the Central and Eastern European, version of the ritual, a conversation needs to take place between the father ransoming his son and the priest. In the Sephardic tradition, that of Asian, African, and Southern and Western European Jews, the exchange between the priest and the father is minimal.

The father tells the *kohen* that his son is a first-born to his Israelite mother. The *kohen* asks if the father wishes to redeem the child. The father answers in the affirmative and offers the priest five pieces of silver. The pieces weigh between 90 and 130 grams, or 3.2 ounces and 4.8 ounces, each. Five silver dollars would do. If one cannot obtain silver coins, one can pay with banknotes or other means of payment. The flexibility of the actual monetary amount of the ransom, and the variety of the means of paying, point to the fact that the ritual is not about money, but about "protection." The parents are "ransoming" their son, and by so doing, making him less vulnerable. He is now properly "free," and therefore better protected from the forces of evil. Not surprisingly, the offering of the silver is symbolic, and the *kohen* returns the money to the parents. This development emphasizes the symbolic nature of the ritual, which is not about additional income for the priest, but about the usage of whatever means priests still have to offer further protection to first-born sons. The *kohen* is using his priestly powers as an intermediary between humans and God to set the first-born free from whatever obligation they have to serve God.

The ritual can be performed anywhere, but in actuality *Pidyon Haben* has turned into a small celebration, a gathering of family and friends in the parents' home, a month after the child's birth. There is no short supply in *kohanim*, and the family often invites a *kohen* who is also a friend or a relative, and so friends and family come to watch and rejoice while pieces of silver are offered to the *kohen*, and then given back. The *kohen* blesses the child with the priestly blessing, "May God bless you and protect you," and adds, "God is your protector, your right side shadow, God will protect you from all evil, and save your life."[14] By celebrating while the son is being ransomed, the parents, at times unwittingly, declare that their first-born sons are special. Jews perform more celebrations on behalf of their sons: *Shalom Zahar* (Peace be upon you, son) on the first Sabbath after a son's birth, a *Berit Milah* (a covenant of circumcision) on the eighth day after a son's birth, and *Pidyon Haben*, the

---

[14] Cf. the *Siddur*, the Jewish prayerbook, *Seder Pidyon Haben*.

ransoming of the first-born sons, about a month or so after birth. Like *Berit*, *Pidyon Haben* has inspired Jewish artists and artisans to create special ceremonial objects, such as plates on which to place the sons or the silver.[15]

The ritual of ransoming excludes, at least in theory, sons born to non-Jewish mothers. In the rabbinical tradition, full membership in the Jewish community has officially been defined by the mother being a member of the community, or, alternatively, by the mother of the children undergoing a ritual of conversion. There is reason to assume, however, that this rule has not been unanimously observed. Communities of Jews made up of men marrying women whom they met in new locales sprang up in a number of places, and while there is no way of determining if such Jews practiced the ransoming the first-born sons, one suspects that they did. Jewish parents sought protection for their sons, whomever their mothers were. The ruling that ransoming of first-born sons is reserved or intended for children of Israelite women can be understood in a number of ways. The constructors of the ritual, or more likely, its modifiers, have defined first-borns as those first born to their mothers, and only Jewish mothers can be expected to observe a Jewish ritual. However, one suspects that there has been a deeper and less "logical" consideration: in Jewish lore, "foreign" women are often conceived of as being physically and emotionally tougher. They, and their offspring, are stronger and better equipped to face the dangers of early infancy. Moreover, non-Jewish women possess powers, at times demonic, that Jewish women do not possess. Their need of protection is less urgent.

Priests and Levites are exempt from ransoming their first-born sons. To begin with, priests cannot be expected to ransom themselves. While regular Israelites pay ransom to a *kohen*, at least symbolically, a *kohen* cannot pay ransom to himself, and *kohanim* cannot pay each other. Such "ransoms" would have little meaning. In addition, priests, *kohanim*, have dedicated their lives to the service of God, and so cannot exercise the privilege of ransoming. They have to remain priests forever more, no excuses, no ransoming. The exemptions of *kohanim* and *Leviim* from paying ransoms for the first-born sons, as well as first-born grandsons, has, however, deeper meaning. Being *kohanim* and *Leviim*, the people who had stayed loyal to God all along, and dedicated their lives to God's

[15] Cf. such a plate in the Wolfson Museum in Jerusalem, www.jhom.com/topics/firsts/firstborn.html.

service, they are under God's special protection. Their children and grandchildren, therefore, are not in need of the ransoming.

The Enlightenment and Post-Enlightenment

Jewish groups influenced by the European Enlightenment and of rational thinking challenged such rituals as the ransoming of the first-born sons. Laws governing "purity and danger" in general have seemed to nineteenth century Jewish advocates of reform and secularization to be redundant, as they could not possess any real power. Like laws of *nida*, preserving bodily purity, during periods of danger, *Pidyon Haben* was declared an accidental, archaic, "superstitious" practice. Influenced by the fledgling scholarly disciplines of History of Religions and Anthropology, Jewish reformers had, like progressive Christians, differentiated between "magic" and "religion."[16] In magic, they saw a primitive stage of what later on evolved into a more rational and enlightened "religion." The understanding of magic, Randall Styers tells us, by enlightened scholars, has not been divorced from communal or theological agendas. Modernists in the nineteenth century promoted "modernity" as oppositional in nature to a past regarded as naive, a mode of differentiation that assumed that the modern is superior both intellectually and morally to modes of thinking and action that preceded it.[17] The Jewish modernists worked to suppress the magical in Judaism as a means of reinventing their tradition. They wanted a Judaism that they could be proud of and feel at home in, one that is in tune with the ideals of the Enlightenment. The reformers wished to preserve those components that seemed completely in line with what they, and other nineteenth century thinkers, considered to be enlightened and rational. *Pidyon Haben*, like ritual baths, seemed redundant. Secular Jews simply disregarded the ritual, just as they disregarded the laws of *nida*. As a rule, "secular" Jews have not abandoned all ties with their tradition, and continued to celebrate the holidays, for example. But they were highly selective, and *Pidyon Haben* was one of numerous rituals for which they had no use. The Re-

[16] Yaakov Ariel, "Christianity Through Reform Eyes: Kaufmann Kohler's Scholarship on Christianity," *American Jewish History*, vol. 89, no. 2 (June 2001): 181–91.

[17] Randall Styers, *Making Magic: Religion, Magic and Science in the Modern World* (Reflection and Theory in the Study of Religion; New York: Oxford University Press, 2004); Gustavo Benavides, "Modernity," in *Critical Themes for Religious Studies* (ed Mark C. Taylor; Chicago: Chicago University Press, 1998), 186–204.

form movement in modern Judaism, however, decided to abandon the ritual out of principle. The reformers gave up completely on the idea of a separate class of priests, which they also considered anachronistic, and adopted instead the idea that all Israelites are a "nation of priests," with a special role and mission in the world. In addition, the reformers objected to the discrimination embodied in the ritual, as it centered only on first-born sons, thus giving preference to males over females.

The movement towards return to tradition in the Reform movement in the latter decades of the twentieth century has brought the ritual back, albeit with significant changes. Priests do not take part in it any more, and rabbis carry out the priests' role. And the ritual is egalitarian in nature, intended for girls, as well as boys.

The Conservative movement has retained the, mostly symbolic, role of the priesthood and did not object to the ritual of *Pidyon Haben*. But the Conservatives have insisted that the ritual, which is often practiced in the privacy of the home, among family and friends, be supervised by a rabbi, thus asserting the role of rabbis as leaders and mentors of their communities. Like the Reformers, they, too, have retained it then in a non-priestly manner.

Ironically, the ritual of ransoming of the first-born son (or should we now say first-born child?) is, in relative terms, celebrated now more than ever before. In the late modern era there has been a dramatic increase in the percentage of first-borns among boys, as for the most part, Jewish mothers do not have more than one boy. Most mothers complete their pregnancies and give birth to healthy children.

Within the realm of the Conservative, Reconstructionist, and Renewal movements, as well as some liberal Orthodox circles, women, and men, too, have worked in the past generation to transform the liturgy so as to include females, as rabbis, as priests, and as participating laypersons. Parents have come to regard first-born girls as equal to male offspring and in need of being ransomed as much as boys. The renewed popularity of the ritual points to a larger development in contemporary Judaism:

The ushering in of a post-Enlightenment era, the reenchantment of the world and the resurfacing of the "irrational."[18] In the last genera-

[18] Cf. Yaakov Ariel, "Hasidism in the Age of Aquarius: The House of Love and Prayer in San Francisco, 1967–1977," *Religion and American Culture* 13, 2 (Summer 2003): 139–65.

tion, Jews, both in America and Israel, have rediscovered the "magical" elements of their tradition, putting again *mezuzot* and *hamsot* on the entrances to their homes, reading horoscopes, and studying Kabbalah. It is perhaps no wonder that in the 1980s the Israeli Society of Coins and Medallions issued a set of five silver shekels to be used in the ceremony of *Pidyon Haben*. The ritual has come back, and is, in relative terms, celebrated now more than ever before.

Conclusion

The ritual of the ransoming the first-born sons has survived since Mishnaic times until today. While modern Jews, influenced by the Enlightenment, and treating the observance of the commandments selectively, have abandoned many other rituals, they have retained or re-instituted this particular one. The official rationale for the ritual notwithstanding, the persistence of its celebration should be understood in terms of "purity and danger." The ransoming of the first-borns should be viewed as a rite of passage that comes to reassure that everything has been done to protect the newly born, including in the realm of the supernatural or the "magical." While everyone is aware that the *kohanim*, the descendents of the ancient priests, do not mean to take the first-born sons away, parents know that other forces might do so. In parents' minds, the first-borns, more so than other infants, were vulnerable, and in need of God's mercy.

Contrary to the way many Enlightenment Jews viewed their tradition, Judaism included numerous elements that nineteenth century scholars of religion would have placed in the realm of "magic." In fact, Judaism can serve as a case study that shows that differentiating between religion and magic can be ill conceived.[19] Within the Jewish traditions, one can find schools of thought and practices that fall into the different categories, and, more often than not, weave the two together. Especially in the realm of childbirth, Jews have mustered as many weapons as they could find to protect mothers and babies. Lacking modern medical means, Jewish parents throughout the centuries, like all parents, have had to face high mortality rates among their new-borns. In the psychological climate that such a harsh reality created, it was no wonder

---

[19] Howard Eilberg-Schwartz, *The Savage in Judaism: An Anthropology of Israelite Religion and Ancient Judaism* (Bloomington: Indiana University Press, 1990).

that parents sought protection from 'evil forces' and approached God and his guarding angels, asking them to spare their children. To protect themselves and their children, pregnant women would wear special amulets, often with inscription that came to assert their righteousness and keep the evil spirits away. The good, protecting angels, Michael, Gabriel, and Rafael, would be called upon to stand near by and see that disruptive *shedim* and *shedot* would not harm the mothers or children. At the twenty-first century, Jewish anthropologists and folklorists are well aware of what has been called by modernists "non-rational," "popular," or "magical" elements of the Jewish tradition.[20]

First-borns were particularly vulnerable, as they were precious "first fruits" that signified the fertility of their mothers and the beginning of a family, with more children to follow. Moreover, an awareness that God, like the gods of their neighbors, saw the first-borns as "His," prompted the Israelites to make every effort to "ransom" their boys and liberate them from whatever demands the Deity might have over them, so as to ensure a favorable attitude on the part of God and his angels. Giving up on a rite of passage that comes to protect the new-borns, especially first-born sons, was something Jews would not easily do, and, at the turn of the twenty-first century, having re-examined and re-surfaced "irrational" elements in their tradition, they re-instituted it.

---

[20] See, for example, Issachar Ben Ami, *The Adoration of Saints Among Moroccan Jews* (Mekheqre Hammerkaz Lekheqer Haffolqlor 8; Jerusalem: Mages Press, 1984).

Slaughter and Innocence: The Rhetoric of Sacrifice in Contemporary Arguments Supporting the Death Penalty

Randall Styers, University of North Carolina, Chapel Hill

"There is pow'r, pow'r, wonder-working pow'r, in the blood . . ."[1] So begins the chorus of Lewis E. Jones's famous 1899 hymn. This refrain echoes a theme common in nineteenth century American Christian revivalism, the atoning power of the blood of Jesus. Both the hymn and its theme have remained prominent in American evangelical culture through the past century.

As demonstrated by the essays in this volume, sacrifice was a central idiom of religion in the ancient world. As Christianity emerged within this context, the theme of sacrifice became reconfigured in doctrines of the atoning significant of Jesus' death. As Paul Capetz has stated it, the early Christian insistence on the unique character of Jesus' crucifixion as an atonement for sin "provided a rationale for a form of religion without the literal practice of sacrifice." On the basis of this innovation, Capetz continues, "sacrifice comes to be understood in both the New Testament and later Christian writings in a metaphorical and symbolic sense."[2] Yet the precise nature of this metaphor remained a subject of theological dispute, and the doctrine of Jesus' substitutionary sacrifice evolved through Anselm's formulation of atonement as satisfaction into Reformation theories of atonement as propitiation and expiation rendered to satisfy the demands of divine justice.[3]

---

[1] Lewis E. Jones, "There is Power in the Blood," *The Baptist Hymnal* (ed. W. H. Sims; Nashville: Convention Press, 1956), 193.

[2] Paul E. Capetz, "Response to Anna Case-Winters' 'Who Do You Say that I Am? Believing in Jesus Christ in the 21st Century,'" *The Covenant Network for Presbyterians*, 9 November 2002. Cited 20 July 2005. Online: http://www.covenantnetwork.org/sermon&papers/capetz.html .

[3] See Dale S. Recinella, *The Biblical Truth About America's Death Penalty* (Boston: Northeastern University Press, 2004), 76–79.

Recent theologians have underscored the violent subtext within traditional formulations of this doctrine. Joanne Carlson Brown and Rebecca Parker have argued that the doctrine of substitutionary atonement implies that suffering is divinely ordained by a "bloodthirsty God" and thus forms the core of "an abusive theology that glories suffering." They see traditional understandings of the atonement as valorizing a form of " 'divine child abuse'—God the Father demanding and carrying out the suffering and death of his own son." Brown and Parker conclude that Christianity must move beyond this theology: "We must do away with the atonement, this idea of a blood sin upon the whole human race which can be washed away only by the blood of the lamb."[4] The womanist theologian Delores Williams amplifies this critique as she underscores the specific ways in which the traditional Christian themes of substitutionary atonement and sacrificial suffering have served to legitimate—and rationalize—the sacrifice and suffering of those on the margins of society.[5]

In response to such concerns, Christian thinkers have worked to formulate alternative understandings of the soteriological significance of Jesus' life and death.[6] But the doctrine of substitutionary atonement remains dominant within contemporary American evangelicalism. It is in this doctrine that the notion of the sacrificial power of blood remains most alive in the cultural imagination of American evangelicals. And nowhere are the social implications of this theme of the potency of sacrifice more overt than in contemporary arguments in support of the death penalty.

A number of contemporary scholars of religion have pointed toward important parallels between the practice of capital punishment and human sacrifice. In a provocative 1995 article, James McBride argues that the death penalty in contemporary America constitutes a religious ritual of scapegoating that should properly be seen as violating the anti-establishment provision of the First Amendment to the Constitution.

---

4 Joanne Carlson Brown and Rebecca Parker, "For God so Loved the World?" in *Christianity, Patriarchy, and Abuse: A Feminist Critique* (ed. J. C. Brown and C. R. Bohn; New York: Pilgrim Press, 1989), 1–30, 26.

5 Delores S. Williams, *Sisters in the Wilderness: The Challenge of Womanist God-Talk* (Maryknoll, N. Y.: Orbis Books, 1993).

6 See for example J. Denny Weaver, *The Nonviolent Atonement* (Grand Rapids, Mich.: Eerdmans, 2001). Anna Case-Winters, "Who Do You Say That I Am?" *The Covenant Network for Presbyterions*, 9 November 2002. Cited 20 July 2005. Online: http://www.covenantnetwork.org/sermon&papers/case-winters.html.

McBride builds his claim first by asserting that the rationale for capital punishment ultimately turns not on a concern with individual justice but on a broader sense of the collective good, "a deep-seated *irrational* belief in the need to execute the condemned, even though they might be factually innocent, in order to defend the well-being of the social order as a whole." Invoking René Girard's theory of religious violence and scapegoating, McBride argues that the death penalty functions as "a surrogate for the bloodletting that would otherwise ensue if the state did not substitute its own ritual of government-sponsored executions for the extra-legal spiral of citizen violence." Proponents rationalize capital punishment "not as a legal recourse to punish the individual but rather as a social mechanism to vent the violence that would otherwise destroy the social order." Thus, McBride concludes, with the state endorsing one particular bloodthirsty—and ultimately theological—perspective over alternative soteriologies or visions of the social good, the death penalty assumes an unconstitutionally "numinous character."[7]

In a related vein, Brian K. Smith has mapped many of the parallels between the practice and ideology of capital punishment in contemporary America and traditional sacrificial rituals. Smith's analysis focuses particularly on the ritualized nature of modern executions, the selection and role of the victim in the drama of death, and the intensity of public debate concerning how capital punishment is to be interpreted and portrayed. In Smith's view, "capital punishment seems to be freighted with more symbolic than rational purport." So, for example, the defendant in capital cases comes to serve as "the representative of all crime, of 'disorder' and social 'chaos,' of the 'breakdown of values' ... a direct challenge to the power of the state." Like McBride, Smith invokes Girard's perspective on the ways in which the criminal justice system fulfills the social objectives of sacrifice. Smith quotes Girard as follows: "Like sacrifice, [the judicial system] conceals—even as it also reveals—its resemblance to vengeance.... In the case of sacrifice, the designated victim does not become the object of vengeance because he is a replacement, is not the 'right' victim. In the judicial system the violence does

[7] James McBride, "Capital Punishment as the Unconstitutional Establishment of Religion: A Girardian Reading of the Death Penalty," in *Capital Punishment: A Reader* (ed. G.H. Stassen; The Pilgrim Library of Ethics; Cleveland: Pilgrim Press, 1998), 182–202, particularly 186, 198 (emphasis in original). And see René Girard, *Violence and the Sacred* (trans. P. Gregory; Baltimore, Md.: Johns Hopkins University Press, 1977).

indeed fall on the 'right' victim; but it falls with such force, such resounding authority, that no retort is possible .... In the final analysis, then, the judicial system and the institution of sacrifice share the same function, but the judicial system is infinitely more effective."[8]

McBride and Smith offer many suggestive links between capital punishment and human sacrifice, but shifts in the debate over capital punishment in recent years have provided even more confirmation of the sacrificial nature of state violence. A growing body of data has demonstrated the degree to which the American criminal justice system is plagued with error, and proponents of the death penalty have been forced to confront more directly the possibility that state violence may stray from its proper victim. When pressed to abandon arguments based purely on individualized guilt and retribution, advocates of the death penalty have come to rely even more overtly on a logic of sacrifice. If individualized justice can no longer be taken for granted, the collective functions of bloodletting assume greater centrality for defenders of capital punishment. The purpose of this essay is to examine recent arguments in support of the death penalty, particularly those most widely circulated in public debate, that specifically address the possibility of executing the innocent. We see in these responses a broad range of utilitarian and theological arguments that rationalize the death of innocent victims in satisfaction of a greater social good, a rhetoric redolent with the ideology of human sacrifice.

Christian reflection on the morality of the death penalty has a long and complex history, and theological concerns have played a central role in American debates over the morality of capital punishment since the formative years of the republic.[9] In 1956 the Methodist Church became the first major American denomination to formally oppose capital pun-

---

[8] Brian K. Smith, "Capital Punishment and Human Sacrifice," *JAAR* 68/1 (March 2000): 3–25, 15–16, quoting Girard, *Violence and the Sacred*, 22–23. See also Mark Douglas, "Theological Arguments and the Case against Capital Punishment," in *The Leviathan's Choice: Capital Punishment in the Twenty-First Century* (ed. J. M. Martinez, W. D. Richardson, and D. B. Hornsby; Lanham, Md.: Rowman and Littlefield, 2002), 109–14. Glen H. Stassen, "Deliverance from the Vicious Cycles of Murder," in ibid., 115–37, 127.

[9] See James J. Megivern, "Religion and the Death Penalty in the United States: Past and Present," in *Capital Punishment: Strategies for Abolition* (ed. P. Hodgkinson and W. A. Schabas; Cambridge: Cambridge University Press, 2004), 116–42. Idem, *The Death Penalty: An Historical and Theological Survey* (New York: Paulist Press, 1997). Stuart Banner, *The Death Penalty: An American History* (Cambridge: Harvard University Press, 2002). Philip E. Mackey, *Voices Against Death: American Opposition to Capital Punishment 1787–1975* (New York: Burt Franklin & Co., 1976).

ishment, and the Methodists were soon joined in this abolitionist stance by most other mainline Protestant denominations.[10] Yet Christian religious leaders have also led the movement to retain capital punishment. There is substantial support for the death penalty among conservative Christians, and the vast majority of American executions over the past decade has taken place in the highly evangelical South. Subtly recognizing the utility of religion in swaying popular opinion—the "pow'r in the blood"—prosecutors have regularly quoted the Bible to juries in support of the imposition of capital punishment.[11]

Despite a number of important abolitionist efforts through the nineteenth and twentieth centuries, in the late 1960s most American states and the federal government retained a death penalty for murder (and, in some states, for rape and certain other offenses). As opposition mounted in various quarters to the American system of capital justice, a massive litigation effort was undertaken in a number of states challenging the death penalty as violating the Eighth Amendment to the Constitution which forbids the government from inflicting "cruel and unusual punishments." The United States Supreme Court responded with the landmark 1972 ruling, *Furman v. Georgia*, in which a five to four majority concluded that the predominant system for administering the death penalty was unconstitutional because it granted juries unbridled discretion in determining exactly which defendants would suffer the penalty. Following the *Furman* decision, many state legislatures prescribed new legal standards seeking to meet the Court's objections to the arbitrary application of the penalty, and in a set of decisions in July 1976 the Supreme Court upheld various new state death penalty statues purporting to limit jury discretion. Over the thirty years since these decisions, the death penalty has persisted—and expanded—in the United States, but debate concerning its morality and social value has also continued throughout

[10] See James J. Megivern, "Religion and the Death Penalty in the United States," 119–20.

[11] Robert L. Young, "Religious Orientation, Race, and Support for the Death Penalty," in *Leviathan's Choice* (ed. J. M. Martinez, W. D. Richardson, and D. B. Hornsby), 69–79. And see Dale S. Recinella, *The Biblical Truth About America's Death Penalty*, 5–12, 352. See also T. Richard Snyder, *The Protestant Ethic and the Spirit of Punishment* (Grand Rapids, Mich.: Eerdmans, 2001). Chris Hutton, "Flaws in Capital Sentencing: Skewing the Reasoned Moral Response," in *Leviathan's Choice* (ed. J. M. Martinez, W. D. Richardson, and D. B. Hornsby), 271–98. Thomas Berg, "Religious Conservatives and the Death Penalty," *William and Mary Bill of Rights Journal* 9/1 (December 2000). Cited 24 March 2004. Online: http://papers.ssrn.com/sol3/papers.cfm?abstract_id=259152 .

American society, and the Supreme Court has been forced to address an array of issues concerning the constitutionality of the practice. The fundamental tension at the heart of the death penalty decisions from the 1970s—between the need, on the one hand, for individualized justice and, on the other, for the uniform application of law—has never been successfully resolved.[12]

In 1974 the great American constitutional scholar Charles L. Black first published his famous treatise against the death penalty, *Capital Punishment: The Inevitability of Caprice and Mistake*. In this book Black argues that the twin evils of caprice and error inescapably pollute the morality of capital punishment. A judicial regime that does not punish all unlawful killing with death must rely on some system of legal standards to determine which defendants will be selected for the punishment. But the promulgation of such standards itself inevitably entails increased opportunity for error in their administration. Without standards, the selection for execution is hopelessly arbitrary; with them, error is inevitable. Black summarizes the dilemma:

> "Mistake" and "arbitrariness" therefore are reciprocally related. As a purported "test" becomes less and less intelligible, and hence more and more a cloak for arbitrariness, "mistake" becomes less and less possible—not, let it be strongly emphasized, because of any certainty of one's being right, but for the exactly contrary reason that there is no "right" or "wrong" discernible. ... in one way or another, the official choices—by prosecutors, judges, juries, and governors—that divide those who are to die from those who are to live are on the whole not made, and cannot be made, under standards that are consistently meaningful and clear, but ... they are often made ... under no standards at all or under pseudo-standards without discoverable meaning. ... *mistake* in these choices is fated to occur.[13]

This reciprocal relation between caprice and mistake in the imposition of capital punishment is inevitable, Black explains, but it is also morally

---

[12] See *Furman v. Georgia*, 408 U.S. 238 (1972). And see Charles L. Black, Jr., *Capital Punishment: The Inevitability of Caprice and Mistake* (2nd ed.; New York: W.W. Norton, 1981), 19–21, 111–56.

[13] Charles L. Black, *Capital Punishment*, 28–29 (emphasis in original).

unacceptable, since "death is different": "the infliction of death by official choice ought to require a higher degree of clarity and precision in the governing standards than we can practicably require of all choices, even of choices for punishment." Abolition is the only moral response.[14]

Black's arguments focus on the range of opportunities within the American criminal justice system for this interplay of caprice and mistake to take shape: decisions as to the charging and plea-bargaining of crimes; problems in the trial and verdict phases; the mystifying array of issues arising in sentence determination; and the various types of arbitrariness that come into play after sentencing (particularly in the appeal and clemency processes). As Black points out, innumerable aspects of these processes are prone to error, particularly those involving the determination of various psychological factors relevant to the defendant's state of mind (intent and motive) and decisions concerning factors aggravating or mitigating the severity of the crime.

The possibility of error is surely a major factor in determining the morality of capital punishment, and many legal scholars and social theorists have joined Black in arguing that the risk of executing the innocent is an overwhelming ground for abolishing the death penalty. During debate on reinstituting the death penalty in the United Kingdom in 1994, British Home Secretary Michael Howard explained that this very issue had led him to abandon his support for the death penalty. Howard concluded that "the fault lies not in the machinery but in the fallibility and frailty of human judgment."[15] Michael L. Radelet and Hugo Adam Bedau offer a stark assessment of the propensity to error and inequity in the American criminal justice system:

> The problem of wrongful convictions is important because it is part of a much larger issue: once we decide that some of

---

[14] Charles L. Black, *Capital Punishment*, 29–30. See also Jeffrie G. Murphy, "Crime and Punishment," in *Philosophy of Law: An Introduction to Jurisprudence* (ed. idem and Jules L. Coleman; Boulder, Col.: Westview, 1990), 113–56, 156, arguing that that death is uniquely "incompensable" in the degree to which it deprives its victim of the possibility to develop "a morally coherent personality." And see Elizabeth A. Linehan, "Executing the Innocent," *Papers of the Twentieth World Congress of Philosophy, 10–15 August 1998*, The Paideia Archive. Cited 24 March 2004. Online: http://www.bu.edu/wcp/Papers/Huma/HumaLine.htm .

[15] See Stephen Nathanson, *An Eye for an Eye?: The Morality of Punishing by Death* (Totowa, N.J.: Rowman and Littlefield, 1987), particularly 122–30. Elizabeth A. Linehan, "Executing the Innocent." Peter Hodgkinson, "Capital Punishment: Improve It or Remove It?" in *Capital Punishment* (ed. P. Hodgkinson and W. A. Schabas), 1–35, 12.

> our citizens will be executed, all the evidence shows that our government officials do a positively horrible job in selecting who should live and who should die. Some are selected because of their race or class (or the race or class of the victim); some because of pure arbitrariness; some because they are not like we are. ... many today end up on death row not because of the brutality of their crime but because of the incompetence of their defense.[16]

Moral concerns over error have also long been a major factor in Christian opposition to capital punishment. In its 1958 statement calling for the abolition of the death penalty, the American Baptist Church (Northern) included among its primary grounds both "the fallibility of human agencies and legal justice" and "the immorality and injustice of capital punishment for persons later proven innocent."[17] In a 1961 tract in opposition to the death penalty the Mennonite theologian John Howard Yoder quoted Lafayette's challenge to capital punishment: "I shall ask for the abolition of the penalty of death until I have the infallibility of human judgment demonstrated to me." Yoder argued that error is always possible (even if unlikely), given the fallibility of all human judgment and institutions, and in this light it is morally wrong for society to "lay claim to *absolute* authority over life."[18] Many citizens share a deep sense that the possibility of error in imposing the ultimate punishment is a strong argument against capital punishment.

But such concerns have been inadequate to sway the majority of the United States Supreme Court. In its 1993 decision in *Herrera v. Collins*, a six to three majority of the Court rejected the appeal of a convicted murderer on the grounds that new evidence could prove his factual innocence. Writing for the majority, Chief Justice William Rehnquist held that a claim of actual innocence alone was insufficient for federal *habeas corpus* relief in the absence of an independent constitutional vio-

---

[16] Michael L. Radelet and Hugo Adam Bedau, "Erroneous Convictions and the Death Penalty," in *Wrongly Convicted: Perspectives on Failed Justice* (ed. S. D. Westervelt and J. A. Humphrey; New Brunswick, N.J.: Rutgers University Press, 2001), 269–80, 277–78.

[17] James J. Megivern, "Religion and the Death Penalty in the United States," in *Capital Punishment* (ed. P. Hodgkinson and W. A. Schabas), 120.

[18] John Howard Yoder, *The Christian and Capital Punishment* (Newton, Kan.: Faith and Life Press, 1961), 18–19 (emphasis in original). See also idem, "Against the Death Penalty," in *The Death Penalty Debate* (ed. H. W. House and idem; Dallas: Word Publishing, 1991), 105–79, 167–71.

lation in the underlying state proceedings. Except in the most extraordinary circumstances, the Court concluded, claims of factual innocence are inadequate for legal relief, since *habeas* appeals can be recognized only on the basis of issues of law, not fact. In a harsh rebuke to the *Herrera* majority, Justice Harry Blackmun dissented that "the execution of a person who can show that he is innocent comes perilously close to simple murder." The following year, in his dissent in *Callins v. Collins*, Justice Blackmun personally abandoned the effort to balance the competing objectives of consistency and individualization in applying the death penalty. His declaration has become famous: "I no longer shall tinker with the machinery of death. . . . the inevitability of factual, legal, and moral error gives us a system that we know must wrongly kill some defendants, a system that fails to deliver the fair, consistent, and reliable sentences of death required by the Constitution."[19]

Despite—or perhaps because of—the constricted logic of the Court's majority in *Herrera*, the concern with factual error has become increasingly significant in public debate concerning capital punishment over the past decade. New forms of DNA testing have demonstrated how pervasive error can be in the American criminal justice system, and evidence of the fallibility of fact-finding in capital cases continues to mount.[20] A recent study from the University of Michigan identified 199 murder exonerations—73 of them in capital cases—over the 15-year period from 1989 (the year of the first DNA exoneration) through 2003. The study concludes that the high rate of exoneration of death-row

---

[19] *Herrera v. Collins*, 506 U. S. 390 (1993); and *Callins v. Collins* 510 U. S. 1141, 1145 (1994). McBride, "Capital Punishment as the Unconstitutional Establishment of Religion," 183–84, offers the following assessment of the majority's logic in Herrera: "prisoners are not condemned because they are guilty; they are guilty because they are condemned. In other words, whether or not they committed the crime is irrelevant; insofar as they stand condemned, they are legally guilty, regardless of the question of their factual innocence." See also Randall Coyne, "Marking the Progress of a Humane Justice: Harry Blackmun's Death Penalty Epiphany," *University of Kansas Law Review* 43 (1995): 367–416.

[20] See, for example, Amnesty International, "Fatal Flaws: Innocence and the Death Penalty in the United States," 12 November 1998. Cited 25 July 2005. Online: http://web.amnesty.org/library/Index/engAMR510691998 . Jim Dwyer, Peter Neufeld, and Barry Scheck, *Actual Innocence: Five Days to Execution and Other Dispatches from the Wrongly Convicted* (New York: Doubleday, 2000). Westervelt and Humphrey, eds., *Wrongly Convicted*, particularly Michael L. Radelet and Hugo Adam Bedau, "Erroneous Convictions and the Death Penalty," 269–80. Kate Zernike, "Executed Man May Be Cleared in New Inquiry," *The New York Times*, 19 July 2005. Cited 26 July 2005. Online: http://nytimes.com/2005/07/19/national/19death.html .

defendants (a group which presumably receives the highest standard of American justice) raises significant questions as to the reliability and accuracy of the system of capital justice.[21] Michael L. Radelet and Hugo Adam Bedau echo these concerns: "All of the cases of the vindicated prisoners teach us that the criminal justice system goes to great lengths to hide its mistakes. People released from death rows today are not released because of the system; they are released in spite of it. If the main ingredient in a successful exoneration is luck, one can only wonder how many executed prisoners were not only unlucky but also innocent."[22]

The possibility of error assumed center stage in the American death penalty debate in early 2000 when the conservative Republican governor of Illinois, George Ryan, announced a moratorium on his state's imposition of capital punishment. During the prior 23 years, 13 Illinois death row inmates had been exonerated because of new evidence shedding doubt on their guilt; during that same period, Illinois had executed only 12 inmates. In response to this record, Ryan stated: "Until I can be sure that everyone sentenced to death in Illinois is truly guilty; until I can be sure, with moral certainty, that no innocent man or woman is facing a lethal injection, no one will meet that fate. I cannot support a system which, in its administration, has proven so fraught with error and has come so close to the ultimate nightmare, the state taking of innocent life." Two years later, just before leaving office in January 2003, Ryan declared Illinois' system of capital justice "an absolute embarrassment ... a catastrophic failure" and issued a blanket commutation of all death sentences in the state. He explained his decision: "Our capital system [in Illinois] is haunted by the demon of error: error in determining guilt and error in determining who among the guilty deserves to die."[23]

---

[21] See Samuel R. Gross et al., "Exonerations in the United States 1989 Through 2003," *The Journal of Criminal Law and Criminology* 95/2 (2005): 523–60.

[22] Michael L. Radelet and Hugo Adam Bedau, "Erroneous Convictions and the Death Penalty," 275. See also Death Penalty Information Center, "Innocence and the Death Penalty." Cited 25 July, 2005. Online: http://www.deathpenaltyinfo.org/article.php?did=412&scid=6 .

[23] See Erik C. Owens and Eric P. Elshtain, "Religion and Capital Punishment: An Introduction," in *Religion and the Death Penalty: A Call for Reckoning* (ed. E. C. Owens, J. D. Carlson, and E. P. Elshtain; The Eerdmans Religion, Ethics, and Public Life Ser.; Grand Rapids, Mich.: Eerdmans, 2004), 1–19, 1–3. And see Carl M. Cannon, "The Problem with the Chair," *National Review*, 19 June 2000. Cited 24 March 2004. Online: http://www.nationalreview.com/19jun00/cannon061900.html . For Governor Ryan's subsequent reflections on his decision, see George H. Ryan, "Reflections on the Death Penalty

Ryan's actions energized a broad movement seeking to persuade other governors and state legislatures to impose moratoria in order to reform—or abandon—the system of death. The factors that Ryan found persuasive prompted even conservative commentators to question the legitimacy of the death penalty. In an influential article in the *National Review* shortly after Ryan's imposition of the Illinois moratorium, Carl M. Cannon argued that conservatives in particular should be wary of the imposition of government power in cases of life and death. Conservatism, Cannon points out, is built on a fundamental distrust of government and a deep sense of human fallibility, and conservatives should thus be particularly cognizant of the possibility that the criminal justice system could systemically err. Cannon asserts that "the true horror of the death penalty has made itself plain. The right question to ask is not whether capital punishment is an appropriate—or a moral—response to murders. It is whether the government should be in the business of executing people convicted of murder knowing to a certainty that some of them are innocent." Cannon concludes with a pointed moral query: if a society enforces the death penalty knowing that some innocent defendants will be killed, do all the members of that society share in the implicit guilt of murder?[24]

But just as a majority of the Supreme Court has been able to discount the concern with innocence, so also many other proponents of the death penalty have been undeterred by the growing body of data suggesting that the criminal justice system is riddled with error. Instead, advocates of capital punishment have reformulated their arguments in support of the penalty. In many cases these proponents have directly acknowledged the possibility that innocent people have been, or could be, executed. This possibility seems unavoidable, given that law, whatever its provenance, must be administered by fallible and limited human beings. And thus confronted with this inescapable risk, proponents argue that capital punishment is appropriate, even if the innocent are killed. It is in these arguments that the logic of human sacrifice becomes central.

Moratorium," in *Religion and the Death Penalty: A Call for Reckoning* (ed. E. C. Owens, J. D. Carlson, and E. P. Elshtain), 221–30. In June 2000, just months after Governor Ryan's imposition of the Illinois death penalty moratorium, the Southern Baptist Convention for the first time explicitly endorsed "the fair and equitable use of capital punishment by civil magistrates as a legitimate form of punishment." Dale S. Recinella, *The Biblical Truth about America's Death Penalty*, 9, 351–52.

24 Cannon, "The Problem with the Chair."

In the face of claims of error in the administration of the death penalty, the most common initial response is to deny that error is a significant problem. A 1981 report prepared for the United States Senate Judiciary Committee by South Carolina Senator Strom Thurman asserted that in light of various procedural safeguards, the risk of error in capital cases had been reduced to "a mere theoretical possibility."[25] More recent advocates have acknowledged that DNA and other evidence has established that error occurs, but, they argue, these very exonerations offer an ample indication that the system of justice is self-correcting. The high rate of reversals in death penalty appeals can thus be cited not as evidence that the system of capital trials is flawed, but as evidence that the appellate process is succeeding—in the words of former law professor and now United States District Court Judge Paul G. Cassell, "a reassuring sign of the judiciary's circumspection before imposing the ultimate sanction." Cassell asserts that the current system of justice "extend[s] extraordinary generosity to murderers," and he concludes that "contrary to urban legend, there is no credible example of any innocent person executed in this country under the modern death-penalty system."[26] As Joshua K. Marquis states it, "[t]here are indeed stories of people wrongfully sent to prison and even death row, but they are so few and the situations so easily remedied that they are hardly the basis for abolishing the ultimate punishment for the worst murderers."[27]

Researchers such as Hugo Adam Bedau and Michael L. Radelet have documented a number of cases in which they believe innocent defendants have been executed,[28] and many defenders of the death penalty direct their efforts toward seeking to debunk those specific claims. In

---

[25] Strom Thurman, "Executing Innocent People," in *Reviving the Death Penalty* (ed. G.E. McCuen and R.A. Baumgart; Hudson, Wisc.: Gary E. McCuen Publications, 1985), 96–100, 99.

[26] Paul G. Cassell, "We're Not Executing the Innocent," *Wall Street Journal*, 16 June 2000. Cited 24 March 2004. Online: http://www.fed-soc.org/Publications/practicegroupnewsletters/PG%20Links/casselldeathpenalty.htm .

[27] Joshua K. Marquis, "Truth and Consequences: The Penalty of Death," in *Debating the Death Penalty: Should America Have Capital Punishment? Experts on Both Sides Make their Best Case* (ed. H. A. Bedau and P. G. Cassell; Oxford: Oxford University Press, 2004), 117–51, 149. See also Dudley Sharp, "The Risk of Executing the Innocent," in "Death Penalty and Sentencing Information in the United States," *Justice for All*, 1 October 1997. Cited 19 March 2004. Online: http://www.prodeathpenalty.com/DP.html .

[28] See for example Michael L. Radelet, Hugo Adam Bedau, and Constance E. Putnam, *In Spite of Innocence: Erroneous Convictions in Capital Cases* (Boston: Northeaster University Press, 1992).

pursuing this strategy, Paul Cassell declares that "the risk of mistaken execution is virtually non-existent. ... the criminal justice system is doing an admirable, if not indeed perfect, job of preventing the execution of innocent defendants. ... modern-day examples of executed innocent defendants remain as rare as unicorns." An important tactic in this effort is to downplay the error rate by highlighting the difference between legal exoneration and factual innocence. Thus, proponents argue, while numerous defendants have been legally exonerated, those exonerations fail to prove that the defendants were factually innocent of the crimes with which they were charged.[29]

There are indeed few cases in which it can be definitively established that an innocent defendant has been executed, but, as Charles L. Black pointed out in the 1970s, this claim is relatively meaningless. Not only is there no legally meaningful way in which a claim of innocence can be formally established, but since the defendant is dead, there are few parties motivated to pursue such claims or to develop or maintain the evidence that would be needed to legitimate them. And while there is surely an important difference between legal and factual innocence, legal error is as relevant as factual error in determining who should properly be executed. The execution of a defendant who fails to meet the legal criteria for the death penalty is a morally significant error in the administration of justice, regardless of factual guilt or innocence.[30]

But even as proponents of the death penalty downplay the significance of error as a practical concern, most will acknowledge the lingering possibility that the innocent can be executed. Faced with this possibility, advocates of the death penalty commonly turn to various forms of utilitarian, consequentialist calculus to bolster their position. Some of the more rudimentary versions of this calculus simply argue that all life is difficult (or, in the vernacular, "to make an omelet, you must break some eggs"). As Wesley Lowe explains it, "I must point out that in this im-

[29] See Paul G. Cassell, "Statement before the Committee on the Judiciary, United States House of Representatives, Subcommittee on Civil and Constitutional Rights," 23 July 1993. Cited 19 March 2004. Online: http://www.law.utah.edu/faculty/websites/cassellp/TESthousehearing.htm . Tom Flannery, "The Death Penalty (A Christian Defense)," *Christianity.com*, 2000. Cites 19 March 2004. Online: http://www.christianity.com/CC/article/1,1183,PTID1000%7CCHID%7CCIID132640,00.html . Dudley Sharp, "Innocence Issues: The Death Penalty," *Pro-Death Penalty.com*, 2005. Cited 26 July 2005. Online: http://www.prodeathpenalty.com/Innocence.htm .

[30] See Charles L. Black, *Capital Punishment*, 170–73.

perfect world, nothing that is worth having comes without risk." In this regard, Lowe quotes syndicated columnist Charley Reese:

> I favor a fair trial, one quick appeal and prompt execution .... As for not being able to correct a mistake, so what? Virtually all accidental deaths are deaths by mistake. Why impose a standard of perfection only on the criminal justice system? There are no perfect human institutions. Our system is, more than any other, designed to protect the rights of the defendant. The chance of a truly innocent person being executed is exceedingly slim. But if it happens, it happens just as things happen to people every day.[31]

Or, as Steven Farrell states:

> The justice of the death penalty is strengthened, not weakened, by the advent of new technologies such as DNA testing, which have recently been utilized to more firmly establish guilt or innocence. It does not logically follow that the death penalty should be abolished because such evidence "might" have reversed the fate of some previously put to death. It's too late for that. What's past is past.[32]

In reiterating this theme, David Anderson asserts that the inevitable fact that innocent defendants are convicted is "part of a necessary evil in every state governed by law. No judicial system can avoid it." As Anderson concludes, "In a harsh and unpredictable world we must accept that innocent people everywhere suffer."[33]

A more nuanced version of this claim seeks to differentiate the pragmatic and moral aspects of the death penalty. For example, H. Wayne

---

[31] Wesley Lowe, "Pro Death Penalty Webpage," 9 June 2005. Cited 26 July 2005. Online: http://www.wesleylowe.com/cp.html .

[32] Steven Farrell, "Thou Shalt Not Kill—A Convicted Murderer?" 27 August 2001. Cited 28 July 2005. Online: http://www.geocities.com/graymada/Farrell/TSNK.html .

[33] David Anderson, "Alternative Sanctions to the Death Penalty Afflicts [sic] More 'Innocent' Ones," in *The Death Penalty: A Defense*, 2005. Cited 28 July 2005. Online: http://www.yesdeathpenalty.com/argument_15.htm . And see David Anderson, "Answers to the Argument Against the Death Penalty," in ibid. See also Gregory Koukl, "The Bible and Capital Punishment," *Stand to Reason*. Cited 19 March 2004. Online: http://www.str.org/free/studies/capipuni.htm , concluding that "life is flawed, not capital punishment."

House has claimed that despite deficiencies in the criminal justice system, "failure to properly apply capital punishment does not make it immoral."[34] In this view, the morality of the death penalty should be determined in abstraction from any consideration of the practical limits of human judgment. The philosopher Louis Pojman amplifies this argument as he explains the moral difference between a miscarriage of justice and murder. In response to opponents of capital punishment who argue that mistaken state execution is morally equivalent to murder (or perhaps even worse, since in this situation execution is a deliberate and dispassionate collective choice), Pojman asserts that wrongful execution is morally superior to murder since in the execution there is no "deliberate intention to kill the innocent."[35] (Pojman here ignores the moral implications that arise not from an intention to execute the innocent, but rather from actually foreseeing that such error is inevitable.)

A second strand of consequentialist calculus seeks to deny that death is different from other types of punishment (and therefore deserving of a higher level of moral scrutiny). While capital punishment is surely an irreparable loss to the defendant and while even the United States Supreme Court has affirmed that "the penalty of death is different in kind from any other punishment imposed under our system of criminal justice,"[36] a number of proponents of the death penalty argue that all punishment is equally significant, inflicting comparably irreparable loss. As H. Wayne House states it: "[t]he courts can release an individual who has been imprisoned for a crime he or she did not commit, but it cannot return the lost time .... This should motivate us to ensure that only the guilty are punished, not to eliminate penalties for all crimes."[37] Other advocates of capital punishment join House in the claim that all punishment inflicts comparable loss and that error in imposing the death penalty is, therefore, no more avoidable—or morally significant—than error in imposing any other type of punishment.[38]

---

[34] H. Wayne House, "In Favor of the Death Penalty," in *The Death Penalty Debate* (ed. H. W. House and J. H. Yoder), 1–104, 78.

[35] Louis P. Pojman, "Unfair Application of Capital Punishment Does Not Justify Abolishing It," in *Capital Punishment* (ed. M. E. Williams; Current Controversies; San Diego: Greenhaven Press, 2000), 91–96, 92–93.

[36] *Gregg v. Georgia*, 428 U. S. 153 (1976) (Opinion of the Court by Justice Stewart).

[37] H. Wayne House, "In Favor of the Death Penalty," 78.

[38] See Michael Levin, "Claims About the Unfairness of Capital Punishment are Unfounded," in *Capital Punishment* (ed. M. E. Williams), 83–87, 84.

A third variation of this utilitarian theme argues that despite the risk of executing the innocent, failure to enforce capital punishment will actually place more innocent victims at risk. Ward Campbell argues that the risk of wrongful execution must be weighed against the benefits of capital punishment: "Counterbalancing the concern that even one innocent person may be executed is the question of whether the death penalty saves innocent lives by deterring potential murderers." Campbell believes that the costs of foregoing capital punishment outweigh countervailing concerns with error. As he concludes: "innocent lives are at stake. On the one hand, there is the remote prospect that an innocent person may be executed despite the most elaborate, protracted, and sympathetic legal review procedures in the world. On the other, there is the possibility of innocent people horribly and brutally murdered in the streets and in their homes with no legal review process at all."[39]

Other proponents of capital punishment make this moral calculus in even more explicitly utilitarian terms. Louis Pojman argues as follows:

> Society has a right to protect itself from capital offenses even if this means taking a finite chance of executing an innocent person. If the basic activity or process is justified, then it is regrettable, but morally acceptable, that some mistakes are made. Fire trucks occasionally kill innocent pedestrians while racing to fires, but we accept these losses as justified by the greater good of the activity of using fire trucks. We judge the use of automobiles to be acceptable even though such use causes an average of 50,000 traffic fatalities each year. We accept the morality of a defensive war even though it will result in our troops accidentally or mistakenly killing innocent people .... That occasional error may be made, regrettable though this is, is not a sufficient reason for us to refuse to use the death penalty, if on balance it serves a just and useful function.[40]

---

[39] Ward A. Campbell, "Critique of DPIC List," 2003. Cited 24 March 2004, Online: http://www.prodeathpenalty.com/DPIC.htm . See also Strom Thurman, "Executing Innocent People," in *Reviving the Death Penalty* (ed. G. E. McCuen and R. A. Baumgart), 96–100.

[40] Louis P. Pojman, "Unfair Application of Capital Punishment Does Not Justify Abolishing It," 93. See also Steven Goldberg, "The Death Penalty Deters Murder," in *The*

Just as society accepts the risks of modern conveniences (automobiles seem to be the favored example), the risk of wrongful imposition of the death penalty is configured as a necessary price paid to enjoy the benefits of public safety.

Paul Cassell inverts this issue as itself an attempt to avoid harmful error in the administration of justice, though the error that concerns him is the error of wrongfully allowing guilty defendants to live. Executions protect the innocent, he says, in three major ways: their incapacitative effects on particular defendants, a general deterrent effect through the broader population, and in anchoring a system of just punishment. He states:

> To justify abolishing the death penalty on grounds of risk to the innocent, abolitionists would have to establish that innocent persons are jeopardized more by the retention of the death penalty than from its absence. In fact, the balance of risk tips decisively in favor of retaining the death penalty. On the one hand, abolitionists have been unable to demonstrate that even a single innocent person has been executed in error. On the other hand, there are numerous documented cases of innocent persons who have died because of our society's failure to carry out death sentences .... Clearly, on any realistic assessment, the innocent are far more at risk from allowing these dangerous convicts to live than from executing them after a full and careful review of their legal claims.[41]

Many of the most publicly active proponents of capital punishment revert to this claim. Dudley Sharp, the Death Penalty Resources Director of the pro-death penalty advocacy group "Justice For All," argues that sparing murderers actually leads to a greater degree of "sacrificing the innocent," when murderers are allowed to kill within prison or after release or escape. While executing an innocent defendant might be morally offensive, Sharp states, a true concern for innocence would steer society toward greater support for the death penalty: "stopping execu-

Death Penalty: Opposing Viewpoints (ed. C. Wekesser; Opposing Viewpoints Ser.; San Diego: Greenhaven Press, 1991), 113–18, 116. Wesley Lowe, "Pro Death Penalty Webpage."

[41] Paul G. Cassell, "In Defense of the Death Penalty," in *Debating the Death Penalty* (ed. H. A. Bedau and P. G. Cassell), 183–217, 208. See also Paul G. Cassell, "Statement before the Committee on the Judiciary." Idem, "We're Not Executing the Innocent."

tions will always put many more innocents at risk."[42] Wesley Lowe offers a personalized version of this moral calculation. To those who ask how he would respond if he personally were to be wrongfully executed for a crime he did not commit, Lowe states: "I would have to consider which is more important to me, my personal safety, or the common good. Common decency and ethics demand that I place the common good far above my personal safety. Therefore, I am morally obligated to take that risk."[43]

This line of argument—the utilitarian cost-benefit approach to error—is not invoked simply by secular advocates of the death penalty. Various religious thinkers also make the utilitarian claim. So, for example, Michael Pakaluk argues that Christians should not be swayed by the possibility of error in administering capital punishment. Instead, they should realize that "since murderers often murder again, innocent persons will also be killed if capital punishment is *not* used." Errors in the system of capital justice are lesser evils than the additional murders they prevent (since those murders are "intended and premeditated"). Therefore, "it is better to make the former sort of mistake."[44] As Bob Enyart states it, "if God's command were enforced, rather than ridiculed, the shedding of innocent blood would virtually disappear in our land. God's wisdom would save thousands of children."[45] In a further twist of this argument, many religious advocates of capital punishment add to the benefit side of the balance a claim that execution aids evangelism in that it provides a stark incentive for condemned defendants to convert.

There are many questions to be raised about the type of utilitarian analysis offered in these arguments. Such calculation is, of course, at its core rather questionable as a mode of theological ethics. But even at a pragmatic level, the argument proves both too much and too little. If we grant the assumption that implementation of the death penalty can deter violent crime through its specific incapacitative effects on particular criminals, then such an argument would appear to apply with equal force not only as to murderers but to many other types of criminals (perhaps

[42] Dudley Sharp, "Innocence Issues."

[43] Wesley Lowe, "Pro Death Penalty Webpage."

[44] Michael Pakaluk, "Christians Can Morally Support the Death Penalty," in *The Death Penalty: Opposing Viewpoints* (ed. C. Wekesser), 67–73, 73 (emphasis in original). See also Dudley Sharp, "Christianity and the Death Penalty," in "Death Penalty and Sentencing Information in the United States."

[45] Bob Enyart, "God and the Death Penalty," *Theology Online*. Cited 24 March 2004. Online: http://www.theologyonline.com/DEATH.HTML .

all); at the very least, there is no obvious limit to the application of the specific deterrence claim. But even in its most limited scope, the specific deterrence argument is ultimately persuasive only if we have a high degree of assurance that we are actually executing criminals who are both guilty and likely to kill again, and the systemic error in our system of justice adds substantial uncertainty with respect to both factors. As for a general deterrent effect from the implementation of capital punishment, the evidence of any such effect has proved quite elusive.[46] The proper comparison is not between execution and release, of course, but instead the far more complex—and indeterminable—question of whether there are substantial numbers of potential murderers undeterred by the possibility of lengthy prison sentences, but diverted from their crimes by the possibility of execution. Stephen Nathanson has made a point central to our evaluation of claims of deterrence, whether specific or general. Faced with the possibility of executing innocent defendants, he argues, any type of cost-benefit analysis in relation to the death penalty would be morally meaningful only if we could actually determine that a substantial number of lives would be saved and that there are "no feasible, morally preferable alternatives to the death penalty, no policies that are available to us and that would be equally effective in saving these innocent lives."[47] Surely the substantial resources expended in the system of death could be used to produce effective alternative modes of restraint and security.

But proponents of capital punishment seem far less interested in the factual merits of the deterrence claim than in a nearly ritualized recitation of its social calculus. And that calculus is permeated with the logic of human sacrifice. Faced with the possibility of executing the innocent, advocates of the death penalty are forced to abandon the claim that their mode of justice is based on individual guilt and retribution. Instead, they move to propound a punitive scheme in which individual victims are expendable in the interests of a greater social good. Error

---

[46] For an overview of this issue, see Michael L. Radelet and Ronald L. Akers, "Deterrence and the Death Penalty: The Views of the Experts," *Journal of Criminal Law and Criminology* 87 (1996): 1–16.

[47] Stephen Nathanson, *An Eye for an Eye?* 124–26. See also Elizabeth A. Linehan, "Executing the Innocent." William C. Bailey and Ruth D. Peterson, "Murder, Capital Punishment, and Deterrence: A Review of the Literature," in *The Death Penalty in America: Current Controversies* (ed. H. A. Bedau; New York: Oxford University Press, 1997), 135–61.

leading to a sacrifice of the innocent might be regrettable, but the deterrent effects assumed to be produced by the system outweigh any moral concerns as to individual injustice. James McBride and Brian Smith both underscore the symbolic import of the system of capital punishment as a mode of sacrificial scapegoating through which society seeks to ritually repudiate evil.[48] This sacrificial zeal is manifest in these efforts to minimize the moral significant of error. The cavalier assurance with which so many proponents of the death penalty can so easily invoke unproved—and unprovable—claims about deterrence in support of their utilitarian calculus demonstrates that the logic of scapegoating thrives in the modern world.

An even more overt sacrificial logic appears in the distinctly theological arguments offered on behalf of the death penalty. Protestants and Catholics diverge in their initial moves in defending capital punishment. For Catholics this position has become more complicated in recent years as the Vatican has become increasingly explicit in its opposition to the death penalty. Pope John Paul II's 1995 encyclical *Evangelium vitae* affirms that capital punishment is appropriate only "in cases of absolute necessity ... when it would not be possible otherwise to defend society." Because of improvements in the organization of the penal system, the Pope asserts, such circumstances will be "very rare, if not practically non-existent."[49] A number of conservative American Catholics have publicly rejected this aspect of *Evangelium vitae*. The most prominent is Justice Antonin Scalia of the United States Supreme Court. In Scalia's view the encyclical implies that the death penalty should be imposed only to protect, not to avenge, but the Justice categorically dismisses this position as an abandonment of "two thousand years of Christian teaching" that the death penalty is a properly retributive exercise of state authority. Indeed, Scalia argues, this innovation is a product not of any developing moral insight within the Church, but of secular Western democracy. "The more Christian a country is the *less* likely it is to regard the death penalty as immoral," since, the Justice explains, "for the believing Christian, death is no big deal." John Paul II's declaration in *Evangelium vitae* is thus a mere novelty that "need not be

[48] See above nn. 7 and 8.

[49] Pope John Paul II, *Evangelium Vitae*, 25 March 1995. Cited 15 August 2005. Online: http://www.vatican.va/holy_father/john_paul_ii/encyclicals/documents/hf_jp-ii_enc_25031995_evangelium-vitae_en.html .

accepted by practicing Catholics."[50] Many conservative Catholics join Scalia in this invocation of tradition in support of execution.

In a related vein, the conservative Catholic writer Solange Hertz defends capital punishment by invoking traditional theological notions of expiation through the shedding of blood. She argues that it was God who instituted the death penalty, God who first imposed it, and God who embedded the penalty in "the very fabric of natural law." Indeed, all human beings stand under the penalty of death "without hope of reprieve" in punishment for the sin of Adam. Since all will die because of the fallen human condition, errors in the administration of criminal justice are irrelevant to our consideration of the morality of capital punishment. It is God, not human beings, who must be avenged when murder is committed: "the penalty is due primarily as *expiation* to God in justice, and only secondarily to man." Since the shedding of blood is necessary for the remission of sin, the death penalty displays a "supernatural dimension ... as an agent for the spiritual good of both society and the criminal." Like Scalia, Hertz sees the decline in executions as paralleling a decline in faithfulness: "It is sober fact that death sentences were liberally handed out in the heyday of Christendom, when the Faith was strong and governments legislated with an eye to the spiritual welfare of citizens whose sights were primarily on future bliss in heaven."[51] Scalia, Hertz, and other conservative Catholics highlight both the Church's historical enthusiasm for capital punishment and the practice's role in a divine drama of retribution.

For conservative Protestants, the initial step in offering a theological defense of the death penalty is to argue that the Bible demands the punishment. Thus, for example, Dudley Sharp argues that the Bible affirms that "government imposition of capital punishment is required for deliberate murder." Sharp continues:

> The Bible clearly asserts, from beginning to end, without any reservations, that righteous judgement [sic] includes the execution of a murderer. In the case of murder, the biblical materials offer the clearest and most sustained justification

[50] Antonin Scalia, "God's Justice and Ours: The Morality of Judicial Participation in the Death Penalty," in *Religion and the Death Penalty* (ed. E. C. Owens, J. D. Carlson, and E. P. Elshtain), 231–39, 235 and 238–39 (emphasis in original).

[51] Solange Strong Hertz, "The Death Penalty," *The Remnant*, 31 March 2001. Cited 24 March 2004. Online: http://ourworld.compuserve.com/HOMEPAGES/REMNANT/death2.htm (emphasis in original).

> for the death penalty. The purpose of capital punishment is justice—deterrence is irrelevant. A person who takes a human life, without proper sanction, forfeits any right to life—no alternative is allowed and the community must not be swayed by values to the contrary .... However meritorious mercy may be, however abundantly evident it may be in God's own dealings, murder was an offense for which mercy and pity were not allowed ... [52]

This claim that the death penalty is mandatory is echoed by Carl F. H. Henry: "Nowhere does the Bible repudiate capital punishment for premeditated murder; not only is the death penalty for deliberate killing of a fellow human being permitted, but it is approved and encouraged, and for any government that attaches at least as much value to the life of an innocent victim as to a deliberate murderer, it is ethically imperative."[53] Such advocates argue that the Hebrew Bible specifically prescribes the death penalty (the most cited proof texts are Gen 9 and Exod 20–21) and that various New Testament texts assume or affirm the validity of capital punishment (Rom 13 is commonly invoked). Others turn to Num 35:33 to argue that "murder pollutes the land, and ... the only way to purge the land of this curse is by enforcing the death penalty." Such proponents conclude, in the words of Randy Alcorn, that "the state is not simply free to carry out the death penalty in cases of first degree murder, but it is *obligated* to do so."[54]

Through both Catholic and Protestant versions of these arguments, there is repeated recourse to the twin themes of the sanctity of (some) human life and the necessity of retributive justice. Questions about the deterrent effects of capital punishment are deemed irrelevant, since the primary purpose of the practice is seen as upholding a cosmic scheme of justice. So, for example, Charles Colson argues that the death penalty is required by the sacred character of human life:

[52] Dudley Sharp, "Christianity and the Death Penalty."

[53] Dudley Sharp, "Christianity and the Death Penalty," quoting Carl F. H. Henry, *Twilight of a Great Civilization: The Drift toward Neo-Paganism* (Westchester, Ill.: Crossway, 1988), 70, 72.

[54] Randy Alcorn, "Capital Punishment: Right or Wrong?" *Eternal Perspective Ministries*, 2004. Cited 24 March 2004. Online: http://www.epm.org/articles/cappun.html . See also Glenn Dunehew, "What About Capital Punishment?" Cited 24 March 2004. Online: http://www.forerunner.com/forerunner/X0131_Capital_Punishment.html . Dudley Sharp, "Christianity and the Death Penalty."

> Justice in God's eyes requires that the response to an offense—whether against God or against humanity—be proportionate. The *lex talionis*, the "law of the talion" [retaliation] served as a restraint, a limitation, that punishment would be no greater than the crime. Yet, implied therein is a standard that the punishment should be *at least as great* as the crime .... To be punished, however severely, because we indeed *deserve* it, as C. S. Lewis observed, is to be treated with dignity as human beings created in the image of God .... The issue in my mind boils down ultimately to just deserts. Indeed, just punishment is a thread running throughout the whole of biblical revelation .... God in fact requires capital justice ...[55]

Dudley Sharp quotes the Protestant minister Reuben Hahn as follows: "God gave to government the legitimate authority to use capital punishment to restrain murder and to punish murderers. Not to inflict the death penalty is a flagrant disregard for God's divine Law which recognizes the dignity of human life as a product of God's creation. Life is sacred, and that is why God instituted the death penalty. Consequently, whoever takes innocent human life forfeits his own right to live."[56]

Of course the possibility of error raises substantial difficulties for this rationale of retribution. Most retributive arguments launch from the assumption that it is the guilty party who will suffer the penalty, and with this premise in place, an abstract notion of justice can be invoked to support the *lex talionis*. But the possibility of error complicates this simplistic moral equation. As discussed above, the conservative journalist Carl Cannon raised the prospect of collective guilt for executing the innocent in his 2000 *National Review* article. In response, Steven Farrell argues that this possibility of error is irrelevant in assessing the morality of attempting to follow God's law:

> God is more just and merciful than that. It seems best to trust, as did our forefathers, that if we do the absolute best we can to uphold His laws, He will judge us by the intent of our

[55] Charles Colson, "The Death Penalty Is Morally Just," in *The Death Penalty: Opposing Viewpoints* (ed. P. A. Winters; San Diego: Greenhaven, 1997), 60–65, 61–64 (emphasis in original).

[56] Dudley Sharp, "Christianity and the Death Penalty," quoting Reuben Hahn, "Human Events" (2 March 1985).

> hearts in those areas where we may have remotely failed. It is He who established the law for the death penalty. His law is good. To abolish His just and compassionate law in defense of criminals, fairly convicted, misses the mark with religion by striking a blow at the laws and justice of God, whose laws are at the root of the American judicial system."[57]

Or, as John A. Kohler states it, "When God instituted capital punishment, He knew that it would not always be carried out fairly. The real solution here is to improve the way in which the law is administered, not to eliminate the punishment for violations of that law."[58] The implication of this perspective seems to be that God is to be far more concerned with some innocent deaths than others. While divine justice appears to relentlessly demand a system of state execution, God is surprisingly tolerant of error in the administration of that system; mistaken executions might even be foreordained.

Other religious advocates of the death penalty readily affirm the limits of human capacity and judgment, but, they argue, those limits themselves should temper our moral concern over error in the system of justice. Since the state can kill only the body, God's broader plan will proceed despite mistakes in its human administration. As Wesley Lowe states it, "[s]ome religious people argue that since we cannot create human life we should not take it. If you accept the premises of religion, then not only can we not create human life, we cannot destroy it. We can only destroy the flesh that temporarily houses the immortal soul. What happens to the soul is God's business, no one else's."[59] Solange Hertz amplifies this theme. She argues that it is only an erroneous assumption of modern secularism that physical death is such a weighty loss: "It is only to be expected that materialists—for whom the immortal soul does not exist, and who believe that this present life of the senses on earth is the only one man has—should be reluctant to punish anyone by killing him. In their eyes this means total extinction." But, Hertz explains, the present life pales in comparison with the "future endless existence in heaven"; execution only expedites our transport to a more significant plane: "When Catholic society puts a man to death, it ter-

57 Steven Farrell, "Thou Shalt Not Kill—A Convicted Murderer?"

58 John A. Kohler III, "Objections to Capital Punishment Answered." Cited 28 July 2005. Online: http://members.aol.com/brwoodbc/cappun.html .

59 Wesley Lowe, "Pro Death Penalty Webpage."

minates only his temporal life on earth, catapulting him into eternity for his final judgment before almighty God." Capital punishment allows the criminal "to render *expiation* to God and to society," and if the punishment is accepted with appropriate repentance, "it preserves his soul from hell and eliminates much of his purgatory. If his contrition is perfect, it's conceivable that he could go straight to heaven!" Indeed, Hertz points out, many prison chaplains have testified to the spiritual benefits of capital punishment in focusing the criminal's attention on the afterlife.[60]

Jesus is enlisted both as a strong proponent of the death penalty and as the prime example of its cosmic efficacy. Since many passages in the New Testament might be read as foregrounding such spiritual virtues as forgiveness, mercy, and love, great exegetical ingenuity is deployed in combing the gospels for reference to judgment and punishment in order to demonstrate Jesus' affirmation of a rigid economy of divine justice and retribution. As Dudley Sharp states it: "Far from releasing believers from prior law, Jesus was a 'hard liner' who made things even tougher, stating that He has come not 'to abolish the law and the prophets ... but to fulfill them,' offering even stronger interpretations than in the original."[61]

To these ends, a number of conservative religious thinkers cite Jesus' crucifixion as itself demonstrating the propriety of the death penalty within the divine scheme. As Jacob J. Vellenga states it:

> Love and mercy have no stability without agreement on basic justice and fair play. Mercy always infers a tacit recognition that justice and rightness are to be expected. Lowering the standards of justice is never to be a substitute for the concept of mercy. The Holy God does not show mercy contrary to his righteousness but in harmony with it. That is why the awful Cross was necessary and a righteous Christ had to hang on it. ... wherever and whenever God's love and mercy are rejected, as in crime, natural law and order must prevail, not as extraneous to redemption but as part of the whole scope of God's dealings with man .... It is significant that when Jesus voluntarily went the way of the Cross he chose the capital

[60] Solange Hertz, "The Death Penalty" (emphasis in original).

[61] Dudley Sharp, "Christianity and the Death Penalty." See also Bob Enyart, "God and the Death Penalty."

> punishment of His day as His instrument to save the world. And when He gave redemption to the repentant thief He did not save him from capital punishment but gave him Paradise instead which was far better. We see again that mercy and forgiveness are something different from being excused from wrongdoing . . . . The law of capital punishment must stand as the silent but powerful witness to the sacredness of God-given life. Active justice must be administered when the sacredness of life is violated.[62]

Michael Pakaluk also argues that the doctrine of the atonement legitimates the contemporary death penalty:

> [I]f "no crime deserves the death penalty," then it is hard to see why it was fitting that Christ be *put to death* for our sins and crucified among thieves. St. Thomas Aquinas quotes a gloss of St. Jerome on Matthew 27:33: "As Christ became accursed of the cross for us, for our salvation He was crucified as a guilty one among the guilty." That Christ be put to death *as* a guilty person, in the place of guilty persons, presupposes that death *is* a fitting punishment for those who are guilty.[63]

In a similar vein, Wesley Lowe argues that Jesus' example confirms the propriety of the bloodletting as the means of atonement:

> [T]he death penalty fits in very well with Christian beliefs, especially if one considers Christ's crucifixion. For man's sins were so great, that only an execution could atone for them. Just as Christ died to atone for Man's sins, so must the murderer die to atone for his, following Christ's example. Without atonement for one's sins, forgiveness and redemption look cheap and frivolous. Christ demonstrated just that when he died on the cross for us.[64]

---

[62] Jacob J. Vellenga, "Is Capital Punishment Wrong?" *Essays on the Death Penalty* (ed. T. R. Ingram; St. Thomas Press: Houston, 1963), 63–72, 69–72.

[63] Michael Pakaluk, "Christians Can Morally Support the Death Penalty," in *The Death Penalty: Opposing Viewpoints* (ed. C. Wekesser), 69 (emphasis in original).

[64] Wesley Lowe, "Pro Death Penalty Webpage."

Here we have the intertwined claims that the shedding of blood is necessary for the atonement of sin and that death is the fitting punishment for guilt.

Charles Colson makes a similar argument. He asserts that the exercise of mercy without blood justice would be:

> a mockery of the sacrifice of the Lamb of God. It ignores the fundamental truth of biblical anthropology: the soul that sins must die; sin incurs a debt that must be paid. Punitive dealings provide a necessary atonement and restore the moral balance that has been disturbed by sin .... Purification comes by way of suffering; it prepares the individual to meet his maker.[65]

Just as there is atoning power in Jesus' blood, so also there appears to be a purifying, retributive power in the blood of the executed. Or, in a widely circulated statement concerning the value of the death penalty attributed to New York State Senator James Donovan: "Where would Christianity be if Jesus got eight to fifteen years with time off for good behavior?"[66]

These arguments are quite extraordinary, particularly since traditional Christian theology has long held that the demand for blood expiation—for all ritualized sacrifice—properly ended with sacrifice of Christ. This issue has long been underscored by American opponents of the death penalty. In the nineteenth century, John McMaster argued that while in the pre-Christian era capital punishment "was necessary to reveal God's character and purposes, and to foreshadow the atoning death of our Savior," "the necessity for capital punishment was swept away by the atonement of our Lord and Savior Jesus Christ."[67] More recently John Howard Yoder has argued that while capital punishment might have been rationalized before the coming of Christ by a logic of expiation in the name of the cosmic order, the strongest reason for abolishing the death penalty, the one "closest to the heart of the gospel," is that

---

[65] Charles Colson, "The Death Penalty Is Morally Just," in *The Death Penalty: Opposing Viewpoints* (ed. P. A. Winters), 62–63.

[66] James Donovan, quoted by Ontario Consultants on Religious Tolerance. Cited 24 March 2004. Online: http://www.religioustolerance.org/exeover.htm .

[67] John McMaster, *The Divine Purpose of Capital Punishment* (London: Kegan Paul, Trench, Trübner & Co., 1892), xv, quoted in James J. Megivern, *The Death Penalty: An Historical and Theological Survey*, 12.

"the death of Christ is the end of expiation."[68] Glenn Stassen affirms this view of Jesus' death, asserting that if the crucifixion is understood to be the unique expiation of human sinfulness, "then it is pagan to insist that others pay the penalty of death as expiation for sin again, as if Jesus had not already done this once for all, for all of us." At the very least, proponents of capital punishment fail to clarify why some guilty human beings—but not all—must pay this extreme punishment. Stassen also points to a further incoherence in the argument that Jesus' crucifixion demonstrates the propriety of capital punishment. As he reminds us, the Christian tradition has consistently maintained that since Jesus was perfectly innocent, his crucifixion was unjust, sinful, a crime of the highest order; "surely if asked, [Christian proponents of the death penalty] would agree that the cross discloses human sin, but when they seek to justify the death penalty, surprisingly, they argue that the cross discloses the death penalty was and is right." In Stassen's view, followers of Jesus should have great qualms about sending others to a similar fate.[69]

In traditional Christian theology, the crucifixion of Jesus would certainly seem to be the pinnacle of human sinfulness, the execution of the one perfectly innocent victim. It is thus quite shocking to see Jesus' execution invoked as the exemplar of the practice's propriety. But Solange Hertz carries this argument to an even further extreme. She indicates that Jesus' innocence in facing execution is itself the proper comparison to use in weighing the possibility of other errors in human administration of the death penalty. As Hertz explains, "[w]hen God set the death penalty in Eden He pronounced it on Himself, to be carried out in the fullness of time through the malicious free wills of his own creatures." The "miscarriage of justice" that occurred in the execution of the blameless Jesus was "beyond any the world could ever imagine," dwarfing all other human injustice in comparison. But this most monumental injustice was itself a central, foreordained component of God's plan of salvation. Even in the midst of such suffering and injustice, Jesus never denounced the death penalty, she argues, making clear that the

[68] John Howard Yoder, "Against the Death Penalty," in *The Death Penalty Debate* (ed. H. W. House and J. H. Yoder), 128.

[69] Glenn Stassen, "Deliverance from the Vicious Cycles of Murder," in *The Leviathan's Choice* (ed. J. M. Martinez, W. D. Richardson, and D. B. Hornsby), 127–28. See also Stanley Hauerwas, "Punishing Christians: A Pacifist Approach to the Issue of Capital Punishment," in *Religion and the Death Penalty* (ed. E. C. Owens, J. D. Carlson, and E. P. Elshtain), 57–72. Dale S. Recinella, *The Biblical Truth About America's Death Penalty*, 80, 90.

penalty of death continues as the proper "wages of sin" for humankind. Indeed, from that point in salvation history forward, "it is Christ who delegates the divine authority to punish by killing, and both Scripture and tradition testify that [the death penalty] is lawfully wielded by those to whom He entrusts the temporal sword in His Kingdom."[70] In the very injustice of the crucifixion itself, Jesus grants a divine imprimatur to state execution.

All humanity must eventually submit to the penalty of death, Hertz continues, which itself accords each human being "a share in making restitution for sin." Thus, "what Christ did was to sanctify the death penalty, transforming it into a sacrament of life for those who believe .... The first of that numberless host of Christian martyrs who would be put to death by constituted authority for testifying to the truth, Christ commanded His disciples to 'Follow me!'" Hertz concludes by drawing a striking linkage among the death of all human beings, the death of Christ, and the death of executed criminals, an equation in which issues of human innocence and guilt become relatively trivial in the scheme of cosmic justice:

> Criminals put to death undergo a penalty no different from the one exacted from the most innocent amongst us. As with everyone else the moment of death ushers them either into heaven, hell or purgatory. The most that can be said is that their lives here on earth are shortened, and they must settle their accounts sooner than expected. This could be a great mercy for them as well as for society, both in terms of expiation and protection from any future crimes they might have perpetrated. The death penalty, from the first one imposed on man by God in the beginning in Eden, to the one imposed on God by man on that Good Friday in Jerusalem, on down to those still being imposed today, transcends human legislation. By divine decree it will perdure until the end of time ....[71]

Many aspects of Hertz's claims here are remarkable. The linkage she draws between Jesus, all mortal humanity, and the executed works to obliterate any meaningful distinction between innocence and guilt.

---

[70] Solange Hertz, "The Death Penalty."
[71] Solange Hertz, "The Death Penalty."

With the exception of Jesus, even the most innocent human beings are seen as partaking in original sin, so all except Jesus are guilty. All human beings must die, even the perfectly innocent Jesus who was executed in satisfaction of God's righteous judgment. The human death penalty is thus a relatively minor subset of the all-encompassing divine penalty of death imposed on all humanity. Any error in the human system of justice pales in comparison to the injustice committed on Jesus, but just as that injustice was explicitly sanctioned by God, so also all victims of the death penalty are properly executed regardless of any qualms about their specific guilt. Any human degree of relative innocence or guilt is ultimately irrelevant to the cosmic drama, a drama that demands the shedding of all human blood in the expiation of sin.

But even as Hertz's sacrificial logic collapses any distinction between innocence and guilt, it also redounds with additional convolutions. She simultaneously devalues the significance of human life on earth (death is no great loss in comparison with the demands and rewards of eternity) and invests the present life with ultimate cosmic importance (our eternal fate depends on how we expend this brief span). This ambivalence concerning the significance of the present world is perfectly emblematized in the fate of the condemned defendant. On the one hand, the merits of the judgment meted out to any particular individual is relatively irrelevant (since all human beings are sinners deserving death, and execution merely speeds one on to eternity). On the other hand, however, it is utterly essential to the divine plan that the government rigorously enforce capital punishment, since the penalty furthers God's sacrificial economy of retribution.

Through all these permutations, we see the rhetoric and logic of human sacrifice. Christian tradition and scripture are invoked as demonstrating the role of bloodletting in the cosmic scheme of justice. Divine decree obligates human society to carry out the death penalty, even though God foresees that error might occur. Error is thus a necessary side-effect of God's plan, a form of cosmic collateral damage. Just as we saw in the earlier utilitarian arguments, innocent victims are discounted as a necessary price paid not only for social order and security, but also for faithfulness. Fortunately, theology offers the solace, thin though it might be, that state violence can kill only the body. With the soul expedited to its ultimate deserts, God will right the scales of justice in the life to come. In this logic, Jesus' crucifixion can be invoked not as the culmination of a sacrificial economy of expiation, but instead as a divine model to be emulated. The death of Jesus is seen as affirming God's demand for blood-justice, and believers are called to take up the cross and follow him. Even Jesus' innocence can be enlisted into the scheme, as demonstrating that God's economy requires not guilty victims, but sacrificial ones.

Donald A. Cabana, former warden of the Mississippi State Penitentiary, provided this assessment of his personal experience in supervising executions: "For those few who are actually authorized by the state to kill another human being, the death penalty becomes a chilling exposé of the darkest emotions of the citizenry."[72] These darkest emotions would appear to thrive in the arguments made by those who advocate the death penalty despite the possibility of executing the innocent. Error is inevitable in any human legal regime, and the sacrifice of the innocent is thus an inescapable risk within the system of death. In the face of this possibility, many proponents of capital punishment actively embrace this form of human sacrifice as the proper means to attain higher social and spiritual rewards. But the rewards of this sacrificial scheme are surely illusive. I leave the final word here to Charles L. Black, who fought diligently in opposition to capital punishment. Faced with the limits of human judgment, Black counseled that humility was a course far preferable to violence: "We did not create life; perhaps it is only a symmetry, whose final secret is hidden from us, that decrees that whichever way we turn we cannot rightly handle the justice of death, but stammer in dilemma before the mystery."[73]

---

[72] James J. Megivern, "Religion and the Death Penalty in the United States," in *Capital Punishment* (ed. P. Hodgkinson and W. A. Schabas), 134, quoting Donald A. Cabana, *Death at Midnight: The Confession of any Executioner* (Boston: Northeastern University Press, 1996), xi.

[73] Charles L. Black, *Capital Punishment*, 155–56.

Indices

Subjects

References

Ancient Near Eastern Texts

Ancient Greek and Roman Texts

Jewish Texts

Christian Texts